A Coup Attempt in Washington?

A Coup Attempt in Washington?

A EUROPEAN MIRROR
ON THE 1998–1999
CONSTITUTIONAL CRISIS

By Peter H. Merkl

palgrave

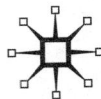

A COUP ATTEMPT IN WASHINGTON?
Copyright © Peter H. Merkl, 2000.
All rights reserved. No part of this book may be used or reproduced in any manner whatsoever without written permission except in the case of brief quotations embodied in critical articles or reviews.

First published 2001 by
PALGRAVE™
175 Fifth Avenue, New York, N.Y. 10010 and
Companies and representatives throughout the world.

PALGRAVE is the new global publishing imprint of St. Martin's Press LLC Scholarly and Reference Division and Palgrave Publishers Ltd (formerly Macmillan Press Ltd).

ISBN 0-312-23831-2 hardback

Library of Congress Cataloging-in-Publication Data

Merkl, Peter H.
   A coup attempt in Washington? : a European mirror on the 1998–1999 constitutional crisis/
  by Peter H. Merkl.
     p. cm.
   Includes bibliographical references and index.
   ISBN 0-312-23831-2
    Clinton, Bill, 1946—-Impeachment—Foreign public opinion, European. 2. Clinton, Bill, 1946—-Sexual behavior—Foreign public opinion, European. 3. United States—Politics and government—1993—-Foreign public opinion, European. 4. Political corruption—United States—Foreign public opinion, European. 5. Public opinion— Europe. 6. Press and politics—United States. I. Title.

E886.2.M474 2000
973.929'092—dc21

                                       00-059150

Design by Acme Art, Inc.

First PALGRAVE edition: January 2001
10 9 8 7 6 5 4 3 2 1
Printed in the United States of America

To my grandchildren,
Ted, Rosie, Sam, Amy,
Alexandra, and Brady,
in the hope that they will inherit this democracy
without the distortions of blind partisan hatreds and media frenzy.

Table of Contents

Acknowledgments ix

A Fable 1

Introduction. 5

CHAPTER 1: *The Prelude, 1994–1997* 33

CHAPTER 2: *A Coup Attempt in Washington?* 83

CHAPTER 3: *Europeans on Sex, Lies, and Audiotapes* 173

CHAPTER 4: *Democracy and the Media Conspiracy* 249

CHAPTER 5: *Damage to the Constitution?* 303

Notes 353

Index 359

Acknowledgments

This book is dedicated, first of all, to the many concerned friends abroad of American democracy and the Constitution who are quoted throughout these pages. Special thanks are owed to my dear friend of so many years, Walter Gelb, whose enthusiastic support and unstinting editorial assistance made this work blossom even though, after his own long media career, he must have had some misgivings about my critique of the contemporary American media. I owe a debt of gratitude also to another friend, Bruno Jactel, of the French Council of State and formerly of the Washington embassy for his advice and assistance. I am particularly indebted also to my friend and colleague, Cedric Robinson, for the benefit of his insights into the lingering crisis of the media in this country.

I would like to acknowledge, furthermore, the kindness of the staff at the Institute of Political Science of the University of Munich who made recent European newspapers available to me on CD-ROM, to supplement the treasures of the newspaper room and library of the University of California, Santa Barbara. And I truly appreciate the great improvements and valuable suggestions made by Palgrave's editors and their assistants, Karen Wolny, Alan Bradshaw, Roberta Scheer, Amy McDermott, Sara Safransky, and others involved in the copyediting of the manuscript. I would also like to thank Sandy Jacobs for her word-processing services.

Finally, I am deeply in debt to my wife, Lisa, whose initial aversion to this subject turned into the most generous support and assistance in the end.

Peter H. Merkl, September 2000, Santa Barbara, California

A Fable

Once upon a time, in the year 1998 to be precise, a tremendous, intergalactic tornado arose. It lifted the entire city of Washington inside the Beltway a mile or two up, well into the ozone, and kept it there, spinning around on its axle, for a full thirteen months. People outside the Beltway, throughout the country, and in friendly neighboring countries, looked up in disbelief at the levitated capital city and its magnificent House of the Constitution. It suddenly seemed to look so different up there. People in other countries, who had always admired and even envied the American Constitution from afar, even thought they could see two distinct and different structures in the distance, separated by an atmospheric layer of refraction that was produced by all the dust raised by the levitation of a whole city.

People speculated endlessly about the tornado. Was it, perhaps, a call for this Washington den of iniquity to rise and face divine judgment for its decades of public immorality and congressional corruption? Or was it rather a sewer explosion in the ancient, ill-kept system of the capital city? There were many malevolent sewer wisps and sprites about, with names like the Melon, the Kenster, the Media, and the Tripster, but their powers, jointly or separately, had never before been so great as to levitate a whole city.

Many surmised it was the tremendous swirl of partisan winds that they had noticed earlier. Others thought that the excess of rising hot air endemic to Washington had fomented this mother of all tornadoes and would keep it whirling for a year.

When the extraordinary event first occurred, there was much confusion as scores of Beltway dwellers found themselves aloft in the Kingdom of Schmooze. Tom the Varmint-Slayer and his little dog, Henry, thought at first they were alone as they searched for the evil Billy the Saxophone King and his wife, Grizabella. But there were Newt and scores of other Angry White Boys gathering around the large Pundit Pond dominated by the roar of the Pundit bullfrogs, the quacking of smaller Pundit amphibians, and the bleating of numerous paper sheep. The deafening noise emanating from the pond helped to keep Washington high in the air, far above the range of common sense and the ringing ears of those below.

The Angry White Boys soon ganged up on Billy the Saxophone King, who, to make matters worse, and even noisier, infuriated them by tooting his instrument whenever they thought they had him cornered. It was only at this moment that the Angry White Boys even noticed that there were girls around as well, and black and brown boys, who gathered to defend Billy against their anger. Barely above the ear-rending din, moreover, the great Christian Choir sang, if somewhat out of tune: "Don't they even feel a sense of outrage at remaining so far beneath my ideals of virtue?"

The people below, however, were more outraged by the undignified howling and carryings-on up there and thought un-Christian thoughts about the Christian Choir and the whole lot of them. They had not been entirely deceived by the sewer wisps, especially the odious Media that had been so busy stirring up the fight in the elevated Kingdom of Schmooze for its own ends: "Why don't you and he fight and I write?"

People in neighboring lands, to the extent they were not too preoccupied with their own problems or with the world's deteriorating situation, watched the developments with astonishment and alarm. Some of them were mumbling, "the sewer wisps have no clothes, the Angry White Boys are blue in the face, and maybe the Christian Choir is singing Satan's tune."

At long last, the tornado began to diminish and, after a last whirling frenzy in February 1999, Washington slowly descended to earth, causing barely a ripple in the quietly flowing Potomac.

Americans were so stunned by the events that for a long time they did not even want to talk about them.

Now, what was this all about?

INTRODUCTION

The Shock Felt Around the World

Most Europeans and most informed observers around the world viewed the American crisis in a totally different light than the American media and conservative Republicans saw it. They were deeply shocked, not by the admittedly tawdry conduct of Bill Clinton but by the manner in which it was exposed and paraded around the American and world press and over the Internet. To Europeans in particular, it was gross public indecency to publish all this salacious material, and they blamed American decadence—which they believe evident in our sky-high divorce and crime rates and waves of television and movie filth and violence. "Also, das ist doch zum Kotzen" (this really makes you throw up) said Chancellor Helmut Kohl of Germany who, like most adults, was familiar with the pervasiveness of marital infidelity and pornography but believed in the sanctity of one's privacy as well as in the normal self-restraint of civilized society not to invade it in this outrageous fashion, least of all for transparent partisan reasons.

"Investigations are perverse in which details of sexual organs, and of sexual practices are publicly discussed," opined the conservative *Frankfurter Allgemeine Zeitung* (September 11, 1998) which was otherwise very critical of Clinton: "This not only offends good taste but it violates the human dignity of those affected—even when it is a matter of the president. It should have been possible to render a legal judgment of Clinton's behavior, a moral judgment about his person, and finally a political judgment without going into the most intimate things." British Labor prime minister Tony Blair, and the conservatives German chancellor Helmut Kohl, French president Jacques Chirac, Italian premier Roman Prodi, and many others soon went out of their way to publicly extend their expressions of friendship and solidarity to President Clinton. Similar support came from around the world on the occasion of a Clinton speech on terrorism before the United Nations, right after release of the Starr Report and the videotape of Clinton's grand jury testimony: the assembled UN delegates all rose and gave him a standing ovation, with rhythmic handclapping. On the front page of the London *Times,* Matthew Parris commented on the videotape: "This was medieval. It was cruel. This was like bear-baiting . . . It was humiliating even to the viewer" (September 21, 1998). They may well all have imagined that such shocking American customs of public exposure might be imitated in their respective homelands and that their various political oppositions might unleash similar peephole campaigns *à l'américain.* In America, contrary to his opponents' venom, Clinton's public approval rose noticeably with the beginning of the impeachment drive in fall 1998 and, at year's end, president and Mrs. Clinton even topped the list of most admired Americans of 1998 in a Gallup poll.

This book is not a defense of President Clinton and his private indiscretions, but it will show the anti-Clinton campaign of 1994-1999 in a rather different light than our media portrayed it. Our press and television punditry hinted that European opinion differed from American attitudes about sex but never told us that the European press was extremely critical of the constitutional, legal, and political issues underlying the impeachment drive.

Europeans were particularly shocked to see the very people who invoked the Constitution and the rule of law in justification of their partisan vendetta—Kenneth Starr, his ultraconservative lawyer friends, and the confrontational Republican leaders in Congress, Newt Gingrich, Dick Armey, Henry Hyde, and Tom DeLay—show so little respect for law and the Constitution. They were convulsed by the irony of the accusers in a presidential lying-about-sex scandal themselves being "outed" as philanderers (Hyde, Bob Barr, Dan Burton, Gingrich, etc.), perjurers (DeLay and Starr), and liars, especially Starr and the media. "Who is this Starr?" I was asked time and again by Europeans concerned about the possible faltering of American leadership in NATO, the Middle East, Asia, and Latin America in the wake of the scandal. It was difficult to explain to Europeans how a man might be said to resemble Elmer Fudd and yet be another Senator Joe McCarthy, or the Torquemada or Grand Inquisitor of furtive sex, all at the same time. Late-breaking revelations in the perpetually Starr-struck American press about the ultraconservative lawyers' groups, such as the Federalist Society to which both Starr and some of Paula Jones's lawyers were said to belong, and of their conspiracy to entrap the unwary president did not exactly relieve European suspicions about Starr's motives.

Europeans love stories of political conspiracies and, unlike Republicans in the United States, listened very carefully when First Lady Hillary Rodham Clinton spoke of a "vast right-wing conspiracy." Major European newspapers readily identified Richard Mellon Scaife, Jerry Falwell, the religious right, and certain ultraright attorneys as the conspirators. To outsiders, there was never any doubt that, after fruitlessly investigating Whitewater and other "culpable" links of Hillary and Bill, a desperate Starr finally had to get lucky with this shameful panty raid. Starr's illegal leaks of grand jury testimony (he denied them under oath before the Judiciary Committee of the House of Representatives) and his ultimate report, which sought to shame and humiliate the president by exhibiting Clinton's and Monica Lewinsky's sexual activities in graphic detail to the world, crystallized how Starr would be perceived in critical European eyes. The roles of the "three witches," as some of my informants called them—Linda Tripp, Lucianne Goldberg, and the weakened Newt Gingrich of 1997-1998—stirring the brew made for a colorful scenario of the scandal. The ingenue Monica, lovelorn, manipulated by the witches and the president, "kidnapped" and mercilessly extorted by Starr's feckless minions, made this scandal a political soap opera that no foreign newspaper could pass by.

As the Clinton-Lewinsky scandal wore on for a full year and eventually wound down in acquittal, European attention to it also began to decline and in time turned toward more pressing issues. But there was none of the pretended amnesia and, perhaps, guilt feelings with which the American media in the spring of 1999 no longer wanted to think about the grand action to which they had been accomplices: the attempt to oust a duly elected president. By the beginning of the next presidential election campaign, our media pundits had even invented a catchy slogan, "Clinton fatigue," to justify not talking about it. As Sean Wilentz observed in *The New Republic* (February 28, 2000), however, the slogan "rests on a fictional premise. By every meaningful standard, statistical and historical, Clinton fatigue is an utter hoax. It is the latest sign of the growing gap between what the public actually thinks and what the pundits [still aloft in the skies] claim the public thinks." Wilentz went on to demonstrate, with the help of history and statistics, that Clinton's popularity as an able president not only continued at a high level but that in this regard he outdid nearly all his predecessors in their final years in the White House. The Princeton historian concluded: "political frustration breeds political self-delusion . . . the experts, having persuaded themselves that Clinton fatigue truly exists, attempt to pass the fraud off on a resistant public."

THE CONSTITUTIONAL CRISIS OF 1998-1999

We have emerged from the most serious constitutional crisis in this nation's history since the Civil War: the 1998-1999 escalation of political and partisan infighting to the level of an attempt to dislodge the constitutionally elected president by impeachment—or, as some say, by an outrageous abuse of the American rule of law and the Constitution. Was it an attempted coup d'état? Who were the plotters and who cooperated with them? By what road, what antecedents, did we arrive at this critical point? Why did a large majority of the American people, according to public opinion polls, resist the plotters for a whole year in the most emphatic way? A constitution is a living though delicate system of principles and structures. Major damage to it is not as obvious as, say, to an automobile after an accident. What may be the effects of this crisis; what would they have been had the coup attempt succeeded?

The world did not stand still long for the upheaval in Washington. The pressure of new events, such as the Yugoslav war over Kosovo, soon distracted Americans from reflecting more on the larger implications of the crisis of 1998-1999. But the truly alarming fact about American public opinion following the Senate acquittal of President Clinton on the impeachment charges, presented by thirteen managers in the House of Representatives in mid-February of 1999, was the seeming public indifference and desire to forget it all. We would really prefer not to think about it any more and not analyze how we teetered at the very brink of upsetting the fundamentals of our constitutional democracy. But how can we live with such collective amnesia that pretends nothing extraordinary has transpired and we can just get on with business as usual? In some American media, apropos of New Year's retrospectives on 1999, or on the twentieth century, the impeachment trial of the twice-elected president of the United States on trumped-up charges was not even mentioned. Worse yet, in other media, mention of this constitutional crisis falsified the impeachment charges against President Clinton into adultery or, by way of jokes, into skirt-chasing. How indeed can we expect our media, prominent participants in the "vast right-wing conspiracy" to tell us the truth about the great partisan battles of 1998-1999 and their antecedents? In the midst of a sea of media-borne lies and under the onslaught of daily, personal, and partisan anti-Clinton venom, I found myself looking for a more balanced, objective point of view on our crisis among the media voices from abroad, and particularly from the advanced democracies of Europe and the Commonwealth. It also occurred to me that, inasmuch as the American media participated in this anti-Clinton conspiracy, this left the vast protesting American majority without a voice in this matter. Perhaps the dramatic chorus from other democratic countries can give unbiased expression to the American public with whom the media abroad seemed to agree on many points.

European observers closely observed what we were doing to ourselves. When Congress first began to talk of impeachment, even conservative European journalists were well aware of the gravity of such a step. As the German *Frankfurter Allgemeine Zeitung*—which was very critical of President Clinton's conduct but, unlike the American media, never claimed that *he* was bringing the impeachment crisis on himself—wrote: "If Congress really starts impeachment proceedings, this will trigger a sensational process the institutional and political consequences of which . . . can hardly be exaggerated" (September 17, 1998).

In February 1999, when it was finally over, there was universal sense of relief, combined with dismay at Congress, not just in Europe but around the world, especially in the Commonwealth countries. The very religious and conservative paper *Hindu* of Madras, put it best: "The impeachment trial of President Bill Clinton by the Republicans must be rated as one of the most disastrous interregnums for the American polity of this century. The scandal exposed the leadership of the entire political spectrum as . . . blindly partisan, pursuing their gamesmanship unmindful of its potential to cause harm to the nation. There were no heroes and only villains." (Quoted in *World Press Review,* April 1999. In this source, the date of publication may be as much as three months after the appearance of the undated original.) Right after the impeachment vote by the House of Representatives in December 1998, the London *Observer* (December 21, 1998) called the vote "horrible theatre" and expressed sympathy with the House Democrats (like Representative John Conyers, the leader of the Democratic minority of the Judiciary Committee) who had dubbed it "an attempted constitutional coup d'état by the Republicans." The *Berliner Morgenpost* (December 21, 1998) also called the turbulent proceedings "horrible theater" and added that the Lewinsky affair had "poisoned the political atmosphere of the United States" and damaged the country's standing abroad. The London *Times* (December 21, 1998) quoted Jack Lang, the chair of the Foreign Affairs Committee of the French National Assembly and former Minister of Culture, to the effect that the "U.S. House of Representatives offered the world a festival of hypocrisy," the proceedings were a "parody of justice," and that American "sectarian fundamentalism" might yet destabilize a great democracy.

For what purpose, on what charges did we undertake this extreme and constitutionally dubious impeachment action of an elected president, the first time in over 200 years of the American republic? For a sex scandal transmogrified into a weak set of legal charges such as allegations of perjury and obstruction of justice? Compare this, for example, to the impeachment charges that the Russian Duma (lower house of the federal parliament) failed to pass with the required two-thirds majority against President Boris Yeltsin, three months after the United States Senate similarly acquitted President Clinton. Yeltsin was accused of (1) instigating the collapse of the Soviet Union, which had broken up into its constituent Union Republics in 1991; (2) improperly using force (rockets) against the Russian parliament; (3) launching the disastrous war upon the separatist republic of Chechnya; (4) destroying Russia's military with his neglect; and (5) ruining the people of Russia with his economic policies. The Russian constitution, to be sure, is rather different from ours, but we can hardly fault Yeltsin's enemies for launching impeachment action for trivial reasons or mere partisanship. But the hardline communist faction in the Duma behind the attempted impeachment of Yeltsin, the Russian equivalent of our Republican impeachment advocates in both houses of Congress, failed to overcome their colleagues' fear of the chaos and constitutional collapse that would have resulted from a successful impeachment in Russia. I shall examine below the cost to our Constitution and political system had the removal from office of President Clinton been successful.

Past American attempts at impeachment of presidents at least had weighty causes. The impeachment of Andrew Johnson, for example, often trivialized by Southern commentators, really was not based on such technicalities as violations of the Tenure of Office Act. It came about because this pro-Southern vice president of Abraham Lincoln had made major efforts to roll back the effects of the Northern victory following years of the most savage bloodletting in American history. The charges of Richard Nixon's proposed impeachment involved major excesses of authority, a cover-up, real obstruction of justice in the wake of the war against North Vietnam, and his persecution of American war resisters. The attempt to impeach Ronald Reagan centered on weapons sales to Iran and on supporting a sanguinary private war in Central America, all in defiance of congressional actions and laws. Clinton's impeachment, by contrast, involved charges of dubious constitutional weight, far short of the formula of "treason, bribery, or high crimes and misdemeanors," and therefore was no more convincing to a majority of the Republican-dominated Senate in February 1999 than it had been to public opinion at home and among our friends abroad.

In January 1998 the witches' cauldron of Washington and the self-styled political class of national politicians and media people went off on their own to pursue the unfolding Lewinsky scandal and impeachment drive against the president with unprecedented abandon. It made the vast majority outside the Washington Beltway predictably suspicious. The louder the media pundits and right-wing politicians shouted for Clinton's head amid the general hysteria of the sex scandal, the more the public opinion polls on the president's job performance veered in the opposite direction. From a modest and fluctuating level of approval that had rarely exceeded the half-mark before the scandal broke, Clinton's performance ratings soared 10 to 15 percent to levels of 60 percent and more, with occasional highs brought on by events such as a stirring State of the Union speech or an air strike against Saddam Hussein. For a while, the Clinton-haters still hoped that, perhaps, the news of the scandal had not yet reached everybody, that many loyal Democrats still believed his lies about his dalliance with Monica Lewinsky and possibly others, or that the full impact had not yet dawned on everybody. Had not Nixon's polls dropped by half during the Watergate imbroglio, and Reagan's slipped from 67 percent to a mere 44 percent during the Iran-Contra investigation?

But Clinton's polls remained sky-high in spite of further leaks, agitation for impeachment, and even William Bennett's exhortations to the American people to show moral outrage. Some European observers noted this amazing phenomenon, reported it in their newspapers and on television, and, in the end, reflected on its meaning for democracy. Those who did not note the extraordinary gap between public opinion and the Washington mob, of course, missed the one true hero of the whole affair—yes, there was one—the skeptical American people who in the end saved the Constitution. In an editorial by Alain-Gérard Slama in the conservative *Le Figaro* of Paris (September 14, 1998), the newspaper concluded, "We must never despair of democracy. In the face of the meanspirited (*infâme*) campaign that was visited upon Clinton, a majority of Americans kept their trust in him." *Le Figaro* was no defender of the president's conduct either, but always faithfully reported the

American opinion polls (for example, August 14, 1998; see also *Frankfurter Allgemeine Zeitung,* September 11, 1998) and contributed thoughtful comments on the American drama. Before the House impeachment vote in late December 1998, the liberal German weekly *Die Zeit* of Hamburg also described the "surreal tragedy in Washington" where "the proceedings [in the House] are deepening the gulf between the powerless and unnerved citizenry and the politicians" (December 16, 1998). At about the same time, the centrist daily *Sueddeutsche Zeitung* of Munich wrote "there has never been a wider gap between a zealous, screaming parliamentary faction and the incredulous but silent majority in the country" (*World Press Review,* February 1999).

WHY PAY ATTENTION TO FOREIGN OPINION?

What is the point of looking at the reflection of certain events in Washington in the European press? What might we learn that we have not already absorbed through observation and from our own media? Obviously, such reflections by foreign journalists and resident Europeans involve a certain amount of filtering, even bias, and it may be rather different from the bias of our own media. European and Commonwealth journalists will probably concern themselves only with the larger outlines of events, not all the minor details and side shows that enrich our own news and understanding for better or for worse. After all, the French, British, or Italian public, respectively, have their own problems and are interested in American politics only to the extent that it may affect them in the long run. I have not made an effort to track how often and to what extent European newspapers reported their American news about the great scandal even though this too might be revealing. To give an example, the percentage of hits on the websites of Germany's four largest newspapers (*Frankfurter Allgemeine, Die Welt, Handelsblatt,* and *Sueddeutsche Zeitung*) shows about one-fourth of the interest during the period in question to have been devoted to the

Lewinsky affair alone. For this book, I selected only expressions of European and Commonwealth opinion and their evaluations of how Washington grappled with the Clinton-Lewinsky scandal and its environment.

In addition, European journalists obviously harbor their own political and cultural biases regarding what they may applaud and what made them uneasy about the great American constitutional crisis of 1998-1999. The journalists and their papers differ from each other along liberal-conservative dimensions, although we shall see that conservative European journalists and newspapers frequently were not greatly impressed by American conservative causes or politicians. They may be, in effect, very critical, just as liberal European voices often condemned the president and the Clinton administration for reasons ranging from personal dislike to left-wing criticisms of Clinton's centrist political position. As Thomas Walkom wrote in the liberal *Toronto Star* (September 1998, quoted in *World Press Review,* October 1998): "What is it about Clinton's presidency that is so liberal? . . . [He] has made America a meaner, more desolate place. This, rather than any inability to keep his fly zipped, is the terrain on which he should be judged."

Furthermore, the personalities of American politicians play a much smaller role in these European and other assessments than do their authors' and readers' understanding of American institutions and offices such as the presidency, the Congress, and the special prosecutor or independent counsel. Almost completely absent from European news reports about American politics are the familiar personal diatribes against politicians, for example about the alleged character of Bill Clinton or of Newt Gingrich, who commanded a fair amount of attention and respect in the European press as he put together his ideological party machine for his triumph in 1994-1996. In the conservative *Sunday Times* of London (January 5, 1997), for example, Andrew Sullivan defended Gingrich as "one of the least sleazy politicians in America" against both a critical American press and low public opinion polls that punished him for his "real action" toward balancing the budget. A rare example of personal polemics was provoked by the Republican appointment of Jesse Helms as chair of the Senate Foreign Relations Committee when John Carlin wrote in Britain's *Independent on Sunday* (February 16, 1997) that this action resembled Emperor Caligula's decision to make his horse a consul of ancient Rome: "Historians may even conclude that, of the two, Caligula made the wiser choice." Carlin cited Helms's opposition to the Chemical Weapons Treaty, the Civil Rights Act, homosexuality, abortion, modern art, and the United Nations, as well as his support for anticommunist Latin American dictators, the tobacco industry, and the gun lobby.

To Europeans, of course, American politics is *not their system,* and they hardly identify with American political parties and interest groups, even when the latter seem to resemble their own points of political identification at home. American uniqueness, in any case, keeps such resemblances to a minimum. They do have a basic, overall grasp of our system and how it should work—or so it is hoped. In fact, there is a great reservoir of admiration in Europe for the American Constitution, democracy, and society. As in much of the rest of the world, America has long been a shining example of constitutional democracy and the undisputed leader of the free world. At the same time, however, this high esteem produces alarm and shock whenever the players of the political system appear to violate their own rules or when important parts of the system falter.

During the 1998 Clinton-Lewinsky scandal, the American press and television occasionally gave us limited glimpses of European (or foreign) press reactions, but they generally did so in rather distorting fashion: they made us think that it was only because of different attitudes towards sex and privacy that many Europeans were critical of how we handled this affair. There was little mention of the worldwide shock at the indecency of the publication of salacious material about our highest elected leader in the Starr

Report and on the Internet. There was even less American media reference to the well-informed European assessments of the legal and constitutional issues raised by the impeachment drive, for example, the partisan interpretations of high crimes and misdemeanors or of the crime of civil perjury. And there was no hint at all that Europeans and, for that matter, members of the old British Commonwealth were highly critical of the American media and how it had handled this scandal. This book hopes to fill in some of the gaps and to restore balance in how others see us, and how, perhaps, we ought to see ourselves.

In sum, seeing our great political crisis reflected in European eyes is likely to give us a rather abstract picture, literally from a distance and without the distortions of an excess of detail or a surfeit of personal and political identifications that might prevent us from seeing the forest for the trees. There may be some extraneous distortions but, on the whole, this reflection will give us a more objective view of what has been transpiring in Washington, a larger vision of the true significance of the American constitutional crisis of 1998-1999. Listening to these comments from Europeans and the Commonwealth is like a quick glance at a mirror. And what could be a better time to glance at the mirror than right after we have been in an all-out partisan catfight, a conflict so passionate that we could see nothing but the flying fur. The objectivity to be gained may be even greater if a large part of our own media turns out to have been very much involved in instigating and aggravating the crisis, and therefore rather unlikely to tell us the unvarnished truth. Finally, there is that phrase in our venerable Declaration of Independence about "a decent respect to the opinions of mankind" to which the authors appealed their grievances against British tyranny. This is obviously a very different situation and yet, let us remember, these are not the voices of our enemies but of our friends and allies, well-meaning critics and commentators.

POISONING THE POLITICAL ATMOSPHERE

It has been commonplace in the American media to speak of the constitutional crisis of 1998-1999 as if it first began in January 1998 and, in a manner of speaking, as if Clinton had personally brought all the charges against himself. The campaign to oust him from office by nonelectoral means, however, began long before that year. It was a manifestation of what Jeffrey Toobin in his book *A Vast Conspiracy* has called the "conspiracy within the legal system to take over the political system."[1] Occasionally in this book I shall attempt a brief chronology of key points of this campaign, separating them as much as feasible from the normal give and take of politics since Clinton first ran for national office. It was quite normal and nonconspiratorial, for example, for Clinton's rivals and critics to attack him during the 1992 primaries, the 1992 and 1996 presidential campaigns, and at any other time on matters of policy, personnel, or partisanship. The ado about Gennifer Flowers in the 1992 primaries, the first *New York Times* investigation of the Whitewater boondoggle and the Madison Guaranty bank failure, and the first beginnings of the draft issue in 1992 thus seemed par for the course, as were the bruising battles over health reform and budget matters in general.

The 1992 presidential campaign among the incumbent, President Bush, and his two challengers, the surprisingly effective Ross Perot with his "infomercials" and the eventual winner, Clinton, culminated in an all-too-typical American mudfight. The rapidly sinking George Bush was neither a "kinder and gentler" campaigner nor a gracious loser. Driven by his poor polls and the dismal state of the economy, at one point he even resorted to unearthing Clinton's State Department passport file. He hoped to raise the hoary old image of communist collaboration or, at least, of Clinton having led anti-Vietnam, anti-American demonstrations abroad.

In an article "Lies, Lies, Lies," *Time* magazine (October 5, 1992) reflected on the fate of truthfulness in that campaign and published a public opinion survey on "who has been less truthful since the start of this campaign?" Bush won the prize of the liars contest with 41 percent overall for lying (1) about his pledge of "no new taxes" (according to 71 percent of the respondents), (2) his non-involvement in the Iran-Contra scandal (63 percent), and (3) an affair with a staff member (30 percent). Clinton followed with 34 percent overall for lying (1) about the draft (40 percent), (2) about his relationship to Gennifer Flowers (50 percent), and (3) "not inhaling" marijuana (68 percent). The public in fact grew exceedingly weary of the mudfight and 68 percent wished that Perot would reenter the campaign that he had temporarily abandoned even though he was doing very well. The liars contest, of course, is also par for the course of our election campaigns, even though most respondents (72 percent) thought there was "less honesty in government today" than there had been ten years earlier.

President Clinton has since complained that no other president of the United States has ever been given such a hard time by his adversaries in the fulfillment of his duties. There may be some truth in this complaint even though all United States presidents, from George Washington on, had to put up with an extraordinary amount of abuse and invective. At the stage when other newly elected presidents were accorded the customary honeymoon, for example, Clinton found himself stymied by a filibuster—the old last resort of southern senators against civil rights laws—opposing his modest efforts to stimulate the stagnant economy. His legislative proposal was never debated on the floor of either house. During his first half year in office, a nasty bunch of media and partisan adversaries also gathered, hooting at every sign of disorganization about the inexperienced Clinton, ready to scream their misogyny and other prejudices—"quota queen"—at his attempts to bring women and minorities into the new administration. Radio talk shows à la Rush Limbaugh turned the air blue with venom in those days, much of it directed at Hillary Clinton. The public discourse in Congress had become so coarse in 1993-1994 that record numbers of senators and members of the House of Representatives seriously began to consider retirement.

Was all this poisoned atmosphere particularly directed at the couple in the White House? Perhaps not, but years later, the First Lady complained about their treatment in Washington, feeling that they had been singled out because they were from Arkansas where Bill had been attorney general and then governor. President Bush, during his failing 1992 campaign for reelection, had indeed concentrated his arrows on Clinton's alleged character issue and pointed to Clinton's background from Arkansas as "the lowest of the low." It is difficult to deny that many of the troubles of the Clinton presidency had their origins in the personal and political animosities and tangled affairs of that state.

The social prejudice against Clinton was also picked up by European journalists who had rarely noticed such displays of nastiness and contempt during the tenures of Clinton's predecessors. In the liberal German weekly *Die Zeit,* for example, Klaus Harpprecht mentioned that Clinton himself had once characterized his social origins as "the product of southern white trash"—of the fast life of Hot Springs, Arkansas rather than as "the man from Hope." Harpprecht went on to wonder whether, perhaps, this was the reason Washington had tolerated the sexual adventures of the patrician John F. Kennedy but not those of Clinton (January 29, 1999). One may indeed wonder where all these fine-feathered right-wing ladies and noble gentlemen had come from in egalitarian America. There is no lack of precedents for this social animosity in American history, beginning with that shown to the first truly democratic president, Andrew Jackson, and on down to Nixon, another brainy president of very modest origins, although much of the visceral hatred shown Nixon may really have dated from his no-holds-barred, red-baiting congressional campaign against Helen Gahagan Douglas. However, much of the mantra about Clinton's alleged lack of character does seem to hide this social prejudice against the brainy upstart who went to the best schools, was a Rhodes scholar, and time and again outsmarted his less competent political antagonists. Americans rarely value brains in their political leaders—and would rather paint them as "tricky Dick" and "slick Willie"—unless those brains have been used to accumulate fortunes. Wherever he came from originally, in any event, Clinton had obviously reinvented himself. His loyal majorities in public opinion polls throughout the crisis were not swayed by the social prejudices of many Clinton-haters and their "classy" media and Washington friends. On the contrary, they took pride in the fact that even a person from such modest antecedents could make it to the White House.

THE RESULTS OF THE 1992 ELECTIONS

As the 1992 presidential campaign entered its final stretch, Ross Perot came back into the fray and his following constituted a crucial obstacle to the reelection of President Bush in certain key states. By October, Bush had recovered somewhat but the chief issue against him continued to be the state of the economy as perceived by the voters. This was Clinton's great opportunity, and his campaign made optimal use of the slogan "It's the economy, stupid" while other issues, such as his relationship with Gennifer Flowers and the evasion of the Vietnam war draft, receded into the background. In the polls, half of the nation actually still feared they would lose their jobs in the next twelve months and two-thirds opined that the country was "on the wrong track" under the hapless George Bush. But the president's attacks on Clinton's character and credibility left a lasting impact on the challenger: a week before the 1992 elections, only 49 percent of the respondents regarded Clinton as "honest and trustworthy enough to be president." But after his first State of the Union address it was up to 69 percent (*Time*, January 25, 1993). In any case, there was no way Bush could have overcome this fatal economic undertow in the elections.

Clinton won a plurality of the popular vote, 43 percent against 38 percent for Bush and 19 percent for Perot, and a comfortable majority of electoral college votes (31 states and 357 votes against 18 states and 168 votes for Bush). Clinton led Bush with minority voters, women, and young people. Bush scored well only among Christian fundamentalists and, barely, among white males, especially the older generation and in the South. Many Republicans took Bush's defeat very hard and swore to make the new president's life miserable. Some added Perot's vote to that of Bush and claimed that Clinton had really lost the election.

The 1992 Congressional elections, in spite of some Republican gains in the House of Representatives, maintained the Democratic majorities in both houses with large margins of 42 in the House and 14 in the Senate. In a country like France—where the president is popularly elected too—such a sweep of presidential and parliamentary elections would have gathered enormous political power in the hands of a newly elected president, but this could not be taken for granted under our stringent separation of executive and legislative powers. The Democratic majorities in Congress, after a quarter century of a nearly unbroken line of Republican presidents, were fragmented, used to self-serving deals with these presidents, and dominated by long-established prima donnas like Senators Sam Nunn, David Boren, Pat Moynihan, and Dan Rostenkowski, the chair of the powerful Ways and Means Committee of the House, whose financial entanglements with the House post office soon landed him in jail. In spite of their perpetual majorities, the congressional Democrats were rarely unified on anything, including resistance to Republican presidents. Their power was shot through with interest politics, venality, and corruption, as the successful campaign of the GOP's Newt Gingrich to overthrow it demonstrated abundantly in 1994. As the *Economist* put it, Clinton's central problem was that "his agenda is as fat as his wallet is thin" (August 14, 1993). If the newly elected Clinton had expected to get his agenda enacted—his New Covenant of job creation, health care reform, education, and training for the work force of tomorrow—with the help of these Democratic majorities, he was sadly mistaken.

From the start, Clinton had presented himself as a centrist, a New Democrat patterned after the Democratic Leadership Council, and this orientation, halfway between the Old Democrats and the Old Republicans, could count only on limited support among the congressional majorities at large. Perhaps his efforts at the beginning of his tenure to balance all the Democratic groups in Congress and to woo a larger following were too feeble. Perhaps his concessions to individual legislators or to established groups among them did not rise to the levels they expected. Perhaps his reform plans were far too ambitious for anyone's taste. It was up to well-meaning Republicans—and to the equal-opportunity political adviser Dick Morris—to tell him later that he should have made major efforts to enlist Republican moderates in his legislative endeavors, like the great health care reform, rather than to rely totally on fragmented Democratic support.

He did receive an offer of Republican support, from Gingrich for NAFTA (North American Free Trade Agreement), an issue opposed by many Democrats in the House. From all accounts, however, Clinton's first years suffered from a fatal political weakness that was probably the main attraction for the large collection of political hyenas and vultures, not to mention the media who gathered and circled their prey in the midst of the storms over policies such as health care reform. And it was from among these opponents, from Arkansas, Chicago, New York, Philadelphia, and, of course, Washington, that various plots began to emerge in 1993-1994 to eject the president from office. One of these plots, with help from many quarters, almost succeeded in 1998-1999, but it certainly started to take shape long before 1998.

THE INCREDIBLE SHRINKING PRESIDENT

Aside from his evident weakness in Congress, the new president naturally would be unable to turn the economy around immediately, despite an encouraging surge of the stock market following his inauguration. At the last minute his predecessor dumped a number of foreign policy problems (Somalia, Bosnia, the Start II Treaty, and Iraq) into his lap with the expectation, no doubt, that Clinton would not succeed in what Bush rightly considered his own area of strength. Campaign promises also were broken or postponed, and some executive appointments were aborted because of alien nanny problems (Zoe Baird, Kimba Wood) or abandoned with great embarrassment to the president (Lani Guinier).

Inevitably, Clinton's new taxes on the wealthy and the energy tax on business, both efforts to cut the deficit, met fierce resistance. Powerful Democratic groups and individuals in Congress felt spurned or took offense at not being sufficiently consulted. Commenting on his disappointing first 100 days—after his sure-footed management of the election campaign—Clinton reportedly admitted: "There's a lot I have to learn about this town [Washington]." At the outset some press voices still gave him and his economic plans the benefit of the doubt. But his public opinion polls soon plummeted from an approval rating of two-thirds in the first quarter of 1993 to 36 percent at the end of the second quarter. After bitter losses and compromises over appointments, tax, and budget battles, the dismissal of the Bush-appointed White House Travel Office staff, and the replacement of George Stephanopolous with David Gergen, *Time* magazine published a picture and cover story entitled "The Incredible Shrinking President" (June 7, 1993).

May of 1993, according to the *Economist* of London (May 29, 1993), was "the worst of months," as Clinton struggled against the image of a tax-and-spend liberal and simultaneously tried to woo the Old Democrats of that description in Congress. *Time* magazine was not alone in turning on the weakened president whose interaction with the press became rather testy on occasion. And yet, this was precisely the time that Clinton's fortunes began to improve: the national job market picked up noticeably (750,000 new jobs since January); the first budget and deficit reduction passed (just barely), as did the national service bill and the crime fighting bill—

promising 50,000 extra police officers, not to mention a photo opportunity with law enforcement; and the "don't ask, don't tell" compromise was adopted for gays and lesbians in the military.

In July, Clinton nominated his first Supreme Court justice, Ruth Bader Ginsburg, and had the opportunity to shine at the G-7 meeting in Tokyo, advancing his international economic policy. In the eyes of the *Economist,* the president had emerged as "a born-again centrist" and "his speeches are littered with references to law and order and personal responsibility." "Talking about reforming welfare" was his test of being "a new kind of liberal" (June 19, 1993). To steady his relations with the media, he brought in Gergen, who had served creditably in several Republican administrations. He also ordered a bombing attack on Saddam Hussein in retaliation for the attempt on the life of visiting ex-president George Bush in Kuwait earlier that year. The signing of a Middle East peace accord further established the new president's role in foreign relations, although major problems with Russia, Somalia, and Haiti soon put his mettle in this field to a severe test.

BLOOD IN THE WATER

But there were also ominous harbingers of lingering issues that would threaten the Clinton presidency in ways beyond electoral decisions and legislative compromises. One of them was the suicide of a long-time friend and attorney, Vincent J. Foster, from which right-wing scandalmongers soon spun an arresting tale of alleged murder arranged by a jealous husband, Bill Clinton, and embellished it with stories of alleged drug trading by Clinton when he was still in Arkansas. A videotape about these juicy rumors, "The Clinton Chronicles," was endorsed by the Reverend Jerry Falwell, a pillar of right-wing agitation for many years. Another ominous issue to emerge was the Clintons' 1978 involvement in Whitewater, a failed land development project in Arkansas, and in the costly failure of Madison Guaranty Savings and Loan, a company managed (or mismanaged) by the late James McDougal. The *New York Times* had published an early investigation of Whitewater during the presidential campaign, whereupon the Clinton campaign commissioned an audit to show the considerable losses of the Clintons from their investment in it. To thicken the plot, the conservative *Washington Times* disclosed that Whitewater files had been removed from Foster's office and shredded before the premises could be searched by law enforcement officers investigating his death. In the fall of 1993, the Resolution Trust Corporation, a new agency charged with managing the outcome of the collapse of savings and loan banks in the 1980s, initiated a criminal investigation of Madison Guaranty. Its failure had cost millions. Former judge David Hale, a one-time McDougal associate threatened by indictment for fraud, had alleged that then-Governor Clinton had pressured him to lend McDougal a considerable sum. There was a surprising consensus among the media that, even if all Whitewater charges were true, the Clintons' responsibility would not amount to much. Yet practically all the major media outlets made the matter into a huge affair, what the *Washington Monthly* (April 1994) called "the great snipe hunt." The *Washington Post* managed to squeeze some 62 articles out of Whitewater—16 on page one—according to Michael Isikoff's book *Uncovering Clinton*, an amazing performance by any journalistic standard. In a later interview with Jim Lehrer (*NewsHour*, January 26, 2000), Clinton himself reflected: "We endured what history will clearly record as a bogus investigation . . . where there was nothing to Whitewater, nothing to these other charges [Travelgate, Fostergate, Filegate] . . . tens of millions of dollars were spent and we got a clean bill of health on that." The sheer accumulation of serious charges, however baseless, served its intended purpose of underlining the character issue and creating the image of a scandal-prone presidency.

Both the *Washington Post* and the *New York Times* editors now demanded to review all the Whitewater documents in the Clintons' possession. When the Clintons and their lawyers, Bernard Nussbaum and David Kendall, balked, they repeated their demand with threats of "going on the warpath" against the White House. George Stephanopolous in his book *All Too Human* describes the clash between *Post* editors Leonard Downie and Ann Devroy on the one side and, essentially, Hillary's and Nussbaum's fear that the peremptory demands were "an invasive fishing expedition that would only create more inquiries." Stephanopolous continues to believe that this refusal to give in to the press sharks was the crucial beginning of the near-sinking of the Clinton presidency in 1998-1999, because "a president's right to privacy is limited by the public's right to know," and reporters and the public should never get the idea that a president's family has something to hide. The media sharks smelled blood in the water.

It seems to me that this was indeed a crucial moment though, perhaps, not for the same reason. It was a turning point because it sharply brought out the point in time when some of our media elites began to succumb to the delusion that the *Post*'s Leonard Downie, for example, had been elected by the American people to be president of the United States or, at least, been appointed a special prosecutor under the now-defunct Office of Independent Counsel Act. The same goes for Howell Raines of the *Times*, the Captain Ahab relentlessly chasing after the great Clinton white whale. The Justice Department, on the other hand, had a right to demand and did eventually receive most of the records in question. There is, of course, a difference between the practical political advice given by Stephanopolous and the constitutional argument that a private firm such as a newspaper has no business making "peremptory demands" and threatening "war" upon the elected representative of the American people.

Emperor Napoleon III of France used to have a so-called reptile fund, a secret slush fund from which obnoxious politicians and the journalistic reptiles of his day could be paid off. I find it shocking that our once-respectable newspapers should have lapsed into this reptilian mode. The *Post*'s example was only the spearhead of similar aberrations by other newspapers and periodicals, as the *Los Angeles Times* and *American Spectator* launched Troopergate, the story of how Arkansas state troopers allegedly procured women for the then-governor of Arkansas (see also chapter 4). Troopergate was generated by an old Clinton foe from Little Rock, attorney Cliff Jackson, and paid for by Richard Mellon Scaife, a Philadelphia newspaper publisher and untiring financial angel of right-wing causes and journals such as the weekly *Standard* and *American Spectator*. According to Gene Lyons writing in the *Washington Monthly* (April 1994), the troopers of Troopergate were a most unreliable source with a record of lying for money. David Brock's account in *American Spectator* (which he later disavowed in a letter to *Esquire* in spring 1998), however, flushed out Paula Corbin Jones who felt offended by her mention—by first name only—in the article. In February 1994, the ever-resourceful Jackson presented Jones and her right-wing attorney to a meeting of the Conservative Political Action Conference, a group of hardline right-wing activists. In a word, half of the right-wing conspiracy was already on the move, long before Bill Clinton ever met Monica Lewinsky, before Kenneth W. Starr was appointed, and even before Newt Gingrich led the Republican party to victory in the House of Representatives. The slogan of impeaching Clinton was first launched by Jackson in 1993, by the anti-abortion Operation Rescue, and by Republican Dick Armey in Congress.

In January 1994, Stephanopolous argued that the White House itself should request an independent counsel to look into Whitewater—to preempt the appointment of a special prosecutor—and he warned the Clintons that Senators Alphonse D'Amato and Bob Dole were already calling for Whitewater hearings and could not be stalled forever. Soon the White House got both, a special prosecutor, Robert Fiske, and a Senate subcommittee on Whitewater, chaired by D'Amato. It is easy to smile about the Whitewater affair now, in retrospect, after D'Amato, Fiske, and even the vengeful Starr wasted years and tens of millions looking for the smoking gun. Starr sent several Arkansans to jail, including Governor Jim Guy Tucker, James McDougal (who died in jail), and his wife, Susan, on contempt charges because she refused to incriminate the Clintons. Rumor also had it that Starr's investigators, even then, often startled their witnesses with questions about past amorous affairs of the former governor, a subject beyond their authorization. A critical assessment of presidential investigations in the British *Economist* years later pointed out how a prosecutor like Starr "can take his inquiry down any side alley he fancies. That is how Mr. Starr ended up, preposterously, questioning Arkansas state troopers on Mr. Clinton's sex life" (July 12, 1997). The final anticlimax occurred at the retrial of Susan McDougal on contempt charges: she really knew nothing incriminating to the Clintons. The feisty McDougal, a true American heroine, spent eighteen months in jail rather than be bullied by Starr. Her attorney, Mark Geragos, in fact made Starr's bullying the focus of her retrial which ended with her final acquittal in 1999.

THE MILITARY ISSUE

Before we get into the heart of the great conspiracy against Clinton, we should examine one more issue of considerable ramifications and longevity, namely, the polemics over young Clinton's relationship to the military, which various groups of his enemies quickly turned into a chorus of condemnation. The bedrock of truth underlying the various yarns was that Clinton in his college days, like many others, had opposed the Vietnam War and evaded the draft. During the 1992 campaign, the ever-ready Cliff Jackson, who had known Bill for many years, including in his days as a Rhodes scholar at Oxford, released a batch of old letters that suggested that Clinton had dissembled about his draft status. This was enough to mobilize an army that pictured him as (1) a representative of the late '60s generation with its loose attitudes toward drugs and sex; (2) a sworn enemy of the military of which, as president, he would be the commander-in-chief; (3) the "first postwar president" who had never fought in the armed forces himself (conveniently forgetting that Ronald Reagan had served only in the War Department's film-making army unit, not in combat); and (4) a draft dodger during the days of anti-Vietnam draft-card burning.

In the heat of the polemics, of course, Clinton's foes never acknowledged that the generational change, though dramatized by Clinton's young age and the heroic World War II pasts of both his 1992 Republican antagonist Bush and his 1996 rival Robert Dole, was bound to happen sooner or later. As the *Economist* put it prophetically, referring to the civil rights march of 1963, "too many of Washington's politicians and commentators remain silently obsessed by the ghosts of the past" (September 11, 1993). Some, we might add, were also obsessed with the ghosts of Watergate and thoughts of revenge for that and more recent humiliations. By now, of course, a very large proportion of American politicians at the federal and state levels are of Clinton's generation, and many still younger, and the general population is younger still. Also, Clinton's disingenuous declaration of "never having inhaled" marijuana and his evident furtiveness in avoiding confrontation over the draft— so as "not to jeopardize a future political career"—make him a rather untypical representative of that rebellious generation. There is no evidence that young Clinton was ever a pacifist or hostile to the American military in general, even though his initial effort to break down the patterns of exclusion and discrimination against gays and women in the armed forces may have given military traditionalists such an idea.

Clinton may be the first post–World War II president who never served in the American military, but this was and is also true of a large majority in Congress, including such younger Republican leaders as House whip Tom DeLay, Speaker Newt Gingrich, former vice president and presidential candidate Dan Quayle, the sons of President Bush (Quayle and George W. Bush chose to go into the National Guard instead and stayed out of the war) and, for that matter, countless middle-class and upper-class American whites whose unquestioned patriotism evidently did not extend to enlisting for combat in Vietnam.

Once the war was over, the draft was abolished and the new professional United States armed services became a volunteer force. But the issue would not die as long as partisan invective kept reviving it with regard to Clinton, sometimes in relation to war, e.g., "sending young Americans into harm's way," sometimes in reference to officers being punished for illicit affairs. Some military officers had to be disciplined for criticizing their commander-in-chief or his foreign and defense policies, a serious infraction of military discipline. Some civilian critics, for example, the poison-pen house cartoonist Michael P. Ramirez of the *Los Angeles Times*, in discussing the invasion of Haiti or the peacekeeping force for Kosovo, contrasted the "Hell, no, we won't go" posture of Vietnam draft protesters with the orders for the now-professional soldiers to face military enemies.

The anti-Clinton attitudes of veterans' organizations also surfaced on occasion, even though the president never missed an opportunity to identify sympathetically with American soldiers. And the issue made its last stand in 1999 when Republicans in Congress and among the media pundits seemed to split in two camps. One camp claimed that he had cut back military expenditure too much. It wanted a bigger defense budget but was reluctant to finance the Balkans conflict or any other current engagement abroad. The other camp tried very hard to push the administration into the use of ground forces in Kosovo, perhaps expecting a lot of bodybags and massive demonstrations as in the Vietnam war. But this time Clinton would be at the receiving end of popular ire in the United States. When the war in Kosovo was won without employing ground forces, furthermore, some of the voices from the latter camp suggested it was somehow immoral to have won without substantial casualties.

CHAPTER ONE

The Prelude, 1994–1997

> [The conspiracy of ultraconservative lawyers behind the Paula Jones suit in 1997] used this lawsuit like a kind of after the fact election, to use briefs, subpoenas, and interrogations to undo in secret what the voters had done [in 1996].
>
> —Anthony Lewis, "Nearly a Coup,"
> *New York Review of Books* (April 13, 2000)

Like a musical overture, the four-year prelude to the impeachment crisis of 1998 presented many of the basic elements that played a role in 1998. On the one hand, there were the political battles of the 1994 and 1996 congressional and presidential elections, including the spectacular rise of the Republican majority spearheaded by Newt Gingrich. The new majority generated much legislative activity but was skillfully outmaneuvered by a resurgent President Clinton who won reelection in 1996, the first Democrat to be reelected to a second term since Franklin Delano Roosevelt. On the other hand, there was in retrospect the by-now familiar conspiracy of right-wing lawyers, judges, businessmen, and media elites trying to undo Clinton's electoral mandate with an onslaught of investigations and charges.

Most of these accusations were either ancient, such as Whitewater and other charges from the days when Clinton was governor of Arkansas, or sex charges both old and new, which shady lawyers and journalists tried to stretch into criminal acts, relying usually more on sensationalism than on their legal aspects. The few accusations of wrongdoing while president of the United States—Travelgate (the dismissal of Bush appointees in the White House Travel Office), Filegate (the acquisition of FBI files on Republican opponents), and campaign finance violations—would have commanded less weight upon closer examination had not the media elites poisoned the atmosphere with their polemical exaggerations and sensationalism. The prelude of 1994-1997, in other words, resembled the hectic year of 1998 in many ways except for the Starr Report and the role of the House Judiciary Committee—and the full House of Representatives—in actually impeaching the president, the presumed attempt at a coup d'état against the Constitution.

If we put aside the media chase and the political failures of the first year of Clinton's presidency, when did the "vast right-wing conspiracy" to hound him from office really come together? To speak of a conspiracy, there is no need to pinpoint an actual meeting of all the conspirators or a precise, coordinated plan or time. Julius Caesar's assassination by Brutus in 44 B.C., very likely, was "in the air" for some time and on many minds in the Roman Senate before it came to fruition. Suffice it to repeat that several lethal anti-Clinton conspiracies were hatched in 1994, one at the end of 1993 (Troopergate), and the conspirators soon found ways to coordinate their respective efforts. Originally the conspirators may have hoped to bring him down in the next presidential election in 1996, which would be, again, only par for the course in a democracy. Some may have hoped merely to squelch the Clinton reform agenda by burying the White House under a battery of extraneous charges. According to George Stephanopolous, Hillary Clinton's fear of quashing health care system changes—after nearly a year of gargantuan labors by her task force of 500, scores of congressional meetings, and all-out assaults from the enemies of reform—may have been first among the reasons why she resisted disclosure of the Whitewater files. In early November 1993, the 1,342-page health care plan had just arrived on Capitol Hill and for the first time invited the broadsides of its many self-interested critics—in Congress, from the health insurance, hospital, and medical associations, and from the media—when the investigation into the financial ties of the Clintons to their long-time friends and Whitewater business partners, the McDougals, got under way. If the White House could be kept on the defensive on Whitewater and on Hillary's legal services to Madison Guaranty—and later on diverse sex charges against Bill—it would be hampered in pursuing its legislative agenda.

In early 1994, long before its formal presentation to Congress, Hillary's health care reform was threatened politically by a rival plan (Cooper-Breaux) with bipartisan support and by the criticisms of Senator Pat Moynihan, a Democrat. Press comments varied from stamping it dead on arrival—and criticizing the president for being too quick to compromise, even of "premature capitulation"—to a flood of hostile distortions—for example, the charge that it was a design for single-payer, or "state-socialized" medicine. And there were political gales blowing elsewhere, including on the remaining Whitewater documents in the Clintons' possession—some still needed to be catalogued, some could not be found in the White House. Attorney General Janet Reno subpoenaed them all and appointed Robert Fiske, a Wall Street lawyer who had served in the Ford and Carter administrations, as special prosecutor to examine all Whitewater-related matters. A federal grand jury was assembled on Whitewater. Some television pundits and newspapers quickly made the spurious connection between Whitewater and Watergate, often by sleight of hand, or slip of the tongue, and some seriously debated whether, if all the allegations were true, they would really suffice for impeaching Clinton.

Why should a decade-old, botched real estate speculation trigger the extraordinary impeachment process of the Constitution? Senate minority leader Robert Dole and William Safire of the *New York Times* threatened to "turn up the heat" on Whitewater while House and Senate Democrats were accused of "dragging their heels" on the investigation of the failure of the Madison Guaranty Savings and Loan bank. Congressional Old Democrats refused to defend Clinton who, the previous November, had ignored their will on the North American Free Trade Agreement (NAFTA). It had passed the House, 234 to 200, with the help of more than 100 Republican votes delivered by Gingrich. It was a magnificent example of what political strategist Dick Morris later called bipartisan "triangulation," and Clinton expressed the hope that in the future he might rally similar "centrist" coalitions for his health care bill, welfare reform, and the budget. The last budget had squeaked through by a whisker. NAFTA had passed the House with the support of 75 percent of the Republican but only 40 percent of the Democratic members who, along with Ross Perot and organized labor, saw little merit in it. The economy by then was booming, but the slogan "It's the economy, stupid," seemed to appeal to free-trading Republicans more than to the Old Democrats.

The Whitewater story ground on through half a year of probing by Special Prosecutor Fiske—who eventually said he could find no evidence of wrongdoing by the Clintons—and the frequently contentious hearings continued before Senator Alphonse D'Amato's Whitewater committee. And there was a new development that already had been part of the "Christmas week surprises" of 1993, Troopergate. By now, every charge against Clinton received the suffix "-gate" for its potential to lead to impeachment: Nannygate, Whitewatergate, Travelgate, Fostergate, and soon, Filegate, and Zippergate or Monicagate. The White House complex had become literally and metaphorically a gated community. Every new charge seemed to encourage the Clinton-haters to hope for a Watergate reprise, this time against a Democratic president. Even *Time*, after repeating frequently that the passage of 16 years and the pettiness of possible charges made Whitewater a minor affair, claimed that it left "a shadow reminiscent of Nixon."

A week later, *Time* (March 21, 1994) even had an essay "Why it isn't Watergate" in which the magazine lamely explained that there was "no evidence of criminal conduct," but that Whitewater was hardly trivial "because, if their veracity cannot be trusted on those matters who can believe them" regarding details of the health reform. The magazine never explained why it was drawing a far-fetched if avowedly negative comparison of Whitewater and Watergate, or why the "noncriminal Whitewater" conduct, by allegedly raising doubts about the truthfulness of details of the Clinton health care reform, somehow left shades of criminality on both. With the first wild charges over the suicide of Vincent Foster, a prelude to the media circus of 1998 began to envelope the punditry of Washington, deliberately blurring the line between fact and fiction.

A profound and disquieting change was also occurring in public discourse that seemed to upset normal political routines in Washington, enabling Clinton's enemies to imagine him already convicted and deposed. As hints of his imminent demise or resignation began to trickle through the media in the most unexpected places— I once spotted a rumor of his fall being "just days away" in the "Best of Today's TV" column of the *New York Times*-owned *Santa Barbara News Press,* of all places—it seemed that the desired reality of a fallen president had taken hold in the minds of rather imaginative and Watergate-haunted media elites and conservative Republicans. The grand rehearsal for the assassination of Julius Caesar had begun as they began to think of him as dead, out of the way, long before Brutus arose, dagger in hand. The would-be Republican conspirators of 1994 and 1998 still had to find a way to turn their runaway dreams into reality. Their Brutus, the conspirator with a method ready to turn far-fetched, anticonstitutional dreams into action, was Kenneth Starr. Nicole Bacharan, a frequent French television commentator on American affairs and the author of the first European book on our 1998 constitutional crisis, *Le piège (The Trap),* subtitled "When democracy loses its head," described Starr: "A devil of a man. Round face and fleshy lips, his grey hair slicked down over his balding skull, looking like a prematurely aged baby. He wears the fine spectacles of a clergyman and affects a permanently sulking mien."[1]

CONGRESS IN REPUBLICAN HANDS

American politics in the watershed year of 1994 ran on two separate tracks, the delusionary one we have just described, the other a series of major political disasters interspersed with some triumphs for the Clintons. The biggest political disaster was undoubtedly the Republican landslide in the congressional elections of November, which, at midyear, even as astute a foreign journal as the *Economist* completely failed to predict. In May the London weekly still called a "major change not too likely" and gave the Republicans only a 20 percent chance of winning a majority in the Senate and none at all in the House (May 14, 1994). But Gingrich, Republican minority leader since November 1993, had a better assessment of the unpopularity of partisan gridlock and of the 20-year Democratic hold on Congress. His Contract for America established a political program for his army of specially recruited candidates for the House of Representatives, and he had 300 Republican members and candidates solemnly pledge loyalty to it on September 27 at the steps of the Capitol.

Though many observers doubted whether most voters really knew the details of the contract, Gingrich's partisans went on to sweep the House elections, turning a lopsided Democratic majority into a Republican one that was firmly in his hands. European observers were fascinated to see an ideologically unified, well-disciplined European-like party emerge in America. As Josef Joffe described it in the centrist *Sueddeutsche Zeitung* of Munich (January 11, 1995): "The mightiest man in America, next to Clinton, immediately began to flex the muscles of his new political machine for a 'revolution from the right,' whipping in 14 hours through an amazing program of 15 votes to reorganize the House of Representatives and to hobble future 'tax-and-spending' initiatives with a requirement of a two-thirds vote." Two months later, Kurt Kister of the same newspaper credited "the strongman of the conservatives in the House of Representatives" not only with "complete control over the themes and progress of legislation," but also with "absolute dominance over his, for American politics, extraordinarily loyal partisan majority of Republicans" (March 15, 1995). The Gingrich juggernaut in the House passed nearly its entire contract agenda within the first 100 days. The Senate too passed into Republican hands shortly after the elections although it conspicuously held back from endorsing the contract. A majority of state governorships (30) had also gone to Republicans, though of a more pragmatic stripe than the disciples of Gingrich, and so had some state legislative bodies in the same election.

Three months after its erroneous prediction, the *Economist* (August 20, 1994) had changed its tune to the expectation of Republican gains in both the House and the Senate. The stunning election result produced considerable comment in the European press. Jonathan Freedland, writing in the liberal *Guardian* of London (formerly of Manchester), blamed Clinton's rout on his being a centrist New Democrat—not right enough for the Right (on health care and gays in the military) and not left enough for the Left (on NAFTA and GATT)—and expressed the expectation that Clinton would be voted out in 1996. Leo Wieland suggested in the daily *Frankfurter Allgemeine Zeitung* that the president really needed more moderate Republican support, because his "motley left-liberal minority coalition" obviously had not worked well in 1993-1994. The Republican landslide also moved the Italian mass circulation daily *Corriere della Sera* (quoted in *World Press Review,* January 1995) to speak of an "American earthquake"—"a referendum on the Bill and Hillary factor and on the Democratic base which is considered corrupt and inefficient." The Italians saw in it an "electoral revolution [like those] in France, Canada, Italy and Japan," voting "against forty years of entrenched government." The *Corriere* was obviously thinking of contemporary Italian politics where "the voters [also] chose a third party of outsiders," businessmen, self-employed people, managers, "aiming at antipolitical" pragmatism, bureaucratic reforms, and efficiency—like Ross Perot or Silvio Berlusconi who had become Italian prime minister in April. That "entrenched Italian government," however, had indeed been entangled in major corruption and, in the end, even Berlusconi was not entirely beyond suspicion.

There was a second major disaster in 1994, the agonizing death of the health care reform that had been in preparation since early in the Clinton administration. Whatever may have been the multiple causes of its demise—its excessively ambitious and complex nature, the awkward and partisan way it was squired through Congress, the bruising battles with the various well-heeled health lobbies, the sudden health industry efforts to slow the alarming rise of health care costs, the extremely aggressive media, and the phony television ad discussions of Harry and Louise—the reform never passed. Some of the more progressive states, however, undertook well-considered reforms to cope with the problems it sought to address, in particular the presence of tens of millions of uninsured Americans. Would it have fared better if the Clintons had enlisted bipartisan input at an early point? When the *Economist* heard Senate minority leader Dole repeat three times at the opening of the Senate debate, "America has the best health care system in the world," it concluded that there was little likelihood the Republicans would have been any help (August 13, 1994). The eventual failure of this central project of the administration, at any rate, played a major role in the electoral disaster to follow.[2] In the meantime, foreign policy crises had also begun to accumulate, from Somalia and Haiti to the confirmation battles in the Senate over the president's plans to reshape his policy-making apparatus.

FROM FISKE TO STARR

There could be no doubt that the Whitewater investigation and other assorted charges interfered with the ability of the Clintons to make the case for their health care reform plan. While no fewer than five congressional committees worked on aspects of their health reform and rival proposals, and health insurance representatives ran the infamous Harry and Louise commercials on television, the ups and downs of opinion polls on Whitewater and on health reform showed a curious connection between the two unrelated issues. In January of 1994, the public still favored the health care reform 50 percent to 33 percent, but in March rejected it 41 percent to 45 percent. With Special Prosecutor Fiske subpoenaing six White House aides and three Treasury officials in March, looking into Foster's suicide, and investigating former Rose law firm attorney Webster Hubbell, now an assistant United States attorney general, public attention to Whitewater moved inversely from 48 percent paying attention to it in January (versus 51 percent who paid little or no attention) to 64 percent in March (versus 36 percent). Talk radio hosts like Rush Limbaugh added their venom to intensify the vague fears and personal biases beyond such logical stretches as *Time* or the *New York Times* would suggest to make the health care proposal somehow seem unethical. The *Times* also pilloried Hillary Clinton's financial gains of 1978-1979 in the commodities futures market in the crudest tabloid style while other media speculated on such questions as whether the Clintons had met all their tax obligations 16 years earlier and since, and whether their hesitation in turning over all records was or wasn't a Nixon-like obstruction of justice. Curiously, back in Watergate days, the impeachment investigation had stopped precisely at Nixon's suspected income tax offenses because it considered them a matter of private and not of public misconduct. The tabloidized major media and the talk radio hosts of 1994 had a field day with speculations and accusations against the Clintons and their erstwhile Arkansas associates.

Eventually Fiske cleared the Clintons of involvement in the Foster suicide and the suspicious White House contacts regarding Whitewater taxes with the Treasury Department. He began to annoy the Whitewater hawks in other ways as well, especially by hampering the congressional investigations of the same subject while he was still working on it. So the conspirators found a way to remove him and replace him with Starr. Right-wing Senators Helms and Faircloth of North Carolina met over lunch with ultraconservative federal justice David Sentelle, evidently with advice also from radio host Floyd Brown of the Virginia United Citizens, "a clearinghouse for Whitewater conspiracy theories" (*Economist,* August 13, 1994). Under the revived Office of Independent Counsel (OIC) Act, Chief Justice William Rehnquist appointed a three-judge panel headed by Sentelle which completed the switch: Starr was appointed in August of 1994 to continue the Whitewater investigation. A solicitor general under President George Bush and prominent tobacco lawyer, Starr was well known to White House counsel Robert Bennett who thought him compromised: Starr had written a brief opposing the claim of presidential immunity against such civil suits as that of Paula Jones, and the tobacco industry was then under siege from the Clinton administration. Bennett felt Starr was no independent prosecutor and should withdraw his name. This promised to be another mammoth investigation echoing the Iran-Contra investigation by Special Prosecutor Lawrence Walsh, who had finally wound up his search in January 1994 after seven years and $40 million. His finding was that President Reagan had indeed "set the stage for criminal activities by others" (who had been indicted, pardoned, or acquitted long ago) and that Vice President Bush had been "in the loop" after all. In contrast to the Whitewater snipe hunt, at least Iran-Contra had been a matter of considerable import to the United States while Reagan and Bush were in office, but Walsh's report was now of little consequence for the two retired presidents. No one would indict them now.

The *Economist*'s editorial, under the byline of Lexington, wistfully coined the phrase "the Clinton gap" to denote the gap between Clinton's sinking public opinion polls and the rising indices of the economy. "Clinton's agenda is still popular, but he isn't . . . Americans are still feeling insecure about the job boom,"

Clinton pollster Stanley Greenberg suggested as an explanation for this gap. "Clinton is failing; he needs some spectacular triumphs such as health care reform or with his crime bill." But "America [was] in a sour mood" at the time of the 1994 elections. To explain the devastating outcome of the elections, Jonathan Freedland of the *Guardian* of London (November 1994) advanced yet another interpretation: "Ronald Reagan was the Teflon president, the leader to whom no criticism, failure, or scandal ever stuck. Clinton is a Teflon president too: in his case, it's the praise, success, and accomplishments that don't stick." The economy was booming and 4.6 million new jobs had been created in the 21 months since he took office, Freedland wrote. Yet the voters did not credit the president, even though in 1992 they had held Bush responsible for a lagging economy.

THE LABORS OF SISYPHUS

"Mr. Clinton always fought an uphill battle," the *Economist* wrote in January 1995. "The failures of his first two years have made it positively Sisyphean . . . No sane man would [now] wager on Mr. Clinton reconquering the summit . . . He arrived [in 1993] full of grand schemes and lofty dreams. Congress was controlled by the Democrats; anything seemed possible . . . Today, Mr. Clinton's schemes and dreams are more or less irrelevant" (January 22, 1995). Was it still possible for the "comeback kid" to reinvent himself yet again or was it "too late: is the Republican tide too strong, Mr. Clinton himself too thoroughly shattered?" Clinton would be president for at least two more years, even if it was true that he had to face putdowns and challenges from many quarters.

Kurt Kister wrote in the *Sueddeutsche Zeitung* (March 15, 1995): "The besieged president in the White House . . . and the Democrats in the House of Representatives have become irrelevant. One-time barons like [Speaker] Tom Foley and [Ways and Means Committee Chair] Dan Rostenkowski were voted out in the elections; others lost their committee chairs and can now hold [their press conferences] only in the cellar rooms of the capitol." Senator Helms, "the mild crackpot" (*Economist,* November 26, 1994) and now the chair of the Senate Foreign Relations Committee, ominously suggested after the election that "Clinton was not up to the job of being America's military commander-in-chief . . . [and] he had better watch out if he comes down here [to North Carolina military bases]." Gingrich at one point claimed publicly that one-fourth of the White House staff used drugs. In public opinion polls, two-thirds of Democratic respondents preferred that Clinton not run again in 1996, and indeed there were rival Democratic candidates popping up literally right and left of him, in particular Senator Bob Kerrey and House minority leader Dick Gephardt, blaming him publicly for the 1994 electoral debacle. He was said to have lost the South, the working and the middle classes. Only the poor, respondents with annual incomes under $15,000, had still voted solidly Democratic. Many of his black supporters were taken aback by his resolute law-and-order stance. "This president is in political trouble," commented the centrist *Financial Times* of London, and the liberal *La Repubblica* of Milan said in late January apropos of his State of the Union address: "The state of the union is good [but] the state of his presidency . . . is not."

"The voters," wrote the *Frankfurter Allgemeine Zeitung* after the November 1994 elections, "evidently are looking to the Republicans to accomplish Clinton's program, crime control, economic growth, immigration, and health care reform." Polls indeed showed that, in the voters' mind, the Republicans had a better handle on the economy than the Democrats, who had never shaken off the tax-and-spend image of Republican propaganda. But the *Economist* also contrasted the likely Republican presidential candidate and Senate majority leader, Bob Dole, with "Gingrich's messianic fervor . . . and the sounds of coronation as the new Speaker ascended on a wave of parties and the adulation of press and peers." "Since November," according to Lexington (*Economist,* January 7, 1995), "it has often been easy to believe that Mr. Gingrich is, if not president (yet) then at least the undisputed leader of his party . . . [His] grip on House Republicans seems so firm that he will be able to ram through much of his agenda."

Admittedly, Gingrich neither pleased Dole (who was already beginning to campaign for the presidential nomination along with seven other hopefuls) nor the public at large, which at an early point seemed to have decided that it did not like him very much. But his contract group flourished and launched long-needed cleanup measures in the House and a reorganization of the chamber, which left him the most powerful Speaker since Joe Cannon in the early 1900s. His well-disciplined following immediately tackled the budget deficit question on a scale that dwarfed the feeble deficit reduction maneuvers of Clinton by a factor of more than three to one—$197 billion as compared to $60 billion in spending cuts over five years—and "instead of reinventing government [Vice President Gore's formula] . . . would disinvent whole chunks of it. Entire cabinet departments [Energy, Education, Transportation, HUD] and government agencies" were targeted by the "new abolitionists" (*Economist,* December 17, 1994 and January 7, 1995). The *Economist* was rather skeptical of these deficit-cutting efforts on both sides—"too much smoke and mirrors"—but there was no doubt that Washington had never before seen the likes of it. But then the Achilles heel of Gingrich was found: an ethics investigation into charges of tax evasion and a $4.5 million book contract from Rupert Murdoch—the latter all too reminiscent of the book deal that Gingrich had used to drive Democratic Speaker Jim Wright from office in 1988.

The near-perfect completion of the first 100 days of Speaker Gingrich and his dedicated freshmen Congress members also witnessed the paradoxical reemergence of a resilient President Clinton. Since the initiative now lay clearly with the Republican majorities in Congress, their critics from the White House and the media could gleefully observe every Republican misstep and mistake: the Senate majority, for example, proved unable, after 115 hours of debate, to achieve the required two-thirds majority for the ballyhooed balanced budget amendment to the Constitution. The House had already passed it 300 to 132. The House, moreover, failed to pass the term limits proposed by the contract, and no fewer than eight Republican presidential hopefuls prepared to fight each other for the 1996 nomination. "The minnows [not sharks] are circling Clinton," wrote Martin Fletcher in the *Times* of London about the Republican presidential candidates (February 21, 1995).

Now Clinton could strike a statesmanlike pose of defending the vulnerable of American society against the ruthless Republican budget deficit hawks and cutters of entitlements for the poor, the sick, the hungry school children, and the (actually quite comfortable) elderly. While Gingrich saw his polls drop lower and lower, Clinton's approval rating surged and his public image as the champion of the middle class soared: 52 percent said the president could be trusted to help the middle class as compared to only 38 percent who expected this of the Republican Congress. This placed him in the desired middle ground of "mainstream values" and "middle-class economics (whatever that may be)," according to the *Economist* (March 25, 1995). Gingrich and his Republican freshmen, by way of contrast, were pushed to the right, even the extreme right in the eyes of the public. The contract—which had seemingly turned the 1994 congressional campaign, ordinarily a bundle of local campaigns, into a national confrontation between Reaganism and the Clintonism of the first two years, especially on health reform—now put the Republicans on the defensive and became a target for Democratic polemics. It allowed their Democratic critics to lambaste their intended tax cuts for the wealthy and welfare cuts as extremism and open greed. Gingrich, who had expressed a desire to become president, by the end of 1995 withdrew his name from the roster of Republican hopefuls.

Tension among Republican factions on many issues also bedeviled their appearance as a unified reform movement, beginning with the emergence of Senate majority leader Dole as the likely front runner in the race for the presidential nomination. "In a city [Washington] dominated by a pair of brilliant, mercurial, slightly squirrelly baby-boomers—Bill Clinton and Newt Gingrich—Mr. Dole is a certified grown-up," Lexington explained (*Economist*, April 15, 1995). However, most Republicans did not exactly "burn for him" but rather thought him a compromiser and "deal-maker," and not a "true conservative." The use of the conservative label for Dole may have been debatable among Gingrich's followers, although the dour Dole, with his background of small-town virtues and hard luck, was probably closer to what Europeans would consider conservative, in particular in contrast to Clinton and his generation.

However, candidate Dole could not ignore the large percentages of skeptical Republican born-again Christians, gun owners, and foes of affirmative action and of raising taxes (he signed the "pledge" against tax increases), besetting him on issues he had voted for at one time or other in his long distinguished career. His pragmatic conservatism simply did not mix well with the radicalism of Gingrich and his band of revolutionaries. The resurgence of the religious right over such issues as abortion, Clinton's controversial nomination of Henry Foster as surgeon general, and the Christian Coalition's Contract with the American Family—a market-tested attempt to emulate the Contract with America with a list of religiously inspired proposals—made life difficult for the Republicans. It hardly helped to unify "that amalgam of supply-siders, populists, libertarians and cultural right-wingers who comprise the ascendant wing of the [Republican] party" (*Economist*, ibid.). When there was talk about a possible liberal Republican running mate for Dole—possibly New Jersey Governor Christie Whitman—the religious right, in fact, threatened to run its own candidates against the Republican ticket. It insisted on a vice presidential candidate solidly opposed to abortion. The pendulum had swung rather far from the 1992 slogan "It's the economy, stupid" to the alleged moral crisis of America of 1995. Economic growth actually slowed down for a while in mid-1995, but that did not seem to matter.

THE GREAT GOVERNMENT SHUTDOWN

Only weeks after President Clinton had managed a timid statement to the effect that, in spite of the assertiveness of the Republican Congress, "the president was still relevant" to the governmental system, Clinton's visibility and role in the bully pulpit received a considerable boost. In the wake of the Oklahoma City terrorist bombing, he found the right words for a shaken nation and his supportive posture produced a leap of ten percent in his approval rating. As Lars-Erik Nelson put it, looking back: "Conservative anti-government rhetoric still seemed popular at the start of 1995, but then, in April, the federal office building in Oklahoma City was bombed, and some of the newcomers [in Congress] were shocked into tempering their language."[3] The *Johannesburg Star* wrote, "Perversely, [Bill Clinton] is doing better as a rather lame duck than he did when his party controlled Congress" (May 25, 1995). His approval rating climbed from the low 40 percent level to well over 50 percent, the best showing in more than a year.

But the great budgetary deficit-cutting debate went on through the summer and fall of 1995. It finally generated an ambitious Republican proposal that promised to lead to a balanced budget in seven years, after severe cuts totaling over $900 billion and the elimination of a number of cabinet departments, federal agencies, and programs—and the promise of $245 billion in tax cuts. From the vantage point of Clinton and the congressional Democrats, the budget cutters intended to savage Medicare and Medicaid (the medical insurance for the poor), push the sick and elderly poor out into the street, and consign children and teenage mothers to poverty—all while exacting a huge tax cut for the wealthy. Senator Pat Moynihan accused the Republicans of "welfare repeal" and chief of staff Leon Panetta exclaimed that they were "shredding the Social Security Act." Clinton and the Democrats similarly wanted to cut the annual deficit but not as draconically and over a longer period of time. It was not to Clinton's advantage, moreover, to tie his reelection campaign to the Old Democrats, according to his new/old political strategist, Dick Morris. The *Economist* commented: "The cold reality is that Mr. Clinton can win in 1996 only by putting a decent distance between himself and his party. And the chances of a Democratic recapture of Congress have if anything worsened since November [1994]," both in the Senate, where a number of Democrats were retiring or switched parties, and in the House, which had lost many moderate Democrats in the 1994 elections (May 20, 1995). Liberal Democrats, for their part, passionately resented the return of Dick Morris, who had once before (in 1982) helped Bill Clinton to reinvent himself as a centrist Democrat and, more recently, also served Republicans such as Trent Lott, the new Senate majority leader: "[They] assail Mr. Morris as Darth Vader, a shadowy force from the dark side, for persuading Mr. Clinton to put forth a balanced budget plan," too (Lexington, *Economist,* July 29, 1995).

The crisis point was reached quickly because the annual appropriations bills of the budget had to pass before October 1 and the House, by September 1995, had passed only one of 13 such authorizations, and Clinton had threatened to veto that because of its controversial budget-cutting details. A so-called continuing resolution was needed as a stopgap spending measure to keep all government agencies at work. Because of its reliance on the same details (the large tax cut and the huge appropriation cuts in Medicare, Medicaid, federal welfare programs, and farm subsidies), the president threatened to veto this continuation bill too, which would shut down half the federal government. These were two "trainwreck scenarios," according to the *Economist* (September 9, 1995). And there was a third one, namely that the government's debt ceiling would be reached in October. This point would mark an unprecedented default on paying the interest of $22 billion on the national debt, the first time in over 200 years that the United States government would have defaulted, risking a fiscal and stock market meltdown. It would have triggered a crisis in the worldwide financial markets. Since only Congress could raise the debt ceiling, the Republican majorities were said to be tempted thus to blackmail Clinton into cooperating with their budget plan. "The Republicans used [the debt ceiling ploy] to make Mr. Clinton look irresponsible—and to make life miserable for Mr. Rubin [the Treasury secretary], whom they have disliked ever since the Mexican bailout" (*Economist*, November 18, 1995). Rubin successfully intercepted their ploy with clever measures to raise the funds for the interest payments, but the government was largely shut down: some 800,000 of the government staff were furloughed as non-essential, including about 80 percent of the presidential staff.

Near-apocalyptic terms and veto threats from both sides flew in the debate as the Republican majorities of both houses prepared their seven-year budget with over $900 billion in deficit cuts (along with the $245 billion tax cut), half of the savings to be realized by cutting Medicare by 20 percent and Medicaid by 30 percent. It was ironic, furthermore, that one year after the painful demise of the Clintons' health reform, the Republicans now discovered that there was a health care crisis after all, namely, the impending financial collapse of the Medicare trust fund that had to be "saved" by drastic cuts. Perhaps, reasoned the freshmen of Gingrich's revolution, Medicare could be turned, like the welfare programs, into (greatly reduced) block grants to the state governments which could use them as they saw fit. Clinton, in a speech before retirees in Florida, called it "a middle-class tax increase on young people whose senior parents will now require their assistance." The *Economist* (September 23, 1995) pointed out that "the Medicare Trust fund . . . has been in trouble before—the trustees have forecast its bankruptcy nine times since 1970—and each time, it had been 'saved' without imposing any pain on beneficiaries." Mentioning its own tough prescriptions such as rationing services, reliance on HMOs, and means testing, and pointing out that there were still 40 million Americans uninsured, the British weekly added: "The history books will record that weak Republican knees and strident Democratic demagoguery both played their part and that these traits are symptoms of a shared sickness: fear of offending the old . . . the sickness may be terminal."

The Republican script for the shutdown evidently called first for the passage of the controversial seven-year budget bill, Clinton's expected veto, and then a still-disputed financial stopgap measure that Gingrich and Dole thought would lead either to the president's immediate capitulation or, at least, to his commitment to their seven-year timetable. Clinton had vacillated and compromised so often— and his position was not that far from theirs—that they were quite confident he would give in. Clinton, however, had seen in the public opinion polls that the outraged American public blamed the Republican Congress for shutting down half the government. He stood his ground, vetoing the first stopgap and a slightly modified second stopgap measure with the explanation that he would not submit to blackmail. He launched counterproposals that dropped the tax cut and lessened the cuts in Medicare. The House freshmen (more than Gingrich himself) seemingly hoped that their strong-arm maneuvers would be the liberating coup that destroyed the federal welfare state. The public might even discover that a truncated federal government stripped of non-essential bureaucrats was quite satisfactory and would lead to the devolution of welfare and other functions to the state level. They had already killed some 30 federal programs and cut many others, even though they were notably reluctant to tackle the vast subsidies of corporate welfare and tax benefits for the wealthy. But now their forceful campaign turned into an embarrassing rout. Moreover, it reflected poorly on the likely Republican presidential candidate, Dole, in spite of his reluctance to participate in the budgetary strong-arming attempt. European observers watched all this with alarm: "Mr. Clinton [once more has triumphed but] may . . . discover a sobering truth about his new strategy [of triangulation]: the point of a triangle can be a particularly lonely and helpless place" (Lexington, *Economist*, November 4, 1995).

European journalists saw the disgust of the American public with this political theater performance: "The audience, meanwhile, grows surlier with each passing hour. Confused, it wonders how the players could have rehearsed all year, only to end in this pathetic state of disarray ... a high-school company could, it seems, perform more professionally," commented the *Economist*. The public was not as naive as the self-styled political class had thought. It was angry but not surprised or shocked by the "farcical ... shadow-play that shut down the government," a farce that had occurred already five times since 1980. Many Americans agreed that, perhaps, the impasse should have been resolved with a one-year stopgap resolution that would let the voters of 1996 decide, as in a referendum, what to make of this confrontation. "The audience groans ... having sat through this perplexing, perturbing and deeply cynical production ... a hail of tomatoes may soon be heading for the stage, not to mention the ballot box" (*Economist*, November 18, 1995). The exasperation even spread to some Republicans, like Doug Gamble, a speech writer for Reagan and Bush. He later called the congressional leaders "these geniuses who squandered the 1994 GOP takeover of Congress" (*Los Angeles Times*, February 10, 2000).

By the time of the Republican presidential convention of 2000, Ronald Brownstein looked back on this moment (*Los Angeles Times*, August 14, 2000) and reflected on how different the "GOP convention [of 2000] might have looked if Clinton had not broken the momentum of the conservative ascendancy after the 1994 election gave Republicans control of Congress. When they swept into power with Newt Gingrich at the lead, the 'revolutionary' generation of young conservatives dreamed of closing the Education Department (among other Cabinet offices), repealing the ban on assault weapons, replacing the progressive income tax with a single-rate flat tax and lighting a bonfire under Federal Registers thick with environmental regulations." Clinton, however, outmaneuvered the Republicans by half-adopting some of their programs, such as welfare reform and a balanced budget. "When public opinion sided with Clinton during the government shutdowns in the winter of 1995-96, the die was cast: He surged into the lead over Republican presidential candidate Bob Dole and then coasted to reelection" (August 14, 2000). The final upshot of Clinton's maneuver and the resulting compromises, according to Brownstein, was George W. Bush's half-adoption of several distinctive Democratic concerns, such as improving public education and the appeal to ethnic diversity.

PRESIDENT CLINTON'S REELECTION

The election year of 1996 opened with the budget issue unresolved and Gingrich "badly wounded from the battles of the revolution" (Lexington, *Economist,* December 16, 1995). As widely expected, Dole had emerged as the undisputed front runner on the Republican side, if somewhat scarred by stiff competition in the primary elections, particularly by right-wing populist Pat Buchanan and flat-tax advocate Steve Forbes. Compared to the impression of "messianic fervor" of a Gingrich, the septuagenarian Dole stood out mostly with his "fervent moderation," said the *Economist* (January 7, 1995), on many things the New Republicans cared about. He had always been a pragmatist on fiscal policy, with a conservative dislike for deficit spending. Dole and Gingrich, not to mention retired General Colin Powell, a Rockefeller Republican, were rivals for Republican attention, if not for the presidential nomination of 1996. "Dole's biggest, unsolvable problem, in spite of the brilliant Republican landslide elections of 1994," wrote the conservative Joffe in the *Sueddeutsche Zeitung,* "is a party as totally split and at odds with itself as the Democrats were in the seventies and eighties." Worse yet, while the Republicans were fighting, "Clinton had stolen all the good Republican issues, budget discipline, crime, welfare reform, and family values. Now, who still needs to vote for Republicans? . . . The [Republican] elephant has become an animal whose tusks are aimed at its own behind" (August 12, 1996). By sending the president a welfare bill that he might accept, of course, the Congressional Republicans had also robbed Dole of his best campaign slogan. Now Clinton appeared the cautious and conservative moderate while Dole was the optimistic radical.

While the Republican young tigers at times squabbled "nastily with their maximum leader [Gingrich]" (Lexington, *Economist*, December 2, 1995), Dole had a presidential campaign to run, against what may well have been one of the cleverest and most effective campaigners of the twentieth century. Gingrich struggled to maintain control over his runaway revolution and some of its perhaps unintended consequences: the landslide of 1994 had swept neo-isolationists into office—e.g., Jesse Helms into the Senate Foreign Relations Committee chair, Trent Lott into the Senate majority leader position, many of Gingrich's freshmen, and even some Democrats on the left. This was at a time when Gingrich himself and two-thirds of Americans (according to a Chicago Council on Foreign Relations survey) wanted the United States to play a more active role in the world, the highest mark of internationalism in twenty years. In fact, presidential standard bearer Dole had always been a Nixonian internationalist, too.

The freshmen, moreover, including the born-again abolitionists of federal agencies, soon began to get around to the more controversial parts of their revolution, such as their campaign against governmental and environmental regulation of business, which stiffened resistance to the contract in some quarters. Furthermore, Thomas Bliley, the "congressman from Philip Morris," had become the chair of the House Commerce Committee at a time when the tobacco industry, which had Congress in its pocket for decades, was entering perhaps its darkest period ever. The Speaker's estranged sister Candace Gingrich came to Washington from San Francisco to represent a lesbian organization, a great embarrassment to Gingrich since "the only thing the Speaker and his sister seem to share is a desperate need for a more flattering haircut." (*Economist*, March 11, 1995). The Speaker's public opinion polls, in any case, by then marked him as the least popular politician in the United States, though probably not among Europeans. But, more than any other hazard, Gingrich and his revolution faced a skeptical if Republican-dominated Senate, which early in 1995 already began to fear a voter backlash against the contract's combination of deep welfare cuts with a huge tax cut for business and wealthy Americans.

Clinton, in the meantime, had not only regained his composure after the electoral disaster of 1994 but could now focus more emphatically upon his original, centrist, New Democrat agenda. Even though the 1994 elections had claimed many moderate Democrats in Congress, leaving proportionally more of the Old Democrats, Clinton was now free to advocate his centrist position. No longer was he constrained to accommodate himself to the dominant congressional Democrats of his first years in the White House. In a bit of whimsy, the *Economist* had even written a 1995 State of the Union speech for him which boiled down to admitting his "big mistake" in allowing himself to be "willingly shackled to the . . . congressional barons in my party" (January 22, 1995). His seeming about-face registered in different ways in the different camps: Secretary of Labor Robert Reich spoke of "a second transition" from New to Old Democrat and back again. Voters were confused, having perhaps associated him with "big government liberalism" and the alleged elitism of the Democratic and New Deal bureaucratic establishment.

Republicans at first welcomed Clinton's seeming conversion to their preferences—if not to the entire hidden agenda of the Contract for America and its subordination of environmental protection and workers' rights to business interests—and his cooperation with their legislative projects. But his relentless focus on economic issues that mattered to the middle class, both wholesale issues such as cutting the deficit and retail ones as with his "politics of miniaturization" (e.g., school uniforms), soon began to crowd them. Some critics viewed him as a "stealth Republican." Others claimed that his crime bill and eventual signatures on welfare reform and deficit-cutting plans really amounted to his stealing Republican issues, or at least, his taking credit for their passage. As the conservative German business weekly *Wirtschaftswoche* of Düsseldorf wrote in amazement over the passage of American welfare reform: "No developed nation spends less on social welfare (as a percentage of national income) than the United States. But for Americans even this cost is too high. By signing the Personal Responsibility and Work Opportunity Act [welfare reform] of August 1996, President Clinton has embarked on the biggest social experiment since Franklin Delano Roosevelt promised every citizen in 1935 'a certain measure of protection.' For six decades the credo that society had a duty to support the poor has endured. With welfare reform, the responsibility will now shift to the individual . . . the reason being less the high federal deficit than a change in American values. For many Americans, the welfare system has become synonymous with government waste and subsidized dependency" (August 8, 1996).

In the year before the final horse race began in August of 1996, the role of the third-party spoiler of 1992, Ross Perot, also crystallized after abortive Republican efforts failed to co-opt or sideline him as a contender for a significant share of the Republican vote. Four times as many Perotistas leaned toward the Republicans as indicated a liking for the Democrats. In August of 1995, all Republican candidates and Gingrich went a-courtin' in Dallas but found Perot uncooperative and his followers bent on their independent course, an angry "radical centrism" (per Republican pollster Frank Luntz) that insisted on bringing only "outsiders" to Washington. This was a bad omen for Dole, the quintessential Washington insider of 34 long years. Before the year was out, Perot announced his intention to be a candidate for president in 1996 and to incorporate his movement, United We Stand, America, as the Independence Party, a third party that would be content to endorse congressional candidates, not nominate any. In the polls, nearly two-thirds of the public had indicated that they would like to see a third party in the running. As in 1992, this had an immediate impact on Clinton's chances for reelection. Lexington commented in the *Economist* (September 30, 1995): "[President Clinton] faces an uphill struggle in a straight contest against a Republican challenger, but in a three-way race he instantly becomes the favorite . . . Now Mr. Perot has reminded everyone that, mouselike as he is, he can still scare the daylights out of an elephant." A few months later, before the last three-week government shutdown was resolved, Lexington added: "The advisers whisper . . . into the presidential ear that he should resist a budget deal [now] . . . because a budget breakdown is the surest way of bringing Ross Perot into the race" (January 6, 1996). Perot's entry did play a role in the end when he won 8 percent of the popular vote—perhaps also denying Clinton the one percent of the popular vote for the majority that he craved—but it was far less consequential than in 1992.

President Clinton entered the year of his reelection unopposed in the primaries. He was cloaked in the image of a statesman in foreign policy on the heels of triumphs in foreign trade (NAFTA, GATT) and in the peace processes of the Middle East, Bosnia, and Northern Ireland. Some eight million new jobs had been created on his watch—soon to grow to ten million—and unemployment fell under six percent. An ever-accelerating stock market was soaring to unprecedented levels, making many of his well-heeled enemies even richer. The president's campaign finance strategy, aside from avoiding heavy expenditures in the primaries, was to raise his campaign funds early and to avoid the financial dry stretch that beset his Republican opponent before the presidential nominating conventions. In his State of the Union speech, moreover, the president sounded his new call that "the era of Big Government is over," although a skeptical American press did not accept this. They claimed instead that the great budget battle still raged over the question of whether the expansive vision of the New Deal and the Great Society was to be replaced by a narrower regime based on laissez faire and individual virtues. Candidate Dole added his own leitmotif, calling the president the obstacle to progress and insisting that Clinton "walk the talk he talks so well." But Dole found it difficult to clearly aim his barbs at this president, who was now matching the Republicans' seven-year plan toward a balanced budget with his own, more moderate, seven-year plan.

How Dole, the master politician of the Senate, fell so far behind Clinton in the polls—over 20 percent behind in mid-1996—is not easy to explain. His rival, Pat Buchanan, called him "an empty vessel, bereft of ideas," and others described his campaign as "brain dead," with "no vision of the future," and scored him for alienating such Republican core constituencies as the anti-abortion forces, the gun lobby, and the freshmen of Gingrich's revolution. "There has been lasting damage to the Republican image," wrote correspondent Stefan Kornelius of Munich's *Sueddeutsche Zeitung,* "caused by the so-called conservative revolution of . . . Gingrich after his electoral triumph of 1994. There was even talk that Gingrich ought to resign" (September 21, 1996). A veteran of three previous presidential campaigns, Dole had hoped to overcome his large gender gap by inviting pro-choice Republican Representative Susan Molinari to address the convention that had nominated him. He promised an economic plan that would combine a Reaganesque, across-the-board 15 percent tax cut with efforts to eventually reach a balanced budget. But nothing seemed to improve his chances, not even his selection of the charismatic Jack Kemp as his running mate and his own ceremonial resignation from his prominent Senate post, which was meant to show how serious he was about running for president.

Three weeks into the postconvention campaign, Kornelius of the *Sueddeutsche Zeitung* still saw "Dole stuck in the doldrums of failure . . . it is a hopeless situation . . . his greatest handicap remains: the voters have not accepted his issues, and his [economic] recovery program for the country seems superfluous. No one believes his tax cut promises" (September 21, 1996). The *Economist* commented dryly on Dole's economic plan: "Mr. Dole's measures look attractive when each is viewed in isolation. In combination, the result looks ugly. Mr. Dole proposes no serious cuts in federal spending, and has promised to leave Medicare, Social Security and defense [the bulk of the budget] . . . untouched. That leaves his promise both to cut taxes and balance the budget on magic" (August 10, 1996). Two months later, the same journal called Dole's plan "simply dishonest: even with a deficit that is now only 1.6 percent of GDP . . . and even on the rosiest projections of the future economic growth." Clinton's tax cut of only $20 billion seemed more cautious and "mostly matched by specific cuts in spending . . . the deepest [due only] when—surprise!—he will be out of office" (October 5, 1996). Still, as Republican Senator William Roth remarked with indignation, "lowering taxes is a Republican idea." But Reagan's old miracle weapon, the large tax cut combined with deficit-raising defense splurging—based on Arthur Laffer's "voodoo economics" (George Bush's phrase)—had failed miserably for Dole.

Clinton, by contrast, had benefited from playing the 1996 Olympic Games (like Reagan in 1984) for political advantage in an election year. Democratic centrism had arrived, even in the British perspective where Labour party deputy leader John Prescott, back in 1992, had taken a dim view of any "Clintonizing." Now Prescott came to Chicago, just before the Democratic convention and signaled his appreciation for both Clinton and the rightward turn of Tony Blair, who won the British elections a year later (Norman Gelb, *New Leader,* September 9-23, 1996). The economy was humming along, at minimal inflation, with 4.8 percent growth in the second quarter of 1996. The budget deficit was forecast to shrink by about $50 billion compared with the previous year. All this made Dole's doleful economic assumptions sound quite unrealistic. The low level of unemployment (5.1 percent) also made Dole's argument for a tax cut to create jobs seem irrelevant. Britain's Lexington wrote, "if the *Economist* were an American voter seeking to make sense of the campaign . . . it would . . . hope that Bob Dole is lying; and . . . that Bill Clinton is telling the truth" (August 10, 1996). Never mind that the much-touted welfare reform really only moved welfare functions to the state level—where presumably they better knew how to take care of their poor—and that, four years later, a study discovered that over $7 billion of the diminished welfare funds transferred there had not even been spent. And now that Clinton prepared to sign the welfare reform bill to "end welfare as we know it" (i.e., the federal guarantee of it), per his 1992 election promise, the British weekly added: "[His signature] looked like a statement of future intent, a demonstration that the new Bill Clinton really does mean to cut government, to eliminate the deficit and to devolve responsibilities [to the state level]."

Kornelius, for his part, was impressed by Clinton's clever use of small election promises: "He holds [the voters'] attention with a minimal program and a politics of small niceties . . . a suitcase full of little surprises, none of them very expensive" (*Sueddeutsche Zeitung*, September 21, 1996). Early in September, moreover, Saddam Hussein had given Clinton an opportunity to show that, contrary to widespread criticism, he was also quite ready and able to wield American military might. Almost eight out of ten Americans approved of his bombing raids, a noticeable factor driving his own popularity polls of 55 percent versus 35 percent for Dole. On almost all policies and issues, Americans credited Clinton with more competence than Dole, save one: on the hoary issue of character, the Senate majority leader and World War II hero was 26 percent ahead of the president. Otherwise, state by state, calculations of Clinton's likely edge in the Electoral College vote gave him 417 votes to Dole's 81, a landslide by any measure.

When it became clear that the Republican presidential candidate was headed for a humiliating defeat, especially after the first presidential debate, Dole did what Bush had done in 1992. His new campaign ads announced that there was a "moral crisis" in the White House and, in the second presidential debate, Dole concentrated on ethics issues. Gingrich, glad to be at the right end of an ethics investigation for once, immediately called for an examination of Democratic campaign finance irregularities and claimed he could "smell a scandal that would make Watergate look tiny." Dole disclosed new "scandals almost on a daily basis," commented Lexington in the *Economist:* "The new Dole strategy amounts to an admission of failure, the failure of any other approach to make an impact on what has remained an extraordinarily static race" (October 19, 1996). Dole had promised to avoid a mudfight in this election, the *Sueddeutsche Zeitung* concluded, but in view of his dismal polls, his advisers got the better of him; "but the voters balk at making this a 'character contest'" (October 18, 1996). Lexington in the *Economist* added that, in this presidential campaign, Dole "belied his own record on many issues" and "All this from a man who touts his [own] 'leadership qualities.'" The *Economist* also praised Clinton's disciplined campaign style and his rapid response team's "prebuttals." The resignation of Dick Morris over his own sex scandal was the only mishap. "The bimbo eruption was Mr. Morris's, not Mr. Clinton's; and by then the Morris strategy had worked its magic. Mr. Clinton had neutralized the 'Republican issues,' from welfare to crime and foreign policy, making him a maddeningly difficult target for Mr. Dole to attack (October 19, 1996)." The *Sueddeutsche Zeitung* was not quite as forgiving in its comment: "The Morris resignation [in the middle of Clinton's nominating convention] highlighted the conservative perception of a crude and sinful White House; it revived the character issue" (August 31, 1996).

Curiously, however, the *Economist* did not repeat its 1992 endorsement of Clinton nor did it endorse Dole, declaring them both "flawed candidates" and the choice a dubious one. In a blistering editorial, possibly inspired by iron instructions from on high, the British weekly explained that "Bill Clinton has been [throwing away his principles] for four years . . . for the difficulty with Mr. Clinton is that he changes so often that it is hard to know what you are supporting, or opposing . . . Four years later [our endorsement of Clinton] looks like a mistake." The editorial writer believed that the 1994 defeat made the president "recast himself as a moderate Republican" but would not trust him to continue in this fashion. Challenger Dole, by the same token, was accused of having thrown his principles away but only for the last year: "The real Bob Dole is the one who spent three decades on Capitol Hill, not this year's dubious character" (November 2, 1996). The *Sueddeutsche Zeitung* editorialized: "The president never succeeded in burying his character questions but Americans have learned to live with him. His sure paternal touch in moments of national tragedy [like in Oklahoma City] have made Clinton seem more endearing. But he also seems strangely slippery . . . hesitant and unsure in his decisions and appointments" (November 5, 1996).

The presidential elections of 1996 ended, as expected, with a Clinton landslide although, to quote *Time* magazine, "Clinton paid dearly for a victory he probably could have had on the cheap" (November 12, 1996)—an observation made also about the 1972 reelection of Richard Nixon with regard to campaign finance irregularities. Clinton and the Democrats lost votes and public respect for similar reasons, especially among Republicans, independents, and even evangelicals who had been planning to vote for them. Nevertheless, Clinton was out in front in nearly all categories of voters (save white males where Dole was ahead by 11 percent), including 50 percent of Catholics, one in five conservatives, one in four members of the religious right, and one in eight Republicans. His gender gap, the difference between male and female voters, was now 16 percent. The Republican party gained in the Senate, but lost nine seats of its House majority (including six of the 1994 freshmen), still retaining 227 versus 207 Democratic (and one Independent) seats.

Democratic congressional campaigners later complained that the president had made little effort in their quest to regain control of Congress, other than raising funds. But then, perhaps, half a Democrat in the White House was better than none. "But would Clinton really have done as well with a Democratic Congress as with a Republican one?" mused the *Sueddeutsche Zeitung* (November 5,

1996), considering his purloining of many middle-of-the-road Republican issues. "Clinton the poacher took something from all the camps, the Old Democrats, the New Left, and the conservatives. He has no unifying vision." Centrism obviously had not yet arrived in Germany in 1996. The House races were fought by both parties not on the customary local issues but as a kind of national referendum for or against the revolution of the Contract for America. By then, unlike in 1994, the public had a real sense of what this revolution was all about. Gingrich claimed that no fewer than 75,000 Democratic ads had named him as the devil to be avoided at all costs. "Gingrich stood for the arrogance of power," according to Kurt Kister's postmortem on the elections in the *Sueddeutsche Zeitung*, " . . . he wrongly believed the voters had given his Republicans a mandate for a 'conservative revolution' [in 1994] when they really only wanted to punish their unprincipled president [of 1993-1994] and the corruption of the perpetual Democratic majority on the Hill" (November 7, 1996).

The *Economist* belatedly (April 5, 1997) came to the defense of Gingrich in an issue entitled "Whatever Happened to the Republican Revolution?". It admitted that voters had not really endorsed the contract and had resented both the government shutdown and Gingrich himself. But it was not fair for the Republicans to now turn on him. For one thing, "the radicalism of the Republicans in 1994-1996 was not all that it seemed. Sometimes they merely appeared vigorous by contrast with the sleepy gatherings that had gone before. And they talked much more than they acted." The British journal was disappointed with the revolution's actual achievements, for example, regarding tort reform, taxes, regulation, and affirmative action. Furthermore, "The disintegration of the Republicans is not to be lamented merely because one coherent ideology and one source of energy have disappeared from American politics," but also because now the Democrats were no longer constrained to masquerade as Republicans walking down the center of the road. "Two years ago,

Mr. Gingrich was celebrated as the most powerful Speaker of this century; now a fellow House Republican describes him as 'roadkill on the highway of American politics,' and his demise is predicted on all sides." Considered weak ever since investigation of his ethics and his reelection with Democratic votes, the Speaker now was said to be without an agenda and, "in encounters with the president, Mr. Gingrich turns to jelly." More than any other reason, his statement that tax cuts could wait until a balanced budget deal had been struck doomed him in the eyes of his former disciples. In the view of the *Economist*, however, "Mr. Gingrich, more honest than Mr. Reagan, has discovered... that taxes cannot be cut much, given America's fiscal problems," such as the social entitlements in the midst of the aging of America: "If Republicans had the courage to be honest, they would thank Mr. Gingrich for refusing to follow Mr. Reagan's road" (April 5, 1997).

It was an election of little passion, in any case: Dole and Clinton were both pragmatic rather than ideological campaigners. The electoral turnout was the lowest since 1924, and 7 percent less than in 1992. Clinton had indeed run more against the unpopular Gingrich of the government shutdown than against Dole. "Clinton's strength had been in his economic policies in the midst of global stagnation [including German stagnation]," commented the *Sueddeutsche Zeitung* (November 7, 1996): "He reduced the annual budget deficit to a mere third of its level of 1992—but there were also his triumphs in foreign policy ... This election signifies the end of the World War II generation among national leaders. Americans certainly knew they were electing a 1968er for president." Clinton was reelected with an increased popular mandate of 49 percent, still not a majority but backed up overwhelmingly by his Electoral College vote, 379 in 32 states as compared to 159 in 18 states for Dole. The American people and the Constitution had spoken out although there were some critical voices. Other reelected presidents such as Eisenhower, Nixon, and Reagan had triumphed by nearly 60 percent. *Time* magazine called Clinton "the better man to enact a Republican agenda" (November 18, 1996), taking care not to speak of *the* Republican agenda as if there had been only one. The famous welfare reform bill signed by the president, on the other hand, also found many bitter critics on the left, who feared for its many victims, especially children in poverty and foreign-born legal residents. "The Clinton political machine has been relaunched for another four years," commented the French weekly *L'Express* (November 14, 1996), and Canada's *McLean* predicted that "after his easy reelection victory, President Bill Clinton will have a much tougher time in his second term" (November 18, 1996).

AMERICAN COMPLICATIONS TO A DEMOCRATIC TRIUMPH

Clinton was the first Democratic president since Woodrow Wilson and Franklin Delano Roosevelt to be elected to a second term. To European and other democratic observers around the world, this looked like the triumph of a democratic constitution. They did not reckon with certain American legal peculiarities that, since Watergate, have increasingly interfered with the straightforward workings of that Constitution. Democratic mandates in America can be subverted by loose cannon prosecutors, lawyers, the media, and, of course, the defeated political opposition. As Perot said on the eve of the elections, "If Clinton is reelected, his second term will be a nightmare of legal problems that will compare with Watergate." *Time* magazine (November 4, 1996) ventured, "that's a stretch" but conceded that the relentless Starr investigation was now nipping at the heels of people near the Clintons, and that Hillary Clinton was the likely target of the search warrants on Travelgate obtained by Starr for the home of Hillary's friend Patsy Thomasson. On Filegate, a federal appeals court gave Starr the authority to investigate whether White House lawyer Bernard Nussbaum had lied to Congress regarding the hiring of Craig Livingstone, a lowly operative who had custody of these FBI files.

There was no question but that John Huang would be questioned after the elections about Asian campaign contributions. A fortnight later, James O. Stewart wrote in the election issue of *Time* (November 18, 1996): "Clinton's resounding reelection all but guarantees that Whitewater and all its progeny, from Travelgate to Filegate, will continue to hound this presidency." The Starr investigation was marching on—mostly barking up the wrong trees, as we now know, but this would hardly deter it—and Attorney General Janet Reno had already approved expanding his jurisdiction five times. The investigations of other targets in the administration—Secretary of Agriculture Mike Espy, Secretary of HUD Henry Cisneros, and Secretary of Commerce Ron Brown—were next. The American Constitution gives little clue to this recurring circus of investigations of administrative officers, although we can assume that Congress, like all modern legislatures, has the power to investigate those it appoints and confirms, to conduct any and all investigations relating to legislation, and to investigate anything and anyone as part of its control function over the executive branch. Since they had attained a majority in 1994, a fair measurement of the escalating Republican investigations is the rising number of days the House Committee on Government Reform and Oversight has spent with hearings. During the 104th session (1995-1996) it was 313 days compared to 195 days under the Democrat-controlled 103rd Congress.

The most consequential legal trap awaiting Clinton, we can say with the benefit of hindsight, was the 1994 civil suit of Paula Corbin Jones against him for $700,000, for "intentionally inflicting emotional distress, violating her civil rights, and defaming her" (read: sexual harassment). The statute of limitations for charges of sexual harassment had run out and such a charge was hardly supported by the facts anyway. According to Jones's sister, "she [Paula] smelled money," and according to the *Economist*, "Clinton-haters smelled blood." The voters did not seem to care, "but the acid of scandal in a president's private life . . . will inevitably corrode confidence in the presidency itself . . . the sniggering—and the bad jokes about the 'distinguishing characteristics' of the presidential penis—is no laughing matter," wrote Lexington (May 14, 1994), and neither was the enormous legal expense to the Clintons and to subpoenaed witnesses.

This civil suit against a sitting president—the principle of presidential immunity from criminal law suits is long established—was hardly a model of American justice and the rule of law to begin with, judging from Jeffrey Toobin's description in *A Vast Conspiracy* and Michael Isikoff's account in his book *Uncovering Clinton*. The eventual explosive power of the Jones lawsuit in the hands of a conspiracy of right-wing lawyers and judges carried the triumph of legal busywork over the Constitution to absurd lengths. The principals of the Jones suit, other than Paula Jones herself and Clinton—who denied remembering her or the alleged incident—were the cabal of attorneys of the secretive Federalist Society, the lawyers of the Rutherford Institute of the religious right, and Starr. Add to this the eagerness of the media to find a presidential sex scandal and of religious right groups, like the anti-abortion activists of Operation Rescue, to supply fuel to the conflagration. Under American law, public personages have no protection from slander and libelous attacks in the media unless they can show them to be intentionally malicious. Given enough "dirty money" from radical-right angels to keep it going and a camarilla of eager right-wing lawyers and judges, any lawsuit can make its way through the courts in America to eventually torpedo the highest office in the land.

"Officials find the experience [of being subpoenaed and interviewed] a nightmare. Their lawyers bemoan an age in which only people with the morals of Mother Theresa can afford to go into public life" (*Economist*, May 28, 1994). With a federal judiciary seeded throughout by the Reagan and Bush administrations with more than 50 percent of arch-Republican appointees, the federal judges were no guarantee of even-handed justice. Thomas Jefferson had hoped the judges would be "mere machines" in the exercise of their function. Alexander Hamilton suggested that they should have "neither force nor will, merely judgment." Moreover, political questions are often "judicialized" (Alexis de Tocqueville) and the ever-hungry legal system tends to swallow politics (Toobin). But in the 1990s, the judges' judgment on the highest institutional matters, more often than not, turned out to be of the narrowest partisan sort. "Modern America has discovered litigation as the continuation of politics by other means" (*Economist,* May 28, 1994).

And there was, of course, the ancient Whitewater affair, that inexhaustible source of investigatorial initiative and partisan invective. If there was any need to point to the congressional Whitewater hearings as a political fishing expedition, Senator D'Amato's committee and Representative James Leach's House Banking Committee provided chapter and verse after the 1994 Republican landslide gave them the respective committee chairs. D'Amato invoked a "national and law enforcement interest" in the 1978 Whitewater real estate development failure and then concentrated on his real purpose, slurring the president in the senatorial hearings. Leach offered high-minded thoughts on the theory of checks and balances while scanning vast amounts of information on Hillary Clinton's investments in cattle futures. At the same time, Starr's team of government-paid lawyers—whose need for witnesses and documents often stymied the congressional examination of the same Whitewater subject matter—were rumored to be beating the bushes of Arkansas for evidence of libidinous bimbo eruptions of then-governor Clinton.

"In a world of conspiracy theories," to quote *Economist* columnist Lexington, "one of the more plausible is . . . that the Republicans' main motive is to embarrass Mr. Clinton as much as possible in the run-up to the 1996 elections." The columnist himself had already offered another such theory to explain the Whitewater mess, tongue in cheek, the "British connection" or "Britgate" from Clinton's days as a Rhodes scholar at Cambridge University. "Far more feverish imaginations have been churning out conspiracy theories by the fax-load. Talk radio and the Internet have helped the paranoia business boom" (*Economist,* July 22, 1995). Despite the eventual failure of Starr and others to pin any substantial Whitewater charges on the Clintons, we should remember that some Arkansas notables were convicted, such as Governor Jim Guy Tucker, the McDougals, and Webster Hubbell, Hillary's partner in the Rose law firm, and that the total Whitewater-related complex from Madison Guaranty to Castle Grande and the Rose law firm was so incredibly entangled that it could indeed stymie even the taxpayer-supported persistence of a Starr for four years.

A number of new scandals for investigation came from the fund-raising practices of President Clinton and the Democratic National Committee (DNC) in the 1996 campaign. These involved invitations to friends and supporters, including of course major financial contributors, to spend the night in the Lincoln Bedroom of the White House. Over 500 guests were served coffee at the White House, according to media tallies, and contributed $26 million to the campaign. Republicans, who themselves raised far more money than the Democrats, pilloried this as a superexpensive, tit-for-tat bed-and-breakfast operation in a national shrine. European observers generally withheld comment inasmuch as they rarely have any equivalent of such national cult objects compared to the White House.

Potentially far more explosive were scandals involving campaign contributions from shady and foreign sources to the Democratic National Committee, such as those from Indonesian James Riady of the Lippo investment group or John Huang and the Chinese connection. The possible linkage of such contributions to Clinton's China policy, or to the Chinese espionage scandal that unfolded in 1999, made this an irresistible target for partisan polemics. The problem was not so much in the fact of scandals on both sides of the aisle—Gingrich also had to answer for a tax-exempt foundation that financed his televised college course—but in what the campaign finance scandal revealed about the legality of buying access to Congress and to the administration. As journalist Michael Kinsley put it years ago, the real scandal is often in what is revealed to be perfectly legal corruption and venality, not in what is found to be illegal modes of corruption. Republican politicians had also accepted and, in some cases, later returned such illegal or dubious cash contributions from abroad, for example, from Hong Kong during the 1994 elections ($2.1 million) as Haley Barbour of the Republican National Committee admitted. But the GOP had long resisted the introduction of effective regulation of so-called soft campaign money, that is, funds contributed to a party rather than to individual campaigns, claiming that such regulation violated the first amendment. This was "the hottest free speech issue of the day . . . ," wrote the *Economist* (January 4, 1997), "[namely] whether the first amendment covers campaign spending." The Supreme Court had given a qualified yes and has since partially reversed itself. Congressional campaign finance had never been subjected to regulation in quite the same, if imperfect, fashion as presidential campaign finance had been in the aftermath of Watergate. Congress, over the years, has been by far the most venal and corrupt branch of our federal government.

Since Kentucky Senator Mitch McConnell was the most prominent spokesperson of the dubious theory that unlimited political contributions were a kind of protected free speech, wags invented a McConnell constitutional amendment to replace the first amendment to the Constitution: "Congress shall make no law restricting the flow of soft money to the Republican party . . ." This went along with the new second (or Charlton Heston) amendment which pointedly left off the confusing part about "a well-regulated militia"—or replaced it with "an unregulated militia of patriots"—and simply asserted "the right of the people to keep and bear assault weapons, cop-killer guns, shoulder-held antitank and anti-aircraft rockets, antipersonnel mines, nuclear suitcase bombs," and whatever else might bring the amendment in line with twenty-first-century weaponry. Efforts at regulating campaign finance were at the heart of getting control of our corrupt money politics, the system that for decades has required elected politicians constantly to raise funds for the next campaign from well-heeled special interests—such as the gun lobby, insurance companies, or the tobacco industry—which held Congress in their pockets regardless of the sentiments of majorities of Americans. Foes of campaign reform like to say "nobody cares about finance reform," or to pretend that, because even an advocate of campaign reform like Senator John McCain has had to solicit and accept such funds to get reelected in the past, he has no right to call for an end to this corrupt money politics.

Finally, we must recall the palpable escalation of polemical language in Congress and in the media that occurred in direct proportion to the budget battles, the electorally unassailable course of Clinton's reelection strategy, and the often wildly speculative media concentration on the latest alleged or real Clinton scandal. In the mid-1990s, the air in Washington and the editorial pages of major newspapers frequently turned purple with partisan vituperation and personal invective the likes of which had not been seen in American politics in a long time. With the frustration of the Clinton-haters and the corporate interests behind the Contract for America (in particular, the embattled tobacco industry which sought to continue profiting from the suffering and deaths of hundreds of thousands) at being unable to diminish popular support for the president's reelection, their growing fury was reflected in the coarsening of political dialogue. Many foreign observers noticed and commented on the new "banana republic style" of American politics in Congress, on the hustings, and in the once respectable press in the United States.

In a column called "Wifewater," an obvious play on Whitewater and the fury directed toward Hillary Clinton, Lexington (*Economist*, January 13, 1996) took on the scandalous article by William Safire in the *New York Times* in which Safire had called the First Lady "a congenital liar": "In Britain's House of Commons, 'liar' is considered an unparliamentary expression and will get a member chucked out of the chamber," wrote a shocked Lexington. This rule of civility particularly applies to using this epithet against a woman member or the wife of a politician in a body otherwise known for its deadly, though rarely vulgar, partisan polemics. Lexington also noted that Safire used no less than fourteen circumlocutions for "lying" in that same *New York Times* article (January 8, 1996), and that an earlier *New York Times* issue had poured the crudest vituperation on Hillary's successful investment in "sow bellies" (commodities futures made to sound like Arkansas razorbacks and rural squalor), pretending that there was something dishonest, dirty, or illegal in speculative investing in commodities futures. Safire at that time even called her investment gains a bribe, among other insulting language. National media condemnation of the alleged La Bubba Nostra corruption of Arkansas politicians was so thick that even Paul Greenberg, a Pulitzer Prize-winning editorialist at the *Arkansas Democrat-Gazette*—who had coined the label "Slick Willie" in 1980—was deeply dismayed (*Los Angeles Times*, August 15, 2000).

The spectacular descent of the *New York Times* into tabloid style, of course, was just as evident with the *Washington Post, Wall Street Journal, Los Angeles Times,* and many other American newspapers owned by them or their parent corporations (see chapter four). And Safire was in good company with many vulgarians in the press, on talk radio, on the floor of Congress, or in press conferences who delighted in calling the president a liar. Chucking out certain foul-mouthed members of Congress may indeed be a good way of restoring to that institution gravitas, the loss of which, on the part of the Clinton presidency, was often alleged by the handful of more literate conservative pundits. The public, moreover, bridled at partisan gridlock with its excessive speech and action: "Washington, old hands agree," to quote Lexington once more, "is gripped by a depressing incivility. Republicans and Democrats are at each others' throats, in Congress and still more viciously, on television" (*Economist*, January 11, 1997). Behind every excess there is a defect, to quote Ralph Waldo Emerson, in this case the defect of political extremism. Extremism is also at the root of terrorism, assassination, and other forms of political violence common in our society. Vituperative and slanderous speech tends to loosen the hold that unstable minds have on reality and on the importance of constitutional rules and moral standards that normally restrain the resort to violence in politics. Violent speech by important opinion leaders often engenders violent deeds by marginal groups and individuals.

A DYING REVOLUTION?

In spite of the investigative time bombs, the reelection of Clinton and of the Republican-dominated Congress created at first a deceptive calm, even a curious sense of political well-being in American politics. "Even at a mere three-months' distance," the *Economist* wrote in wonder, "Bill Clinton's first term has acquired the aura of a golden age." The British weekly mentioned achievements such as deficit reduction and welfare reform and, perhaps, exhaustion after the great health care battles of 1993-1994 and the budget battles of 1995-1996 (April 5, 1997). But there was another mega-event, a black hole in the Republican starry skies of the last two years, as the great revolution of Gingrich and his freshmen seemingly imploded in fragmentation and frustration. Throughout 1996 and even earlier, it had been clear that the Republican Senate majority was not a part of Gingrich's united revolutionary phalanx. The Republican presidential candidate and Senate majority leader, Dole, was far from endorsing the Contract with America, nor did he make its program his own for the campaign. Now the dissension in the party turned on Gingrich, who had barely survived his ethics investigation and had been reelected as a greatly weakened leader. House Democrats had been happy to support his reelection as Speaker now that his ethics troubles had diminished his aggressiveness. But when he retreated on the issue of the big $245 billion tax cut, his foes and rivals within his own party seriously began plotting his imminent demise. An angry letter of protest was signed by 27 Republican House members and as many as 50 House Republicans were rumored to be in favor of his ouster. The internal wrangling over his succession continued, especially among Dick Armey, his deputy Bill Paxon, and majority whip Tom DeLay. His actual resignation, however, only occurred a year and a half later, in the middle of the Republican impeachment drive against the president and after the congressional elections of 1998, in which House Republicans lost five seats instead of gaining 25-40 as expected.

But what about the revolution itself, the thrust of the 1994 upheaval—even though few voters had actually seen or understood the Contract with America at the time—in the House of Representatives and in the state legislatures and governors' mansions? What happened to the revolution of 1994? At the outset, the freshly elected, ideologically committed House members gathered in Baltimore to listen with bated breath to Rush Limbaugh, their guru and an honorary member of their club. The Republicans now had "an extremism that defends little and offends almost everyone" (*Economist*, November 26, 1994). In an effort to help British readers understand the mysteries of American politics, the *Economist* even showed a series of pictures of Barry Goldwater morphing into Gingrich. The House freshmen of 1994, more purely even than the Speaker himself, were the Goldwater hard core, the new abolitionists of the New Deal's federal big government and its social guarantees, the devotees of a Reaganite tax cut and of welfare devolution to the states. In comparison to them, Gingrich was merely "a teenage mutant ninja Goldwater" whose "Newtopia" spoke "a missionary spirit that says to the poorest child in America: 'Internet's for you'" (*Economist*, November 4, 1995). Looking for a cyberbridge to the twenty-first century, he was in many ways like Clinton and Gore, political figures of the same age who also shared some of his Republican premises but did not agree with him on the socially and politically controversial details.

The Goldwaterite freshmen killed dozens of federal programs and severely cut dozens more. Yet even the freshmen did not have the courage of their convictions when it came to cutting corporate welfare, local pork, and the billions of business subsidies estimated by the libertarian Cato Institute at $50 billion and the Progressive Policy Institute at $75 billion a year—in any case, representing a substantial part of the annual budget deficit. More than even the pragmatic Goldwater's, theirs was the Reaganite dream of the big tax cut delivered without pain, but with charm and effortless leadership. Dismantled federal government services would pay for the resulting deficit. But where Reagan had merely sung the praises of individual freedom, wrote the *Economist* with rather a fat tongue in cheek, now there was "a new kind of Republican . . . solid citizens, fathers, religious leaders who shelter orphans from mean streets [as long as they are not pregnant teenage mothers] . . . they do battle against deadbeat dads, permissive liberals, and other agents of social decay. To Republicans . . . , freedom has its darker side: it causes self-expression to displace self-restraint, individualism to degenerate into egotism. When this happens, America is lost" (July 13, 1996). Clinton's centrist position and embrace of some, though not all, of their rhetoric may have helped to drive the revolution into excesses like the government shutdown and to overplay its hand with the American public, or at least it appeared to do so—by juxtaposing the tax cut to long-range cuts in Medicare. Again and again, the wily president managed to make them look bad and to snatch credit for actions endorsed by both sides, seemingly having "protected the most vulnerable from the rigors of the revolution"—and to be reelected for it to a second term in the end.

Was it Clinton's clever political triangulation that eventually killed the Republican revolution? Was it the internal bickering and factionalism among the Republicans? Or was it that Americans in general had never really endorsed the contract and, recoiling from some of its more stringent social and environmental depredations (not to mention the budgetary squeeze and governmental shutdown), turned against Gingrich and his freshmen? By 1997, many Republican congressional and state level candidates had come around to understanding that they could not win their respective races without showing "a kinder, gentler" side, as President Bush had promised in his 1992 reelection campaign—or "a compassionate conservatism," as his son George W. was to champion as a presidential candidate in 1999-2000. They stopped railing at the burdens of environmental legislation on business and replaced their calls for a general tax cut (again) with one for cutting only the capital gains tax. "The result," to quote the *Economist,* was "political mush" (April 5, 1997). Or, to put it differently, they began to look more like Clinton at his most successful and less like the revolutionaries of the contract.

PREPARING THE NOOSE FOR THE PRESIDENT

The invention, in the wake of Watergate, of special independent prosecutors was the basis of Starr's rooting around in the ancient (1978) Whitewater mess and whatever other matters he wished to investigate—including Clinton's sex life. By mid-1997, Starr had spent $30 million of taxpayers' funds to investigate a failed loan of $300,000. When he announced his retirement to become law school dean at Pepperdine University—a decision quickly reversed upon protests from Republican Clinton-haters—this notice brought him an acid comment from the *Economist* (March 1, 1997) which saw him as "fading" fast, having "made a public fool of himself . . . Whatever now becomes of the Whitewater investigation, Mr. Starr looks like a man of flawed judgment." But this was hardly the end of other investigations, such as those of the House and Senate committees on campaign finance (Dan Burton and Fred Thompson, respective chairs). Aside from the obligation to submit a report on his investigation in the end, Starr and other special prosecutors (of cabinet members Mike Espy and Henry Cisneros) were not responsible to anyone or subject to any of the checks and balances that permeate our constitutional system. "As long as [Starr] digs around," editorialized the *Economist* (July 12, 1997), "... he creates a pervasive atmosphere of guilt that even his chief suspects may turn out not to deserve ... At the core of his inquiry are two questions that have a real bearing on abuse of presidential power: whether or not Mr. Clinton lied [regarding Whitewater], and whether his wife obstructed justice. Someone should be investigating those things." The *Economist* obviously approved, despite some doubts about the special prosecutor's unaccountability and the absence of limits on the duration of such investigations and on alleged crimes committed long before the investigatee's present term of office. The *Economist* never explained the nexus between "abuse of presidential power" and the old Whitewater allegations.

Lexington added his account of yet another Senate investigation of campaign finance irregularities, this time chaired by Senator Fred Thompson who had been a Watergate lawyer, a Washington lobbyist, and a Hollywood actor before coming to the Senate. Thompson opened his committee's hearings with the dramatic announcement of a Chinese government plot to buy political influence in the 1996 American elections. His promise to reveal these dark conspiracies involving both parties, but especially the role of the Democrats' John Huang and his Asian connections, kept the pot boiling. But its practical result was mostly to unveil the never-ending thirst of American politics for campaign funds. It also highlighted Thompson's own political ambitions, and the controversy over campaign finance reform, especially the area of "soft money" of which some $264 million had been raised for the 1996 elections alone. We are reminded of Kinsley's rule that scandals are more notable for what they reveal to be legal—the venality of American politics—rather than what is illegal. But this was not the last comment on this subject in the *Economist*; two weeks later (July 26, 1997) it raised the question "why is foreign money, applied to elections, so much worse than the [far more plentiful] American sort?" As Chinese premier Zhu Ronji during his visit reportedly was to quip two years later, "If we [Chinese] really had wanted to influence your elections, would we have sent only $300,000?" Thompson's committee nevertheless continued its spectacular hearings although the fallout for both parties—the former Republican National Committee chair Barbour testified to Hong Kong financing of part of the 1994 Republican triumph—was hardly an unsullied public relations coup. And as for campaign finance reform, a majority emerged in the House to pass the Shays-Meehan bill and, in the Senate, to support the bipartisan McCain-Feingold bill, both of which would have banned soft money and controlled other financing abuses. But the majorities proved no match for the legislative wiles of Senate majority leader Trent Lott and other congressional supporters of the free flow of soft money.

Late in 1997, there emerged one more missing link to the 1998 impeachment action of the House of Representatives that threw a revealing light on the constitutional crisis to follow. On November 5, 1997, exactly a year to the day from the president's reelection, a longtime Clinton foe, Representative Bob Barr from Georgia, introduced a resolution directing the House Committee on the Judiciary to "1) investigate whether grounds exist to impeach Clinton; and 2) report its findings, recommendations, and, if the Committee so determines, a resolution of impeachment." This action, not unlike the Starr investigation up to this point, predated any knowledge of the Lewinsky affair or any legal entrapment for perjury or obstruction of justice. It was a fishing expedition for charges—something, *anything*—to bring against the president. It specifically aimed at that extraordinary emergency weapon in the Constitution against traitors or tyrants in the White House—impeachment. Once before, in early 1994, Republican leader Dick Armey had mentioned impeachment as a way of punishing President Clinton for Whitewater. A New Hampshire Republican, Bill Zeliff, also had threatened Clinton with impeachment over the Waco, Texas tragedy when a large number of Branch Davidians perished by fire. It was an amazing choice of words never before used so lightly against an elected president in more than 200 years, and Zeliff, Armey, Barr and their following evidently intended to use it simply to settle personal and partisan grudges.

At a November 5, 1997 news conference, Barr said the president "has violated the rule of law, and however difficult it may be to go down the dark tunnel of impeachment, at the end of the tunnel there is light." House Rules Committee chair Gerald B. H. Solomon promised to have his committee examine Barr's proposal. Barr indicated that he "was deadly serious about the effort to force the president out of office." The resolution was initially supported by 17 House members, all Republicans and about half from the South. Five more Republicans signed up early in 1998 after the Lewinsky sex scandal broke, and another nine House members in September 1998 after the submission of the Starr Report. Only one supporter out of 32 was a Democrat, G. Taylor from Mississippi. This was, of course, not enough to carry the motion, but by September even the Judiciary Committee chair, Henry J. Hyde—who had rejected such action as recently as January 1998, because "you don't impeach a president with peccadilloes"—had come aboard the impeachment train.

THE HANGING JUDGES

European and Commonwealth press reactions, without exception and unlike our own media, saw this 1994-1997 prelude as the obvious antecedent to the coup attempt of 1998. It featured two rather separate stages of engagement. One was the political battle between Clinton and the new Republican majority in Congress. It began with the president's legislative weakness and failures of 1993-1994. Gingrich's revolutionary House majority spearheaded the Republican landslide of 1994, destroying the Democratic hegemony in the House and Senate and in many states as well, and seemingly boxing in the New Democratic president in 1995-1996 on the crucial issues of deficit-cutting and the budget. To the excruciating frustration of the Republican majority in the House, a resurgent Clinton in the end won the upper hand against the Republican squeeze play and handily defeated Robert Dole in the 1996 presidential elections. Clinton's reelection as a centrist New Democrat, however—associated with welfare reform, deficit cutting, law and order, and personal responsibility—did not help his party reconquer Congress in that election year.

On the second stage, at the same time, a steady onslaught of investigations by the Republican majority in Congress and by rightwing judges, special prosecutors, and the media attempted to undo or overcome the clear verdict of the voters in 1992 and 1996. Targets of the investigations were Bill and Hillary Clinton and various former and current associates and executive officers. The subjects, such as the 1978 Whitewater investment scheme and other alleged missteps of Clinton's years as attorney general and governor of Arkansas, mostly preceded the president's term of office. Right-wing lawyers and businessmen, not to mention some media elites, made great if unsuccessful efforts to find current grounds for accusations, such as Vincent Foster's suicide, the firing of the White House travel office staff, the possible misuse of FBI files on Republican notables, and other feeble charges of cover-up or obstruction of justice, in hopes of producing evidence of malfeasance remotely resembling Watergate.

Clinton-hating newspaper publishers and editors, not to mention talk radio and television, added to this the poisoned atmosphere of ceaseless name-calling, innuendo, and character assassination with the constant repetition of mantras like "trust" and "character," and scurrilous references to the president's "likely impeachment." There were frequent attempts to season their polemics with sex charges, as with Troopergate or references to Gennifer Flowers or Paula Jones. As Starr was to do in 1998, the Clinton-haters often tried to substitute sex scandals for the weakness of their legal or political arguments. Lacking convincing grounds for allegations of criminal conduct, for example, in connection with the Jones case, the ultraright lawyers tried to make up in salacious graphic description what they could not accurately label illegal sexual harassment or worse.

The role of certain members of the federal judiciary and the legal profession gave official sanction to what might otherwise have been only partisan excess and media bile. The firing of Special Prosecutor Fiske and his replacement, by a federal judicial panel, with a far more partisan tobacco lawyer, Starr, is a case in point. So is the subsequent widening of Starr's jurisdiction to help his extended hunt for charges to pin on the Clintons. If there had been any doubts about the partisanship of the three federal judges involved, the August 1999 decision of the panel appointing Starr resolved them to embarrassing lengths. When Starr himself, once more, indicated he was ready to move on to other pursuits—after Clinton's acquittal and the expiration of the Independent Counsel statute—the panel voted two to one for him to continue: Republican appointees David Sentelle and Peter T. Fay voted to go on while Democratic appointee Richard D. Cudahy thought the investigation had run long enough and cost too much ($52 million).

The worst example of judicial malpractice regarding the campaign to undo the electoral mandate of Clinton was the unanimous Supreme Court decision in mid-1997 to permit the civil lawsuit of Paula Jones against a sitting president to proceed on the grounds that "even the president should be subject to the law" and that defending himself against a suit would hardly interfere with the president's fulfillment of his official duties. "Just imagine," harrumphed one of my legally trained European friends, "that Congress were to make your Supreme Court judges, or all federal judges, subject to civil lawsuits from any Tom, Dick, or Harry with a beef about past or present decisions of the court? Critics of Roe v. Wade or a hundred other issues could threaten and intimidate each judge with unrelated lawsuits over property or whatever. Wouldn't this interfere with the judicial work before the court?" I protested that such a hypothetical congressional action made no sense, but he replied: "Do you think that this decision makes sense, a wholesale raid by the Supreme Court upon the Constitutional separation of powers that the court is sworn to defend? Why couldn't this suit wait a few more years—the alleged offense took place in 1991—until the president leaves office? Do you think the judges were unaware of the nature of this case, of the contrived interpretation of facts, the smell of money, and the right-wing sponsors behind it? Your Supreme Court may be a little remote from everyday politics, but not this remote."

CHAPTER TWO

A Coup Attempt in Washington?

This does . . . begin to take on the appearance of a coup [d'état].
— Representative John Conyers,
House Judiciary Committee (December 12, 1998)

I believe [by not resigning] I defended the Constitution against a serious threat. I am sorry I did something wrong [the Lewinsky affair] that gave them the excuse to really go overboard.
— President Bill Clinton,
interview on the *NewsHour* with Jim Lehrer
(January 26, 2000)

It was not so long ago that Europeans and the rest of the world deeply admired American democracy and its venerable Constitution. Eastern Europeans and Russians after the fall of communism in 1990-1991, in particular, paid American institutions and the rule of law the sincerest form of compliment, namely, extensive efforts to import and imitate parts of them. After our triumph in World War II, Western Europeans had also embarked on a long era when our democratic institutions and processes were widely considered the standard against which to measure their own efforts to institute democratic government, even though their governmental structures were, of course, beholden to their respective French, German, and Italian traditions. This pattern of European respect clearly suffered a major lapse with the distribution of the Starr Report and the videotape of the president's grand jury testimony of August 17, 1998 on orders of the House of Representatives. In the conservative French daily *Le Figaro,* Pierre Rousselin wrote: "It is now up to Congress to return to American democracy the dignity that was so seriously lost by the default of three other pillars [of the American system]: The chief executive in unbelievable conduct, a judicial apparatus at the mercy of an implacable prosecutor, and a fourth estate [the media] without self-restraint" (September 11, 1998). The columnist did not explain why he expected salvation to come from, of all places, Congress. Two days later, Charles Lambrosini added in the same paper: "The president may survive [this crisis] but his presidency is shattered (*foudroyé*)" (September 13, 1998).

In one of the great newspapers of the world, the centrist *Le Monde* of Paris, Denis Lacorne, the research director of the Center for International Studies and Research, spoke of the "irresistible decline of American democracy, under the deceptive appearance of 'democracy on the march.'" He attributed the congressional action to three illusions, the "illusion of truth," "of law," and of "parliamentary deliberation": "But judicial truth is rarely the whole truth . . . the questions directed at Clinton were meant to entrap him in perjury . . . and the logic of the law is not the logic of the people . . . Fortunately for Bill Clinton, American [public] opinion has not fallen into the trap that the prosecutor and the Republican majority in Congress set for him" (September 25, 1998). Lacorne then conjured up the concern of the founders of the American republic to protect individuals such as Clinton from the intrusion of a tyrannous state into their private lives and denounced the congressional "deliberations" toward impeachment as mere "illusion." Lacorne's salvo ended with the aside: "Well, at least the cigar was not Cuban . . . The president did not violate the embargo." What accounts for the present estrangement, the expressions of European exasperation, even shock, at events in American national government and public opinion in 1998-1999? Why did so many of my European friends—to the extent that knowledgeable Europeans paid attention and understood the events in a far distant land—call the goings-on inside the Beltway so exaggerated, mean-spirited, or simply incomprehensible?

ILLUSIONS OF PARLIAMENTARY GOVERNMENT

One likely source for their distaste may be misunderstandings based on the different governmental structures that we and they tend to take for granted, particularly in the relations between the national executive and the legislature. Europeans know that we have a separation of powers between Congress and the president—which none of them have—and we know that most of them have some form of parliamentary government in which prime ministers are elected and dismissed by a majority of the lower house of parliament. Optimally, prime ministers are in command of both parliament and the executive branch, quite different from the role of the self-sufficient Congress, which was described by Lexington in the *Economist* as "a bunch of men and women of extraordinary pomposity, as windbagged as the worst Welshman, unable to raise their sights above the most mundane concerns of their local constituents, and generally mildly corrupt . . . a 'permanent government,' made up of incumbents with a rate of reelection that made them look like the noblemen of the ancient regime . . . now, if only they would reintroduce spittoons" (June 26, 1993).

In their hearts Americans and Europeans know very little about the workings of the other system in everyday practice. And both take their own systems so much for granted that even their gut reactions to a governmental crisis abroad are patterned by these basic differences in structure. The first impulse of Europeans on seeing the intense hatred of congressional Republicans against

Clinton was to say "Why don't they just vote him out of office?" without immediately realizing that this is not possible under our system. A prime minister's loss of position, moreover, requires no charges or public trials, and involves no punishment other than being ousted. When prime ministers lose their parliamentary majority by a no-confidence vote or after an electoral defeat, they are simply retired. Impeachment of an American president, the most powerful leader in the world, on the other hand, seems very strange, punitive, and cumbersome, almost archaic to modern Europeans, an extreme solution to an everyday political crisis. The importance of these difficulties in understanding American politics cannot be easily documented with quotations from the European press. They are rather like Sherlock Holmes's story of the dog that did not bark, deep if simple reactions based on complex reasons. We can, however, find out by talking to knowledgeable European friends that they play a big role in mutual misunderstandings.

It is an irony of history that British governmental traditions, after inspiring the American colonists to rebel against the tyranny of Westminster and of George III and to create a republican Congress and president in deliberate, adversarial juxtaposition, gave birth to several other governmental inventions. Among them were the older devices of fighting the fierce battles between king and parliament, such as star chamber proceedings (no pun intended), criminal trials of political opponents by special courts and without any of the usual protections (such as attorneys or habeas corpus) for the accused, impeachment of a public official by parliament, and bills of attainder issued by legislatures to fine or punish an executive officer. By far the most striking of these inventions was parliamentary government, a system of executive-legislative relations that evolved (from the 1740s) over a period of two-and-a-half centuries to its present popularity with most European states. In Britain, its rise was reinforced by the growth of strong political parties and, eventually, by democracy. All three combined to make this a stable and resilient system: if there is a two-party or two-bloc system present, each national parliamentary election is likely to produce a mandate for a parliamentary majority with a prime minister and cabinet whose rule will end when their majority support is lost. It may be replaced by an oppositional majority. But there is only one such national election, that of the House of Commons (the parliamentary executive is not popularly elected) and, under normal circumstances, it gives the voters a real choice between parties A and B, or between the A and B coalitions of parties. Prime minister, cabinet, and parliamentary majority almost invariably belong to the same party or coalition.

Under our separation of powers, or presidential system, the president and the Congress (both House and Senate) are elected separately. Frequently, the White House is occupied by one party and the other party controls one or both houses of Congress. In fact, this kind of divided government has prevailed in the United States for most of the years since Watergate (1974). When the separation of powers was first devised by the framers at Philadelphia, they thought of it not only as a rigorous scheme to make the executive, legislative, and judicial functions as far as possible independent of each other. Putting two or all three into the same hands, according to the Baron de Montesquieu, was considered the very definition of tyranny. They also believed that each branch, pursuing its natural ambition, would check and balance the others—"Ambition must be made to counteract ambition" (Federalist Paper No. 51, James Madison)—in order to keep each from self-aggrandizement and tyranny over the people.

As the new republic got underway, however, this countervailing separation was met by new forces that the founders had viewed dimly. The most significant of these were political parties and the dynamics of popular democracy. The rise of political parties has meant that presidents and legislative majorities in both houses are often of the same party, and thus capable of overcoming most of the intended checks and balances. The rise of egalitarian democracy since the age of Andrew Jackson considerably modified the system further, as did the extraordinary expansion of what had started out as a rather small country with a limited suffrage; now political legitimacy came from popular elections, and both executive and legislative authority derived from the consent of the people.

MISREADING AMERICAN PRESIDENTIAL GOVERNMENT

How, then, might European observers have been misled to erroneous conclusions based on these structural differences? Parliamentary government differs from presidentialism with regard to (1) how executive authority is derived from the people, namely, by having only one national parliamentary election and through the mediating role of the newly elected parliament and partisan majorities in it; (2) the fusion of executive and legislative authority in parliamentary government (which was anathema to the founders of the Constitution); and (3) how to get rid of a duly (if indirectly) elected chief executive.

The first difference very likely led European observers of the well-orchestrated Republican landslide in the 1994 congressional elections to expect the new majorities of both houses to push the Democratic president against the wall. The new House Speaker, Newt Gingrich, probably had the same expectations. A Congress veteran (first elected 1978), Gingrich had prepared the ground with a skillfully compiled party program and recruited and indoctrinated a large number of Republican candidates for House seats. Upon their election, they helped him to pass nine of the ten items (the exception was term limits) of the contract in a few weeks of intense sessions in the House. It was an extraordinary moment in the history of the chamber. Gingrich presided over a signal partisan victory after decades of Democratic numerical superiority. The Republican popular vote for the House now stood at 51 percent to 46 percent for the Democrats, the exact opposite of the 1992 elections, and the Democratic edge among Senators similarly shrank in a few years from 58 (and 42 Republicans) to only 45 (and

55 Republicans), and among state governors from 28 (and 22 Republicans) to 17 (and 33 Republicans). In 1995-1996, after two years of various crises and disasters such as the health reform debate, the Clinton presidency had thus lost its Democratic majorities and, in the opinion of many European observers, seemed destined for political annihilation. A surprising number of Republican voices, especially in the press, explicitly welcomed the resulting dominance of Congress over the presidency. But do the American people really want to change our presidential system in a parliamentary fashion, making presidents dependent for their tenure on congressional support?

To Europeans and Commonwealth observers, this was a familiar situation and they expected the overwhelming new Republican majority to capitalize on its superior numbers. Taking a leaf from Australia's own parliamentary practice, in January 1995 the *Sydney Morning Herald* commented that the American lurch to the right signified a "belief [that] Clinton is a failure" and that the voters wanted to clip his legislative wings. "America is now adrift. To put it bluntly, for the next two years, it is ungovernable." The *Herald* naturally assumed that the 1996 congressional and presidential elections would bring a decision as to which party would be in control from then on. By March 1995, the *Sueddeutsche Zeitung* of Munich wrote: "If we did not know better, we'd think that since January 4 it wasn't just the majorities in Congress that had changed but the entire governmental system. It almost seems as if Clinton was only a [figurehead] president now, while Gingrich had the power of a prime minister" (March 15, 1995). The German newspaper also provided in-depth coverage of the background and the ideas, and enumerated the targeted enemies of the new Speaker: Democratic "social engineers," the counterculture of 1968, and advocates of racial equalization. At the end of the first year of the Republican majority, the British *Economist* commented in a tone of admiration: "Astonishingly, Mr. Gingrich is doing all this from Capitol Hill rather than the White House which is rather like steering a canoe from the front. With few exceptions, the Republicans' discipline in Congress has been iron . . . as though Mr. Gingrich were the head of a parliamentary government. His has been an electrifying performance . . . He has persuaded Washington that what the voters wanted in 1994 was what he was proposing to do" (November 4, 1995). Other European observers were just as impressed if not as eloquent.

Gingrich indeed led his troops into an all-out attack on what he viewed as Democratic Big Government and attempted to hobble such excessive (to him) government activities as business regulation and environmental protection by denying or drastically cutting budget appropriations to most nonemergency government services—in effect shutting them down. The Europeans did not quite understand what he was doing and, even less, the Clinton counteraction of executive vetoes for which there is no equivalent in European parliamentary systems. In fact, thanks to the European executive-legislative fusion, European politics almost never witnesses comparable battles between parliament and executive—not even in France where a hybrid presidential-parliamentary version in recent decades (since 1986) has also featured divided government ("cohabitation" of Gaullists and Socialists) but little overt executive-legislative conflict. In any event, Europeans expected the Republican surge to continue into the 1996 elections and Clinton to be vanquished at that time.

What happened instead illustrates my earlier point about the democratic source of legitimate authority: the Republican popular vote for the House in 1996 indeed remained ahead, 49 percent as compared to 48.5 percent for the Democrats who, despite gaining two seats, were still behind, 208 to 227 seats. But Clinton also won 49 percent (to 41 percent for Dole) and an even larger electoral college vote than in 1992. To European eyes, there were now two competing popular mandates, a Republican congressional mandate and a Democratic presidential one, a very confusing situation compared with the clear outcomes of parliamentary elections in Britain, or Germany, or most older Commonwealth countries.

Would this make for confusing conflict between the branches that so rarely occurs in Europe's parliamentary systems? Europeans are, of course, accustomed to battles over policy between government parties and their opposition, and no strangers to extremes of radical left and radical right partisanship that ravaged their politics time and again throughout the twentieth century. But political struggles between major national institutions such as parliaments and their prime ministers and cabinets—there are also figurehead presidents and monarchs that play no important political role—seem rather archaic and disturbing to them. Such struggles appear to threaten institutional gridlock, or breakdown, or, at least, a diminished capacity to act. A fact that Europeans were less aware of was that, during Clinton's first two years as president and despite an ample Democratic majority in Congress, he could not count on much support from his own party; there hardly was a "Clinton Democratic Party" in the House or Senate prior to the impeachment battles of 1998. As a New Democrat, he was rather isolated and could find support for his policies and budget only by what later became known as triangulation between Republicans and liberal Democrats.

If Europeans were aware of the Republican landslide of 1994 and its likely consequences, they also could not help noticing the significant Republican setback in the 1998 congressional elections and Gingrich's subsequent downfall. The *Sueddeutsche Zeitung* of Munich commented that the 1998 election "heralds an astonishing, even sensational change of trend in American domestic politics. The majority Republicans, bursting with self-confidence up to the election day, appear to have passed the peak of their power. The election will unleash a shock wave through the Republican party that will possibly catch and carry away the party leadership and top representatives in Washington" (November 5, 1998). Gingrich's resignation from both the speakership and the House after the electoral disaster struck Europeans as hardly unexpected. "The failure of [Gingrich's] conservative revolution forces the GOP to develop new concepts and programs," said another German newspaper, the conservative *Düsseldorf Handelsblatt* (cited by *World Press Review*, January 1999). Europeans never expected the chastened Republican majority in the House to proceed with their impeachment drive.

EUROPEANS ON NIXON'S IMPEACHMENT

The third difference, how to bring down a duly-elected chief executive, naturally touches closely upon the question of impeachment and, as we shall see below, whether the Republican impeachment drive of 1998 amounted to an attempted coup d' état against Clinton's electoral mandate. In parliamentary systems, prime ministers generally lose their posts in more or less the same fashion they gain them: in two-party systems, it is usually by being defeated in an election in which the incumbents have to defend what they did with their original mandate from the voters, or how they dealt with new crises and major challenges. Typically, recent French, German, and British governments were toppled by elections that cost them their majorities. Successful parliamentary no-confidence votes have become rare since political parties have become so disciplined, but they may still occur in a coalition government. In the 1970s, for example, Labour prime minister James Callahan of Britain was toppled by the unexpected departure of Scottish Nationalist MPs. His reaction reportedly was: "This is the first time turkeys have voted for an early Christmas." Recent Italian governments fell when one or more of the coalition parties walked out over an important issue, and the same happened to Chancellor Helmut Schmidt of Germany in 1982 when the Free Democrats left his coalition and embraced Helmut Kohl instead. Behind closed doors, moreover, a prime minister or chancellor may sometimes be persuaded by his own party leaders to resign because his actions have disgraced his party. An example might be Anthony Eden's resignation in 1956 following the failed Suez invasion, or Willy Brandt's resignation in 1974 because of a spy scandal. In some ways this resembles, in our own rather different system, the resignation of Richard Nixon in the Watergate affair, when senior Republican congressional leaders prevailed upon him not to wait for his removal by the Senate.

The European reaction to Nixon's impeachment crisis was quite characteristic. When European observers became aware that Nixon had become bogged down defending himself against extended impeachment investigations, and would have to submit to an even-lengthier Senate trial in the midst of the Cold War and the first energy crisis, they were horrified. They had no particular quarrel with the emerging charges—although they seemed to regard them as no worse than some actions of their own political leaders. But America was the leader of the free world and they thought that the government paralysis of a world power surrounded by potential aggressors, large and small, who might take advantage of the situation was intolerable. Some Europeans, such as the West German government, also had a strong preference for Nixon and Secretary of State Henry Kissinger over the opposition and were disturbed to see Nixon fall. European friends told me at the time: "Why can't your modern America have a swift and painless solution, like parliamentary overthrow, instead of this crazy outmoded method of impeachment that Britain abandoned 200 years ago?" Parliamentary overthrow is indeed quick with no trial and no opprobrium haunting the fallen leader. Nor is there a partisan struggle to leave bitter feelings or thoughts of revenge such as those that existed as a motive for the Republican impeachment drive against Clinton—revenge for Watergate and the threatened impeachment of Nixon. There is, of course, a profound difference between routine replacements of the executive impelled by changing partisan fortunes and full-dress impeachment, as specified in the Constitution, to oust a traitorous or tyrannous chief who has become a menace to the survival or integrity of the state itself.

THE AMERICAN WAY OF DUMPING A PRESIDENT

The American method of expelling a chief executive considered a danger to the state is indeed archaic and was abandoned in England after the 1787-1795 impeachment of Warren Hastings, the first governor general of British India. It was still used frequently in seventeenth- and eighteenth- century England, also in the American colonies and in the Jeffersonian era, but never against a chief executive or a president until after the Civil War. Today, European observers balk particularly at the curious American mixture of judicial and political elements which, in their opinions, was used as a continual dodge by the Republican impeachment drive of 1998. On the website of the French left-wing paper *Libération,* for example, questions about the confusing mixture of the two dominated an interview which their correspondent, Jacques Sabatier, conducted with Jeffrey Rosen, an American constitutional expert from George Washington University law school and a staff writer for the *New Yorker.* Leading off the questions were: "Is the [impeachment] process essentially political or juridical?" (answer: both) and "How does it relate to the juridical norms of American courts?" (only in part); followed by "What is the significance of having the Chief Justice of the Supreme Court . . . preside over the [Senate] proceedings" (none) and "Can the Senate acquit the president of a [dubious] perjury charge even when it is not contested?" (yes). Whenever such rarefied legal charges as perjury, subornation of perjury, or obstruction of justice were challenged by the president's lawyers as unproven or nearly unprovable in a court of law, as European observers trained in their own respective legal systems would note, special prosecutor Kenneth Starr and the Republican ultras on the House Judiciary Committee and elsewhere withdrew into the political realm and claimed that impeachment was a political matter after all. The Starr Report, jeered the liberal *Guardian* of London, had "made no attempt to present the whole [legal] truth, but gone straight for his man . . . this is not a criminal process and . . . not subject to conventional rules and safeguards [of the much-invoked rule of law]" (September 15, 1998).

Nicole Bacharan, French television commentator, in her book *Le Piège,* focused on the dubious manner in which ultraright lawyers, especially Starr and his friends, turned the complaint of Jones—"the woman with the Minnie Mouse voice and the forced smiles"—into a "guided missile of the ultraright" against the president.[1] The object of the lawyers, according to Bacharan, was to link somehow the financial charges of the Whitewater affair with the sex scandal of a consensual liaison with Monica Lewinsky, and to sell the "resulting legal mayonnaise" to Attorney General Reno and to the panel of three federal judges who had authorized the special prosecutor to investigate possible criminal conduct of the Clintons in the Whitewater-Madison Guaranty business. Reno, who had been under intense political pressure, and the three judges, in Bacharan's opinion, committed "two grave errors" in agreeing to Starr's dubious request to extend his authority beyond Whitewater: Linda Tripp's tapes of Lewinsky's confidential telephone conversations, Starr's smoking gun, were illegal under the laws of the state of Maryland where they had been made, and it was highly irregular of him to promise Tripp immunity for making them. His second piece of evidence, a tape obtained by Tripp and the FBI during the sting luncheon with Lewinsky at the Ritz-Carlton in the Pentagon City Mall on January 13, 1998, was also illegal because Starr had not yet been authorized to investigate Lewinsky, much less to use the FBI for this purpose. On that tape, a flustered Lewinsky had loosely suggested that Clinton and Vernon Jordan had wanted her to deny the affair. She said that in an effort to convince her friend Linda Tripp, who pretended to be skeptical. "It was a little white lie," according to Bacharan. The second error was to conflate a criminal suspicion, regarding Whitewater-Madison Guaranty, with obviously non-criminal conduct, the Lewinsky affair, which even the alleged white lie could not turn into a crime.[2]

When Clinton, who holds a law degree from Yale University, was found to use excessively legalistic formulas or to engage in legal maneuvers and evasions in his dealings with the Jones grand jury, propagandists of the impeachment promptly asserted that such legalisms were contrary to commonsense political understandings. So, for example, with the grand jury and Clinton's definition of sexual relations, he insisted that his "inappropriate relations" with Monica Lewinsky did not amount to full sexual relations, and Lewinsky, in her statements on the Linda Tripp tapes, had called it "just fooling around." When an editor of the prestigious American Medical Association's journal, in the midst of the Senate trial (January 20, 1999), released a survey report on college students' understanding of the term "sexual relations" that stated 60 percent of the students also considered oral sex not to constitute sexual relations—a response in keeping with popular language use in much of American society—he was fired. On the other hand, the impeachment campaign and its supporters were always quick to insist that their effort was not about sex at all but involved charges of perjury and of obstruction of justice for which other Americans had gone to jail. Skeptical Europeans were not impressed by such arguments.

The most authoritative American legal assessment of the operations of Starr's Office of Independent Counsel (OIC) is that of Jeffrey Toobin, a former United States assistant attorney in Brooklyn and associate counsel with Iran-Contra special prosecutor Lawrence E. Walsh. In *A Vast Conspiracy,* Toobin shines an appropriate light on the personnel of the OIC, distinguishing in particular the more professional first set of counsels of the Whitewater investigation—who moved on in 1997, having found no smoking gun of Clinton wrongdoing there nor in Travelgate, Filegate, or Fostergate—from the more partisan and gung-ho counsels who joined up at a later date. One of the latter was W. Hickman Ewing, Jr., who ran the OIC operation in Little Rock and raised eyebrows with his obsession with ferreting out Arkansas girlfriends of Clinton's past. He, rather than Starr, deserved the image of the relentless, born-again Christian prosecutor pursuing presidential sex as if it was an impeachable crime, according to Toobin.[3] Another was Jackie Bennett who, among other things, arranged the sting luncheon of Tripp and Lewinsky on January 13, 1998 at the Ritz-Carlton, complete with listening devices and FBI agents, but without prior authority from Reno or the Sentelle panel to expand the OIC investigation to the Lewinsky affair. Starr mostly stayed away from the operation of the office and never met any of the witnesses. "Starr's lack of experience as a prosecutor was such that he exercised almost no critical judgment on the key decisions made by his office," Toobin claims.[4] Inexperience and ineffectual leadership of the OIC, of course, do not spare Starr the full responsibility for its acts and for his egregious lies about them in press conferences, on television, and under oath before Congress.

"The American judiciary," wrote the conservative *Le Figaro* "has gone crazy (*devenue folle*) and demonstrated the absurdity of its omnipotence" (August 18, 1998). The emphasis on judicial definitions was particularly the tenor of the final impeachment debates in the House of Representatives and in the Senate. To legally trained European ears, however, this meant that critical, judicially formulated charges would be tried in a political kangaroo court by a mob of journalists and politicians, yet with the serious consequences of a regular court trial and no possibility of judicial appeal.

The American judiciary received low marks from Bacharan's *Le Piège* for its naiveté about the ultraright twistings of legal reasoning: the acceptance by the Supreme Court, in a May 27, 1997 decision, of the right to accuse and try a sitting president with a civil suit—leaving it to the courts to decide whether or when such pursuit might interfere with the president's duties—showed "an astonishing naiveté . . . of the nine sages," considering the likely ado and media circus involved. "The decision of the Supreme Court opened a huge breach [in the wall of the separation of powers]: Henceforth there would be the possibility of politically motivated groups to tarnish the reputation of the president, to demand that he prove his innocence, to absorb his time and financial resources... and thus to paralyze the execution of the political program for which he was elected."[5] Toobin describes the hectic scene at the Supreme Court, the excited "justices... primed, for the historical moment, [who] scarcely let a lawyer on either side complete a sentence without jumping in with questions... Despite the political differences among them, the nine justices shared a hard-won disengagement from the ways of the real world and their [unanimous] opinion in the Jones case sang out their collective ignorance."[6] Arkansas federal judge Susan Webber Wright—who earned some praise from Bacharan for her determination not to let this dubious Jones case become an "affair of state"—also is criticized for being "as blind as the nine sages of Washington." In making decisions on small matters, "she did not see how she put at risk the great [American] democratic ambition to protect the rights of the individual by precisely balancing the [governmental] powers."[7] Her vacillations in the end served the worst purposes of the witch hunt for the president and the public exposure of decades of his private life.

If these perspectives soured Europeans on the process of impeachment in general, the Republican hot pursuit of it in the fall of 1998 raised further alarms. At this point, the instances of high-handed conduct of the Office of Independent Counsel in the Lewinsky investigation were still largely unknown here and abroad, thanks in part to the media conspiracy not to investigate and not to mention them. The unfolding prosecution and impeachment was regarded skeptically by most Europeans, but some conservative European papers such as Rupert Murdoch's British tabloid *Sun* ("The Lying Fornicator Must Go") and some left-wing papers critical of Clinton's centrist policies (for example, on welfare policy) were rather unsympathetic to the president.

The British prestige press often likes to feature one opinion leader arguing against another in a weak gesture of even-handedness: sometimes one called for Clinton's resignation and the other was critical of the conduct and arguments of the impeachers, or of the idea that the alleged offenses rose to the level of impeachability demanded by the American Constitution. Those critical of the impeachment drive took particular umbrage at what they saw as violations of Clinton's rights as an accused person in a court—for instance, the refusal of the House Judiciary Committee and of Starr to give him a copy of the Starr Report before its submission to the committee and even before its publication in the media, an outrageous violation of the rights of the accused in any court, American or European. The fifth amendment that normally shields the accused citizen from having to incriminate himself is completely useless for a president in the hot seat of a major investigation. The American Constitution is not very helpful with details on such rights under impeachment and neither are the Federalist Papers nor the precedent of Andrew Johnson's impeachment after the Civil War.

In 1868 President Andrew Johnson, Abraham Lincoln's vice president and successor, a Southerner not elected to the presidency, drew the ire of the radical Republican majority in Congress with a series of actions designed to undo the severity of Reconstruction measures in the defeated South. He did this mostly when Congress was not in session and in defiance of its express will. His lack of a popular mandate and the fact that the Union had just concluded an immensely bloody and fratricidal war with the South (which made him seem a traitor of sorts to the Union) exposed him to impeachment by the House and near-removal by the Senate. He survived by one vote and served out his term.[8] The only other serious effort at impeaching a president in 200 years came to an end when Richard Nixon resigned to avoid certain removal by a large Senate majority. "Watergate," according to Carl Bernstein of Watergate fame, "was about a vast and pervasive abuse of power by a criminal president who ordered break-ins and fire-bombings, impeded the free electoral process, instituted illegal wiretaps and used the Internal Revenue Service as a force for personal retribution . . . [He also involved] the CIA and FBI in the cover-up of these activities" (*Los Angeles Times*, September 27, 1998).

In spite of the seriousness of the charges, the Watergate scandal so upset the nation that it weakened Presidents Ford, Carter, and Reagan and militated against yet another impeachment effort, this one against Reagan on the occasion of the Iran-Contra scandal of the 1980s. Again the charges were very serious, illegally selling arms to hostile Iran and supporting a secret war in Central America (with shocking assassinations and thousands of civilian casualties), but there was pronounced public resistance to an impeachment drive against President Reagan—and, for that matter, against George Bush, who claimed to have been "out of the loop" of the Iran-Contra plans while he was Reagan's vice president. The extraordinary death toll of civilians at the hands of American-supported right-wing military dictatorships and armies, or counterinsurgents such as the Nicaraguan Contras, in Guatemala, El Salvador, Nicaragua, and Honduras was largely hushed up in the American media at the time. Only recently, on the occasion of President Clinton's official 1998 visit to Central America, could the American public read in the press about the massacres and genocidal actions against Mayan villagers by American-supported forces during the 1980s.

DEFENDING THE CONSTITUTION

There is a very obvious reason why impeachment as a means of banishing an elected president has been used so rarely in the 200-some years of the republic: as with all elective offices (and especially in contrast to the shadow cast upon the constitutional deliberations in Philadelphia in 1787 by the unimpeachable King George III) the logical remedy for a poor choice of elected officer lies in not reelecting the person. Such a means of correction is not available, for example, with regard to federal judges or executive officers below the president. The remedy of impeachment was added only because, in the interval of a four-year term and surrounded as the young republic was by powerful empires with likely designs on it, a president might have been tempted to betray the nation's integrity or independence, to be bribed to commit treasonable actions, or to jeopardize the safety and integrity of the new federal state with "high crimes and misdemeanors" against this state. This was the emergency for which the impeachment process was inserted into the Constitution. The framers must have turned in their graves to learn the twisted interpretation given to their language by the impeachment advocates of 1998-1999. To quote Republican John Dean, Nixon's counsel who, back in Watergate days, had turned against his president: "[Previous impeachment proceedings] stand in stark contrast to the we-don't-give-a-damn treatment of President Clinton by the Republicans now running the show" (*U.S. News and World Report,* December 21, 1998).

When the Starr Report of September 1998 urged the House to consider impeachment charges against Clinton, European observers had not yet heard of the unscrupulous and underhanded actions of the OIC under Starr. But they were rather skeptical of the claims of Starr and Judiciary Committee chair Henry J. Hyde that they were defending "the rule of law." Europeans simply considered this a sex scandal and took a dim view of the pornographic disclosures of the report. In an editorial entitled "Hell is American," the liberal *Le Monde* called the Starr Report "an American curiosity, simply exotic to our Latin culture . . . In four years of investigation, the prosecutors only found this: the pitiful lie of a seducer [*Le Monde* gallantly assumed the affair was *his* initiative]. And of this [Starr] is making a *crime de l'état* [crime of the state], even several, subject at least to incarceration . . . An inquisitor . . . of practically unlimited means threatening reluctant witnesses with perjury [charges]." The French daily described the selective documentation of Starr's legal arguments and the salacious passages of the report: "What does it matter [to the law] if . . . the president lied under oath about whether he ejaculated or not, that Miss Lewinsky twice achieved orgasms, or that a cigar was used in an erotic game," clearly implying that these *passages cochons* (swinish or sex passages), not the legal charges, were the important features of the report (September 13-14, 1998). They became even more suspicious when they noticed how the impeachment forces in the House seemed to disregard all the caution signs established by the Constitution and by American law.

Balanced assessments of the facts of the case for impeachment stood out even in the readers' letters to the Murdoch-controlled London *Times:* as Laurence J. Olivier wrote after Clinton's acquittal in the Senate, for example, "Elements of the Republican party have gone to extraordinary length to try to unseat the president, conducting an unprecedented judicial inquiry into numerous allegations against Clinton. All that they finally managed to unearth was a sexual misdemeanor which, in most countries would not be considered worthy of mention" (February 13, 1999). Or, tongue-in-cheek by another reader after Clinton's impeachment in December by the House: "Sir, if it is true that Clinton cheated at golf . . . then never mind other evidence; he surely has to go" (December 21, 1998).

After the contentious and unsuccessful impeachment of Supreme Court Justice Samuel P. Chase in the early nineteenth century, followed by other judicial impeachments since, a consensus had established itself in America to protect the process from partisan abuse: a person about to be impeached should have advance notice of the charges, have a right to counsel, and enjoy protection against self-incrimination, all points that were flagrantly disregarded at crucial turns of the case against Clinton. It was "a parody of justice," to quote Geneva's *Le Temps* (September 13, 1998). European legal eagles also were shocked by the unlawyerly manipulations of the House leaders, such as the use of undisclosed rumors and secret files on serial Jane Does in the "evidence room"— that were never exposed to the rules of evidence or cross-examination in a court of law. They were also scandalized by the transparent attempts at sensationalizing the Senate proceedings with live witnesses, whom the Judiciary Committee of the House had never bothered to invite to its proceedings. The perorations of the impressive-looking Chairman Hyde—Americans of my generation may be reminded more of the cartoon image of Al Capp's stemwinding Southern Senator Phileas Phogbound—impressed Europeans less with their content than with his looks. "I can believe the stories of his 'youthful indiscretions,'" said one Frenchwoman. "He must have been a handsome devil back then. Still is."

The Constitution sets forth a series of stop signs for reflection on the road to impeachment, the first of them being the formula of causes for which a president may be impeached: "treason, bribery, and high crimes and misdemeanors." Obviously these reflected the new republic's fear of a return to tyranny—as experienced under George III and his parliament—or major foreign and domestic threats to the new American state and society. In November of 1998, the Judiciary Committee understandably felt that it ought to seek expert counsel from a long list of constitutional and political experts, attorneys, and historians in order to determine whether Starr's charges against Clinton rose to the level required by the Constitution for impeachment. The constitutional experts summoned before the Subcommittee on Constitutional Issues all emphasized the high threshold for presidential impeachment—as compared to the much lower threshold for the impeachment of federal judges, who serve for life and "good behavior" and never face the test of election or reelection. In his testimony before the committee, Bruce Ackerman of Yale University raised the question: "Does the conduct alleged in this case constitute such a threat to the very foundations of the Republic that it is legitimate to deprive the people of their freely elected choice as president?" He quoted James Madison, one of the fathers of the Constitution and an author of the *Federalist Papers*, as saying at the Philadelphia convention that a lower standard than "high crimes and misdemeanors" would transform the four-year presidency into an office "whose term will be equivalent to a tenure during the pleasure of the Senate," making it a kind of parliamentary government, in other words.

The original, unedited version of the Constitution included the phrase "high crimes and misdemeanors *against the state.*" The last three words were removed by the Committee on Style, who considered them redundant. Ackerman warned that impeachment in this case "will be setting a precedent that will haunt this country for generations to come." Whenever congressional majorities and the president were of different parties, impeachment would become an easily available partisan weapon that would shift the United States "toward a British-style system of parliamentary government for decades to come." Gary L. McDowell of the University of London, who emphasized the impeachability of a perjury charge (but not just any false statement under oath), if it could be proven, also warned of "the effect [that] the exercise of this extraordinary constitutional sanction would have on the health of the republic . . ." Regarding the impeachability of civil perjury, Jeffrey Rosen has pointed out belatedly that Americans courts, until Reconstruction, did not require defendants to testify under oath, believing their testimony to be self-serving and unreliable. It seems unlikely, then, that the authors of the impeachment clause could have meant to include civil perjury among the "high crimes and misdemeanors."

Matthew Holden, Jr., of the University of Virginia, in his testimony also cautioned against "the continual avoidance of [the subject of] the costs and benefits of impeachment when considered in relation to the whole political system" and expressed the fear that "impeachment investigations, trumped up or otherwise, will virtually be mandated by going forward on this one." He expected impeachment of all federal judges and executive officers to become a routine frequently employed in the ideologically combative days to come. Cass R. Sunstein of the University of Chicago insisted that "the charges made thus far by Judge Kenneth Starr . . . do not, if proved, make out any legitimately impeachable offenses under the Constitution . . ." and that the question "whether perjury . . . is an impeachable offense depends on what it is a false statement about."

It could be so only if the perjury is about conduct involving "serious . . . abuse of office," not a cover-up of a consensual sex affair. So much for the impeachment charge of perjury.

Later, *Le Monde* (January 15, 1999) noted the irony of having Chief Justice William Rehnquist presiding over the impeachment trial of the Senate, "a profoundly conservative man" who wrote a book about the impeachments of Supreme Court Justice Chase and President Andrew Johnson, *Grand Inquests* (1993), but "would also defend the constitutional tradition [of America] and a restrictive conception of impeachment, limited [indeed] to 'high crimes and misdemeanors.'" In an accompanying brief biography in the same issue, Patrice de Beer explained that Rehnquist, a Republican, shared the conservative views on abortion, affirmative action, and other issues but did not hesitate to declare that Republican President Nixon deserved removal by the Congress. "[Rehnquist] has manifested a certain skepticism toward the process of impeachment and [also] a concept of 'high crimes and misdemeanors' that is sufficiently restrictive and limited to actions that threaten the state." If Andrew Johnson had been removed, the French paper said, it would have cast a great shadow upon the independence of the presidency (*Le Monde*, January 15, 1999). In *Grand Inquests,* Rehnquist indeed warns against a partisan Congress removing a president from office for any but the most serious of causes. But the Chief Justice also has the reputation of a strong partisan. He appointed the panel of Judge David Sentelle, a fierce Republican partisan, and this panel, ignoring the word "independent" in independent counsel, appointed equally fierce Republican Judge Starr, thus subverting the intent of the OIC statute. Rehnquist and Antonin Scalia, another rather partisan figure, also seem to have browbeaten the Supreme Court into denying presidential immunity to civil suits, such as that of Paula Jones, while a president is in office, thereby setting the tracks for the impeachment caper of 1998-1999.

When most of these experts from the nation's most highly renowned universities testified that they did not agree with the committee majority, Hyde's committee simply chose to ignore their advice as well as that of several hundreds of unsolicited opinions of historians and constitutional experts. One appeal from over 400 prominent American historians, including Arthur Schlesinger, Jr., and Sean Wilentz, emphasized particularly the danger of "leaving the Presidency permanently disfigured and diminished, at the mercy as never before of the caprices of any Congress... a precedent for the future harassment of presidents." It warned against turning our system into one of parliamentary government, quoting James Madison who did not want to see the president serve only "during the pleasure of the Senate," and thus abandoning our system of checks and balances. There, of course, lies the rub of protest against this assault on the Constitution: do we really want a parliamentary form of government? But the committee did not argue constitutional law with the experts, even though many of its impeachment-minded members were lawyers, ex-prosecutors, or ex-judges, but gave the transparent excuse that all contrary advice must be inspired by a pro-Clinton bias. To make their case appear more convincing, furthermore, the committee invited testimony from average persons who had gone to jail for perjury and another who had lost her job because of an extramarital affair at her place of work. European correspondents ignored this silly gesture.

The Constitution also limits the punitive effects of successful impeachment to removal from office and to barring the convicted person from holding any other federal office of "honor, trust or profit." The framers preferred to leave punishments of life, limb, and monetary fines to the courts. One of the authorities testifying on the process of impeachment before the committee, political scientist Samuel H. Beer of Harvard University, likened removal from presidential office without further punishment to a parliamentary vote of no-confidence, "a way of supplementing the principal mechanism of democratic responsibility by quadrennial elections... The Congress ... must act in lieu of the people between quadrennial elections." But Professor Beer warned the

House against such use of its power in the face of a twice-elected president and opinion polls that showed that the true sovereign, the American people, did not support such extreme action. In the same vein, Ackerman of Yale University argued that "only a truly democratic [newly elected] House [not a lame-duck Congress] had the authority to impeach a duly elected president"—in other words, the 105th House with its pre-election majority had no right to pass impeachment charges for the 106th House which had a different composition and a new mandate. This was another warning that Chairman Hyde and his team chose to ignore. My European friends often commented also on the Republican myopia of not seeing, in the heat of partisan and personal hatred for Clinton, that the Republican House majority was ruining the presidency for future Republican presidents.

Finally, the framers had instituted the two-thirds requirement in the Senate for the removal of an impeached president, an evident barrier against excessive partisanship or "popular passion," reflected in the likely impeachment fervor of the House of Representatives. In the cases of both Presidents Andrew Johnson and Clinton, the two-thirds clause performed exactly as intended: it saved them from removal. And thereby it also protected the delicate balance between Congress and the presidency, but only up to a point. In Clinton's case, the Constitution would have been severely and permanently damaged by a successful impeachment on such flimsy charges. "It is eminently important," was the editorial comment from the conservative Swiss *Neue Zuercher Zeitung* after Clinton's acquittal, "that a president cannot be chased from office on bagatelle charges. With this decision [to acquit], the Senators made clear that they want to keep the presidential office strong and to limit means of the Congress to correct a popular mandate after the elections." The editorial was critical of Clinton's conduct and gave even-handed play to the arguments on both sides, while withholding judgment on "whether it was right to impeach a president for trying to hide a private affair but certainly not threatening the state, the governmental system, or society" (February 13-14, 1999). Impeachment on flimsy charges without removal—the innovation of 1998—of course has now become a process that can be repeated at will and in the same irresponsible fashion by any volatile majority of the House.

After the president was impeached by the House, Alain Frachon, in an article entitled "The End of American Compromise" in *Le Monde* (December 26, 1998), juxtaposed the long-customary spirit of compromise in American politics with what the *New York Times* had called the work of "a party of extremists, of absolute right-wingers . . . , alien to the political and cultural notions of the majority of Americans." Frachon wrote: "The rupture is not just ideological. It touches also upon the workings of the institutions which . . . is, from away back, without precedent. In using the weapon of impeachment for a lie that was indeed under oath but of no bearing upon an affair of state, the Republicans have applied an *intègriste* (extreme purist) filter to the reading of the Constitution, banalizing the use of the impeachment procedure." Using such standards, said Frachon, neither Reagan nor Bush with their great and public lies about affairs of state (Iran-Contra and Iraq) would have escaped impeachment. "By lowering the threshold for the use of this procedure, the Republicans modified the constitutional architecture, redefining the balance of powers between legislature and executive at the expense of the latter [and] introducing an element of parliamentarism, one way, into a presidential regime" (December 26, 1998).

"A village gathering for a public execution" was how Jonathan Freedland, a foreign correspondent for the *Guardian* (September 12, 1998) described the scene of confusion inside the Washington beltway, upon the presentation of the Starr Report. "The gallows are ready, but the court is still uncertain." The *Guardian* was quite acerbic about Clinton, but Freedland could not pass up the opportunity to sneer at Starr, who "invoked the ten commandments, Magna Carta, and the beheading of Sir Thomas More," and who described his task as "to vindicate the rule of law" and exhorted the House to fear "the judgment of the people . . . of history, and the moral law." With evident approval, Freedland cited Democratic minority leader Dick Gephardt, who had referred to the president as the one person chosen by the entire American people: "To overturn him is to overturn the will of the electorate" that had elected him for the second time in 1996. There, of course, lies the essence of the charge that this impeachment drive against Clinton was an attempted coup d' état against the legitimate constitutional authority deriving from popular election. The choice of unusual, extreme, and improper means to this end further separates this campaign from legitimate, constitutional uses of the impeachment power, such as the impeachment of Johnson, the attempt to impeach Nixon over Watergate, and the proposed attempts to impeach Reagan and Bush over the Iran-Contra affair.

European observers were particularly shocked about the odd reasoning that related the extreme action of impeachment to the intense hatred of the impeachers. As the *Los Angeles Times* (December 20, 1998) wrote after the impeachment of Clinton: "It is impossible to ignore or downplay the element of personal loathing for Clinton that underlies so much of what has been said and done in the impeachment process. To many of Clinton's fiercest critics the "character flaws" that came to national attention in his first campaign for president should by themselves have disqualified him from office. The refusal of the nation's voters to agree with that view in both 1992 and 1996 [and in the public opinion polls] only fueled their resentment and hostility." Europeans compared this to a naughty child stomping his foot and refusing to apologize to his sibling for attacking him: "But I hate him so." A child so furious he does not care if he burns down the house—that is, the Constitution—in his rage. What kind of an excuse is that for an adult? Such pathological hatred calls for stern, perhaps even psychiatric, intervention was the European reaction. The reference to "character" and "values," especially after the revelations about philanderers, liars, and perjurers among the House Republicans, was viewed with skepticism. What matters in a democracy is that the majority and the Constitution have the last word.

The validity of the Republican challenge to Clinton, in the view of some observers on the continent, was diminished further by the fact that the Europeans attributed Clinton's continued high approval rating to the American public's awareness that this impeachment was "no isolated event but a part of extensive, systematic, and objectively unjustified Republican efforts to overthrow Clinton." To the *Neue Zuercher Zeitung,* "This point makes all the difference. No one in the United States and abroad could miss the fact that, from the very beginning [in 1993], Clinton headed the Republican hit list . . . a victim of years of investigations by the special prosecutor, whom the Republicans supported without hesitation . . . and who in his efforts to tie the chief executive to any violations of law he could find, frequently went beyond the limits of acceptable conduct. The Lewinsky Affair was merely the last and, as it turned out, most consequential act in a concerted conservative drive to get rid, by judicial means, of this disliked but politically unassailable president" (February 13-14, 1999).

This respected Swiss daily was one of the few foreign media that not only mentioned the American public opinion polls on Clinton's performance but really appreciated them: "Why did the majority of the American people cling so stubbornly to Clinton, for weeks and months on end? Why wouldn't . . . the citizenry believe that he is an amoral criminal whose removal is every good citizen's duty—as the Republicans had told them time and again?" But "the Americans simply saw through this whole scheme and their opinions were not without effect. There can be no doubt but that without the firm and ever newly manifested support of the people, Clinton would not have survived this ordeal." The *Neue Zuercher Zeitung* also ascribed "an extremely dubious role in this entire story to the [American] mass media" (see chapter 4). Ennio Caretto, writing in the centrist *Corriere della Sera,* was withering in his comment on the reception of the Starr Report by the House: "The Republicans have not only inflicted a gratuitous humiliation on President Clinton. They have also strengthened the impression that American politics is a jungle and that the Constitution, which was written 200 years ago, needs to be rewritten at this point. Never before have American institutions and, in the last analysis, democracy been so disgraced, not even at the apex of the Watergate scandal" (quoted in *World Press Review*, November 1998). Klaus Lutterbeck, writing in the German weekly *Stern*, blamed "the hair-raising Independent Counsel Law of 1978 . . . that gives the special prosecutor powers that are really intolerable in a democracy . . . Hardly any other civilized country would have put up with what Starr put together [in his report]. Even less that the people's representatives made this calumny available to the whole world via Internet" (February 11, 1999).

A DIFFERENT KIND OF CONSERVATISM

In European eyes the coup character of the events in Washington had various and at times contradictory aspects that reflected European difficulties in understanding American politics in the 1980s and 1990s, and in general. One such aspect was the nature of the new American conservatism of the eighties, which did not resemble what they, from their own historical experience, understood as conservatism. We need to understand European perceptions of the Reagan administration in order to fathom their attitudes in 1998. The Reagan era, aside from its emphasis on market forces and, in their opinion, an exaggerated hostility to the welfare state, exuded a kind of cultural and religious conservatism Europeans could not understand. The news magazine *Der Spiegel*, for example, at the time reported on the new American president, Reagan, far more in terms of his pronounced machismo, misogynism, antifeminism, and frequent biblical references, than of his economic philosophy that did not resemble conservatism on the continent. Aside from the purple rhetoric, in fact, Europeans perceived mostly the international economic policies of the Reagan administration—for instance, the very high American interest rates that were designed to lure a lion's share of European investment capital across the Atlantic to finance the huge American budget deficits of the 1980s. Reagan's domestic rhetoric, so comforting to Americans in the eighties, left no great impression on European observers. Conservative columnist Josef Joffe formerly of the *Sueddeutsche Zeitung* of Munich, (now at *Die Zeit* of Hamburg), still considers both Reagan and Margaret Thatcher "revolutionaries of the right" and not conservatives (January 11, 1995). By the mid-1980s, European critical attention, moreover, had shifted further toward what Europeans viewed as a new saber-rattling American aggressiveness abroad that manifested itself in threats of a nuclear Armageddon against the communist "evil empire." The loose talk of a "trial nuclear attack," if actually carried out and drawing a Soviet response, might have incinerated Central Europe as well.

First disclosures of the Iran-Contra affair in the European press, furthermore, dealt little with the arms-for-hostages dealings with Iran that upset America and triggered investigations by special prosecutor Lawrence E. Walsh as well as defensive strategies by the Reagan administration. Instead, Europeans were shocked to discover the extent to which exaggerated American anticommunism had helped to direct, finance, and conceal the vast slaughter of civilians in Nicaragua, El Salvador, Guatemala, and Honduras. The rape and murder of Catholic nuns, the assassination of Archbishop Romero, and the killing of tens of thousands of civilians, mostly Indians, by military units and death squads of far-right Central American leaders backed by the Reagan administration deeply disillusioned European opinion about America. Even conservative European Catholics were horrified at the American role bolstering these savage operations. For example, a West German community development organization in Central America, sponsored by the conservative Konrad Adenauer Foundation of Helmut Kohl's governing Christian Democrats, had to pack up hurriedly and under loud protest leave its humanitarian project behind. Catholic church organizations that had previously agonized over the choice between conservative Catholic doctrines and the leftist theology of liberation recoiled in horror from the murderous, even genocidal military regimes backed by the United States in the name of anticommunism.

Fifteen years later, one European journalist, John Carlin, writing for the London *Independent* (May 10, 1998), still bitterly remembered the secret Central American wars of the Reagan administration as "the barbarism Reagan's government was prepared to encourage [in Central America] in the name of democracy . . . They were real people, those Salvadoreans, Guatemalans, Hondurans, and Nicaraguans . . . I saw their disfigured corpses and mutilated limbs." Carlin wrote this apropos of the renaming of Washington National Airport for President Reagan and added, "[they ought to] be hauling him up before a tribunal for his crimes." Our media scarcely reported European discomfort with our Central American policies in those days, probably thinking they were covered by the Monroe Doctrine. At that time, one of the most vociferous congressional defenders of the Iran-Contra missteps of the Reagan administration on the floor of Congress was Henry Hyde, who had been elected to the House in 1974 from suburban Du Page County, one of the most Republican constituencies in Illinois. Two decades later, as a result of the Republican landslide of 1994, he became chair of the Judiciary Committee of the House of Representatives. He chaired the committee—and the House managers before the Senate—in the impeachment drive against Clinton. Hyde had defended the political use of lying in connection with Iran-Contra and the defense of Oliver North, but now he would not hear of any distinctions between big political lies and lying to cover up such infidelities as he himself had committed.

Hyde's reputation is also connected with his anti-abortion amendments to budget bills, usually in the form of riders banning federal funding of abortions except in cases of incest, rape, or danger to the life of the mother. Republican administrations usually let his amendments stand but President Clinton fought them, which may well be one of the explanations for Hyde's bitter hostility towards Clinton. Hyde also defended in Congress the School of the Americas in Georgia, a United States military college for Latin American officers who, among other things, were taught the full gamut of techniques for fighting insurgencies and civil wars, including assassination, torture, and various other ways to "neutralize the enemy." The roster of graduates of this "school for assassins" of the seventies and eighties includes some of the vilest of Central American military instigators of massacres, including Colonel Roberto D'Aubisson of El Salvador—Roberto d'Escuadron to his detractors in reference to the death squads he was said to control—reputedly the force behind the assassination of Archbishop Romero. The CIA director of those days, William Casey, was also a major political pillar of the inner circle of the Reagan administration's covert Central American policy until his illness and death removed him from the grasp of the Iran-Contra investigation.

The consequence of all this was to alert European perceptions of American politics to the fact that the Reagan years had wrought a profound change in American politics. It was a change from what had, at least to the outside observer, seemed a politics of moderation, of the middle of the road even in the darkest days of the Cold War and of Vietnam—another time when Europeans, especially those left of center, had been exceedingly critical of American policies abroad. European estrangement during the Reagan years should also be contrasted with the relatively sympathetic attitudes of Europeans toward Nixon, a president who was quite popular with European public opinion.

The unfavorable European perceptions of the Reagan era shaded over into an awareness of the ever-deepening polarization of American politics in the eighties and nineties. There was some comparability between the self-styled conservatism of the Reagan following and that of British prime minister Margaret Thatcher, though more on economic grounds. Europeans would probably call economic Reaganism or Thatcherism a kind of Herbert Spencer-type neoliberalism or economic libertarianism. Among British Tories, too, Thatcher was a new kind of commercial middle-class leader, quite different from the old-style Tory aristocrat or upper-class figure motivated by an attitude of noblesse oblige and paternalism toward the lower orders. During Reagan's tenure in the 1980s, also, a new kind of self-styled American conservative pundit and institute or think tank arose, which dominates the Washington scene today. Later, the New Republicans of the 1994 landslide arrived, all quite different from and antagonistic toward most Old Republicans who had led the Republican minority in the House before Gingrich. These new American conservatives have few if any equivalents in European conservative parties today, another reason why European observers view them skeptically and with little comprehension. And they also harbor a deep-seated hostility toward the Old Democrats in Congress, although this hardly explains their hatred for Clinton, the New Democrat.

THE DRUMBEAT OF CONSERVATIVE REVOLUTION

Since the 1992 and 1996 Republican primaries, foreign observers have watched Pat Buchanan talk up the culture wars between right-to-lifers, gun owners, economic materialists, and what used to be called conservative Reagan Democrats, on the one hand, and liberals, internationalists, and secular humanists on the other. They have listened to Gingrich and others speak of a "conservative revolution" of family and other values that was about to sweep the country. This oxymoron, conservative revolution, meant little to American ears, or we understood it as the kind of politicians' big talk not to be taken literally. To historically aware Europeans, however—and most educated Europeans know their history very well—this phrase had very ominous overtones. Germans, for example, are well aware of the self-styled "conservative revolutionaries" in their own political history, ultraright-wing literati and demagogues in the 1920s and 1930s, who had nothing but contempt for the democratic politics and constitution of the Weimar Republic of Germany. Theirs was a romantic, folkish nationalism, cultural conservatism, and hero worship. One of them, Arthur Moeller van den Bruck (1876-1925), coined the term "the Third Reich" when he wrote a utopian book with this title. His authoritarianism and racial ideas, including anti-Semitism, inspired many future Nazi propagandists, even though hardly any of these conservative revolutionaries actually joined the Nazi party or showed more than passing interest in its rise. Some, in fact, were imprisoned as suspicious subversives at the beginning of the Third Reich, as were many conservatives and moderates. But they were precursors, extremist propagandists whose writings helped Adolf Hitler and his rough following take over the state although the conservative revolutionaries themselves looked down upon the crude, plebeian Nazis as unworthy representatives of their "spiritual revolution."

Educated Italians, too, associate "conservative revolution" with some of their extreme right-wing writers, such as the influential Julius Evola (born 1898). His writings of cultural pessimism made him a forerunner of Mussolini's fascist movement and state, although he never joined the Blackshirts and maintained a critical distance from the Italian dictator—it was a matter of mutual distrust. In the 1960s and 1970s, Evola's writings deeply influenced Italy's neofascists and ultraright terrorists as well, and they seemed to learn from him an attitude of desperate cultural and political destructiveness that is hard to fathom. France also had its conservative revolutionaries in the 1930s, both right-wing intellectuals and political organizers who gave the country dozens of authoritarian fascist movements, large and small, and like Evola were great admirers of the German Third Reich and its crusade against Bolshevism. Since the 1970s, there have been a number of right-wing journals of the *nouvelle droite* and writers like Alain de Benoist and his Nietzschean doctrines, a kind of missing link between moderate French conservatives and the extremist *Front national*.

Americans may find these comparisons rather alien and, to say the least, not the most plausible match to our contemporary Gingrichites or Republican ultras. Europeans, of course, are not saying that Starr, Hyde, Barr, or DeLay are neofascists or neo-Nazis. They merely try to understand strange American phenomena, like the zealots of this recent impeachment episode, by comparing them to extremist groups and experiences of their own respective national traditions. They have to discount some aspects, in particular, the very different social and historical contexts of each movement. European societies in the 1920s, 1930s, or even in the 1970s were as different from the United States in the 1990s as can be.

However, some telling analogies still remain. True conservatives in any context are not receptive, if not necessarily hostile, to social or political revolution in any form. In truly democratic systems, they are not likely to spread their conservative values by violence or coercion. The revolutionary temper, whatever its goals, is inherently irreconcilable with conservatism. Self-styled conservative revolutionaries in any Western society, therefore, have been highly suspect, especially if they wrap themselves in the flag of the country or try to hide their fervor behind religion, the rule of law or a distorted interpretation of the Constitution. The skepticism of European observers toward self-styled American conservative revolutionaries, in other words, is quite understandable even if there is nothing quite like the big European fascist movements of the twenties and thirties to be found in America today. This is not to deny that there are small right-wing American extremist groups, such as the Ku Klux Klan, which once played a powerful role, or Aryan Nations to which Buchanan's campaign cochairman Larry Platt was linked, or the segregationist Council of Conservative Citizens with which House Republican Bob Barr and Republican Senate majority leader Trent Lott were associated by press reports. In the meantime, of course, the extremist character of the zealots of the 1998-99 impeachment drive was confirmed, rather surprisingly, within the Republican leadership when the presidential convention of George W. Bush in 2000 pointedly excluded them from the limelight. Neither Hyde, Armey, Barr, DeLay, nor Starr, nor the issues of the impeachment drive, were allowed to play a role. The Bush people obviously thought of them as an extremist diversion from their new centrist drive for the White House.

Even if Europeans did not specifically associate the Republican anti-Clinton campaign with their own varieties of extremism, similar words abounded in European press descriptions. Two years after the president's reelection, the conservative *Le Figaro* (December 11, 1998) spoke of "Republican extremism (*jusqu'au boutisme*) holding Bill Clinton hostage." The French daily marveled at "Congress advancing against the popular will . . . Is a bad alcove secret as much of a menace to the American constitution as were the evil operations . . . of Richard Nixon?" The same newspaper also focused on conspirators such as *Pittsburgh Times* publisher Richard Mellon Scaife, a financial angel to extreme-right causes, "the bitterest critic of the leftist line of Clinton's presidency" (September 10, 1998) and "the right-wing radical Rutherford Institute" that paid the second set of Paula Jones's lawyers (November 17, 1998). *Le Figaro* did not consider these any more conservative than it regarded "Starr, the *flic du sexe* (policeman of sex)" a genuine conservative (November 20, 1998).

At the time of the 1996 presidential elections, the *Sunday Telegraph* of London, in a widely reprinted review of conspiracy theories linking Clinton to Vincent Foster's suicide and other alleged crimes, had talked about Scaife, the heir of $800 million of the Mellon fortune who had invested $2 million in the anti-Clinton campaign and paid former *New York Post* reporter Chris Ruddy to investigate first Whitewater and then the Foster affair (October 22, 1995). The liberal *Le Monde* similarly characterized the Federalist Society to which Starr and other attorneys of the anti-Clinton cabal belonged as "the most radical [right] wing of the Republican party." After the House had impeached the president, Alain Frachon wrote in *Le Monde:* "The influence of the Christian fundamentalist right has changed the nature of the congressional Republicans [and given them], . . . a vision of society unlike that of the Democrats or the . . . Old Republicans, nor . . . of the majority of the electorate" (September 13-14, 1998).

This extremist drift, to Frachon, explains the decisions of the Republican leaders in Congress: "The likes of Bob Livingston, Tom DeLay, and Henry Hyde don't hesitate to demand the removal of a twice-elected president by the American people, [who has been] supported by the opinion polls—and this on the morrow after congressional elections that largely repudiated those same Republicans." Frachon added that these extremist leaders also squelched the censure option despite its support from a majority of the people and of Congress, and rejected the advice of senior leaders like "Gerald Ford and Robert Dole who both considered impeachment totally out of proportion . . . The sense of compromise, long at the heart of the workings of the political-institutional American system, is [simply] no longer a part of the Republican repertory" (December 26, 1998). Other French journals, such as *L'Express*, called the Republican radicals "intégralistes" (referring to the integrity or purity of the nation, as in the French debate over integral nationalism) and "anti-Clinton kamikazes" (February 4, 1999), while the German news magazine *Der Spiegel* thought Clinton a "victim of antiblack hatred": "They hate him as they did Eleanor Roosevelt for inviting blacks to the White House," said Gore Vidal in an interview with the German journal. The magazine pointed to all the southerners among the House managers presenting the case for impeachment before the Senate: this "impeachment," *Der Spiegel* said, echoing Karen Grigsby Bates and William Raspberry, "is the political equivalent of a lynching" (February 8, 1999).

The opprobrium in European eyes was shared equally by the "perverse prosecutor" (*L'Express*, February 18-24, 1999) even though the foreign correspondents did not yet know half of Starr's actions in the entrapment of the president. Nor did they know much about the anti-Clinton activists in the House and among the House managers of the case before the Senate. The latter were likened by Klaus Lutterbeck, in the popular German weekly *Stern*, "to the 19 Marineland dolphins jumping in the air three times a day, every day, as programmed in Lewinskyland, Washington" (February 11, 1999). Europeans simply did not take the accusations seriously, considering the sources. The revelations about the sexual pasts of Hyde, Speaker-elect Livingston, committee counsel David Schippers, Representatives Dan Burton and Helen Chenoweth, as well as Republican Whip DeLay's record on perjury and Barr's on abortion, hardly helped to authenticate their moral crusade against Clinton. To skeptical Europeans, Clinton's alleged character flaws were simply those of his pursuers.

A CHRONOLOGY OF 1998

It is not without pitfalls to set up a timetable for the events of 1998, much as the mind strives for markers to jog our memory and to bring some chronological order to the political hysteria of that year. For obvious reasons, foreign journalists in Washington tended to hunger even more for such a chronology. They found themselves in the dark about crucial turns in the story because they naively relied on what the devious Starr and the hysterical American media wanted the public to believe. To illustrate: when the story became so compelling that the foreign media began to focus heavily on it, *Le Figaro* (August 17, 1998) published a chronological sketch starting from January 7, the date of Lewinsky's deposition before the Jones grand jury, to August 6, the day of Lewinsky's revised testimony before the grand jury. In this chronology, just as in the official Starr Report, Lewinsky's "bosom friend," the mysterious Linda Tripp, only appears on January 12, when she supposedly took her secretly recorded tapes to Starr, enabling him to obtain authority to expand his investigation to the Lewinsky affair. As in the Report and in the media at the time, there is no mention of Tripp's earlier relationship to Starr's OIC, before which she had been called to testify repeatedly, dating back to the Foster suicide of mid-1994 (she was the last person to see Foster alive). She had testified again in connection with the Travel Office affair. Instead, just as in the Report and in the American media, Tripp was at first pictured in the foreign press only as a concerned citizen—later she even claimed to have identified with "poor Monica" as if she were her mother—taking criminal evidence to the law (see also *London Times* of February 13, 1999).

The deceptions regarding Tripp's true role were moments of comic grandeur, not unlike the television discussions to follow which Gore Vidal, in *Der Spiegel*, later characterized acidly with "William Bennett . . . always yammering in front of television cameras about 'Monica . . . little Monica' . . . as if she was a five-year-old kindergartner with braids and dental braces who had fallen into the clutches of a pederast" (February 8, 1999). Or the efforts of the *Los Angeles Times* or of Ken Bode of *Washington Week in Review* (PBS) at the time to depict 22-year-old Lewinsky as a child in need of protection from the appetites of older men. Tripp's "evidence," aside from reporting her private conversations with Monica, were the 23 hours of telephone confidences in Valley-Girl-speak about Lewinsky's relationship with "the big creep." None of it was criminal, or related to the alleged criminal conduct by the president, such as telling Lewinsky to lie about their relationship in her deposition or promising her a job if she did. Starr later tried mightily but unsuccessfully to assert such offenses, and in the end prevaricated in his Report that she had been told to lie, in direct contradiction to her repeated testimony of record.

In his book *Uncovering Clinton* and in earlier accounts, Michael Isikoff details the tawdry story of how Lucianne Goldberg, a New York literary agent, manipulated Tripp. And friend Tripp manipulated and frightened Lewinsky into supplying—perhaps initially only material for a book that Tripp wanted to write and Goldberg intended to publish—the "evidence" for the conspiracy against the president. At the turn of 1997-1998, the Jones suit in the hands of teams of the right-wing conspirators, the surprising cooperation of the Supreme Court and other federal judges, the escalating Tripp caper, Starr's collusion with Jones's lawyers and manipulation of his legal powers, and the media conspiracy to topple the president together formed what the French call a *conjuncture* of history, an accidental confluence of several crucial factors that brought the attempt to overthrow the president to near-triumph. Isikoff relates his sudden realization, at the time of the illegal sting of Lewinsky on January 13, 1998, that "this was not about sex, or even about the Paula Jones case. This was about a Special Prosecutor launching a secret criminal investigation against the president—and targeting his supposed girlfriend in an effort to nail him." [9] And again, "Starr's probe . . . was flawed from the start. It began . . . instigated by a scared but devious woman [Tripp, worried about the illegality of her secret taping], who had gotten ensnared in her own plotting."[10]

Isikoff thought Starr's sting operation of Tripp, secretly taping Lewinsky at lunch at the Ritz-Carlton (January 13, 1998), with FBI wiretappers and agents standing by, was "nuts," and the resulting criminal charges of "obstruction of justice" and "subornation of perjury" simply out of place when "applied to the angst-ridden babble of two lonely women."[11] According to Isikoff, Lewinsky had claimed at the sting lunch that she was going to lie under oath and wanted Tripp to do so too. Curiously, this sting operation received no comment in Toobin's book even though Starr had not yet been authorized to expand his investigation to Lewinsky. The OIC then used this dubious evidence to obtain authority from the Department of Justice and the panel of federal judges to seize Lewinsky on the day prior to Clinton's deposition before the Jones grand jury on January 17. The OIC deputies threatened her and her mother, Marcia Lewis, with criminal prosecution if Lewinsky did not cooperate and testify down to the last salacious, titillating details of her affair with the president. She was even asked to wear a taping wire while speaking with Clinton, Jordan, and Betty Currie, the president's secretary, another fact the OIC later chose to deny.

Bacharan, in her book *Le Piège* describes the "mafioso strategy" behind the efforts of the Jones lawyers and Starr to "get the president by any means," even though there was little likelihood they would find anything that the courts would term a crime. On the one hand, there was the new legal twist invented by the cabal of attorneys now arguing that Jones was *discriminated against* because other past Clinton liaisons who were Arkansas employees allegedly had been awarded promotions, perks, or other rewards. They were never able to supply a shred of evidence for this theory. This was claimed to be a violation of the Clinton administration's Violence Against Women Act of 1994, an ex post facto fallacy even if provable. But the insistence of the Jones lawyers on "interrogating every past girlfriend of the president"—an interrogation authorized by Judge Susan Webber Wright—was only a juristic trick "unlikely to find a crime." It was a convenient vehicle, by "leaking the gathered information to the media, . . . for damaging the president." Starr prepared a "juristic entrapment" by "provoking a lie under oath," a strategy "sufficiently common in American law enforcement: When you cannot find a crime, or establish the guilt of a suspect, you try to make him commit another crime, in this case you push him into lying under oath, perjury." The new lie has nothing to do with the crime of which the accused is suspected. You have now created a crime instead of having found one.[12] Like most Americans, I never expected to find our system of justice described in such terms by a knowledgeable French observer.

According to Bacharan, "Starr excels at this art and has no equal in playing with the words, interpreting them, destroying the testimony of a witness . . . If all else fails, [he] has another weapon . . . plea bargaining under pressure: One intimidates the suspects, or the witnesses, threatening the most terrible consequences [if without foundation], and then guarantees they will not be used against them if they cooperate." In other words, one gives them immunity for transgressions they have not committed, which is more or less the principle of Mafia protection. "this may seem legitimate in order to protect society from a serial killer or drug baron, though it is often used for minor offenses. But this time the godfather is a special prosecutor [against the president of the United States] who has the most extensive powers ever conferred in the history of America.[13] Bacharan here describes the theory but may not be aware of Starr's absentee stewardship of OIC where he apparently did not even have contact with any of the witnesses.

Bacharan then relates the story of the detainment and intimidation of Lewinsky on January 16, 1998, at the Pentagon Food Court by armed FBI agents and OIC lawyers, their threats of jailing her for up to 27 years on various baseless charges, the de facto denial of her wish to call her lawyer—all of which, along with the OIC leaks of grand jury information, Starr has denied, under oath before the House Judiciary Committee and millions of American television viewers—plus their implied threats against Lewinsky's mother. "[Lewinsky] is bullied by the policemen and subjected to an intensive interrogation like a murderess . . . but the threats are evidently false." The only possibly valid charge against Lewinsky, and a stretch at that, was that she had lied about her relationship with Clinton in her deposition. The deposition, however, had not even been sent off to Arkansas at that point. Had she been permitted to call her lawyer (Francis Carter), he would simply have withdrawn her affidavit and the case against her would have collapsed, along with the "opportunity to turn her into a pliable witness against the president." All this was to serve the "ferocious desire of Kenneth Starr to have the head of the president, no matter under what pretext . . . Now it only remained to make Bill Clinton fall into the same trap and push him into denying his relationship to the young woman under oath" the following day before the grand jury.[14] "Why did they assemble a grand jury [in the Jones civil suit]," one of my European friends asked, "when there was no evidence of a crime having been committed? Don't you have to have a crime first and then decide who should be indicted?" Toobin points out that, for the second set of Jones lawyers, "the opportunity to examine Clinton under oath had been the principal reason the Dallas lawyers agreed to represent Paula Jones . . . They had entered the case . . . as much to humiliate the president as to compensate their client."[15] Without having him under oath, of course, how could they contrive to entrap him?

THE STARR REPORT: A PENCHANT FOR THE SALACIOUS

The emphasis on graphic descriptions of alleged presidential sex had been the hallmark of the various right-wing lawyers and the anti-Clinton media dating from the Gennifer Flowers report of the 1992 primaries to the beginnings of Troopergate. In the Jones case, lawyers insisted on the allegedly unusual anatomical details of Clinton's genitals that Paula Jones rather implausibly was said to recall. In December 1997, when the Jones lawyers learned about the Clinton-Lewinsky affair, according to Isikoff, one of them told a coconspirator: "You can rest assured we're all over that like flies over feces."[16] The eager revelations of titillating details continued with the January 1998 leaks about cigars, oral sex, semen-stained dresses, telephone sex, ejaculations, and orgasms, fed to the media by whoever had possession of Tripp's recollections and tapes of Lewinsky's confidences, especially by the OIC. The original intent had evidently been to "flip" Lewinsky and her mother by dire threats coupled with promises of immunity for testifying against Clinton. Starr, according to Toobin, could have made the deal to deadly effect in February but failed to accept the immunity agreement offered him then—and thus missed his chance of toppling the president. Lewinsky herself did not testify extensively before the OIC team until the end of July 1998, when she was promised conditional immunity—the chief condition was not speaking out about her relations with, and extraordinary mistreatment by, Starr's office. Tripp was not deposed until the end of June, although all her tapes and other testimony had been in the hands of the OIC since January, and parts of it even earlier.

The booster rocket for either impeachment or resignation was the Starr Report which tried to pump up the sex scandal to its most shocking intensity. Unfortunately for Starr, and fortunately for Clinton, the American public by then had gotten used to what might have been explosive disclosures back in February. For his purpose of publicizing the confidential material, Starr had obtained secret and extraordinary judicial authorization to submit secret grand jury testimony and supporting evidence to Congress long before either the president or Lewinsky had even testified further to the investigators. His 450-page report was replete with salacious details and graphic descriptions of sexual encounters—even idle speculations on whether Bill might divorce Hillary and marry Monica, highly conjectural comments that the European press considered completely inappropriate (*Guardian,* September 15, 1998). It was transparently meant for public distribution, though prefaced with a specific list of eleven possible impeachment charges of a legal sort—perjury, subornation of perjury, lying, obstruction of justice—for the House Judiciary Committee, which hardly required the smutty details. For good measure, and again unnecessary for documentation of the legal charges but obviously intended to humiliate the president, Starr subpoenaed Clinton for a DNA sample to match semen stains on Lewinsky's infamous cocktail dress which Starr had confiscated earlier. An additional five volumes of 7,800 pages (including Xeroxed texts) of "Appendices and Supplemental Materials" added vast amounts of undigested, disorganized material which, to quote Renata Adler of the *New Yorker,* "is an attempt through its own limitless preoccupation with sexual material to set aside, even obliterate, the relatively dull requirements of real [court] evidence and constitutional procedure" (*Vanity Fair,* December 1998).

Another 36 volumes of materials were deposited for later access by House members, followed soon by huge amounts of further documents amassed by the OIC in its years of investigating Whitewater, Travelgate, Filegate, the death of Vincent Foster, and more (including some Jane Doe files for the evidence room). As Adler pointed out, the approach of the OIC appeared to be modeled on the habits of corporate defense attorneys in product liability suits—to bury plaintiffs' attorneys in such vast and ill-arranged masses of documents that would be physically impossible for the latter to read it all or to find the clues they are seeking.

The release in September 1998 by order of Congress led to the publication of large sections of the Report in the press and on the worldwide Internet, with generally little or no editing out of the most salacious parts, neither here nor abroad. The Madrid daily *El País* (September 14, 1998) describing the distribution of the Starr Report by Congress, said it was "not fit for minors," and quoted the hypocritical disavowal by the *New York Times:* "It gives us no pleasure... " Unlike many other European papers, however, *El País* had already succumbed to the prurience of its readers and printed eight pages of excerpts, including some of the more salacious parts. In the American press, except for a few readers' letters, most of which were not published, there were few protests at the dissemination of such graphic descriptions of oral sex and the like through television and family newspapers where children and preteens would see them. Instead, the media editors and Republican pundits and politicians editorially rolled their eyes and said "what are we to tell our children" about this, as if children could have become aware of it without the flagrant breach of journalistic taboos regarding indiscriminate, graphic disclosure of sexual aspects of alleged crimes. When challenged, the Republican editors often pretended that the pornographic aspects really lay in the acts committed by Bill Clinton with Jones and Lewinsky, and not in the dissemination of graphic details.

European journalists were far more skeptical. As Pierre Georges put it in a piece called "The Ballad of the Sinner" in *Le Monde:* "With the sorrowful mien of the tormented tormentor, the Torquemada of the bedroom," Starr, recommended that certain "scabrous details, swinish passages (*passages cochons*) not be shown to children." He turned up his nose, so to speak: "What admirable hypocrisy (*tartufferie*) . . . how better to sell this merchandise? Let's not add indecency to the sordid [facts]!" (September 11, 1998). Some German newspapers such as the Hamburg *Morgenpost* and many radio stations simply refused to touch this "American pornography" and declared themselves to be a "Monica-free zone." On the other hand, the conservative *Frankfurter Allgemeine Zeitung* wrote: "Investigations are perverse in which details of sexual organs and of sexual practices are publicly discussed . . . It would have been possible to render a legal judgment of Clinton's behavior [of which the Frankfurt daily disapproved strongly], or a moral judgment, without [public] investigations that go into the most intimate things" (September 11, 1998). *Le Figaro* (September 11 and 13, 1998) printed two pages of the report, including sexual details, but not without mentioning Scaife's money for the *American Spectator* which "dug up Paula Jones in 1994" and financed a "Pepperdine University chair for Starr [actually a deanship]." An editorial by Charles Lambrosini in *Le Figaro* also suggested that "a majority of Congress . . . is no less impure than Clinton . . . but is now engaged in an irresponsible crusade." And the following day, "one does not know whom [the Starr Report] dishonors most, the president, the prosecutor, or those who have authorized the distribution of the texts" (September 14, 1998). The Italian liberal *La Repubblica* commented: A "puritanical and infantile America" risks world economic prosperity and stability because of "a little clandestine sex in the White House" (September 13, 1998).

From the British birthplace of American common law, a *Guardian* editorial said that Starr mentioned the issue of sex more than 500 times in his report. The British daily, however, would have preferred that Clinton resign upon this public humiliation and degradation (September 15, 1998). In the *Irish Times,* Fintan O'Toole, columnist, author and drama critic, wrote that "humiliating the President is . . . the strongest achievement of the Starr Report . . . driving him out by sheer force of shame. What could be the legal point 'about the cigar and the account of who touched whom where'?" On the Internet, the report even triggered Ireland's (and some other countries') protective mechanism to protect children from pornography (September 12, 1998).

O'Toole sharply contrasted the graphic sex aspects in the Starr Report with its slipshod legal arguments: "The report is scientific when it comes to describing the sleazy detail, but . . . vague and slipshod on the supposed heart of the matter—alleged breaches of the law." O'Toole went over the legal reasoning with considerable scorn, for example the argument of Clinton's alleged abuse of authority, the accusation of witness-tampering with Betty Currie in the Jones case (in which she was not even a witness), and others (*Irish Times,* September 14, 1998). In the same vein, Adrian Hardiman, a senior counsel, pointed out the gross disparity between Starr's allegations and the evidence produced in his "hugely hyped" report. Hardiman dismissed out of hand former president (and nonlawyer) Jerry Ford's opinion that the constitutional formula of "treason, bribery, high crimes and misdemeanors" meant "whatever a majority of the U.S. House of Representatives considers it to be in a given moment in history." Starr, in his opinion, had embarked on a "grossly discreditable and unethical strategy" in his pursuit of the president, "knowing that Clinton [and his lawyers] will not be able for weeks or months to [con]test the evidence" with legal arguments. Hardiman thought the intent of Starr's tactic was to "provoke Clinton's resignation without a hearing . . . There is no other explanation of the inclusion in this report of so much salacious detail . . . To put it bluntly, this is the most egregious as well as the most expensive attempt in history to prejudice or even avoid a hearing by damaging pretrial publicity." Of course, Clinton himself had given "a wily and unscrupulous opponent this opportunity" when he gave in to temptation (*Irish Times,* September 15, 1998).

In the liberal German weekly *Die Zeit,* Robert Leicht considered "the worldwide distribution of the videotape [of the president's testimony before the federal grand jury] a historically unique and simply obscene violation of the due process of [American] law and the rules of a fair trial," especially since it was allegedly made only because a member of the grand jury might be absent. Leicht doubted that the prosecutors could have been "after truth in an ongoing trial [but were] out to destroy a person in preparation for, or in lieu of, impeachment [and] removal from office." He cited the many legal absurdities: charges of perjury in a civil trial (on behalf of Jones) that the judge had already terminated, relating sexual harassment to the consensual Lewinsky affair, the release of Clinton's secret grand jury testimony worldwide—"a flagrant perversion of justice and travesty of zealous prosecution, whether for political motives or for a fringe moralistic craze" (September 24, 1998). There was no doubt that the once so highly respected integrity of American law and justice in European eyes had taken a tremendous beating, which was being administered by Starr, the "fanatical agent of scandal" (October 15, 1998), and "an irresponsibly acting Congress." Leicht later added: "What authority does a special prosecutor have who belongs to the political opposition and receives his ammunition from there?" (*Die Zeit,* January 29, 1999). French and Italian newspapers, as we have seen, were under no illusion either about the "more or less independent" (*Le Figaro,* December 31, 1998) independent prosecutor's ties to the ultraright conspiracy of lawyers and judges, politicians, the press, and the religious right.

True to the right-wing dedication to salacious sex scandals, Isikoff says, Starr and some of his OIC deputies were convinced they needed the sexy details in their Report to Congress, while some of the saner associates wanted him to delay public release at least until House members had read it. But Starr insisted on instant release of his pornographic Report to the world because "it wasn't the [OIC's] job to intrude into the House impeachment process." This incredible rationalization did not deter him from strongly intruding by specifically *advocating* the impeachment of Clinton, quite unlike the Watergate investigators 25 years earlier. He seemed surprised when his ethics adviser, Watergate counsel Sam Dash, resigned because Starr had expressly engaged in urging impeachment to an eager House Judiciary Committee. *New York Times* columnist Anthony Lewis also found this highly objectionable. The salacious conspiracy, of course, also included a number of Republican members of the House and Senate, especially those anxious to keep a collection of interesting testimonies about other alleged sex partners, Jane Does reportedly numbering in the dozens, in their evidence room in the Capitol.

Le Figaro's chronology of August 17, 1998, also failed to mention the sting luncheon of January 13 and the crucial events of January 16 when Lewinsky was seized by armed and burly FBI agents and OIC lawyers and threatened with 27 years in prison. Mike Emmick, one of Starr's deputies, reportedly told her "perjury, subornation of perjury, obstruction of justice, witness tampering were all felonies for which she would have to go to jail for as long as 27 years." She was kept a virtual prisoner for eleven hours so that she could not warn her attorney, Francis Carter, her mother, or the president's men of her unauthorized detention. Starr later denied, with mealy-mouthed circumlocutions—while testifying under oath before the House Judiciary Committee and, on television, before half the nation—that she had been prevented from leaving and not allowed to call her attorney, one of the sacred rights of American law enforcement in European eyes. One of the legal eagles among my European friends guffawed about Starr's lame excuses: "If I was told by the goons of OIC that I might have to go to jail for 27 years, I would not dare leave the room either."

Unaware of the conspiracy, Clinton was to make his deposition the next day before the Jones jury and, Starr correctly assumed, did not admit the true nature of his dalliance with Lewinsky. *Le Figaro*'s timetable, probably based on American media reports, only mentions for January 16 that Starr obtained authority to extend his investigation to Lewinsky via "legal discovery" for the Jones suit and, for January 17, that Clinton denied the affair under oath before the grand jury. The OIC deputies did not tell Attorney General Reno that Starr had long been in touch with the Jones attorneys. By what judicial and prosecutorial skullduggery he was authorized to investigate a not-yet-existing criminal offense, or rather to manufacture it, namely Clinton's alleged perjury, still awaits further investigative journalism. Isikoff and Toobin in their books tell a lot and, perhaps, Reno will some day fill in the gaps. When an immunity agreement was finally signed, Starr specifically forbade Lewinsky to discuss with the American media the coercive events of that January 16, 1998. There is certainly plenty of material for liberal conspiracy theories here about the plot to get Clinton.

One such explanation, certainly not implausible, appeared in the London *Observer*, where Ed Vulliamy traced it all to the tobacco industry, "their chargers on Capitol Hill," and "the industry's ace attorney, Kenneth Starr" (October 11, 1998). What was Vulliamy's evidence? Starr's appointment in summer 1994, following that famous luncheon of North Carolinian Senators Helms and Faircloth with Judge David Sentelle, also from North Carolina and a Helms protégé. Even after his appointment, Starr continued to work for the tobacco industry (especially Brown and Williamson), along with other private business, a major conflict of interest considering the antitobacco campaign of the Clinton administration. As Vulliamy explained, the tobacco lobby had long had half of the Congress in its pocket through its huge campaign contributions and was trying to head off an antitobacco bill that would cost the industry $516 billion over 25 years. The bill mandated an end to cigarette advertisements directed to children and to teenagers, and would have established the right of the Food and Drug Administration (FDA) to police nicotine addiction. Judge Sentelle had been a close associate of Starr and had quashed Oliver North's conviction back in Iran-Contra days. The revival of the OIC statute gave these ultraright conspirators the opening to dump Starr's predecessor, Fiske, who had found nothing untoward on Whitewater or against the Clintons. Faircloth and Fiske, also a Republican, were old enemies from their days under the Reagan administration, Vulliamy related. What a triumph indeed for the tobacco industry to harass and possibly remove their antagonist in the White House.

LE FIGARO CHRONOLOGY REVISITED

To review *Le Figaro's* chronology once more, it did mention the great American media storm of revelations about Clinton's involvement with Monica Lewinsky after his deposition January 17. With few exceptions, the media moguls had recalled many of their star reporters to Washington from the impending first-time visit of the Pope to Cuba—one of the last communist states in the world. In an article, "Sex Rather than the Pope," the *Sueddeutsche Zeitung* of Munich commented on January 23, 1998, that obviously the papal visit was considered trivial when matched against the leaked stories of semen-stained cocktail dresses and the like. But how did the American media know in advance that this was about to break, and that there would be leaks of what the European press soon came to call *les cochonneries* or *Schweinereien,* most likely invented, embellished, and leaked by the OIC investigators themselves—the media never bothered to do their own research? From the vantage point of a foreign correspondent, Kornelius of the *Sueddeutsche Zeitung* described the media circus in Washington when the Monica Lewinsky story broke: "The news about Miss Lewinsky was not yet six hours old when they began to mention 'impeachment' which, by general consensus, was said to be triggered [not by the sex scandal itself but] by charges of 'subornation of perjury' or 'obstruction of justice.'" The barbaric strains of American witch-hunt law had been unleashed by the wiles of a vengeful prosecutor, who took advantage of the pillow talk of a young and foolish woman tape-recorded by her "maternal friend," Tripp. "There was a mob of hundreds of media photographers and journalists in a media feeding frenzy outside Starr's office" (January 24, 1998).

To European ears, the American drama was still rather incomprehensible and *Sueddeutsche Zeitung* quickly supplied personal background on Starr for its readers, "the man who, incredibly, connects Whitewater with the sex life of the American president. This man [Starr] is powerful and not a few say he abuses his office for his campaign to overthrow Clinton . . . he cannot pursue the Lewinsky sex affair but only whether Clinton and Vernon Jordan suborned her perjury" (January 26, 1998). *Le Figaro* also reported Clinton's televised interview with Jim Lehrer on January 21 and mentioned the finger-wagging speech in which he denied it all. The French paper also related that the *New York Times*—ever ready to print all the news that fits its editors and publishers—on January 29 claimed it knew of a Clinton-Lewinsky tête-à-tête of December 28, 1997 when he had allegedly "told her to lie." *Le Figaro's* chronology also listed the federal court decision of April 30, 1998, denying that Clinton's executive privilege would shield his closest advisers from having to testify, and the July 17, 1998 ruling of the Supreme Court that his bodyguards also were not excused from testifying whether they had accidentally or deliberately seen any of the alleged sexual encounters. In the European view, this was another example of the federal judiciary elevating a clandestine sex affair to the level of criminality, and another gross invasion of privacy. On August 17, the day *Le Figaro's* chronicle ended, Clinton testified on the charges against him before a federal grand jury, maintaining that he had not lied under oath before the Jones jury because he had not had sex (in the full, conventional sense of the word) with Lewinsky. But in a television address shortly thereafter, he called it "an inappropriate relationship" and expressed his regrets to his family and the nation—not regretfully enough to many, including some in his own party. To Dieter Buhl writing in the German weekly *Die Zeit,* his televised *mea culpa* "only fortified the camps" (August 30, 1998).

In spite of its relative ignorance, its negative judgment on Clinton, and the fervor of the American media, conservative *Le Figaro* was no pushover. A day after the chronology (August 18, 1998) appeared, the French daily balanced its assessment again between speaking of "the obsessional special prosecutor, Kenneth Starr who has searched for years . . . upon any pretext [for prosecuting Clinton]" and expressions like "What buffoonery (*pantalonnade*)!," and pronouncing the presidential institution as shaken and "the greatest democracy . . . in weeks of a collective delirium." *Le Figaro* considered it "the grandeur of American democracy to dare demand, from time to time, that [even] the president should account for himself. But not for his private life" (August 18, 1998). The Italian daily *La Repubblica* similarly castigated Starr who "surprised the most cautious and conservative lawyers with his singular interpretation of his mandate . . . He feels authorized, contrary to the opinion of most American lawyers, to investigate Clinton's private life." *La Repubblica* took a dim view of Starr's "beginning with an illegal act, Tripp's wiretaps," and of the "moral level of investigating Clinton's associates by illegal and questionable methods" (August 18, 1998). In early September, when the Starr Report was released, the same paper also questioned Starr's charges "because for four years now he had vainly persecuted Clinton from Whitewater to Lewinsky" (September 9, 1998). The European press was also highly critical of Starr's insistence on obtaining a DNA sample from Clinton.

The Paula Jones suit was dismissed by Justice Wright on April 1, 1998 for insufficient evidence of a "violation of her civil rights" because the judge, according to Toobin, had finally lost patience with the media manipulations of Jones's lawyers. On November 13 her lawyers accepted an $850,000 settlement—without Clinton's apology. The two teams of right-wing lawyers promptly began to haggle over the prize until Judge Wright, following Clinton's acquittal before the Senate, permitted them to demand more money from the Clintons. In the first weeks of September 1998, the Starr Report was indeed delivered as a "referral" to the House of Representatives for purposes of impeachment. The House then voted 363 to 63, without permitting the White House lawyers to see it first or to present a rebuttal, to release the report in full to the media, including the worldwide Internet, an action widely criticized abroad as the distribution of salacious pornography. As Toobin among others has pointed out, it was only when they finally received copies, some time later, that the White House attorneys realized how thin a legal case Starr had against the president. The apparent strength of the case had evidently depended on the pornographic bells and whistles, not on juristic logic.

It should be noted that, at this point, more than a hundred Democratic House members were said to have favored the release of the Starr Report and, perhaps, even impeachment until the Democratic House leadership rallied them against the Republican onslaught. The initiative of the anti-Clinton drive had clearly passed to Starr who, unlike the Watergate investigators, proceeded to urge the House to launch impeachment proceedings based on his 11 partly repetitive or overlapping specific charges. The Republican majority on the House Judiciary Committee warmly accepted Starr's recommendation, his report, and a videotape of Clinton's August interrogation by a federal grand jury. The videotape, made allegedly for the benefit of an absent juror—and contrary to expectation not particularly shocking nor embarrassing in the opinion of American journalists—was promptly released to the public as had been the pertinent confidential materials of the Jones grand jury hearings in connection with the Starr Report. Starr evidently took "elaborate, early precautions," wrote a knowledgeable editorial in the *Guardian* of London, "to ensure that he would be within his powers to submit secret grand jury testimony and other supporting evidence to Congress [which then released it], obtaining a previously secret judicial authorization to do so in July, before either Mr. Clinton or Ms. Lewinsky had testified again to investigators" (September 11, 1998). Such releases of normally secret grand jury proceedings again demonstrated the bias shown by the judiciary in the drive to impeach Clinton. Bacharan thought that the use of a federal grand jury in this case was merely a pretext so that Starr could "put witnesses under oath and intimidate them," which, of course, is not normally the purpose of a grand jury.[17]

European correspondents picked up on the moral ambiguities as well as on the drama of the delivery of the Starr Report. The *Sueddeutsche Zeitung* described it as "the final [if long-expected] explosion which left the American body politic prone and shattered while most members of Congress fled the desolate Washington scene, many without a copy of the Report, just to get away . . . Many members of Congress now are horrified . . . ashamed to have voted for publication of the [salacious] Report, often only days after working on antipornographic legislation. Newspapers warn against reading the Report . . . television reporters refuse to read passages aloud" (September 14, 1998). Unlike many larger European papers, the Munich daily did not publish it and reported, at first with some glee, that there was no official German version of it, and later that there was now only an expurgated, child-safe German Internet version (September 21, 1998). The paper did mention some of the salacious details and said: Starr defends the specificity of the sexual details because " every phase of the relationship is part of his chain of proof . . . the demonstrated intimacy of Monica Lewinsky, for example, the president fondling her genitals . . . these are the foundations of his accusatory brief, the intimate details to prove his case for Clinton's alleged perjury" (September 14, 1998). Where the president's testimony obviously clashed with Lewinsky's—or with the version of her testimony that the investigators had her repeat twenty times, only to pick out the lines most in agreement with their case—the paper cautioned, "in American civil suits a witness's statement alone is not considered sufficient proof of perjury." I can imagine what European readers must have thought about the sex-mongering lawyers of OIC, a kind of lawyering they are not familiar with.

Following the distribution of the Starr Report and grand jury videotape, plus other materials of the Starr investigation, the House voted 258 to 176 to initiate an "open-ended inquiry" into the president's conduct, that is, formal hearings on whether the charges sufficed to launch impeachment proceedings. The tactics of Starr and of the Republican ultras in the House of Representatives to "go for broke" with the release of the Report did not meet with universal applause from all of the president's critics and produced further musings among European correspondents. Kornelius of the *Sueddeutsche Zeitung* reported that "even the critics of President Clinton fear that Starr's precipitate action and the panicky publication of the Report by Congress have not been the best strategy . . . The expected storm of public disgust seems to have backfired [regardless of public opinion on Clinton's indiscretions] . . . While Clinton undoubtedly has been guilty of legalistic subterfuge and lost authority with his moral lapse, Americans can understand him and relate to his high-wire acts [to escape condemnation]." Moreover, "just a few hours after submission of the Report, the much-vaunted bipartisanship collapsed . . . because at least the more fanatical Republicans [in the House] just want to punish Clinton. Chairman Hyde, for his part, over Democratic protests, now is fishing for special authority to press his prosecution" (September 14, 1998). The anti-Clinton mob, in other words, was far too eager to succeed in its endeavor in an orderly fashion. Hyde was quoted as saying when the Lewinsky scandal first broke in January, "Don't bother me with this story, it will never overthrow a president" (*Sueddeutsche Zeitung*, July 30, 1998). But now he was as impatient as any other Clinton-hater.

THE ELECTIONS OF NOVEMBER 1998

Starr had obviously timed the release of his Report to trigger a final stampede toward impeachment by influencing the imminent congressional elections of November 1998. They did cast a disturbing shadow over the public and House debates with respect to impeachment: while the congressional candidates for the most part avoided the issue, many partisan commentators suggested that the outcome of these elections would be a kind of plebiscite on the impeachment of Clinton. One Republican political scientist, who expected Republican gains of at least 25 seats in the House and six in the Senate, declared such a landslide would constitute a mandate for impeachment and might give the Republicans a majority for decades to come, just as Nixon's unfinished impeachment had benefited the Democrats after Watergate. On average, the opposition has gained 25 House seats in the second term off-year elections of any incumbent president. Evidently quoting American historians of elections, the correspondent of *Le Monde* (November 3, 1998) even spoke of 40 to 50 House seats. If the Republican gains were less spectacular, they might still signify a congressional mandate for censuring the president for his conduct. As it turned out, however, the Republicans actually lost seats in the House—though none in the Senate—which was widely interpreted as a notable Republican midterm defeat and an electoral signal to squelch the impeachment proceedings, especially against the background of consistent public opinion polls opposing impeachment and supporting Clinton's performance in office. Without exception, the European press (and many American papers) interpreted the Republican electoral defeat of November 1998 as a vindication of the president and death knell for the impeachment drive.

The well-financed Republicans were so confident of victory because they expected their anti-Clinton base of voters to turn out in large numbers while the Democratic base was reported to be demoralized by the scandals of the president and was expected to stay away from the polls in droves. However, with rare exceptions (at the last minute, the Republican advertisements still made impeachment a campaign theme), neither side seemed anxious to make Clinton's impeachment a prominent issue in the electoral contest. Nevertheless, there can be little doubt that substantial Republican gains in this election would have been touted as a GOP mandate to proceed with the impeachment. Instead, however, the elections turned into a Republican rout: with the help of organized labor and special appeals by Hillary Clinton to women voters, the Democrats won five seats in the House, though they failed to regain control of it. In the Senate, they managed to hold the line, and two prominent Clinton-haters, Senators Lauch Faircloth and Al D'Amato, lost their seats. Starr must have been very disappointed. The *Guardian* wrote, "The American electorate . . . delivered a blow to Republican hopes of impeaching President Clinton" (November 4, 1998). A day later, *Guardian* correspondent Jonathan Freedland spoke of "President Houdini and his death-defying escape from the threat of impeachment" and mentioned that "two of the president's most ardent pursuers [Senators] D'Amato and Faircloth . . . were toppled." He also reported that in exit polls, 60 percent of the voters wanted Congress to drop the matter without even starting the hearings announced for the following week. "They are sick of the intrusive poking around of Kenneth Starr" (November 5).

A *Guardian* editorial also called the "voters' message" a referendum on Clinton, confirming what the polls had been saying throughout this "tawdry Zippergate affair" and McCarthyite probe. The liberal German *Frankfurter Rundschau* commented with glee on the elections and the subsequent fall of Gingrich: "Newt Gingrich tripped himself up. Four years ago he waved the banner of morality and traditional American values on the barricades of the 'conservative revolution' . . . But a conservative revolution is problematic [here]. For one thing, and despite the historical legend, Americans are not very revolutionary" (quoted by *World Press Review*, January 1999). Gingrich's role in the impeachment drive in summer and fall, and even after the electoral defeat, may have been behind the scenes but was obviously crucial. As Petra Pinzler wrote in the German *Die Zeit* of the "failed revolution" of the Republicans, "Gingrich's conservative revolution stumbled for lack of pragmatism . . . the 1994 triumph of [his] 'angry white men' eventually petered out" (November 12, 1998). The weekly commented critically on Gingrich's resignation as Speaker and as a member of the House in response to this electoral rout. Many Americans agreed and this was reflected also in the positive approval ratings of the president's performance. The conservative *Frankfurter Allgemeine Zeitung* wrote of a vote of confidence in Clinton and the clear popular rejection of the impeachment plans (November 5, 1998).

Le Monde also expected "the elections to be inevitably interpreted as a sort of referendum on the future of the American chief executive" and, in case of a Republican victory, "a new élan to be imparted to the impeachment drive" (November 4, 1998). An editorial in *Le Figaro* said "the Republican *putsch* has misfired" after making this a referendum on impeachment. "The ideologues of the crazy right (*droite folle*) have been rejected." The paper spoke of a smiling Clinton who "has saved his presidency." *Le Figaro* now expected the impeachment effort to be dismantled even though the Republicans still commanded a narrow majority in the House and an ample one in the Senate (November 5, 1998). The Italian *La Repubblica*, finally, headlined "America absolves Clinton" (November 4, 1998) and "The vindication of Clinton" (November 4 and 5, 1998), and proclaimed that "the specter of Monica has vanished." Its Washington correspondent, Vittorio Zucconi, who had been very critical of Clinton, wrote "The good sense of the people, that instinctive moderation which in democracies restrains the intemperance of politicians and mass media seems to have won again" (November 4, 1998). Far from such instinctive moderation, however, the same Hyde who on October 4 had still declared "we can't vote for impeachment without the Democrats," proclaimed two days after the elections, "We must finish the impeachment [of the president]" (*Le Figaro*, November 5, 1998). He wanted to accelerate the process because he was very concerned about the changing numbers when new Congress members would be sworn in.

To the surprise of most foreign observers and many Americans as well, however, the Republican Clinton-haters in the House took up their impeachment proceedings again. Two weeks after the elections, they arranged for Starr to present his charges in a two-hour televised session, part of the 12-hour impeachment debates in the old House chamber where Judiciary chair Peter Rodino's Watergate hearings had taken place a quarter of a century earlier. Starr essentially repeated the substance of his Report, but he was also questioned by Abbe Lowell, the Democratic committee counsel, and others. Starr seemed rather defensive when denying—under oath—charges of grand jury leaks, of having kept his links to the Jones lawyers a secret, and of detaining Lewinsky on January 16, 1998. On conclusion, he received a standing ovation from Republican members of the Judiciary Committee. "The elections and Gingrich's resignation have changed everything," wrote a surprised Kornelius, "but how do you stop this parliamentary steamroller?" (*Sueddeutsche Zeitung,* November 20 and 21, 1998).

Hyde then sent the president a list of 81 questions relevant to the charges and demanded answers. By December 12, he and his followers had prepared four impeachment charges against President Clinton: (1) perjury before the Jones grand jury; (2) obstruction of justice; (3) perjury before the federal grand jury; and (4) abuse of power. The fourth charge referred mostly to the "unsatisfactory" presidential responses to the 81 questions. "For months now . . . the American political class has postponed all discussion of domestic decisions . . . and ignored pressing problems . . . It is beyond description what's going on inside the Washington Beltway these days," wrote the liberal German weekly *Die Zeit* (December 16, 1998).

The Judiciary Committee approved all four charges with about the same partisan majority of 20-21 Republican to 16-17 Democratic votes. After an extremely contentious partisan debate on December 19, 1998, the Republican lame-duck majority of the House finally passed two of the four charges: perjury before the federal grand jury (not, however, before the Jones grand jury) and obstruction of justice in the Jones civil suit (which by then was long settled and had been dismissed by Judge Wright). Hyde was impatient with calls for Republicans to heed the message of the elections and of the public opinion polls: "This may be naive and stupid . . . " he was quoted in the *New York Times*, "but I just think a thermometer is not a terribly useful thing on matters of conscience and matters of principle . . . Look, if Jesus Christ had taken a poll, he would never have preached the gospel." His remarks mirrored the Republican contempt for democratic elections.

European observers were unsparing in their comment: "Those who love America will wonder why the most powerful country in the history of the world at the peak of its power has descended into madness," wrote Gavin Eisler in the *Scotsman* of Edinburgh (end of December, quoted in *World Press Review,* February 1999). The Toronto *Globe and Mail* said, "Friends of the U.S. abroad can only be appalled and profoundly discouraged by the descent of the American political class into the sniggering, bitter, snooping, and contemptuous world that passes for democracy in Washington and New York today. So far . . . it is the American people who have kept their sense of humanity, of proportion, and of justice." *Le Figaro* wrote, "There is definitely something rotten in the kingdom of democracy." And the *Indian Express* of New Delhi suggested: "What is now unfolding in the Senate is not a battle between truth and lies but a vaudeville of vindictiveness . . . the high concept of impeachment has been reduced to the low politics of revenge" (*World Press Review,* March 1999). What a sorry model we had become to aspiring democracies around the world.

The first impeachment charge, alleging that the president had given "perjurious, false, and misleading testimony to a federal grand jury," passed the House with a vote of 228 to 206. It was a largely partisan vote: only five of the 228 Republicans voted no while five of the 206 Democrats voted yes. As Lars-Erik Nelson has pointed out, this alleged "perjury" was actually Clinton's refusal to plead guilty to the Starr formulation, including the *passages cochons,* of his relationship with Lewinsky (*New York Review of Books,* November 5, 1998). It is important to note that the House majority specifically rejected the charge that the president had perjured himself before the Jones's grand jury which, technically, he had indeed done. The second impeachment charge accused the president of obstruction of justice in the sexual harassment suit of Jones and passed by 221 to 212 votes. Twelve Republicans voted against it. Five Democrats voted yes; if they had voted no, the charge would not have passed. Clinton's supporters held that he had merely "lied about extramarital sex"—something any married man might do to protect his marriage and family—and did not violate his constitutional functions. Supporters of impeachment claimed that perjury and obstruction of justice were serious offenses, regardless of the motive, and violated the president's oath of office to enforce the laws.

This "steamroller" that could no longer be stopped (*Sueddeutsche Zeitung*), or "the infernal machine" or "doomsday machine" (*Le Figaro,* January 8, 1999), had reached critical speed, a quasi-automatic process aimed at impeachment, and gathering so much momentum that it seemed unstoppable. The passage of two of the impeachment articles completed the role of the House which now chose twelve managers under Hyde's leadership—all white males, Republican, and zealots on impeachment—to present the case for removal of the president before the Senate. *Le Figaro* (January 8, 1999) called Hyde the "chief accuser" and "the other adulterer spouse," and the manager team, "the 13 enraged men" (*hommes en colère*) or "Republican hardliners."

The actions of the House in this matter raised storms of protest in Congress and throughout the country. Polls ran 70 percent against impeachment. Among other mass actions, e-mail campaigns ("Move On") were organized to resist it and, after it had passed, over $10 million was collected in pledges of campaign money and grass-roots promises to help defeat the Republican impeachers for reelection in the year 2000. All along, the Republican base had been the main force pushing their representatives in the direction of impeaching the president. But now, in many areas, even Republicans protested their party's actions in Washington and some ostentatiously changed their voter registration to independent or Democratic. As *Die Zeit* commented on December 22, 1998, "this impeachment brings America into the deepest governmental crisis in 25 years [since President Nixon's resignation] . . . Washington's mood is feverish. Common sense accounts for little. Delusion reigns."

In his end-of-the-year essay in *Le Figaro*, Académie Française member Jean d'Ormesson called 1998 "the year of the sexual tragicomedy of the president of the United States." He commented that, in spite of American efforts to make it look like a legal matter, the emphasis on sexual details was "like in a hard Feydeau comedy" (a popular writer of sex farces) (December 31, 1998). Similar comparisons were evidently on the minds of many senators despite the enormous pressure for impeachment brought to bear upon them by Republican ultras, inside and outside the august chamber, and by Senate majority leader Trent Lott. A majority of senators, both Democrats and Republicans, were not eager to see their dignified proceedings in a once-in-a-century trial disrupted by the raucous and rancorous scenes that had characterized the House debate in mid-December.

THE SENATE WRAPS IT UP

If the Republican supporters of impeachment in the House and at the grass-roots felt a sense of despair at their chances for ultimate success in removing the president, they did not show it at the end of the year 1998. On the contrary, they came up with the novel doctrine that it was enough to impeach and not remove. Perhaps they were content to have vented their hateful anger, or were embarrassed to abuse the Constitution further by actually removing the president and causing permanent and obvious damage. Or, as proclaimed by another special prosecutor (Smaltz) after a jury threw out his case against Agriculture Secretary Mike Espy following a very brief deliberation: impeachment in itself will send a message. He never amplified what for, or what message. In the case of the president, some suggested quite contrary to the Constitution that his impeachment would serve as a kind of censure, but the censure option was rejected again and again by the Republican majorities in House and Senate. Only the Senate could remove an impeached president and, given the size of the Democratic minority in the Senate, 45 to 55 Republicans, an impeachment motion as partisan as it had been in the House was most unlikely to gather the required support of 67 senators, two-thirds of the chamber. From its very beginning, the effort of Hyde and his twelve managers to oust the president was destined to fail.

When the House reconvened on January 6, 1999, newly elected Representative Jay Insley, who had campaigned on this issue, moved to rescind the impeachment resolution of the House on the grounds that it had been passed by a lame-duck Congress. But the membership narrowly overruled him, again on a partisan vote, 221 to 197. If the Senate had wanted to terminate the impeachment motion (which under the Constitution it had to consider) it could have done so as soon as a floor motion to proceed had demonstrated that more than a third of senators were opposed to impeachment. "There is nothing that will kill this thing," said Tom Oliphant of the *Boston Globe* on the *NewsHour* with Jim Lehrer (January 29, 1999). But there was also an extraordinary amount of pressure on the Senate to proceed. A well-organized campaign, presumably of the Christian Coalition, against early plans to abort the impeachment inundated the Senate with hundreds of thousands of calls in the first weeks of January. House Republicans, furthermore, attempted to lobby their Senate colleagues intensely on, of all things, partisan interpretations of the Senate procedures governing impeachment, a subject of few precedents but great defensiveness among the senators. Despite all this pressure, the Senate leadership managed to come up with a unanimous, bipartisan agreement giving each side 24 hours to argue its case and reserving 16 hours for Senate discussion and a chance to request live witnesses. The insistence of the House managers on calling live witnesses, allegedly to confirm the facts of the case—including preferably all of Clinton's *petites amies,* as Bacharan called the Jane Does—proved the most contentious and most likely to lengthen the trial. The Senate parried the pressure of the House and settled on a compromise involving only videotapes of interrogations of Lewinsky, Jordan, and Sidney Blumenthal, a presidential adviser; it also refused to admit further materials not previously discussed in the House debates from the stash of the OIC and the House Republicans' secret collection. "Amid the Republican majority [of the Senate]," Mével wrote in *Le Figaro* on January 10, 1999, "many more would like to have Monica Lewinsky testify [live] in order to sully the image of Bill Clinton a bit, since they cannot remove him . . . but, in all formality, so as not to dirty their hands." Twenty-five Republican senators broke ranks to vote against live testimony. In restricting the additions of evidence, barring the media, and restraining the House managers from turning its proceedings into a circus, the bipartisan Senate majority acted as a court of law would act.

The European press picked up on several of the themes even though daily coverage abroad notably began to drop along with the temperature of the proceedings in Washington. The German weekly *Stern* (February 11, 1999), after calling the American impeachment proceedings "the most aberrant political farce of all times" and claiming it had "gone bankrupt," added: "But Clinton's pursuers don't give up—their last hope is Jane Doe no. 5, Joan Brodderick," who accused Clinton of a kind of date rape said to have occurred 21 years earlier. *Stern* explained that Starr earlier had the FBI investigate Brodderick but evidently found no usable ammunition: "She is entirely absent from his official Report which [otherwise] is simply replete with shameless, irrelevant detail"—but is mentioned in the "secret part of the Report" and part of the materials in the evidence room of the Capitol. The magazine also reported that the Murdoch-owned Fox television news program still reported her tale in early February 1999 after the White House lawyers had demolished the entire case presented by the House managers.

The German weekly then reported that, the previous December, the counsel of the Republican majority of the Judiciary Committee, David Schippers, had referred to "statements about further serious offenses [of Clinton] that cannot yet be published." The weekly commented that Schippers, too, had been "outed" for having had a mistress for 25 years, as well as a wife and ten children. It then quoted Tom DeLay's promise of "a quick two-thirds Senate majority if only the senators would spend a little time in the evidence room," and it mentioned DeLay's "outing" for perjury in a 1994 trial involving his former business partner. Finally, the anti-abortion stand of House manager Bob Barr was contrasted with his eager role in his second wife's abortion, as revealed by Larry Flynt of *Hustler* magazine. Needless to say, *Stern* believed that such monstrous hypocrisy reflected negatively on the Republican impeachment drive.

The European journalists were impressed by the high quality of the White House defense—compared to the weak and repetitive indictment presented by the House managers; they seemed particularly taken by Cheryl D. Mills, who alone represented both women and African Americans among the otherwise all-male and lily-white legal teams. "A lioness in the Senate arena," Stefan Simons of *Der Spiegel* called her, "who dismantled with rhetorical elegance the three-day constructions of 13 middle-aged Republican House Managers. [She] perhaps turned the atmospheric tide," after Charles Ruff had characterized the charges against the president as "trivial" and "constitutionally dubious" (January 25, 1999). In the French weekly, *L'Express,* P. Coste described the "anti-Clinton kamikazes" and their "image of obtuse intègristes." Their fury was "suicidal" considering the next elections, and they were "crazy to go on with this, to push it further." Coste noted Clinton's popular approval rate of 72 percent and stated that the Republican polls were "in free fall." He did not approve of "the hateful bias of the Starr Report" either (February 18-24, 1999).

The London *Times* published a cartoon of Clinton with "humble make-up" being applied to his face. It called Clinton's acquittal of all charges, without a censure vote, "the greatest triumph of his turbulent political career . . . after his affair with the besotted young White House trainee." It quoted several senators on the reasons for their votes for acquittal and added Hyde's resigned admission of defeat: "We hoped that the public would move from its total indifference to concern. That hope was unrequited." Somehow Hyde never noticed that the public was largely hostile to his efforts, not just indifferent. The *Times* added: "As an event it was rather like listening to the football results when you already know who has won . . . [or waiting to see] if the losing team will manage to put the ball in the back of the net at all . . . [Chief Justice] Rehnquist . . . declared Clinton United had won" (February 13, 1999). The paper also noted that the House managers refused to shake hands with the president's lawyers whereas the senators did, and even laughed and slapped their backs: "That was a horrid game and they couldn't wait for it to be over." And, finally, referring to the 1998 elections and the polls: "The American people have shown their contempt for the Republican effort to twist the Constitution for partisan political ends."

When the trial began, *Le Figaro* (January 8, 1999) also reported that the verdict was known in advance: "A curious trial." On the eve of acquittal (February 12, 1999), Mével wrote "Clinton's acquittal is not in doubt . . . the only suspense . . . is the extent of the defeat inflicted on his Republican enemies . . . they are facing rejection [by the public]." The Republicans, the French paper added, are torn between "the battalion of those elected with the 'conservative revolution' of 1994, from the South and West . . . [and] the others, at once more centrist and more classical [conservatives]." In the title of a report on Starr's last minute threat to indict Clinton on criminal charges while he was in office, *Le Figaro* referred to him as "an obstina[te] evil ghost" (February 13-14, 1999). The *Irish Times* commented that "Mr. Clinton's popularity in the country and the shaky nature of the perjury and obstruction of justice charges ensured that the Democrats mounted a strong opposition to . . . a 'Republican witch hunt'." The daily noted the end of bipartisanship except for five Democratic defections in the House vote, while in the Senate there were ten Republicans who defected on the charge of perjury and five on obstruction of justice. The paper quoted Bill Bennett, the self-appointed czar of American virtues: "The hard truth is that many Americans are not merely tolerating Mr. Clinton; they are embracing him" (February 12, 1999).

On the final day, just as the Senate proceedings of the day were to begin, a heckler shouted from the gallery: "God Almighty, take the vote and get it over with." And the Senate, which had taken only three weeks with the impeachment trial, voted 45 to 55 against the charge of perjury and 50 to 50 against that of obstruction of justice, thus narrowly denying the impeachers even the satisfaction of a majority. Removal would have taken a two-thirds vote, and so the president was acquitted of all charges by a wide margin. The motion of censure, sponsored among others by Democratic Senators Dianne Feinstein and Joseph Lieberman, had already been dropped earlier for lack of support and the threat of a filibuster by Senator Phil Gramm. The half-hearted coup attempt had failed.

NO TROOPS IN THE STREETS

As related earlier, Representative Bob Barr had already made a motion to impeach Clinton in late 1997, long before anyone in Washington had been aware of the Lewinsky affair. Faced in some American press editorials and newspaper readers' letters with the charge that the fall 1998 impeachment drive was an attempted coup d' état against the president, Barr reportedly said: "How can this be a coup? There are no troops in the streets, no tanks." This answer then made the rounds among the Republicans, was taken up by Representative Ed Bryant, and was repeated also in readers' letters in the newspapers. As a description of historic coups, however, it is inaccurate. It is true that wherever a coup or *golpe* is initiated by the military, for example, in Third World countries, the military *golpistas* will use the instruments most available to them. In some notable and major instances in developed industrial societies, however, like the right-wing takeovers in Germany, Italy, or France, there were neither troops nor tanks. It is worth looking at these examples not only to refute Barr and others, but to recall why European observers are quickly alarmed by extremist, right-wing stratagems in American politics. The takeovers of Mussolini, Hitler, and of the Vichy government of France typically began with at least some nonviolent steps that were perfectly legal and in partial accord with the constitutions of those nations.

Mussolini's Blackshirts, for example, chose the old Roman symbol of law and order, the rods and axe of the *lictores* (magistrates). Like the Nazis and other European fascists later, they claimed they had to "cleanse the country with [an iron] broom," a phrase that seems utterly ludicrous today though it was believed widely in their day. Then as today, extremists will accept such patent rationalizations. Il Duce's march on Rome in 1922 was hardly seen as the strong-arm threat to the government that it appeared to be later—there were "no troops in the streets"—but rather as a challenge to the police, the army, and the king to intervene against them with force. It was a calculated bluff relying on, among other things, the fear of the king that he might be replaced by the pro-fascist Duke of Aosta if he did not give in. The blackshirted, ragtag marchers had specific orders to run away if the police or soldiers began shooting at them.

The bluff made Mussolini, then leader of a miniscule party, prime minister of Italy to head a government coalition of liberals and conservatives. And then began the step-by-step takeover with legally (and violently) manipulated elections (under the *Legge Acerbo*), the murder of Giacomo Matteotti, and, in 1926, the consolidation of dictatorial powers in the hands of Il Duce. Sympathetic judges, police prefects, and other administrative officialdom, plus the support of the Vatican and many priests, played a major role in squashing the opposition with a modicum of legality. The lapse of France upon defeat by Germany in 1940, from the liberal regime of the Popular Front into the collaborationist right-wing dictatorship of Vichy France, was also nonviolent: it was through laws, ordinances, judicial actions, and police conduct that Vichy officials oppressed its citizenry, especially French Jews and the Resistance, not with tanks and troops.

When their Munich beer-hall *putsch* was suppressed violently in 1923, the early Nazis learned that they could not simply succeed by a show of violence or coercion. So, when Hitler was released from jail in 1925, he resolved to try it via the electoral and political route, amassing a huge ideologically committed movement that won elections. By 1932, with the impact of the Great Depression and mass unemployment, he had gathered 37 percent of the seats in the Reichstag and was considered eligible to form a government. With the collusion of a half-dozen conspirators of the highest rank, including President Paul von Hindenburg and former chancellor Franz von Papen, Hitler became German chancellor *without* violence or coercion. Thus the actual Nazi takeover also began not with troops—the army insisted on being neutral—but with the legal appointment on January 30, 1933, of Hitler as chancellor of a cabinet that had a large conservative (German National People's Party or DNVP) majority.

The new government even boasted a majority in parliament for the first time since 1930, and there was at first no violence. Even the paramilitary storm troopers generally paraded around with torches like the Ku Klux Klan (in uniforms but without robes and hoods). But sympathetic judges and police authorities had long actively proceeded against defenders of the Weimar Republic in local governments, in the bureaucracy, and in politics, wherever they could in the name of "law and order." For years the Weimar Republic had been under this right-wing siege, and the victims of this prerevolutionary stage ranged from the moderate left to conservatives who had refused to knuckle under to the

Nazis before Hitler actually came to power. One of the most effective steps leading to the takeover by Nazis and conservatives was the nonviolent 1932 ouster of the republican state government of Prussia by Chancellor Franz von Papen and the lifting of the ban on storm-trooper activities throughout this large state. This nonviolent coup against Prussia at first appeared to be legal until a challenge before the highest court finally, long after the Nazis had come to power, ruled it unconstitutional; the Nazis promptly overrode the decision.

Even after Hitler's appointment, the Nazi coup proceeded slowly and gradually by at least semilegal steps for half a year until the Hitler regime had consolidated its grip on power: on February 22, 1933, some 40,000 storm troopers were legally deputized as auxiliary police, presumably to stop street violence. This was the prelude to political arrests and the first concentration camps (Oranienburg, Dachau) for political opponents. Then came the spectacular *Reichstag* fire—evidently not set by the Nazis, as first reported, but by the mentally unstable anarchist Martinus van der Lubbe—which provided a welcome pretext for suppressing the German communist party and unleashing violent terror upon all opponents in the elections of March 5, 1933. Still, no tanks or troops. In mid-March, the would-be dictator had his minions take over all local and state governments nonviolently (if under threats), on the theory that their respective electoral bases of authority had to be "adjusted" to the majority won by the "national revolution" of Nazis and conservatives in the preceding Reichstag elections. On March 21, 1933, special tribunals were established and a law passed to arrest political opponents. Two days later the Reichstag passed the infamous Enabling Act that suspended the bill of rights in the constitution and conferred dictatorial powers upon Hitler.

All these measures proceeded more or less legally, and in avoidance of violations of law and order, without troops in the streets though increasingly in the presence of storm troopers.

Three steps of more doubtful legality completed Hitler's dictatorial control: the smashing of the trade unions (May 2, 1933), a law purging the entire civil service of "unreliable" elements (June 30), and the suppression of all political parties other than the Nazi party and its affiliated organizations (July 14), all still without troops in the streets. Nazi policies toward the Jews also mostly followed, at first, a five-year path of increasing discrimination and segregation by legislation and executive orders rather than by outright violence until the state-arranged pogrom of the Night of Broken Glass (*Kristallnacht*) in November 1938. The Nuremberg Laws resembled the legal base of southern segregation and South African apartheid. Between skillful nationalistic propaganda, manipulated public opinion, and discreet threats of violence, the bulk of the German public simply failed to react to the reality of the 1933 takeover—especially since the media were effectively brought under Nazi control in 1933—until it was too late.

Naturally, memories of these right-wing coups without troops in their own respective histories haunted Europeans when they observed ultrarightists in American politics belying their high expectations of American democracy. "After this affair," editorialized the conservative, anti-Clinton *Frankfurter Allgemeine Zeitung* (September 11, 1998), "America no longer appears as the perfect state of law in which even the president is not above the law." Europeans became alarmed when seeing the blatant disregard of the Republican leadership for the electoral defeat in the congressional elections of November 1998, and the contempt for the public opinion polls that left no doubt of the American public's overwhelming disapproval of the impeachment drive. They were not impressed by the transparent Republican rationalizations of their conduct; for example, that Abraham Lincoln would not have freed the slaves had he followed (nonexistent) opinion polls, a bromide repeated by Starr. "Are Americans really likely to fall for such silly talk?" was the refrain among many of my European friends.

A SCANDAL MADE BY THE LAW?

Europeans were particularly alarmed by the roles of judges and prosecutors in the American scandal, as we have seen. There is a strong negative stereotype of the prosecutor in most European countries, an image of a Torquemada, a Grand Inquisitor, or of a totalitarian (fascist or communist) bloodhound looking for political prey. Europeans are also suspicious of the American system of judicial supremacy in which, unlike most Western democracies, the courts have the last word over legislative and executive decisions. They are skeptical of an imperial judiciary that willfully violates the separation of powers and tells other branches how they should carry on their business. And they are no more enamored of judges with seemingly political motivation—in Roman law systems the roles of judges and prosecutors tend to be much closer than in American law.

The presentation of the Starr Report, wrote Alain-Gérard Slama in an editorial in the conservative *Le Figaro* (September 14, 1998), "is an extreme manifestation of . . . a revolution of the judges," and he expressed the fear that some day it might come to a France that has not forgotten the hanging judges of the Vichy era. Currently there is a major judiciary reform in the offing in France, a reorganization aimed at making judges more independent. But not everyone looks with equanimity toward greater judicial independence which, in some cases, might entail abuses *à l'américain*. Slama was also highly skeptical of the Starr approach to crime. In French law (and the law of all modern nations), first a crime is committed and then the guilty person is found and prosecuted. Starr, however, "first seized upon a 'guilty' person, Clinton, then tried to find a crime to pin on his mark, and finally set out to make him lie under oath in a situation in which most people lie. In French opinion, it was a travesty of justice: the role of justice is to look into a crime or misdeed, not to provoke one." Starr's kind of justice follows that of the Queen of Hearts in *Alice in Wonderland;* to quote William

Raspberry: "Sentence first—verdict afterwards . . . They 'know' Clinton to be so unworthy of the office to which he has been twice elected that any legal pretext for removing him serves the cause of righteousness" (*Santa Barbara News-Press,* December 4, 1998).

Germans and Italians share this sentiment about the proper roles of judges and prosecutors in law enforcement. They remember all too well their judges of the fascist era, like the screaming chief justice Roland Freisler of the Nazis' People's Court, who sentenced the anti-Hitler plotters of July 1944 to the gallows after stripping them of any shred of humanity and dignity in court. Europeans do not share the American idealization of the crime-fighting, corruption-busting district attorney, who cleans up vice and dirty politics and, in the end, is elected governor or president. Even the *Toronto Globe and Mail* icily commented on Clinton's impeachment by the House: "There are two things wrong with the impeachment . . . : its provenance and its relevance. It is rooted in a cynical, partisan legal trap and it concerns a purely private matter rather than a matter of state . . . Clinton is guilty of minor crimes and misadventures [rather than 'high crimes and misdemeanors']" (quoted by *World Press Review,* February 1999).

For an essentially political campaign against the president, there was indeed a surfeit of judicial involvement with overwhelming partisan bias at nearly every turn: the firing of Special Prosecutor Fiske and Starr's appointment in 1994 by a panel of three senior federal judges headed by the very partisan and controversial Sentelle, who was himself selected by the Republican Chief Justice Rehnquist; the denial of the president's immunity from a civil lawsuit while in office, first by a federal appeals court in 1996 and, a year and a half later, by a unanimous Supreme Court; the appointment of grand juries for the Jones case and for the prosecution of the president; the authorization of Starr's "legal discovery" fishing expedition on behalf of Jones to interrogate Lewinsky and other Jane Does, as well as the president himself, under oath. At every turn, the federal judges were standing behind the scandalous abuses of Kenneth Starr. Finally, there were the court decisions denying the claims of executive privilege for the president's closest advisers and even his secret service bodyguards against testifying, thus forcing them to incur extraordinary legal expenses. Future presidents may have to serve in a glass house and under the heel of the imperious judiciary.

Added to the $100 million expense of the OIC were the millions of dollars of private legal expenses imposed by this process upon the Clintons and dozens of witnesses. There was also the post-impeachment decision by Judge Wright to permit the right-wing lawyers of the already dismissed and settled Jones civil suit to collect additional funds from Clinton. Europeans, used to inexpensive legal services and fee schedules for lawyers, thought the imposition of astronomical legal expenses on witnesses was a barefaced attempt to intimidate and push those people out of public service and to punish them for having worked with the Clintons. Is this what you call the rule of law?, I was asked repeatedly. Should it surprise us that European legal eagles saw in this the last straw of judicial supremacy? American judges, unlike the judiciary elsewhere—even in Britain the judges are subordinate to Parliament's decisions—can overrule Congress, state legislatures, and even the people voting on initiatives and referenda. Some Europeans knowledgeable about comparative law and constitutions call the role of the American judiciary in the impeachment affair a kind of judicial dictatorship; none would call it the rule of law, but, more likely, the rule of lawyers, in this case of right-wing lawyers with no respect for democracy and the Constitution.

Germans and East Europeans also remember all too well their experiences with communist show trials, prosecutors, and political justice under communist party dictatorships throughout Eastern Europe. Again, these were travesties of justice, political repression made particularly vile because the communists (like some Republican prosecutors and the House managers of the impeachment trial) claimed justice, morality, and sometimes also their equivalent of the rule of law, "socialist legality," as rationale for their decisions. The high-handed conduct of the OIC in the detention of Lewinsky, to European minds, invited comparison with the Soviet KGB, or East German *Stasi,* both of which also liked to have suspects "brought in" (*zugefuehrt*) by a "friend" and to threaten them with the possible prosecution of their mothers. Starr's ultimate explanation, that his prosecutorial methods were no different from what American prosecutors commonly do, of course, gave a black eye to the entire profession. Many prosecutors, in fact, emphatically denied it was true.

Isikoff and Toobin in their books have chronicled the involvement of a cabal of ultraright lawyers and prosecutors from the beginnings of the Jones civil lawsuit in 1994 when Starr—not yet appointed the special prosecutor on Whitewater—drafted his friend of the court brief for the first set of Jones's lawyers. The brief sought to persuade the federal judiciary to penetrate presidential immunity from such civil suits while in office in a transparent ploy to destroy the presidency; presidents are immune from criminal suits. As Whitewater prosecutor, Starr won convictions against some Clinton associates, but not against the Clintons themselves. He became so discouraged that, early in 1997, he was ready to quit and retire to a Scaife Foundation-supported law school deanship at Pepperdine University, a conservative private college in Malibu, California. Irate Clinton-haters on his staff and among his ultraright attorney friends, and anti-Clinton editorial writers persuaded him to reverse this decision.

At this point, however, the Supreme Court's unanimous decision (May 27, 1997) allowed Jones's civil suit to proceed. Her lawyers could start deposing witnesses under oath and go to court within a year. Clinton's attorneys, consequently, offered to settle with Jones, but she and her husband refused, influenced by Susan Carpenter-Macmillan to hold out for a much larger sum, and a personal apology or perhaps a book contract. Jones's first set of right-wing attorneys at that point quit in exasperation, whereupon the religious right's Rutherford Institute engaged a team of Dallas right-wing lawyers to represent her. The ultraright cabal of attorneys from New York, Philadelphia, and Chicago, including those from Starr's Chicago law firm of Kirkland and Ellis and from the ultraright Federalist Society, helped to write briefs for them. They had been "waiting to do so for three years," according to Isikoff, and henceforth, continually plotted strategy to turn the Jones lawsuit into a vehicle to bring down the president. Setting aside the media and the politicians, Isikoff concludes that in the end, "the conspiracy, thoroughly right-wing, may not have been vast but it had done the job."[18]

The new team of Jones' lawyers also changed her complaint against Clinton from sexual harassment and millions of dollars worth of "emotional distress" to one of "violating her human rights" by sexual discrimination, the basis for further undercover "legal discovery" investigations, even of Clinton's consensual partners, past and present. A cooperative Judge Wright approved a monstrous demand of Jones's attorneys that the president identify all women, other than his wife, with whom he had proposed to, or did, have sex in a period of five years before and five years after the alleged incident involving Jones (1991), provided they were federal or state employees or had been "procured" by state troopers. This was another example of the criminalization of private conduct and of the attempt to plant the sleaziest suppositions—without a shred of evidence—into the minds of the public and the law. Such evidence of hand-in-glove cooperation between ultraright lawyers with their outrageous schemes and the judiciary scandalized European legal observers, who are not accustomed to the criminalization of private conduct for political reasons. When historians look back upon the judicial decisions of this period, they may come to share the European shocked reaction. The postponement or abandonment of official investigations and prosecutions of alleged felonies, like the secret taping of Lewinsky by Tripp—who wasn't even indicted for violating Maryland state law until mid-1999, much less convicted—or the high-handed actions and instances of apparent perjury by Starr and his OIC associates, could hardly persuade Europeans otherwise.

Journalists knowledgeable about the rules of evidence in American criminal law also were stunned to see that the Office of Independent Counsel plotted an FBI sting, wiring Tripp to tape Lewinsky on January 13, 1998, on the basis of Tripp's earlier and illegally obtained tapes and hearsay, and evidently without prior authority from the Justice Department and the Sentelle panel of federal judges. In a switch that deserves to be an exhibit in Constitutional Law 101, this new tape of a frantic and confused Lewinsky talking excited gibberish to her friend at lunch was then used to get belated authority for the sting *after it occurred,* and to seize and threaten Lewinsky on January 16 for her alleged criminal acts as revealed by the illegal sting.

Europeans still ask, why are Starr and his deputies Jackie Bennett and Hickman Ewing not under investigation and subject to disciplinary procedures, such as disbarment, for such thoroughly unprofessional conduct? The OIC's only excuse, if hardly valid legally, was revenge for Watergate and their crusade to obtain Watergate-like tapes and an insider's testimony on the president. Isikoff also relates the hilarious chase for possession of Tripp's Lewinsky tapes among the Jones lawyers, (who wanted to spring the tapes on Monica or Bill during their respective grand jury depositions), Tripp's old and new attorneys, Starr, and Isikoff himself (who was perceived as a time bomb by all the conspirators because he knew and was likely to publish the whole story in *Newsweek).* "Like the Maltese Falcon in the . . . Bogart movie," writes Isikoff, "the tapes had assumed mystical status: whoever acquired them, it was imagined, would acquire strange powers over the Clinton presidency."[19] But this was not Watergate, only a tawdry sex scandal, and Tripp's tapes were illegally obtained, vapid, and mostly worthless as evidence in court.

Isikoff's role in all this was ambiguous, having been privy to the evolution of the Jones case and its intended exploitation by Clinton-haters from the very beginning in 1994. "It wasn't my job to help Starr to sting the president," he said to himself in alarm in early January 1998, after having fully briefed the OIC team. But his own deadline for publishing what he knew in *Newsweek*—the story was killed at the last minute by his editors—actually pushed the OIC into misguided action on January 13, 16, and 17 for fear that his account would ruin their surprise and reveal the duplicity and dubious authority for their course of action.

Finally, Isikoff recoiled from the avalanche of consequences triggered by OIC in which he wanted no part: "[Maybe] Starr . . . [didn't] have more serious evidence of felonies by Clinton and [Vernon] Jordan [such as telling Monica to lie and promising her a job if she did] . . . In that case, the independent counsel's office had just committed a monumental blunder that would discredit Clinton's enemies once and for all."[20] Regardless of Isikoff's musings, however, the hectic year of 1998, the Lewinsky affair, and the anti-Clinton impeachment campaign were perched atop a slippery slope.

We would be remiss if we did not also acknowledge the horror of many knowledgeable European observers regarding certain barbaric recesses of American law reminiscent of Charles Dickens's *Bleak House*—where the malevolent likes of the ultraright lawyers live like poisonous spiders at their webs, ready to grasp and devour their unwary marks with the lowest legal tricks, which surpass at least a European continental lawyer's sense of what should be fair and right. Short of comparisons with Mafia tricks, people who grew up on Roman law simply could not understand how American law permitted the transmogrification of Jones's original complaint and civil suit against Clinton—a simple matter of criminal law on the continent—into a *mafioso* extortion. It was this that allowed Starr to compel the president, through the monstrous method of legal discovery, to disclose under oath decades of his sex life, and in the process sullied his public persona to the ultimate extent possible. As the *Sueddeutsche Zeitung* (January 24, 1998) of Munich editorialized in the midst of the American media frenzy over the Lewinsky affair: "That the escalation is now beyond all bounds has little to do with the original accusation [of Jones, or the Lewinsky disclosures] and a lot to do with the American legal system. What our local legal standards would have made no more than a political embarrassment, now hangs by the coils of conflict-aggravating procedural rules: Doing the Jones case as a civil suit with 'depositions' and interrogations under oath is . . . a dangerous radical privatization of public criminal law relations. It is dangerous because it can be abused for dishonest purposes, such as the 'legal discovery' of 'patterns of sexual behavior' . . . fishing expeditions beyond all boundaries of shame, comparable indeed to the witch hunts of old."

The unidentified writer of the editorial was obviously a surefooted legal expert on both Roman and common law. "As with the old witch hunts, you entrap the accused into 'perjury' by threat of an 'obscene vivisection' [the legal discovery of alleged patterns of witchcraft sexual behavior] . . . the perjury becomes a secondary [but crucial] offense, and the prosecutors can forget the primary offense [Jones's allegations or witchcraft]. The law thus has created the violation it is supposed to avoid." With this perception of the vagaries of American law, it is small wonder that European observers reacted with such intense dislike of Starr and his legal prosecution of what they saw in terms of the primary offense, namely, a very weak case of sexual harassment dressed up as a violation of Jones's civil rights. Under Roman law, such legal trickery could not proceed and would probably have triggered disciplinary proceedings or worse against the overzealous prosecutor.

WAS IT A COUP ATTEMPT?

"Impeachment is America's lawful coup, the democratic substitute for beheading the king," crowed *U.S. News and World Report* on December 21, 1998, a day after impeachment passed the House. The news magazine evidently was so carried away by the stormy debates that it forgot that "the democratic substitute" for beheading kings is supposed to be, first and foremost, elections to the chief executive office. The most recent congressional elections (and the public opinion polls) in the view of many observers, American and foreign, had spoken out forcefully against this beheading of the president. But then, some American media voices such as Elsa C. Arnett, in a Knight-Ridder News Service article about the eager public audiences at the House managers' presentation before the Senate, spoke of the "beauty of democracy" in the title of her piece, quoting one visitor. She might have said the same about crowds gathering for a lynching. Back in the Jim Crow era, media voices often called lynchings an expression of democracy in action. Another visitor, at least, was quoted as saying, "I think this is a witch hunt" (*Santa Barbara News Press,* January 15, 1999).

Did European and Commonwealth journalists believe they saw in the impeachment a coup attempt against the president of the United States or the march of democracy against tyranny, possibly in defense of the rule of law? Some European newspapers and other media—especially those owned by Murdoch—wanted to see Clinton resign or removed from office (see chapter 4). The *Economist,* for example, after years of rather sympathetic coverage, reacted to the breaking of the Lewinsky scandal with a cover story, "If It's True, Go," and insisted that the president should resign if he "lied even just a little bit" about his relationship to Lewinsky (January 31, 1998). The weekly never explained its severe stance.

The liberal *Guardian* of London began in a strongly anti-Clinton vein—especially Martin Woollacott in the *Guardian Weekly* of August 30, 1998—quoting George Will on the president as "a man who represents the doctrine of permissible perjuries, innocuous lies, and oral sex in the workplace" (September 12, 1998). The paper hoped that "the people through Congress [would] not . . . permit Clinton to drag out this thing." But it balanced this call for ousting Clinton with a piece in the same issue by Polly Toynbee, who wrote, "The office of presidential investigator has as much proper place in the body politic as a lethal parasite," and described Starr as a tapeworm eating its way through "the entrails of this largely uncorrupted presidency." Toynbee found Clinton's conduct—the alleged perjury and obstruction of justice—"understandable in the face of gross invasion of his privacy." The *Guardian* subsequently became more critical of the course of the impeachment campaign as it unfolded, and as the Republicans ignored all legal and constitutional restraints, such as the definition of high crimes and misdemeanors. The conservative *Frankfurter Allgemeine Zeitung,* initially highly critical of Clinton, became alarmed by the turn toward impeachment: "What Congress is embarking on now resembles a constitutional walk on a tightrope" (September 17, 1998). By the time of the November elections, and even more after Clinton's acquittal, the paper breathed a sigh of relief. An editorial by Leo Wieland even opined rather optimistically: "The system has passed the test without any apparent damage to its institutions . . . Americans are not worried about their democracy and have no reason to be" (quoted by *World Press Review,* April 1999).

But the vast majority of foreign opinions, as we have seen, were alarmed by the extremist (by American constitutional and Western democratic standards) character of impeachment used as a weapon of partisan strife and personal hatred in this case. "Impeachment is the constitutional equivalent of an atom bomb," wrote *Le Figaro* (December 14, 1998) which had observed the revival of the impeachment drive after the November elections with consternation, because "the voters had practically pardoned Clinton for his escapades" (November 22, 1998). *Der Spiegel* also accused Starr of having "committed a coup d' état trying to annul a democratic election" (February 8, 1999). In the German weekly *Die Zeit,* Petra Pinzler characterized the impeachment vote in the House by reporting "America [was] in the deepest government crisis . . . the zealots don't care any more what the people think of [their actions] out in the country. With all their might, they are trying to push President Clinton out of office" (December 22, 1998).

In the London *Times,* (December 21, 1998), Anthony Howard pointed out that even Nixon never had to suffer "the congressional yoke" like Clinton, the first elected president ever to be impeached. Howard thought that, with his impeachment, the president was no longer in control of his situation: "Any pebble [but not Livingston's resignation] can from now on start an avalanche that could sweep Mr. Clinton out of the White House." The *Times* of that same date carried a brief survey of the reactions of the press around the world to the impeachment of Clinton, which bears out my assessment here. The London *Observer* also called the impeachment vote "an attempted coup d' état by the Republicans" (December 21, 1998). A "constitutional coup d' état," of course, is a coup against the Constitution, not one justified by it; it is a gross abuse or violation of the constitutional order, even if it involves no "troops in the streets."

Crucial to European reactions were also the undemocratic nature of impeachment and the disregard of the House Republicans for the electoral verdict of November, 1998. They saw the coup as aimed at the two bases of political authority in the United States, the Constitution and the sovereign people. And they deplored the partisan zealotry and vituperative language behind it. The attempt to get around Clinton's electoral mandate, European journalists noted, of course began with the elections of 1992 and 1996. It involved dubious investigations that had been going on for four years by the time the Lewinsky scandal was revealed and explicitly aimed at impeachment: the Foster suicide had been investigated at least six times, Whitewater even more often, and nothing had been pinned on the Clintons. The crude violations of legal principles along with ritual defenses of the rule of law did not escape the attention of European journalists, nor did the deliberate misinterpretation—despite the testimony of the constitutional experts—of the key phrase "high crimes and misdemeanors," which "in the eighteenth century . . . probably meant [only] offenses against the state," as the *Guardian* put it. But this definition did not suit the "right-wing bias of the [House] Judiciary Committee" (September 10, 1998).

Finally, the public persona and conduct of Starr, and what the British journalist Andrew Sullivan called an "army of finger-wagging moralizers, epitomized by . . . Starr and energized by Christian conservatives" in the *Guardian* and the *New York Times*, drew skeptical reactions from European journalists (*Guardian*, November 4, 1998). Europeans were no strangers to sex scandals of public figures (see chapter 3), hypocritical moralizers, and attempts at political exploitation of such scandals in their own countries. When Clinton won reelection in 1996, the visceral hatred against him and his preemption of Republican issues—such as welfare reform, crime and deficit cutting, issues for which Republicans somehow claimed proprietary rights—rose to a fever pitch. As Mike McCurry, his press spokesperson, had said earlier, once Clinton appropriated all the main centrist, Republican-style policies, the Republicans could win only by trying to "totally destroy him as a human being . . . to turn him into a liar . . . a cheat . . . a philanderer."[21] The intensity of the anti-Clinton hatred, of course, provided the fuel for the relentless drive for his impeachment via a sex scandal transmogrified into the perjury trap.

But there were two alternative solutions to the Republican dilemma, other than the unconstitutional recourse to impeachment. One was the possibility of a censure resolution that could have expressed all the sincere (and insincere) moral disgust with the president's sexual conduct. The disgust was not all hypocrisy, especially not among Democrats such as Senators Dianne Feinstein and Joseph Lieberman, and such a resolution would have put Clinton's critics on record for morality rather than for trying an end run around electoral mandates and the Constitution. Congressional censure of a president was neither unconstitutional nor unprecedented, but it would not involve any punishment other than shaming Clinton, according to the constitutional prohibition of bills of attainder and the protection against deprivation of life, liberty, or property without due process of law. The Republican House majority effectively squelched the censure option, giving various dubious reasons, erroneously claiming that it was unconstitutional or unprecedented. There were many precedents: for example, Andrew Johnson's impeachment was preceded by a lopsided vote expressing the disapproval of the House. It was obviously not enough for the partisan hatreds of 1998, though European journalists were often appalled at the, in their opinion, overwrought and punitive language of draft censure resolutions.

But the real reason for the House Republicans' rejection of censure was surely the desire to offer no alternative to impeachment, even if that would have captured substantial bipartisan support. In the Senate, the same thinking seems to have prevailed although it was most unlikely that the impeachment charges would get the required two-thirds majority. Censure of the president would have required only a majority and, considering the lingering doubts about the constitutionality of impeachment, would have avoided the question of the dubious level of the charges and the excessive partisanship behind such an extreme action. In many ways, it seemed a politically viable alternative to the two-thirds requirement. This would certainly not have been true of the idea of a finding of fact resolution by which some Clinton-hating senators wanted to pass the same charges as in the articles of impeachment. Fortunately, the Senate had the good sense to reject such an obviously unconstitutional subterfuge.

The other alternative to impeachment was much more attractive and may well have been the original goal of Starr, Hyde, Barr, DeLay, and the rest. When Starr sprang his perjury trap on January 17, 1998, and the deputies in his office began to feed bits of salacious information to the ever-hungry media, touching off and further supplying a feeding frenzy and media circus, he probably expected a resounding chorus among the media and the public for Clinton's resignation. There was, indeed, such a chorus, but Bill Clinton, following the advice of Dick Morris, decided to go on the counter-attack, including his finger-wagging television address, declaring that he had "no sexual relationship with that woman, Miss Lewinsky." Many prominent American pundits who had immediately stated that, within days or weeks, the president would have to relinquish office, were proven wrong. The American public, while dismayed at his private indiscretions, soon rose to defend his public performance—his performance rating rose from under 60 percent to nearly 70 percent—against what it surely perceived as a partisan-inspired attack on its electoral mandates of 1996 and1998.

To his credit, Clinton did not resign then, nor with the presentation and distribution of the Starr Report, nor after the House actually impeached him, to the great chagrin of his enemies and detractors. His repeated response was that he had been elected by the American people to do a job for them and he was going to stick with this job until the last day of his term. There was more than a hint of contempt in his refusal to permit the scandal to keep him from "the problems, challenges, and opportunities of America," from giving yet another rousing State of the Union speech, or from troubleshooting visits to Northern Ireland and the Middle East (see also *La Repubblica/Oggi,* January 14, 1999). Had he relented or caved in, the great conspiracy would have realized its goal and removed him without having to defend its weak legal arguments and low tricks, and without having to persuade House and Senate Democrats. Voluntary resignation would also have resolved the clumsiness of the procedures of an impeachment case and the lack of cooperation on the part of the American public and the congressional Democrats.

At various stages of the final drive, the vast conspiracy mobilized large numbers of pundits, newspaper editors and publishers, and Republican politicians (also a rare Democrat or two) to demand that Clinton resign. European papers took note of the more than a hundred American newspapers that insisted the president resign, among them the *Philadelphia Inquirer, Detroit Free Press, Des Moines Register, Denver Post,* and *Orlando Sentinel*

(*Guardian*, September 14, 1998). Often, as with the *Atlanta Constitution*, it was the publisher's will overriding the editors that put the resigning option on page one or in an editorial. At times even majorities of the public shared this opinion. On the eve of the impeachment vote, there was briefly a majority (58 percent) suggesting that he resign if he was impeached. It did not last beyond the actual vote to impeach him, which the public had strongly opposed (London *Times*, December 21, 1998).

PARTING SHOTS

The first reactions of European journalists to the more dramatic moments of the American crisis were rarely recorded in their newspapers: at the climactic House debates before Christmas 1998, one could hear foreign correspondents of various countries mutter their respective versions of "My god, they are foaming at the mouth," in describing the Republican ultras in the House. But their own habits and their editors' blue pencils would never have permitted such language in newsprint. Their earlier admiration for Gingrich and readiness to expect that his revolutionaries would assert themselves in 1994-1996 over a seemingly lame-duck executive—in the manner of a parliamentary regime—may also have moderated their reactions to this emotional climax. Regarding the self-controlled appearance of a statesmanlike Senate, however, they were not deceived about the presence of similar ultras among the Republican senators, in particular such figures as had been swept by the Republican landslide from provincial obscurity into offices of leadership. Foreign Relations Committee chair Jesse Helms, the improbable heir of many distinguished Republican foreign policy statesmen of the past, was impossible to overlook. Another example was Senate Judiciary Committee chair Orrin Hatch, whose contribution to constitutional stewardship since his ascent to power consisted mostly in blocking hearings on the president's judicial nominations, especially when the nominees were minorities or women. This is a novel interpretation of the constitutional proviso that federal judges are to be nominated and appointed by the president "with the advice and consent of the Senate." And then there is Majority Leader Trent Lott, of the Council of Conservative Citizens background, who owed his ascent to Robert Dole's 1996 candidacy for the presidency. Lott was largely unknown outside the Senate before that time.

When Clinton, after months of Saddam Hussein's defiance of the UN arms inspection team, launched bombing raids on Iraqi positions on the eve of the House impeachment debate, Lott was the only prominent Republican to protest this military enforcement action. He ignored the traditional rule that partisanship stops at the water's edge or when American soldiers are in harm's way. The Washington punditry, of course, crowed that this was a "wag-the-dog" operation—even though they had known about it for months—that is, merely a diversion from the imminent impeachment debate in the House. In the fall of 1999, Helms and Lott refused Democratic requests for hearings and debate on the Nuclear Test Ban Treaty for a whole year, a treaty that embodied the hopes of half the world for a nuclear-free future. In the fall of 1999, the two staged what anti-Clinton columnist and political scientist Ross K. Baker, among others, dubbed "impeachment drama, Act Three" (*Los Angeles Times,* October 15, 1999). In spite of the president's pleas (even in writing) for postponing the decision, they brought about an immediate Senate vote on the treaty, knowing that, with its current flaws, it would fail to garner the required two-thirds vote. The transparent intention was to humiliate the president before our allies, Britain, France, and Germany, whose leaders had pleaded in the *New York Times* for an endorsement by the Senate. Helms wanted this senatorial vote sent to the president "with his regards to Monica," according to media reports. Lott had rejected a compromise proposed by senior Senators John Warner (Republican) and Pat Moynihan (Democrat), with Clinton's agreement, to send the draft treaty back to committee for further study until after the general elections of 2000. Lott also ignored written pledges by Clinton and the Democratic Senate minority leader Tom Daschle to withdraw and not to reintroduce the treaty until after the elections. Finally Lott and Helms tried, unsuccessfully, to extract a pledge from Clinton that he would never call for ratification of it during the coming electoral campaign.

"There was throughout the current test-ban debate the stench of old scores being settled," wrote Baker. After the Senate impeachment trial, ". . . many Republican Senators decided to lie in wait and ambush him on a vote . . . of great personal importance to him and . . . his often-expressed goal to leave behind a legacy of accomplishment." As of this writing, the coup plotters are still at it and may continue to be so for at least the rest of the Clinton administration, and possibly beyond. The defeat of the draft treaty on a partisan vote of 51 to 48— three Republicans voted for it along with 45 Democrats—of course also demolished the image of American leadership in the world on this and other important foreign policy matters.

CHAPTER THREE

Europeans on Sex, Lies, and Audiotapes

> ... the president suffered a terrible moral lapse, a marital infidelity; not a breach of the public trust, not a crime against society... It is a sex scandal. H. L. Mencken said at one time, when you hear somebody say, "this [case] is not about money, it's about money." And when you hear somebody say, this is not about sex, it's about sex.
> —Senator Dale Bumpers before the United States Senate (January 21, 1999)

> The leaders of the political and journalistic establishment [in Washington] never had much use for the Clintons and this hostility contributed to the atmosphere that overtook the city almost overnight—that of a decorous lynching party.
> —Jeffrey Toobin, *A Vast Conspiracy*

While the American media were evidently most reluctant to tell us how European observers regarded the legal and constitutional aspects of our 1998 crisis, they did occasionally give us a hint about European impressions of the real, or imagined, American

Puritanism behind the impeachment drive. This is a subject worth a closer look: Are European attitudes on political sex scandals, or on sex in general, really all that different from those of the majority of Americans?

"You know what this whole business reminds me of," said one of my European friends in August 1998. (He had become familiar with everyday American life while attending an American high school under an American Friends Service exchange program.) "When I was at the . . . high school in Georgia, some of the boys just for fun used to pick on fellow classmates at the local swimming hole. They pulled down their swimming trunks to embarrass them. They called it 'pantsing' and, I think, Judge Starr just pantsed your president with his Starr Report and DNA test." When I protested that such relentless exposure and the threat of impeachment went far beyond any teenage boys' pranks, he shrugged: "Maybe Starr doesn't know the difference. Neither Clinton nor Starr have acted like mature, responsible adults."

His sentiments echoed European press reactions to seemingly incomprehensible actions and counteractions. As the Italian daily *LaRepubblica/Oggi* put it with an almost audible sigh: "The agonizing pantomime is now moving toward the final act [impeachment]." Citing the cigar and other props of the pantomime, the paper continued: ". . . a case of sex, of arrogance, of stupidity, and of false testimony has embarrassed and humiliated America now for eleven months." The daily noted that Gingrich, a major mover behind the scenes, fell after the Republican party was disgraced in the November elections. He had still arranged for $10 million in anti-Clinton ads at the last minute. "Clinton for his part showed himself to be petulant, legalistic, and so contemptuous [of the impeachment circus] that he would not concede to the Judiciary Committee even the smallest admission of his guilt . . . His lawyers admit that he has done what he has done but they say that this does not meet the [Constitutional] standards for impeachment" (*La Repubblica/Oggi*, December 9, 1998).

In the meantime, other European newspapers, much like the American public, left no doubt that they thought little of the legal case for charges of perjury and obstruction of justice, such as had been kited upon the sex scandal. As the *Guardian* put it apropos of the videotape of presidential testimony before the grand jury, "the Republicans may have blundered badly . . . What we watched [on television] was not sex, lies, morals, or the good of the nation. It's politics, stupid," all partisanship between Clinton and Gingrich (quoted in *World Press Review,* November 1998). Columnist Lexington wrote in January 1998, in a somewhat more nuanced fashion—in the same issue that bore the title "If It is True, Go": "The [American] provincials have told the Washington insiders, 'it's a man's world, and men don't always make faithful husbands.' So drop your moralizing talk, and yet popular majorities believe that Clinton is guilty as charged" (*Economist,* January 31, 1998). Even the *New York Times,* in a lucid moment, carried a piece by Frank Rich saying: "[We are] the unwashed masses, too stupid or amoral or selfishly prosperous to get on with the program of the Washington Establishment" (November 7-8, 1998).

If the European press had any doubt that it was indeed a sex scandal, Christopher Cannon, one of the House managers, soon dispelled it in connection with his insistence that Lewinsky and others be questioned live before the Senate and national television. As *Le Figaro* correspondent Jean-Jacques Mével wrote, "the accusers of Bill Clinton of course pretend that interrogating his silent mistress before the Senate is a principle of justice rendered well . . . After all, 'Monica Lewinsky is at the heart of this affair,' as Cannon . . . said so eloquently: 'Without her, it will be hard to see the point of it'" (January 8, 1999). Christoph Bertram, an editor and well-known foreign policy commentator of the liberal weekly *Die Zeit* of Hamburg, was no less skeptical of such legal charges as lying and suborning of perjury "because of a little amorous entanglement in the White House," and asked instead, "Can snooping into the most intimate sphere of the first man of the state in order to topple him really be allowed?" (January 29, 1999). We shall come back to the important line that Europeans (and most Americans) insist on drawing between public and private conduct of their leaders. Bertram also expressed his doubts that, if we consider the prurient nature of most current American prime-time television offerings, the cause of all this could really be just American prudishness and Puritanism—another theme we will discuss below to distinguish American and European sexual attitudes.

Another frequent contributor to *Die Zeit,* Klaus Harpprecht, wrote in the same issue: "The civilized world can only shake its head over the American excitement although we suspect behind it a political intrigue of depressingly underhanded villainy (*Niedertracht*) . . . In Paris, Rome or Bonn these would be considered such banal bed adventures we would smile about them. In 2,000 years we Europeans have gotten accustomed to the fact that [extramarital] sex is a privilege of power" (January 29, 1999). A cursory comparison of sex scandals in high office in Europe and America may also be appropriate although the results of such comparisons may surprise many American readers.

We hardly need Larry Flynt and his sex-driven magazine to remind us that American politicians have been no angels in this respect, and that many younger men among them are still as frequently besieged by eager female groupies as Clinton, Gingrich, or Livingston with his *"galipettes"* (*Le Figaro*'s term). Unlike most political groupies, Monica Lewinsky was not even brought to Washington and into the midst of a constitutional crisis by a personal interest in politics. What is more surprising to European observers is the ease with which American conservatives can ignore the sinners in their midst and concentrate hypocritically on Clinton. Europeans can be at once more playful and teasing about this subject—to quote *Le Monde* editor Edwy Plenel, "We have a very French way of looking at things. We think a president who has affairs is charming" (September 14, 1998). The implication is that he or she at least is not just a cold, power-motivated robot, but "has a life." They can also be stern and disgusted with American prurience and decadence: "Watching the [American] news and talk shows of the great channels, we learn more about provocative undies, presidential toilets, uncleaned cocktail dresses, and unsmoked cigars than any healthy Central European would care to know" (Andreas Kilb, "Impeach TV" in *Die Zeit*, January 14, 1999).

HOW DIFFERENT ARE EUROPEAN ATTITUDES ABOUT SEX?

Differences in this context between most Americans and most Europeans seem to begin at the nexus between sex and American law, or sex and current politics, in this country. Europeans, of course, have experiences with their own lawyers, including politician-lawyers and prominent orators in their parliaments and courtrooms. They also have their unfavorable lawyer stereotypes, lawyerly tricks, shysters, German *Winkeladvokaten* (attorneys of doubtful reputation), French *avocats marrons,* and Italian *avvocatucci,* which may represent negative experiences in Europe. One may even cite Shakespeare's line, "The first thing we do, let's kill all the lawyers." A political lawyer in Europe may be revered as a great fighter for the rights and freedoms of citizens or minorities before the awesome power of the state—or pitied as a Don Quixote flailing away in impotence. In other words, a political lawyer in Europe usually has a positive image. Contrast this with the views of Jeffrey Toobin, who blames much of our recent Constitutional troubles on the triumph of public interest lawyers (including Thurgood Marshall and the Legal Defense Fund of the NAACP) over "traditional American law practice."[1] What is completely new to Europeans, however, is the new American genus of the political sex lawyer who wallows in salacious details—not just the simple facts lawyers may wish to establish in divorce, domestic abuse, or paternity suits—in order to embarrass a public figure. The very phenomenon of the Starr Report as a kind of pornographic land mine set to topple the chief executive officer, or the use of "distinguishing genital characteristics" in a sexual-political harassment suit for the same purpose, makes European mouths drop open.

By the same token, Europeans—who are quite familiar with sex journalism comparable to the work of David Brock, Matt Drudge, or Michael Isikoff—are not surprised by American tabloid stories or book-length exposés such as those that the Arkansas state troopers, Lucianne Goldberg, Linda Tripp, and others in the Clinton-Lewinsky saga hoped to get rich on. The American celebrity cults are not without parallels in Europe and it hardly matters whether the celeb involved is a sports, entertainment, or political star, as long as facile sex journalists can spin a best-selling yarn about the person for money and prurient titillation. What is novel to European sensibilities, however, is the injection of Christian crusading morality into such sexploitation fare or into political sex-lawyering. The combination of all these elements in a Starr or in the second (Rutherford Institute) set of Paula Jones's lawyers, or in the rhetoric of certain persons in Congress simply surpasses the understanding of Europeans, who may even see in it yet another moral abomination from America. Europeans by and large respect religious scruples and genuine reactions of shock about sexual indiscretions, but they are exceedingly suspicious of any transparent manipulation of religious feelings for political purposes. They are similarly suspicious of the motives of political sex lawyers who appear to use sexual shock images for obviously political aims. Under such circumstances, Europeans generally found it difficult to take the American Constitutional drama of 1998-1999 very seriously.

It is obviously daunting to attempt generalizations about European attitudes toward sex, except to point out that they are generally quite far from the overheated and stereotypical imaginings of Americans of every age, sex, occupation, and social origin. American conceptions of what Europeans are like in this respect feed largely upon the longstanding oral traditions of emigration from Europe, which tend to picture the old country in every way much worse than the virtuous society we have been building on this side of the Atlantic. Inherent in the exodus state of mind, as more recent European immigrants to the United States may confirm, is the urge to justify leaving the old sod and reinventing oneself in the New World. But there are also the expectations and, sometimes, the experiences of recent, mostly single American visitors to Europe, such as American soldiers stationed there during World Wars I and II and the Cold War. British soldiers and civilians used to characterize these brave boys—and their social pursuits among native women—with the words "they are oversexed, overdressed, and over here." American soldiers very likely sought and found native young women who appeared to them rather easier and more sophisticated than their high school girlfriends back home.

In a similar fashion, generations of single young civilians, especially college students from the United States, have roamed Europe at the age of their awakening sexual maturity, bringing back memories of encounters with young Europeans of the opposite sex, each other, and even European prostitutes that seemed quite different from their high school sweethearts. Young people mature so quickly at that stage in their lives that many have attributed the striking differences between their own naiveté of yesterday and today's awakening mostly to the European location or some inherent frivolity of their young European acquaintances. We can only speculate how the misleading impressions of youth and the old oral tradition of "feelthy French postcards," French kisses, and the like have come together to form simplistic stereotypes. Reality is demonstrably different, very different.

For a start, there are very similar gradations among the different groups of European societies in this respect as we find among Americans. There are chasms of difference, and of mutual moral condemnation, between "sinful" European big cities and the more traditional, often religiously inclined rural and small town attitudes on sex and family matters: in Paris, few people would raise their eyebrows at the raunchy movies and sitcoms that dominate Hollywood and American television and get exported to Europe. People in the provinces, in *la France profonde,* however, are inclined to run the entertainers and the standards of entertainment of Paris and of America out of town on a rail.

Constant battles rage, for example, over the issue of public nudity, which also tends to separate European countries north of the Alps from their more prudish fellow Europeans in Southern and Catholic Europe. There is frequent friction between the Mediterranean natives and the scores of Northern and Western European nudists who want to frolic in the altogether on Mediterranean beaches. Values clash also in Catholic areas north of the Alps. In the big Catholic city of Munich, a German state capital, for example, nudist *Freikörperkultur* (FKK) lobbying persuaded the city council years ago to permit sunbathing, clothing optional, in a number of rather public, designated locations of the city. In some nearby villages, however, where inns and lakes welcome tourists from the metropolis, local churches and community councils have fulminated in helpless rage against visits by "those exhibitionists." Farmers finally sprinkled organic fertilizer, generously contributed by their livestock, on their beaches and meadows to discourage their "indecent" use. The great European battles of public morality, in other words, have not yet been decided either, just as in the United States. They are still being argued with great passion by different groups, in various locations, by younger and older generations, and issues change over time. Educated, urban Europeans, who often like to pontificate about sexual liberalism in Europe, are generally a very biased source on this complicated subject. Individuals and groups differ widely and violently on such subjects as the permissibility of extramarital sex and of abortion in all their complexity of social settings. There are also tremendous regional and national differences. These were even greater, for example, in the 1970s before divorce and abortion became more or less legalized in Catholic Italy, Spain, and Portugal.

There is no essential disagreement between Europeans and Americans on the basic dimensions of growing up although there are considerable differences in attitudes about childhood, maturity, and the hazardous transition of adolescence in between. Europeans are, in many ways, still very conservative about gender roles even though the legal status and roles of women have become more equal with those of men since the 1960s. Their female representation in legislative bodies, to give a concrete example, rather puts the United States in the rear guard. There are other differences as well. Western Europeans familiar with the American scene are often critical of how some Americans, in their opinion, tend to push their children, especially girls, into a precocious awareness of their sexual attractiveness or premature attitudinizing about the other sex. Europeans feel very strongly about the sanctity of childhood. There are also some who suggest that physical maturation may actually occur somewhat earlier in the United States than in the old country, and that this difference accounts for the seemingly greater sexualization—the "oversexed" nature—of American life in all its aspects.

At the other end of the maturation process, adult European men and women are very proud of their adultness, which to them means being mature and responsible, not as in the American usage of "adult movies" or "adults only," somehow sleazy and degenerate. There is very little of the American cult of youthfulness. On the contrary, European societies think of adolescents as rather unfinished, slightly demented adults whose judgments are questionable until they get a little older and become serious, that is, ready to settle down. Mature Europeans are preoccupied with the pursuit of personal happiness which, unlike the American constitutional phrase of the "pursuit of happiness," is understood mostly as sexual happiness and comforting companionship rather than as the pursuit of economic independence or materialistic wealth. To this day, materialism is not a highly respected social value among the enshrined icons of European societies.

In the midst of the dreadful distractions and disruptions of World War II, for example, French men and women sought that little oasis of adult personal fulfillment, *le petit bonheur*, and it did not always have to be marriage and family as long as it was love and intimacy. Husbands and fiancés were lost in the war, families torn apart, homes destroyed by air raids and combat. But love, to each in his or her fashion, endured, however fleetingly. In this context and to this day, the exact details of such liaisons did not matter much to others and were generally covered by a strong sense of privacy. Except in conflicts and contested divorce cases, it was nobody else's business whether a couple was legally married and exactly how they carried on their sexual relationship. The big difference in those days, and in many ways still today, was that even small-town and rural European societies, the havens of traditional morality, were profoundly disrupted by war, occupation, and postwar developments while American society remained more or less intact throughout the era of the great wars.

The American penchant for standardizing social behavior, moreover, and sermonizing about marriage and sexual interaction hardly exists in European societies; even priests and ministers have learned to express themselves on that subject with great caution only. Moral crusaders à la Starr are considered comic figures or, at best, "a kind of Teutonic knight, a monk-soldier of conservatism, lost in an America whose moral permissiveness . . . [Starr thinks] Clinton incarnates" (*Le Monde*, September 13-14, 1998). *Le Figaro* compared the special prosecutor to the obsessed Captain Ahab chasing the white whale of Clinton (September 11, 1998). In August 1998, *Le Figaro* had already characterized *le scandale Lewinsky* as "a comedy of manners, or a drama of power" (August 17, 1998). "One does not know whether to laugh or cry: . . . the most powerful man on earth [Clinton], at the head of a democracy that would like to stand out as a model, obliged to give a detailed account of his sex life" (August 18, 1998).

Inevitably, particular hostility focused on the special prosecutor, the snoop who poked his nose into things that are, by common consensus, private. As Germans like to say, "*Wer andern in der Nase bohrt, ist selbst ein Schwein*" ("He who picks other people's noses is himself a swine"). The Europeans obviously do not understand the rude American teenage custom of "pantsing" a fellow male. They understand it even less when it is done by adults, before the entire world, and evidently for political manipulation only. This was a very important reason for the almost universal contempt shown the special prosecutor by Europeans from the very beginning. His actions were considered indecent and his report pornographic.

COMPARING POLITICAL SEX SCANDALS

Europeans are quite aware that regional differences still exist in Europe and how they may relate to political scandals at the highest levels. The liberal Swedish daily *Dagens Nyheter* of Stockholm commented at the beginning of the scandalous disclosures about Clinton and Lewinsky, "The French public simply shrugs its shoulders when their politicians commit adultery [as do liberals in Nordic countries, but not so the Anglo-Saxons]." On the other hand, "we Swedes do not condone drunk driving [by our political leaders] . . . For women, [anywhere and in any case] there's an entirely different rule book." (February 2-8, 1998). No doubt the Swedish daily was correct in its assessment of Scandinavian attitudes and even more so with regard to the French, as we have already seen. Years ago, when *Paris-Match* went public with the story of President François Mitterand's grown illegitimate daughter, the magazine was widely criticized and shunned for egregiously bad taste and invasion of the president's privacy. It is hard to imagine today's United States media showing such restraint even though a few decades ago—in the days of Presidents Roosevelt, Eisenhower, Kennedy, and Johnson—they did. The French public also proved most understanding when the president's mistress put in a very public appearance at his funeral. Mitterand and President Giscard D'Estaing had numerous lovers, as did many of their ministers (e.g., Roland Dumas and Laurent Fabius). This was not considered a secret as much as a matter of universal press discretion.

In Spain, Portugal, Greece, and Italy, too, high-ranking politicians such as the great Andreas Papandreou, or the Italian prime minister Bettino Craxi (not to mention Benito Mussolini in another era) had their well-known mistresses. Their sexual peccadilloes never disqualified them from high office. The liberal daily *La Repubblica* of Milan wrote tongue-in-cheek about the leaked grand jury testimony in Washington in February 1998 in an essay, "One of Us": "The real-life drama enveloping the Clintons . . . seems like a funny, absurd and incomprehensible skit. Our [unelected] presidents never had such problems because they were either too religious or too old and ugly. Besides, Italians would not have worried about it . . . because it is considered good manners to lie about matters of love. Even in the face of the strongest evidence, denying everything might save the marriage and thus society, even the state and the church . . . !" Hence, "in the comfort of our tolerant culture . . . we Italians would have understood, nudged each other with eye-winking smugness, and supported 'the traitor,' considering him 'one of us.' If . . . [our prime minister] had committed indiscretions with a young television star, wouldn't we consider him more worthy and more attractive?" (February 2-8, 1998).

We are faced with an amazing consensus in Latin countries in Europe and in Latin America that expresses the conviction that a male politico's affairs may be "charming" and that they may show that he "has a life" beyond political statesmanship. Their attitudes toward political leaders, perhaps, tend to be rather cynical. But it is unlikely that we Americans could persuade them to regard their presidents and prime ministers as super-boy scouts, ever ready to play the selfless hero. As Annick Cojean in *Le Monde* (February 15, 1999) quoted a former Watergate prosecutor with evident approval:

"With presidents as with [famous] basketball players, we must not make them into role models."

Germans, like other Central Europeans, are also accustomed to mistresses and untidy family relationships in high places, from Chancellors Willy Brandt, Helmut Kohl, and Gerhard Schroeder to state governors and cabinet ministers like former finance minister Oskar Lafontaine, the late Franz Josef Strauss, and many others. To quote a German colleague, "All these years in Bonn, everyone knew about all the relationships among politicians and bureaucrats . . . who with whom . . . and who was gay or straight. These are not matters of political importance. At best, they are the subject of ironic jokes." There is the underlying assumption that men are men, women are women, and gays are gays—or, as the French would have put it with a shrug: "Of course she was smitten with this powerful, good-looking man, and of course the 50-year-old Casanova fell for her charms. Get over it."

Europeans are far less tolerant of financial corruption among their leaders, and they have had their share of that kind of scandal and its likely outcome: shameful dismissal. German journalists reacted with exasperation when the Clinton-Lewinsky story was first leaked from the grand jury records. As Kurt Kister wrote in the centrist *Sueddeutsche Zeitung*: "This affair is a manifestation of the putrid moralism of a certain group of [American] conservatives. Since the Republicans cannot keep up politically with President Clinton now, a gang of fanatics is trying to destroy the man with libel and Mafia-like tricks . . . their present aim is as transparent as were the aims of all their earlier attacks on Clinton" (January 1998, quoted in *World Press Review* March 1998). It is worth noting that, even at the onset of the scandal and clearly before disclosure of all the facts of the story, Kister did not picture Clinton but his accusers, most of all Starr, as the cause of the scandal. This at a time when the foreign correspondent could hardly have known much about Starr's dubious prosecutorial methods. The mass circulation, conservative *Bildzeitung* of Hamburg (byline Udo Roebel) was more specific: "On the one hand, a president carried away by his instincts, on the other hand, a special prosecutor who is such a prude that he thinks dancing at a wedding is a sin. What is the outcome: a nation that seriously discusses whether oral sex amounts to a sexual relationship or not. Poor, prudish America" (February 1998 quoted in *World Press Review* March 1998).

So, what about the Anglo-Saxons whom the Swedish *Dagens Nyheter* credited with less tolerance for sexually wayward politicians? Decades ago, British author Anthony King compared British and French scandals and suggested that British politicians, for whatever reason, more likely had sex scandals whereas their French equivalents more often succumbed to financial corruption. This judgment, of course, may also reflect the media coverage more than the actual incidence of different kinds of scandals. Who could forget the Profumo scandal of 1963 when the British Conservative party felt it really needed a more virile image and brought the dashing John Profumo into its government as defense minister? Unfortunately, the sexy defense minister had among his lovers a call girl whom he shared with a Soviet military attaché. Profumo was deposed by fears that his pillow talk might have been recorded by the KGB. But it was not his sexual activities per se that toppled him. Only a few years ago, the Conservative government of John Major included among its rising stars David Mellor, whose graphic details of an affair with a young model were sold to the tabloid press— shades of Gary Hart and Donna Rice or of Gennifer Flowers in the United States. In this case, Mellor's career was ruined, more because of the unseemly publicity than his conduct. In the Clinton-Lewinsky case, of course, the media circus and the Starr Report made sure there would be plenty of "unseemly publicity."

The current Blair cabinet has included several well-known gays who, for a while, preoccupied the tabloid press in Britain; unlike the United States media in the Lewinsky affair, it was a story only for the tabloids. Of these cabinet ministers, Welsh secretary Ron Davies was induced to resign after he picked up a Rastafarian on

Clapham Commons in South London, a notorious gay cruising area, and was robbed. Nick Brown, the agriculture minister, was threatened with being outed by embarrassing details from a former lover, but he remained in office. His lover had tried to sell his story to Murdoch's *News of the World*. Peter Mandelson was outed "on the telly" by a journalist but he was really forced to resign because of his lies in an unrelated matter, the details of a large interest-free loan to buy a luxury house in London. The loan came from Treasury minister Geoffrey Robertson, a millionaire businessman. The Mandelson affair also precipitated a rebellion among BBC staffers when their bosses tried to muzzle reporters on this subject.

A fourth openly gay cabinet secretary, Chris Smith (Culture), has been untouched. It appears that, in Britain, it is not homosexuality in itself but dramatic and embarrassing circumstances in the outing that may lead to a cabinet member's resignation. Only tabloids like Murdoch's *Sun* may still run headlines like "Tell us the Truth, Tony? Are We Being Run by a Gay Mafia?" Respectable newspapers such as the *Independent* will not touch such reporting unless it becomes a scandal for other reasons. The public, as demonstrated in public opinion polls, is far more tolerant of sexual preferences than the *Sun* and, if anything, wary of those who point a finger at the accused.

This aspect, however, may be evaluated quite differently in Latin countries such as France or Italy where, even today, there is strong macho prejudice against homosexuality that has little to do with being on the left or the right. One of the most homophobic regimes in Latin America is that of communist Cuba under Castro. The bearded leader has jailed some homosexuals for as long as he has incarcerated some of his political enemies and rivals. Not so long ago, a Socialist French prime minister Edith Cresson surprised journalists with a statement that, in her opinion, as many as 40 percent of British men were gay! It should also be noted that—unlike in the cases of United States Representatives Bob Livingston, Henry Hyde, Dan Burton, Helen Chenoweth, and Bob Barr—the term "outing" in British usage occurs more in relation to homosexuality than to disclosures about heterosexual marital infidelity. When Liberal Democratic leader Paddy Ashdown was revealed to have had an affair a few years ago, he not only retained his leadership office but his public approval ratings actually improved.

How then did the British press and its readers react to the sex scandal in Washington? Generally speaking, newspapers like the *Guardian, Independent, Financial Times,* and London *Times* expressed sadness, disbelief, and bemusement. Even the *Sun*'s readers thought it "a sorry waste of time." The *Guardian Weekly,* in connection with criticizing the "cycles of prohibitionism" in America, wrote that "when they are not busy trying to outlaw sex, tobacco, or alcohol, Americans enthusiastically pursue them like no other people on earth" (June 14, 1998). The newspaper reiterated its conviction that, in mid-1998, the United States was once more in a prohibitionistic phase, especially regarding "tobacco, booze, and body fat." The *Guardian* also called Clinton's behavior "stupid, infantile, pathetic, caddish, [and] laddish," when it was first reliably confirmed, but insisted that it did not justify impeachment (September 14, 1998). However, the weekly *Economist* followed the bandwagon of certain American media organs, evidently expecting, or calling for, Clinton's resignation. Of course, we have to remember that a foreign journal's call for the resignation of the American president more likely reflects only its opinion and not a conspiracy among publishers and editors to topple the chief executive (see chapter four).

The broadsheet press in Britain often presents spokespersons on different sides of controversial issues in a feeble effort to appear unbiased. The *Irish Times* reported, at the time of the public release of the Starr Report, that many Americans were upset that the president had brought the hallowed American presidency—and presumably also the premises of the White House—into disrepute. But the paper quickly added that Presidents Warren Harding, John F. Kennedy, and Lyndon Johnson had also carried on sexual dalliances in the White House (September 12, 1998). Unlike other crises of major proportions, the uproar over this scandal, wrote *Irish Times* columnist Fintan O'Toole, left no hope of leading to a reform or a better future: "The very idea of public morality has ceased to be credible . . . instead of morality there is [only] moralizing . . . [and] self-righteous zealotry" (September 11, 1998).

Le scandale Lewinsky generated more general accounts in the European press of historical American sex scandals and peculiarities, some of it culled from American sources. Thus Petra Pinzler of *Die Zeit* approvingly quoted Steven Brill of *Brill's Content*: "Will the country (the United States) now be ruled only by the abstinent [after George W. Bush's admission of a youthful alcohol problem], faithful, never inhaling, in short, by faultless presidents?" (October 1, 1998). The same issue of *Die Zeit* reported that an estimated 22 million Americans watched the videotape of Clinton testifying before the federal grand jury in August 1998. Starr had the normally secret grand jury testimony taped, because a member of the grand jury might be absent, with the obvious intention of eventually releasing it to the public. It also printed in translation the famous piece by Pulitzer prizewinner Maureen Dowd of the *New York Times* in which a "most powerful man in the United States" obsesses about Lewinsky's thong underwear and in the end identifies himself as Starr. *Die Zeit* also published a comment on the Starr Report by Sophie Freud, the granddaughter of Sigmund Freud, on the front page. Her judgment on the report: "Simply ridiculous and petty" (September 24, 1998).

Die Zeit also gave voice to an American political scientist, Robert G. Livingston, who pointed out that "President Clinton [was supposed to be] an ethical role model for young Americans" (October 15, 1998). The parallel thought of inspiring the moral and sexual conduct of the young probably had never occurred to a president of France or a premier of Britain, Germany, or any other European country. Unlike the White House to Americans, the French president's Elysée Palace or London's No. 10 Downing

Street are not national shrines and French presidents and European prime ministers have never been expected to act like boy scouts. European journalists are familiar with, although their respective countries do not share, the American reverence for the symbols and even buildings of the nation that allegedly were defiled by Zippergate and by Clinton using the Lincoln bedroom as a high-priced bed-and-breakfast to raise campaign funds. Some European newspaper accounts embellished this further, by claiming the White House had "in reality become a magnificent bordello for . . . furtive trysts." They described President Johnson's "women alarm" which warned him of the arrival of Lady Bird Johnson (V. Zucconi in *La Repubblica,* December 6, 1998). Others went over the litany of American presidential sex scandals beginning with Thomas Jefferson and on to James Buchanan, Grover Cleveland, James Garfield, Woodrow Wilson, Warren G. Harding, Dwight D. Eisenhower, Franklin Delano Roosevelt, as well as Kennedy and Johnson. The message was, a sex scandal in the White House? What a yawn.

As the *Johannesburg Mail and Guardian* put it: "What is all this unseemly fuss about a routine extramarital gobble? . . . Why are we being so prissy?" (February 6, 1998). If the American media and the Clinton-haters did not make such a fuss about it, we could all get on with the business of the country and the world, the Johannesburg paper suggested. A Canadian journalist wrote: "Has the forty-second president, who has admitted John Kennedy is his [ideal] hero, self-destructed in truly mind boggling fashion? Or is he the victim of an unprecedented right-wing smear campaign?" (Linda Hurst in the liberal *Toronto Star,* January 24, 1998). We Americans may be offended by seeing our dirty laundry aired and judged all over the world, but the disclosure and distribution of it, even the opening up of such disreputable perspectives, of course all started right here, with Starr's report and the congressional decision to make it public.

THE PUBLIC-PRIVATE DIVISION

Few aspects of this Washington scandal exercised European opinion as much as the alleged breach of the wall between the private life and the public functions of the president. To quote the French liberal *Libération*: "Monicagate is a surrealist vaudeville because it telescopes two previously separate universes of sexual intimacy and the constitutional order into one—affairs of the flesh and of the state end up under the same sheets" (September 14, 1998). Before we can look further into this question, however, we need to remind ourselves that the public-private distinction has been used in several rather different contexts and is not without some ambiguities. Aside from its economic definitions—as in private enterprise, state regulation, and publicly offered stock—its pertinence to matters or persons of certain other, nonpolitical professions often seems to differ from the standards being claimed here for a country's top leaders. For clergy of any church, for example, private misconduct of any kind cannot be shielded by pointing to satisfactory job performance. Movie stars and other performing artists, on the other hand, often try to project their private persona, after careful and frequently deceptive molding, into the public spotlight for the purpose of increasing their visibility and income. Who could forget the egregious lies, even made-up stories of debauchery, told by the publicity agents of big Hollywood stars over the decades? But there are many cases of ministers unfrocked or, for different reasons, of stars disgraced and even banished for conduct that may not be illegal, or was never proven in a court of law.

For business executives and management in western democracies, the standards of sexual conduct have recently been raised from rather dismal depths—where, in particular, the owners of an enterprise were able to get away with all kinds of sexual transgressions, including against their employees—to considerable diversity and uncertainty. Sexual harassment, for example, was common in

America prior to its uneven proscription a few decades ago. In leading European countries like France and Germany, by comparison, the first wave of legal protections for women employees against their bosses' sexual desires was adopted in the 1920s and 1930s, right after the expansion of gainful female employment outside the home: labor laws flatly prohibited sexual liaisons between a (usually) male boss and female employee, even if mutual consent was claimed or clearly established. A second wave of European concern and attempts at regulation occurred in the 1970s, about the same time regulations were introduced in the United States under such labels as workplace hostility and continual unwanted sexual attention, especially if it made further employment and promotion dependent on sexual favors. This is not to say that violations no longer occur. According to *U. S. News and World Report* (December 14, 1998), over 15,000 complaints are filed with the Equal Employment Opportunity Commission each year, and there is a major industry offering advice and legal counsel to all the parties involved.

Beginning with a series of court cases that gradually built up to acknowledgment of the right to freedom from sexual harassment at work, the concept at first seemed to spread a good deal of confusion and resistance all the way to the United States Senate. There, during the Supreme Court confirmation hearings of Clarence Thomas, Senator Orrin Hatch colorfully expressed his exasperation with Anita Hill's accusations by calling them "that sexual harassment crap." In the case against Clinton, to quote *Le Monde* on December 22, 1998, only the prosecutors' "big lie somehow made consensual sex into the sexual harassment [charge of Paula Jones's] case"—for the purpose of legal discovery—and even into a legal analog for rape charges if the House managers had been permitted to dredge up Jane Doe no. 5. In current American law, according to Toobin,[2] fudging the distinction between consensual and coercive sex (or harassment) has become the rule rather than the exception. The Violence Against Women Act signed by Clinton also failed to draw an unequivocal line, a failure that came back to haunt him.

It is small wonder that legally trained European observers show contempt for such slippery practices of American law and of prosecutors under cover of legal discovery. European Union and especially German privacy laws, we should add, now offer much stronger protection from government or other prying eyes (or ears) than American laws afford in practice. Tripp's 23-hours of secret recordings of Lewinsky's confidences would immediately have landed her in jail on criminal charges had she committed her eavesdropping in Germany rather than in Maryland, where, at this writing, even pertinent statutes have hardly begun to be observed. In Maryland there was no indictment until mid-1999 and the case may lead no further than did the prosecution of Starr and his minions for prosecutorial misconduct. That the Office of Independent Counsel (OIC), according to Michael Isikoff, initially agreed to provide immunity to Tripp in return for her (eagerly offered) tapes and testimony simply boggles European legal experts. It took Lewinsky a very long time, wrote Isikoff, to suspect what her friend was doing to her. In fact, it was not until Tripp had "shopped" her to Starr and the Jones lawyers, as the *Guardian* put it (September 15, 1998), that she was suspicious enough during her illegal "sting" on January 13 to search Tripp's purse for listening devices during an unguarded moment.

As a consequence of public reactions to Nazi spying and (East German communist) Stasi surveillance of private lives, Germans today enjoy broad protection from the inquisitiveness, for example, of commercial operations which in the United States routinely vet our credit card purchases and other buying habits for marketing purposes. Germans and, since the adoption of a European Privacy Code, other European Union member nations view Starr-like invasions of privacy as an intolerable, totalitarian horror that only a Nazi or a *Stalinist* communist could find acceptable. In the United States, according to the *Economist* (February 10, 1996),

Big Brother is doing his bit: "In the struggle against crime, terrorism, deadbeat parents, illegal immigrants, and even traffic jams, government keeps an ever-closer eye on more and more of its citizens." Commenting on the Lewinsky scandal, the conservative Danish *Weekendavisen* of Copenhagen put it well when it editorialized: "How can this sort of thing be allowed to go on in a *civilized* society? Sensationalism is king. Tapes of private conversations recorded under doubtful circumstances are published without the consent of the parties concerned . . . We have observed societies before that did not draw a line between private and public lives. This is the way it was in Eastern Europe before the fall of communism" (January 30, 1998).

Among politicians here and in Europe, the dividing line between public function and private life seems to be drawn quite differently. To begin with, politicians' marriages are often notoriously troubled whether they serve in Congress or American state legislatures, or in London, Paris, or Rome. The simple reason is that the representatives' spouses and family, if any, generally remain back home while the legislator (mostly male) is surrounded by secretaries, lobbyists, and political groupies eager to supply good company. Twenty and thirty years ago, before the new concern with sexual misconduct or harassment had gripped Washington—that is, before the investigation and ouster of Oregon's senator Robert Packwood—scores of married male representatives and senators kept mistresses in Washington. Stories were told of the so-called monkey girls who would see off their midwestern representative or senator at the train station, whenever he headed home to his real family. In those days, easily three-fourths of Congress might have been exposed for infidelity, compared to a conservatively estimated 21 percent of married males and 13 to 15 percent of married females in the general population, if sociological estimates are to be believed. This was one reason why observers expected to see many more hypocrites, especially older members of Congress, to be exposed as adulterers, when *Salon,* Larry Flynt's *Hustler,* and others began their share of the politics of personal destruction among the impeachment-minded Republicans. If this was indeed only a scandal over Clinton's sexual misconduct, his congressional pursuers and their counsel David Schippers, not to mention the nation's media captains, were an unlikely posse on his tail.

Again, the general public in America clearly drew the line between public and private lives of politicians more the way the Europeans do. What else could it mean that large majorities in public opinion polls again and again gave President Clinton high ratings for his public performance while expressing their discomfort with his private conduct? Perhaps they were also scandalized by the dubious legal maneuvers of Starr and company on the occasion of the authorization for extending Starr's Whitewater mandate to the Jones lawsuit: "By confusing perfectly legal private behavior with a possible case of public financial corruption [a crime] . . . the highest judicial authorities of the United States engaged in a grave perversion of the law . . . ," Nicole Bacharan wrote. "Nothing would authorize searching for proof of alleged financial wrongdoing [Whitewater] in the private sex life of the president. And even less could the Paula Jones suit [of criminal harassment] justify asking the president about his private relations with a consenting adult."[3] Similarly, Lars-Erik Nelson in the *New York Review of Books* ("The not very grand inquisitor," November 5, 1998) questioned the legal assault on Lewinsky: "It is hard to believe that Starr thought he had a serious criminal case against Lewinsky . . . Rather he was . . . terrorizing her so that he could bring perjury and obstruction of justice charges against Clinton . . ." Nelson also mentioned Starr's violation of federal conflict of interest guidelines; his use of hearsay testimony and disregard of the rules of evidence; his direct approach to a witness with an immunity deal when the witness had an attorney, a violation of American Bar Association (ABA) guidelines; his cavalier disregard for grand jury secrecy; and his use of a perjury trap.

After impeachment passed the House, the ever-quotable and outable Representative Henry Hyde was quoted by the London

Times (December 21, 1998) as saying "something is going on, repeatedly, that has to be stopped, and that is the confusion between private acts of infidelity and public actions." He was in good company, at least as far as European observers were concerned. This was even reflected in the Russian official *Rossitskaya Gazeta*, which is no stranger to past totalitarian invasions of privacy. Vladimir Lapsky commented in response to the Starr Report: "Who in the end is violating the principles of morality to a greater extent, Clinton or his opponents? It is they, his opponents, who have brazenly invaded his private life; it is they who have humiliated the popularly elected leader of the country" (September 1998). Klaus Lutterbeck, writing in the magazine *Stern* of Hamburg said, "hardly a day passes without having the unchained prosecutors and media reveal new salacious details in the private lives of [American] politicians. Since the conservatives realized how irresistible a peek through the keyhole is, all barriers of common sense have fallen" (February 11, 1999). And, speaking about the shocking invasion of Lewinsky's privacy, Lutterbeck added: "Soon, when the political class in Washington wakes up from its year-long intoxication, the hangover will be great. Big Brother, the specter of the [totalitarian] snooper state, won another battle. Never was more [taxpayers'] money spent to exploit the private details of a single life [Lewinsky's]." In the interest of objectivity, however, we must not forget the extraordinarily loose lips of Lewinsky who had confided most of the details of the affair to Tripp and ten others long before she was debriefed by Starr's deputies.

A letter writer to the *Los Angeles Times* (September 19, 1998) commented, "For the first time in my life, I am actually frightened of being an American. I could never have imagined that someone could—legally—so exploit the most private and personal moments between two human beings; could so violate their precious right to privacy that has been a cornerstone of our society . . . Which one of us is next?" This, to be sure, continues to be the prevailing opinion in this country too, as Representative Henry A. Waxman put it, "Most Americans believe the government has no business prying into consensual sex between adults" (*Los Angeles Times*, September 27, 1998). But the rationale of the Starr investigation and of the impeachment inquiry clearly, and with a vengeance, violated the private boundary suggested by Waxman.

Some Republicans disputed Waxman's view on the borderline between private and public conduct: to quote a reader's letter in the same newspaper, "Bill and Hillary Clinton have publicly damaged the institution of marriage . . . and have set a bad example to not only their daughter but the future generations of our children. Clintons, we're tired of you both. Take your sideshow back to Arkansas . . ." [never mind the lawful election of President Clinton in 1996] (October 14, 1998). I could quote hundreds of domestic statements to the same effect, for example, a Republican reader's colorful election-time argument that the Democratic party had come "forward as the party of adultery, fornication, and perjury" and that "to the supporters of Bill . . . these are all 'private' issues" (October 12, 1998).

THE SHOCK OF STARR'S PEEP SHOW

The violation of the privacy rights of Clinton and Lewinsky was one set of issues shocking to European minds. A rather different issue was the nationwide and worldwide publication of the hard-core pornographic Starr Report—one American commentator called it "at $40 million the most expensive, taxpayer-financed piece of pornography in the world"—upon the authority, yet, of a bipartisan vote of the House of Representatives. At the time of its dissemination, the House Committee on Telecommunications, Trade and Consumer Protection was holding hearings on protecting children from pornography on the Internet. European journalists, of course, noted the report's obsession with presidential sex. The *Sueddeutsche Zeitung* of Munich (September 30, 1998) reported a computer analysis of the 50,000-page report which found the word "sexual" appeared 406 times, "sex" 164 times, and "breasts" 62 times. There was little reference to law, but the word "perjury" occurred 40 times.

Europeans (and most Americans) have always known that every human being in the world has body parts that are better covered in public, and that every human being frequently engages in private activities ranging from defecation and urination to sexual contact that, with or without the consent of the principals, are not to be exposed to public view, least of all to immature children. The distribution of graphic descriptions of sexual details in the Starr Report, of what *Le Figaro* (September 14, 1998) called *"les bucco-génitales* (oral sex), but no penetration, the cigar, everything," was universally regarded as an unprecedented gross indecency, even though many newspapers, here and abroad, printed some of the most salacious excerpts, and the material was available on the Internet. That this was done under the authority of Congress at taxpayers' expense and that it was about a president instantly made it a dramatic example of American decadence to the world. *Le Monde* (September 12, 1998) expressed its shock about the availability of "the crudest details now on the Internet." Referring to the explicit details, the paper also wrote: "These details . . . are only anecdotal. They tell Starr's truth . . . All this man wants is to destroy another man" (quoted in *World Press Review,* November 1998). The reader will recall how important the pornographic emphasis had been to Starr, his deputies, and his right-wing coconspirators—it was practically their modus operandi and distinguishing mark.

We need to emphasize again that nearly all Europeans blamed Starr and the House of Representatives for this universal shock, not Clinton. After the fact, there was a never-ending procession of foreign heads of state, and not just our most important allies, who publicly expressed their solidarity and sympathy with the president as a man and a world leader. Quite contrary to what many Republicans were saying about the way Clinton's conduct had made America a laughing-stock around the world, evidently the world was still saluting the president, and hence the American people who had elected him. When Clinton addressed the UN General Assembly on common actions against terrorism, following the bomb attacks on American embassies in East Africa, he received a long standing ovation with rhythmic clapping by the assembled delegates from around the world. Chief executives everywhere, from Australia to Rome and Madrid, expressed support for the embattled president. French President Jacques Chirac put in a telephone call to the White House, assuring Clinton of "all his friendship and esteem in the personal ordeal that [Clinton] was going through" (*Le Figaro,* September 14, 1998; see also *El País* of Madrid of the same date). The conservative French paper also reported that most of the world press was exceedingly critical of Starr and his report. Prime Minister Romano Prodi of Italy called Clinton "a great president" and recalled his "deep friendship with him" (*La Repubblica,* August 8, 1998). Most Europeans could not fathom the extreme partisan hostility that appeared to have brought on a shocking and unseemly, pornographic pillorying of the highest elected officer of the United States.

The liberal *Le Monde* was also critical of the selective documentation in the Starr Report—"What an astonishingly bad novel!" wrote Pierre Georges (September 11, also 13-14, 1998)—and particularly of the fact that Starr "based his report solely on Monica's testimony regarding sexual relations [with Clinton], from a woman who says she has been lying all her life . . . it is only hearsay so far; he has not proven his charges" (*Le Monde Hebdomadaire,* August 15). We too need to remember this awareness of the legal weakness of the Starr Report to understand why most European journalists showed little respect for the legal case that Chairman Hyde and the House managers later tried to make of it. Conversely, some European press comments were not exactly favorable to the president as a man and some predicted (à la parliamentary no-confidence vote) his imminent fall: "The president of the United States . . . caught in his zipper," snickered *France-Soir* (September 13, 1998). The

Italian *La Repubblica* marveled, "How could a lousy (*riprovevole*), squalid but banal sex story become the second constitutional crisis of this century in the U.S.?" (September 11, 1998). *La Repubblica* correspondent Vittorio Zucconi had at first been very favorably impressed with "that wise old man of great impartiality, Henry Hyde" and declared that President Clinton had "forfeited his right to privacy" by his conduct and would soon be gone (September 12, 1998). After the Republican defeat in the November elections, however, he changed his tune. At about the same time as the Starr Report was issued, the attempt of Malaysian Premier Mahathir Mohammed to oust his vice premier, Anwar Ibrahim, on the basis of dubious sex charges did not enhance the credibility of the accusations brought by Starr and Hyde either: Malaysia as a model for America?

There was also universal alarm at the thought of the pornographic Starr Report falling into the hands of children. "Struck with a red card (the kind handed to European ballplayers when they are sent from the field for committing fouls), requiring parental authorisation," wrote Jean d'Ormesson at year's end in *Le Figaro* (December 31, 1998), ". . . unworthy enough to be prohibited to minors under sixteen, the American tragicomedy leaves the Oval Office . . . and the presidential alcove to take on planetary dimensions." Other European newspapers such as the *Sueddeutsche Zeitung* and the *Irish Times* also expressed concern about the American porn on the Internet, although in Germany and Ireland there are automatic processes to seal children's access to pornography but not always to such documents as the official Starr Report. Nicole Bacharan brought to light a *60 Minutes* broadcast of 1987 in which an American judge had declared: "The media must never reproduce explicit or implicit descriptions of sexual acts. Our society must be purged of perverts who furnish pornographic materials to the media, pretending they have a societal mission in the name of the 'right to know' of the public. Pornography is pornography, whatever the source."[4] Bacharan added: "That judge was Kenneth Starr. No one makes a better pornographer than a true Puritan."

Some aspects of Italian attitudes also come to light from the coverage of *La Repubblica,* which reported with distaste on Starr's imposition of the DNA test on Clinton and on Lewinsky's testimony that "we did it twelve times, always in such a way that, according to him, he would be able to deny that he had sexual relations with me . . ." "What a love story!" correspondent Zucconi wrote: "This is a serious narrative and not a porno cartoon for horny [*fornucolosi*] teenagers" (August 7, 1998). A day later, an essay entitled "Sexygate" appeared in the same newspaper, written by the retired political scientist Giovanni Sartori, once considered the most eligible bachelor of Florence. Sartori wrote tongue-in-cheek: "It is normal for a 50-year-old who has been married since age 20 to have a fleeting and occasional interest in a much younger woman. And it is completely normal that he would deny it. He acted like a gentleman" (August 8, 1998).

The Germans were no less critical of the Starr Report and the grand jury videotape. Robert Leicht wrote a piece entitled "The obscene Puritans" in the weekly *Die Zeit* (September 24, 1998): "The president of a world power was deconstructed. . . . The fourhour interrogation was broadcast worldwide and the intimate life of a person dragged around the globe." Leicht was not exactly in sympathy with Clinton but was skeptical of the "St. Vitus' dance of the search for truth by the extremist [*Exzesstaeter*] Starr, aided by an irresponsible Congress." A German daily in Regensburg, *Mittelbayerische Zeitung,* was more direct when it expressed some skepticism about whether a presidential candidate who, like Al Gore, comes across as a model family man now could be trusted in the future: "Thanks to Viagra, even a Methuselah like Reagan can't be considered for the office of president. What is needed is a eunuch" (quoted in German embassy newsletter, reporting on German press reaction in September). Nicole Bacharan had an even better idea: Shouldn't one install a prosecutor "in the bedroom of the presidential mansion to make sure that only the right sexual relations, with the right partner, take place? Or, better yet, that the presidential couple is truly in love and not like so many couples that merely stay together for the sake of convention, or of the children?"[5]

Later, *Le Figaro* took fiendish delight in reporting how Hyde had to admit to a "youthful transgression that had been prolonged well beyond age forty" (December 19-20, 1998) and in reporting the quest of Larry Flynt—his *Hustler* magazine had promised a million dollars to women who would attest to having had illegitimate affairs with important Republicans in Congress—to torpedo the new Speaker-elect Bob Livingston and other holier-than-thou House Republicans with disclosures of their own sexual transgressions: "Starr, the inquisitor of the White House, at last has found his match in Larry Flynt . . . Starr had his hour of glory with his famous report that detailed by the millimeter how Bill Clinton and Monica Lewinsky touched each other." Correspondent Mével described Flynt's investigative apparatus, his threats to expose a dozen Republican representatives and his background: "The lower house of Congress never deserved its name better." He quoted Flynt, "My sole aim is to demonstrate the hypocrisy of the political class," and described him as "the anti-Starr, the *bête noir* of the religious right, the sexual hypocrites (*pères-la-pudeur*), and the segregationist rearguard" (*Le Figaro*, December 23, 1998). *Die Zeit* also commented, "The *Hustler* makes politics, what else can we say about the state of America?" and described the outing of Bob Barr, the anti-abortion fighter, for alleged adultery and his role in his former wife's abortion (January 14, 1999).

Americans were probably of divided mind about *Hustler*'s threat of revelations for money, but a *Washington Monthly* editorial put the issue squarely: "Republicans who attack Larry Flynt for offering $1 million for dirt on them fail to mention Richard Mellon Scaife's $2 million investment in dirt on Bill Clinton" (March 1999). Europeans were neither surprised by the revelations—"they reaped the whirlwind" was a typical reaction—nor did they show much sympathy for the pompous phrase of "the politics of personal destruction." *Le Figaro* was no less snide in characterizing the White House reaction to the impeachment charges of obstruction of justice as a "conspiracy of silence" to hide the "torrid amourette of the Oval Office." The conservative paper then described the frustration of American television journalists and House Republicans trying to persuade the football-watching public in January and February that the Lewinsky affair was just about to turn into the "trial of the century" before the Senate. At the same time, the newspaper reported on the 300,000 Christian Coalition petitions that demanded an "iron broom" be used on the White House, and on the extraordinary flood of telephone and e-mail messages that was directed by both sides at the House of Representatives and the Senate between the impeachment and the beginning of the Senate trial of the president (December 21,1998).

As former senator and 1972 presidential candidate George McGovern put it, "How, it is asked by those of the [William J.] Bennett school, can the public accept as president an adulterer, especially one who denies it even under oath?" (*Los Angeles Times*, September 27, 1998). Actually, by then the president had admitted to an "improper [but not a sexual] relationship" on television and, as McGovern was quick to add, had "clearly repented and asked for forgiveness," and many had indeed forgiven him. Some, however, had not. As a fall-back strategy to shocking Clinton into resignation—especially if the American public refused to be unspeakably outraged by oral sex, stained dresses, and cigars—Starr and Hyde had the secret stash of additional Jane Does as well as the labored legal accusations of perjury and obstruction of justice for the impeachment proceedings. This was the same case later made by the House managers before the Senate and dismissed by Senator Tom Harkin as "a pile of dung." European observers had difficulty following all the byzantine turns of the great conspiracy. They were also mystified by the strange American mixture of Puritan moral crusades and the moral perversity of the Starr Report, a shocking effluent from the darkest Bible Belt.

THE DARKEST BIBLE BELT

Europeans reacted to the Starr Report from the depths of all their violated taboos: hard core pornography made available to the whole world, including children, the shocking invasion of the privacy not only of President Clinton but of Monica Lewinsky, the transparent mendacity of a sex case used for partisan purposes and, what to them, at least, appeared to be religious hypocrisy. We must remember that, by any standard, Europeans are less religious than Americans to begin with: when they learn that among Americans of today, 94 percent believe in God, and 80 percent think that "religion is very important in life," Europeans are very much aware that, for better or worse, they can hardly muster half these numbers among their own (London *Independent on Sunday,* July 27, 1997). They also have little understanding of the American phenomenon of televangelism, and even less of cases such as those of Jimmy Swaggart or the Bakkers.

European reports on such American curiosities, however, rarely stop with attributing "neo-Victorian Puritanism" to us, as did the French liberal weekly *L'Express* in an article about the Jones lawsuit and about two humorous books about American gender relations, *The Rules* and *The Code* (June 12-18, 1997). Secular Europeans like to add something about "a lot of hypocrisy" to most discussions of religion in politics. The American conjuncture of sex and religion invariably strikes European funny bones because they do not understand and, perhaps, cannot take the outcome seriously. Who knows what might be hiding under the well-coiffed waves on the president's head?[6] In London's *Independent on Sunday* ("Holy War on Capitol Hill," July 27, 1997) John Carlin gleefully reported that the half-million member Concerned Women of America condemned the Disney corporation for "promoting homosexuality and subverting family values" in its personnel policies. There had been resounding echoes of approval of the Disney condemnation and threats of a boycott from the 15 million members of the Southern Baptist Convention.

Even before the Lewinsky scandal broke, Erich Schmidt of the conservative *Neue Zuercher Zeitung* reported that 23 American states have laws making heterosexual oral sex illegal. Georgia law declares it sodomy and threatens a man with five years in jail—even if he did it with his own wife—and forty years if he had a prior conviction for this offense. Georgia law describes more than ten forbidden sex practices, according to the Swiss newspaper. The state intended to post these prohibitions in all Atlanta hotel rooms before the Olympic Games. But "that noble effort had to be abandoned because many foreign visitors could not be expected to read English well enough [especially not such specialized vocabulary] and the organizers were afraid to use pictures instead." A good laugh at American expense. Schmidt concluded that "a goodly measure of small-mindedness and above all, of hypocrisy" was to be found among Americans (April 16, 1997). European journalists are well aware that former Speaker Newt Gingrich was a representative from Georgia and some had read Gail Sheehy's article on his childhood, his women, and his love life in *Vanity Fair* (September 1995). Another Republican hypocrite pursuing the president on sex charges, they concluded.

Figures such as Rev. Jerry Falwell, whose long political career extends from the days of defending Southern segregation, to the Moral Majority, to his campaign against allegedly homosexual Teletubbies like Tinky Winky, have not escaped the amused attention of European correspondents. Falwell is easy to lampoon but his sponsorship of a widely distributed anti-Clinton videotape, the "Clinton Chronicles"—which alleges the president was involved in drug dealing and murder in Arkansas, and, later, in the murder of his friend Vincent Foster in Washington—surpasses all understanding. People who ordered the videotape, moreover, received a follow-up message from former right-wing Congressman Bill Dannemeyer, calling for Clinton's impeachment (in 1994!) and intimating that Henry Hyde was already studying the law on this subject.[7]

"Doesn't this man of the cloth [Falwell] have any respect for the third Commandment," was the deeply shocked response of a Scandinavian Lutheran clergyman friend of mine who had spent many months in the United States. He gave me his summary opinion of the American religious right, cautioning that he was reluctant to question anyone of sincerely Christian beliefs. But there were three grounds on which he found the religious right profoundly flawed. First, he thought them "too political" and too involved in American election campaigns, even power mad. Secondly, the minister regarded Pat Robertson, the Christian Coalition, and most televangelists as "money mad" or "money-grubbing" in ways that offended his own Protestant beliefs. Finally, he considered them profoundly lacking in Christian charity and forgiveness: "What kind of Christian would take such a harsh, unforgiving view of his fellow man?" When I reminded him that many of the conservative ministers who refused to accept the president's pleas for forgiveness questioned Clinton's sincerity, he shook his grizzled head and said emphatically: "Mere humans have no right to doubt a sinner's sincerity, not even ministers. Only God can look into the heart of a person and tell if he is sincere. These ministers are not speaking for Him when they preach hatred." He was not alone in this judgment. A German colleague, upon seeing the Clinton grand jury videotape, hummed an old ditty under his breath: "Wir sind alle kleine Suenderlein. S'war immer so, s'war immer so" (We are all little sinners. T'was ever so, t'was ever so). Who are all these Republican prosecutors, congressmen, and media people—most of whom have done their share of sinning in their time—who are they to cast the first stone?

When the Republican majority in the House impeached the president, many Europeans felt that "the Moral Majority, the Christian conservative majority in Congress imposed its behavioral code on politics in the midst of an unprecedented culture war" (*Die Zeit*, December 22, 1998). More often than not, however, secular Europeans attribute these American oddities, as *Die Zeit* did, simply to "Puritan dreams of a 'city on the hill' that bring about two, three, or four waves of Puritan [revivalism] each century, just as if the collective soul of America yearned to burn off its sins in cleansing fires of overwrought morality." The Gary Hart affair of 1988 was "an orgy of hypocrisy . . . the moralists lack the most humane element of Christianity, the readiness to forgive," wrote Klaus Harpprecht in *Die Zeit* (January 29, 1999). Frank Rich in the *New York Times* was close to this view, perhaps, when he wrote in November 1998: "Americans sense that the government prosecutor (Starr) . . . is an avatar for the political movement that wishes to revive punitive divorce laws, enforce state sodomy statutes (especially against homosexuality), roll back Roe v. Wade, and police libraries, TV, movies, and the Internet for smut . . ."

The apologies of Clinton, on the other hand, drew a surprising and uniformly hostile response in the European press where cartoonists had him apologizing to, among other addressees, the Statue of Liberty (*Le Monde Hebdomadaire,* August 22, 1998), Buddy the dog, and Socks the cat. *Le Figaro* (September 11, 1998) spoke of "pathetic contrition." *The Guardian* (September 11, 1998) called it "serial groveling toward his family, supporters, and the nation" and wrote of "his almost tearful shame and remorse statement" about sinning and of his tearful repentance at a prayer breakfast with religious leaders. The conservative *Frankfurter Allgemeine Zeitung* wrote that "Clinton is a president without pants. But this embarrassment is followed up by still another one with his [public] apologies to each and everyone, an exercise the hypocrisy of which is hard to top" (September 11, 1998). The liberal *Die Zeit* (September 17, 1998), in an article *"Die geilen Puritaner von Amerika"* (The Wanton Puritans of America), was no less dismissive of "Clinton's groveling self-accusations." Even Bacharan is snide in her remarks: "Head lowered, Bill Clinton beats his chest to confess his sins.

[Everywhere] he repents, apologizes, asks for forgiveness . . . he does not forget his dog."[8] *Le Monde,* too, felt turned off by "Clinton's remorse, beating his breast" (September 11, 1998). *Le Figaro* was even more critical of Clinton's renewed apology on the eve of impeachment by the House (December 13, 1998).

Why this distaste for Clinton's apologies? European journalists are obviously unfamiliar with the Bible Belt culture in which lusty sinning and public, tearful, and abject repentance are well-established routines. But even if we grant that most European commentators viewed this sex scandal as a rather secular and cynical partisan enterprise, this spontaneous reaction to Clinton's apologies calls for additional explanation. The European ethos of masculinity is simply not inclined toward apologizing in matters of sex, least of all publicly. Real men, Europeans believe, may love and make mistakes, but they don't apologize. Clinton, to many Europeans, is simply too eager to please, forever fishing for acceptance, and lacking in assertive manhood. He is the man who, in the midst of the counterculture years, didn't inhale, is "reluctant even in his affairs" (*Die Zeit,* September 17, 1998), and, instead of consummating his relationship with the eager Lewinsky, is half-hearted in sex. This may be a caricature of superficial perceptions but it is at the heart of European attitudes.

EUROPEAN WOMEN SPEAK OUT

Refracted through the eyes of women on both sides of the Atlantic, the Lewinsky scandal takes on rather different dimensions from the perspective of the "angry white males" who undertook to unseat an elected president with it. To start, the gender gap (the sum of the gender differences between male and female voters)—which had burdened Republican election campaigns especially since the Reagan era, including the electoral performance of the great communicator himself—had grown further with Clinton and extended to many of the policies he championed, for example, in the fields of health and education. In European eyes, misogyny and a phobia of feminists have been distinguishing marks of the new American conservatives from Reagan to Limbaugh. American women voters responded to the same stimuli and the conservatives had paid for this at the polls.

Feminist groups in the early nineties had adopted what the London *Independent,* in 1994, called "feminism with a friendly face": a determined drive to help women candidates at all levels, as well as Bill Clinton in 1992, to win public office. This often required soft pedaling important issues and avoiding personal offense as much as possible—even among the angry white males. So it sometimes fell to press voices in friendly foreign countries, for example, to take a stand opposing the Republican campaign against welfare mothers, a code phrase for black and Latina mothers in the inner cities of America. As the *Toronto Star* wrote, with reference to Jonathan Swift's *A Modest Proposal,* this was "a trend that was picking up steam across America, especially with conservative Democrat Bill Clinton in the White House, who had pledged to 'change welfare as we know it'... The far-right position of yesterday, forcing welfare mothers to work for their dole while leaving their children with strangers," or unattended, was now "the moderate position on welfare." It was all aimed exclusively at women, poor women, the *Toronto Star* wrote, because the family-value conservatives wanted only their own women to stay home and mind the children. Those on welfare should go out and get a job (quoted in *World Press Review,* June 1994). The children might be given up for adoption or, according to Newt Gingrich, put in orphanages. In Europe, even conservatives find such views appalling. Among southern African American families, indeed, almost half (45 percent) are headed by women and another 6 percent by single men. In the richest society on earth, children in poverty are legion.

Militant Republicans often expressed the hope that the sex scandal might roll back the Democratic advantage with women voters, especially if they succeeded in portraying the president, with the help of the secret stash of Jane Doe materials, as a sexual predator whose proclivities extended to alleged sexual harassment and even rape. Prominent Republican and conservative Christian pundits, moreover, made great efforts—through design or ignorance—to confuse positions and muddy the waters. A favorite ploy, for example, was to express mock surprise that women's organizations, like the National Organization of Women (NOW) and other feminist groups that they had always hated, were *not* up in arms about the Lewinsky scandal. This was intended as a double-bladed strategy, both to smite the despised feminists and to pretend that the women's agenda was mostly against all sexual misconduct, particularly that of a certain Clinton who still enjoyed vast popularity among women voters according to current polls and was frequently defended by women representatives and senators. Republican newspapers and pundits often sought to fudge the issue by interchanging the phrases sexual harassment, which is illegal, and sexual misconduct, regardless of whether the latter was illegal or merely immoral, as in adultery or extramarital sex.

Sometimes, the conservatives of the Christian Coalition missed the point with the best intentions. In 1995, when Ralph Reed launched his Contract with the American Family, the *Economist* asked why there had been no women at the microphones of the Christian convention: "Why should a campaign to strengthen the family be taken seriously when it appears to be championed entirely by men?" (May 20, 1995). The British weekly answered its own question: You cannot ignore 1.6 million activists of the Christian Coalition who dominate the Republican party in 18 states. Annick Cojean, writing for *Le Monde* (February 15, 1999), however, expressed her agreement with Betty Friedan's statement that "it saddened her to see how they used the women to attack [Clinton] . . . how in the name of their [supposed] defense, they stymied the only president whose heart had always been on the side of their cause."

It is doubtful whether these obfuscations left much impact on American women. European women's reactions, on the other hand, followed rather different rationales. In August 1998, the conservative *Le Figaro* asked half a dozen women for their opinions and printed them. The result portrays a range of typical attitudes. None really focused on the president's sexual misconduct which, in the United States, was considered the heart of the matter. One woman, a writer, said: "I don't understand how a country can humiliate itself to such a degree—by any account I have never understood that country." She expressed instinctive contempt for Starr. Another woman burst out: "You could die laughing: All the protagonists are grotesque . . . a woman who does not clean her dress . . . It's a good summer read." I have heard other European women similarly pick out the stained cocktail dress as an object of their disgust in conversations. A third woman, asked by *Le Figaro,* opined: "Clinton has bad taste in women, a weakness for inflatable dolls. But as a gentleman he must lie. He has no right to reveal his private [sex] life . . ." Another woman called the scandal "a disgusting affair" and immediately attacked Starr as "a pit bull, who is revolted by his ideas of the left," referring to the prevalent continental press view of the centrist Clinton as a man of the left.

A fifth woman respondent called the United States "utterly stupid for paying attention to such affairs" and expressed her support for the president. Such ready support resonates with the 80 to 90 percent of Italian women who voiced their support for the president in public opinion polls, presumably without even knowing the details. Finally, there was the French historian Elisabeth Badinter who replied: "What they did to Clinton is an offense to the human rights of man. There's no worse humiliation. He's been violated and this calls for great commiseration. It is as if he had been stripped naked." She felt that he had a right to lie and expressed shock at the intrusive questions asked by the prosecutor about his private life (*Le Figaro,* August 19, 1998).

Writing in *Le Monde* after Clinton's acquittal, Annick Cojean called him "a president so human, so human" and approvingly quoted people who were on his side. "The cause of . . . the

Republican party is so grotesque. To have an adventure and to lie and hide it is no crime against the state." She also cheered a group of students she saw leaving school and chanting. "He lied, I would have lied, you would have lied . . .' What an affair! . . . they suspend the whole country because of a sex affair . . . That's obscene, and not of Clinton but of Kenneth Starr . . . it's as if it was about Baghdad or Kosovo." She concluded, "Charges of sexual harassment must not include consensual relations between two adults. This has all gone far beyond common sense. They have intermingled the public and the private spheres, and politicized the laws. And I am fascinated by the firm resistance [to this] of the American people" (February 15, 1999).

Polly Toynbee in the *Guardian* of London was more philosophical about the matter: "Adultery is . . . commonplace and widespread, always was, always will be. It is not a crime but a private matter between those involved. It is private even when it happens on the Oval Office desk . . . Whatever salacious delights are paraded before our fascinated gaze on the Internet, it is none of our business . . . Most sex if exposed in public is absurdly embarrassing." Toynbee added somewhat naively that if Clinton had admitted his dalliance at the outset, he would have been widely applauded. She excused his resistance to the legal charges because "it [the defense] is understandable in the face of [such] gross invasion of his privacy" (September 12, 1998). The *Irish Times* (September 11, 1998) approvingly reprinted a *Washington Post* piece by Megan Rosenfeld and Michael Colton defending Lewinsky's privacy rights against the invasions of the Starr Report: "Millions of people now know more about Lewinsky in some ways than they know about their closest friends." It also cited a California schoolmate of Lewinsky at Brentwood High School who said: "Starr . . . has humiliated her. How dare he take this young woman and degrade her to the world, and pass it on to Congress."

The European press generally pictured Lewinsky as a victim, not only of Starr and Clinton, but also of the American media. "The mouth of Monica," wrote Jean d'Ormesson in *Le Figaro* (December 31, 1998), "has marked the year of grace, or disgrace, of 1998." Other European journalists noted with disgust that when *Time* magazine featured her picture, only her mouth was in sharp focus, but the rest of her face was rather blurred. After Clinton's acquittal, they commented, *Cosmopolitan* magazine (which has European editions) featured an article on "blow jobs" (fellatio) and why some women like them. To Europeans, this article was evidently another sign of American decadence. Some foreign journalists also noted that it was during the government shutdown, when most of the White House staff was away, that Clinton and Lewinsky first got together. These European sympathies, however, did not keep the European journalists from acid commentary on Lewinsky's active love life, pregnancy, and abortion during the time that she was supposedly pining for Clinton. Describing her as a blabbermouth, they observed that, without her eager revelations to ten or more friends, Starr's investigators might have had to invent her tale. Her taped conversations with Tripp implicated and denounced many other people, including her father, which was yet another reason for her to fear the unauthorized disclosure of the illegal tapes and the Starr Report materials, according to *Der Spiegel* (March 8, 1999). Europeans believe that an illegally taped person has the right to deny her consent to such disclosure and that it is particularly shocking when an officer of the law condones such violations or violates this right.

Bacharan in her book *Le piège* emphasizes the legal and political aspects of the situation, but she also follows it from Lewinsky's romantic point of view. She thinks that "the young woman absolutely had a right to carry on an affair with Bill Clinton, and absolutely had the right not to reveal it. And it was no fault of hers, much less a crime to want to hide it." Bacharan considers it criminal of Starr and his minions to threaten and intimidate Lewinsky with phony charges. "Nothing justifies the spying and sequestering of this young woman other than the ferocious desire of Ken Starr to have the head of the president, no matter under what pretext."[9] Bacharan is even more critical of Lewinsky's ordeal after the immunity agreement in the summer of 1998 when a team of Starr's investigators worked her over for many days: "What followed was a rape (*viol*) of the intimate life of a young woman who had nothing to reproach herself for with regard to the laws of her country." Every day, for several hours, she was subjected to the debriefing by the prosecutor's assistants. She had to tell everything, in minute detail, and accept a consensual search of her apartment, calendars, bills, check stubs, correspondence. Only the investigation of her purchases at the bookstore caused an uproar since it was contrary to American conceptions of human rights. Like Nixon ordering the burglary of Daniel Ellsberg's psychiatrist, Starr even subpoenaed the two psychologists in whom Lewinsky had confided several years earlier because of her depression, following her romance with the president: "The two shrinks spilled everything," even though they had been paid not by the court but by the Lewinsky family; they did so without regard to their professional obligation to maintain her confidentiality. "She told them that she, indeed, had orgasms with Bill—an orgasm! Here was the proof of the crime [of Bill]. It was a sexual relation after all, thought Starr." And only then did he call her to testify before the grand jury and his attorneys went all over it again, "a veritable festival of pornography."[10] When one sympathetic juror wanted to know what exactly had happened on the day of her arrest (January 16, 1998) and insisted in spite of prosecutors' objections and her evident fear to tell, Lewinsky refused to talk until her tormentor of that fateful day, Starr's deputy Mike Emmick, had left the room. Even American legal eagles raised their eyebrows at such "jurisprurience."[11]

European journalists were also outraged by the interrogation of Lewinsky's mother, Marcia Lewis, to extort from her information about her daughter's relationship with the president, an illegal prosecutorial maneuver in some European countries and considered profoundly immoral in all of them. "Can't the snoops stay out of the relationship between mother and daughter?" They were even more disturbed by reports that Lewinsky at one time was made to believe that her mother would have to go to jail if she, Monica, did not cooperate with Starr's office. As Bacharan wrote about the interrogation of Marcia Lewis: "When she appeared at the door [afterward], pale, undone, her lips trembling, her condition raised general indignation. How can one, at the end of the twentieth century in America, make a mother testify against her child, under such humiliating conditions, and because of a [sexual] peccadillo?" Lewinsky's father, on television, called the OIC investigators "Gestapo types . . . we have not seen anything like this since the Spanish Inquisition, Joseph McCarthy, the Third Reich."[12]

Bacharan's description was echoed by Peter Kornelius of the *Sueddeutsche Zeitung* (February 19, 1998) who reported a statement by Lewinsky to the effect that Starr had made her immunity contingent on her testifying to more than actually happened. The European press without exception reacted instinctively against the high-handed conduct of the independent counsel's office. In January 1999, when Lewinsky was forced by threat of withdrawal of her immunity to return to Washington in order to help the House managers in the Senate trial, photographs of her cloak-and-dagger "abduction" with her baseball cap pulled down to hide her face appeared all over European newspapers. The weekly *Die Zeit* (January 28, 1999) spoke of "the outrage that an American judge [Norma Holloway Johnson] forced Miss Lewinsky to testify before [the managers] who had no legal power over her." In spring 1999, when Lewinsky, to publicize her book *Monica's Story* (written with Andrew Morton), appeared on British television and autographed copies, the British media compared her to Princess Diana, another woman used by powerful men and then discarded. Her book signings drew large crowds, particularly young women. Some of this British reaction may, of course, have been intended by the publisher's media campaign to sell Lewinsky in print and on the screen. But it was hardly flattering to either Clinton or Starr.

PERCEPTIONS OF HILLARY CLINTON

It seems appropriate to add here a word or two about European perceptions of Hillary Rodham Clinton who, from the depths of ultra-right opprobrium in the early Clinton years, rose to belated media applause at the precise time that her husband was trapped by the ruses of the wily Starr. At the height of the impeachment drive, the European press frequently featured articles about the First Lady along with other persons of the high drama, but they did not forget her earlier tribulations with American talk radio hosts such as Limbaugh and other right-wing figures. On the eve of the congressional campaign of 1998, Michael Schwelien, for example, reminded readers in the weekly *Die Zeit* of Hamburg (October 29, 1998), how Emmett Tyrrell had already vented his spleen against her in 1992 in the ultra-right, Scaife-financed *American Spectator,* how the *National Review* in 1993 had described her as a "smiling barracuda," and how William Safire in the *New York Times* in 1994 had called her "a congenital liar." Schwelien commented on Hillary's belated acceptance by the United States media as, perhaps, the result of her humiliation by the Lewinsky scandal in which she so courageously "stood by her man." She had already gallantly done so in the midst of the Gennifer Flowers scandal of 1992 and it had done her little good. The conservative *Die Welt,* a large German daily, also paid tribute to the timely support of the First Lady in 1992, 1994, and again in 1998: ". . . he can still count on help [in the congressional elections] from his wife who was more hurt by his White House affair than anyone . . . In the land of soap operas, Hillary Clinton is showing signs . . . of overcoming the crisis on an emotional level, and with the public's help . . . But is all this enough to survive impeachment?" (September 12, 1998).

Bacharan also followed Hillary Clinton's fate and achievements 1992 with sympathetic comment. She described Hillary's pivotal role in 1998, from denouncing "the vast right-wing conspiracy" to her successful campaigning in the November elections, especially with appeals to women voters not to give in to the Republican juggernaut: "She, who once [in 1993-1994] was the most detested woman in America," wrote Bacharan, "has now become its darling, rising like the most popular political star."[13] At the end of the year, Hillary was once more chosen "the most popular woman in America" by a survey. In early September 1998, Safire surprised both Americans and Europeans with his sudden change of tune when he was apparently swayed by the defiant public admission of "improper relations" by Clinton—the same televised, and belligerent admission that angered even some Democrats on Capitol Hill—the man Safire had earlier accused of stealing the 1996 elections with Asian campaign contributions. In his essay in the *Guardian*, "Hang in There, Bill," Safire praised the president for *not* showing "remorse" and for refusing to resign, an action that would have weakened the presidency. He credited "his stalwart wife . . . [who] rejected such self-flagellation" (September 10, 1998).

But the European coverage was not all positive. Back in 1994, Arve Solstad wrote in the liberal *Dagbladet* of Oslo that the First Lady inspired enthusiasm in some people but fear in others (quoted in *World Press Review,* February 1994). In 1996, Martin Walker did a piece on spouses of presidential candidates in America, in which he conceded that Hillary had been made a scapegoat. He added, however, that "a ridiculously high proportion of the Clinton presidency's woes can be blamed on the widespread discomfort with her role," as with the health care reform and her missing legal records (*Guardian Weekly*, July 26, 1996). European responses to her exploration of a possible senatorial candidacy in New York, on the other hand, were overwhelmingly positive. The *Financial Times* of London, for example, referred to her as "formidable Hillary" who had "frozen the New York senatorial race . . . Whatever she decides, the post-impeachment world would appear to be Mrs. Clinton's oyster" (quoted in *World Press Review*, April 1999).

This may also be the place to mention the seemingly towering rages attributed to Starr against uncooperative women, beginning with the First Lady when she could not or would not produce the records on Whitewater or her own law firm records. Bacharan has described how she was subpoenaed and deliberately made to walk through the press mobs and photographers on her way to testifying before the independent counsel. Starr's fury against Susan McDougal and Julie Hiatt Steele are legend. The European press did not cover these cases to any length, although individual Europeans whom I know reacted passionately to the stories of brutal harassment by the Office of Independent Counsel. This was particularly true of the "Joan of Ark[ansas]," Susan McDougal, who was imprisoned on contempt charges sanctioned by the judge and mistreated most cruelly for 18 months—some of the time, despite major back trouble, in shackles and solitary confinement "like a murderess."[14] Part of her punishment consisted of being dragged from jail to jail in a van—in a colored jailsuit that would denote to other prisoners in the van that she was a stoolie, a snitch, and provoke aggressive and insulting behavior on their part—and through a jury trial on charges of embezzlement from Nancy Mehta (wife of symphony conductor Zubin Mehta)—which a jury threw out in the shortest of sessions. Starr and the presiding judge ordered this mistreatment because McDougal flatly refused to tell incriminating lies about her old friends and business partners, the Clintons. Eighteen months for silence! Some Europeans were as deeply shocked by the abusiveness of the OIC and American justice as they were about the arrest and intimidation of Lewinsky on January 16, 1998. "Are there no men in your country who will stand up to Kenneth Starr?" asked one European lawyer friend.

The case of Julie Hiatt Steele centers around Kathleen Willey, a White House volunteer who, according to her former friend, insisted that Steele confirm Willey's story of having been groped and kissed against her will by Bill Clinton, a story contradicted in part by none other than Linda Tripp. Steele at first complied with Willey's request and then emphatically retracted her statement for *Newsweek* magazine, which infuriated the special prosecutor. He launched an investigation of her—for what crime?—seizing bank statements and interrogating family members, and discovered that she had adopted a Romanian orphan in 1990. Bacharan writes, "He let her know that the child could be taken away from her if they discovered the slightest irregularity in the transaction, and indicted her for perjury. A veritable Mafia extortion."[15]

Steele was finally tried in the spring of 1999 on three counts of obstruction of justice and one of making false statements, the only trial resulting directly from the Lewinsky affair. The unrelenting prosecutor hoped to demonstrate that Steele had somehow been pressured by the Clinton people to change her account, just as Lewinsky was supposed to confess that she had been pressured or bought off with the offer, via Vernon Jordan, of a good job. The trial ended in a mistrial and, once again, the special prosecutor had to make do without corroborating evidence to charge the president with obstruction of justice. Starr's reported rages about uncooperative women, a European psychiatrist told me, fit very well into his psychological portrait as an anal-obsessive Freudian type. And so did the story told by Starr's aged mother, that as a small boy he liked to sit in front of the television, polishing his shoes. According to American press reports, his mother also insisted that he was "a normal boy," although no one had questioned this fact.

Jeffrey Toobin also mentions the curious contrast between Starr's reported courtliness toward women and his consistent failure to employ female deputy attorneys. Toobin comments on Starr's obsession with appearing tough and macho, even when it may have hurt his pursuit of the president and when more experienced deputies in his office offered more balanced advice (for example, regarding the immunity agreement with Monica Lewinsky). If Starr had accepted the agreement offered to him in February 1998 by her attorney, William Ginsburg—rather than stalling for five months in hopes that she might become even more terrorized into cooperation with his schemes with the passage of time—the president might actually have been forced out by the furies of the media circus of early 1998. Starr was apparently haunted by the thought that he might appear as something of a Caspar Milquetoast even though his approach to running the OIC was anything but hands on.[16] He and his deputy Jackie Bennett also seem to have thought of the entire White House as "an organized crime family," which justified resorting to high-handed measures such as subpoenaing press adviser Sidney Blumenthal for allegedly bad-mouthing the OIC among his press contacts. After his grand jury interrogation (February 26, 1998), Blumenthal responded appropriately by telling a press conference how he had been forced to disclose his conversations with all the major newspapers, magazines, and television networks—he named them all—and "what reporters had told me about Ken Starr's prosecutors." For once, the media became alarmed at the bullying by the OIC.

To make matters still worse, Starr in one of his asides to the press, which waited at his doorstep while he put out the trash, claimed that "[Blumenthal's] lies, distortions about civil servants [meaning himself] to be spread about . . . have no place in our First Amendment universe."[17] Starr evidently had not read that amendment to the Constitution in some time. His attitude toward the White House staff and the first couple was quite typical of Clinton's pursuers. As Toobin relates, the "belief was pervasive among those who tried to drive the president out of office . . . that some grander conspiracy was sure to be uncovered [next week or next month] just over the horizon. Of course this evidence was never located because it did not exist . . ." There was also a curious, paranoid expectation of some dreadful retribution threatening from the Clintons, a theme frequently echoed by Linda Tripp, the Joneses, the Arkansas state troopers, and other Clinton foes.

LYING: THE TRUE ESSENCE OF POLITICS?

As the Senate trial began to wind down, the news magazine *Der Spiegel* (February 8, 1999) reminded its readers that, back in

1976, "when [presidential candidate] Jimmy Carter promised the American people he would never lie to them . . . Senator Frank Church had said: He [Carter] just denied the true essence of politics." Indeed, all politicians lie, are expected to lie, and may often admit it if they are pinned down. Conservative, and even Christian, politicians worth their salt also lie a lot, and they are more likely to lie about it as well, which is, of course, a valid reason to distrust them, particularly when they bandy about words like "trust" and "character." Why politicians lie so much—media people are another profession steeped in lying—may stem at least in part from the need to reconcile varying constituencies with conflicting goals and policies. To get elected or reelected, an effective politician simply has to tell different stories to different groups, and, perhaps, also at different times. Some of our most successful recent presidents, especially Reagan, were extraordinarily skilled in telling whoppers and little white lies that were vital to their leadership and charisma. In Reagan's case, this skill earned the president the appellation of "the great communicator," who could tell apocryphal stories about welfare queens in Cadillacs and name a fearsome nuclear missile the "peace keeper." I am mentioning all this because of the prominent role that the charge of lying, made against President Clinton by grass-roots Republicans, played in rationalizing their support for the impeachment campaign. Would it surprise the reader to learn that the impeachment-minded Republicans also lied a lot during their campaign to topple the president and that, in fact, much of Washington politics is based on a sea of prevarications?

As *Time* magazine reported (November 30, 1998) when Starr testified before the House Judiciary Committee, he said: "No one is entitled to lie under oath simply because he or she does not like the questions or because he believes the case is frivolous or . . . politically motivated . . . The Supreme Court has emphatically and repeatedly rejected the notion that there is ever a privilege to lie." Neither Starr nor *Time* cited an actual Supreme Court opinion for this hazy claim but it seemed to satisfy *Time*'s journalists. Bacharan commented that the special prosecutor, "to justify his enraged chase, clamored like a child stomping his feet after being disciplined: 'We must get at the truth. There is never an excuse for perjury. Never, never, never.'" But this statement is false, says Bacharan, who obviously knows her American law: "Lying under oath is not necessarily [always] considered a crime. For there are lies and there are lies. For a witness to lie before the judge in order to protect a criminal or denounce an innocent person is not the same as lying to protect oneself . . . one must prove that the lie is 'intentional' and 'material,' that it is sufficiently important to change the outcome of a trial."[18] In a civil suit, furthermore, it is most unusual to prosecute a witness for false testimony.

Clinton's lying about his consensual relationship with Lewinsky clearly had no such effect upon the question whether Clinton had sexually harassed Paula Jones. In other words, in this and in pretending that there is no difference between civil and criminal perjury, Starr and his helpmates on the House Judiciary Committee boldly lied to us. At least Starr and his deputies—not to mention the exprosecutors among the impeachers in the House—must have known that *their lies* were deliberate and would have an enormous impact on the outcome of their case against the president. The House managers, furthermore, like all newly or reelected House members, had sworn to perform their duties in accordance with the Constitution of the United States. In other words, they lied under oath. And, again, the media blithely repeated all these lies without checking their veracity and legality. With our first president, George Washington, at least—notwithstanding the cherry tree tales of Parson Weems—lying enabled General Washington to operate a superb spy network and to leak disinformation to the British troops, which may have done as much for American independence as the sufferings of his brave winter soldiers during the protracted war of independence.

Starr carefully timed the release of his report so that it would influence the congressional elections of 1998 and, he hoped, produce a mandate for impeachment. Of course, the opposite happened. Three days after the Republican electoral disaster of November 3, 1998, the *Los Angeles Times* reported in an editorial on November 6, 1998 that almost two thirds of the people were tired of the whole Lewinsky matter and were against impeachment. In addition to that, exit polls revealed that well over half of the voters were dissatisfied with how the scandal was dealt with by the Republicans in Congress. Under these circumstances, the editorial asserted, "political common sense demands that the impeachment hearings be concluded quickly, for the benefit of all." Similar passages could be found in a number of other newspapers. Starr and the House Republican leadership, however, chose to ignore the voters' message just as they had ignored a year of public opinion polls opposing their attempts at removing Clinton. They simply pretended that the electorate had *not* said no in an unambiguous way.

This was one more operational lie to grease the skids for the removal of the president. An operational lie is a deception intended to facilitate a course of action quite at variance with what the deceivers are actually saying. The first such lie had been shared more broadly with the media: it was that the Clinton-Lewinsky scandal had begun only in January 1998 and that, somehow, the president had brought it upon the country at that time. The Lewinsky affair started in late 1995 and was long over before Starr's minions descended upon her and undertook to manufacture the perjurious difference between what they knew from the Tripp tapes and from her affidavit and Clinton's testimony before the Jones grand jury. The campaign to drive the president from office by hook or crook, however, also had begun long before 1998, in December 1993 with Troopergate, and perhaps even earlier. Such operational lies clearly affect the outcome and shift guilt and innocence around.

The second blatant lie—there were many major lies embedded in the process of disgracing the president—was the claim that this was "not about sex" but a matter of "defending the rule of law against tyranny," to quote Chairman Hyde. The third operational lie was that the Starr Report (regardless of Starr's dubious methods) contained not just bits of evidence—uncorroborated by witnesses and untempered by challenges from opposing counsel—for examination by the Judiciary Committee but that it was the final set of charges of Hyde and his team, who took them as transmitted by Starr and never even chose to question witnesses other than Starr. As his ethics advisor Sam Dash pointed out, Starr had no mandate to advocate anything but only to dig for facts relevant to the investigation. A fourth operational lie was Starr's denials under oath that the OIC had been leaking crucial information to the media and that they had set up the entrapment of Lewinsky and Clinton in perjury with the transparent maneuver described above. We also know from many sources that Starr and the OIC lied again and again about their early contacts with the Jones lawyers, including the OIC denial necessary to obtain Reno's approval for extending their investigation to the Lewinsky affair.

To try to cover up these operational lies with the rationalizations that Jesus and Lincoln did not base their fateful decisions on public opinion polls either was another obvious pack of untruths. Before the House voted a second time on its impeachment charges, in early January of 1999, it was an operational lie also to proceed with the impeachment with the help of the lame-duck Republican Congress members who had already been defeated. Starr also waited until after that election before admitting that, after four years of investigation, he had come up empty-handed on all charges regarding Whitewater, Foster's suicide, and assorted-gates. Under the circumstances of an imminent election, which he hoped would encourage proceeding with the impeachment, this was another crude manipulation of the facts, an operational lie. On other occasions, too, he pretended that there were still charges imminent when there were apparently none.

A sixth and truly monstrous lie was perpetrated when the Republican House leadership pretended that the Constitution intended the extreme remedy of impeachment of the president for offenses such as this sex scandal and the dubious legal charges of civil perjury and obstruction of justice that OIC tried to base on it. Even the Republican-dominated Senate failed to support these charges with a majority vote, much less the required two-thirds. Hundreds of America's most respected constitutional experts and historians told the Judiciary Committee that Clinton's offenses—even if proven beyond a shadow of a doubt, which they were not—would never reach the level required by the Constitution for presidential impeachment. The committee leadership simply ignored the expert advice and, in some instances, claimed the experts must be biased in favor of the president. One does not have to defend Clinton to be aware that all these operational lies highlight the glaring contradictions in Clinton's prosecution for lying.

Knowledgeable European observers, of course, noticed all these lies and logical disconnects, as we have seen, just as they had become aware that this sex scandal was being prosecuted by a number of hypocritical Republicans—Hyde, Burton, Chenoweth, Gingrich, Barr, Livingston, and the half dozen more that Flynt had promised to expose in his *Hustler* magazine. The shell game of using a sex scandal to advance legal charges, and to use the sex charges to drive the president into resignation, is in itself a monument to the mendacity that characterized the impeachment campaign from 1994 to 1999. To most Europeans, the whole case, whether sex charges or legal charges, reeked of hypocrisy and partisan hatred, despite the American media and the Washington crowd choosing to ignore the obvious.

The United States media began reluctantly to catch on to their own one-sided approach only at a rather late stage, around October and November 1998, and not always seriously enough to investigate it. In fact, even in the pages of major newspapers such as the *Los Angeles Times*, a curiously schizophrenic attitude prevailed throughout the year and a half following the Starr Report. On the one hand, the papers began to publish almost all the dubious facts about the right-wing conspirators and their quest. As early as

September 24, 1998, a *Los Angeles Times* editorial criticized the OIC and the Starr Report for falsifying Lewinsky's clear denials that she had been urged to lie and promised a job if she did. On October 11, 1998, the paper reported the right-wing conspiracy and named the lawyers involved while Starr was still falsely denying that he had been plotting with the Jones lawyers and had permitted Tripp to inform them of Lewinsky's affidavit. (*Los Angeles Times,* September 24 and October 11, 1998).

On the other hand, every now and then, the paper's editorials, cartoons, and features seemed to indicate that the writers evidently had never read the ugly revelations about Starr, Tripp, and Hyde in their own newspaper. On the last day of 1999, for example, the paper reprinted its report of the House impeachment vote of December 20, 1998, as part of its millennium series, "Stories that Shaped the Century." The reprint was accompanied by a commentary by Richard A. Serrano, repeating all the old invective and distortions without mentioning the conspiracies of financial sponsors and right-wing lawyers and institutes disclosed in earlier issues of the paper. It began with the image of Clinton's finger-wagging denial of sexual relations with Lewinsky and claimed: "Had he told the truth, the Year of the Scandal might have ended right there." There was no mention of the deliberate misinterpretation of the Constitutional requirements for presidential impeachment. The article went on to state that the Senate then tried him "on the charges of hiding his Oval Office sexual romps with . . . Lewinsky," (not civil perjury and obstruction of justice). It did not mention that Paula Jones's suit was dismissed, nor add that Clinton paid Jones $850,000 and was fined another $90,000 for contempt of court. Starr's departure was noted as that of the prosecutor who "never got his man, Bill Clinton" and who was criticized for "acting more like a black-masked inquisitor than a white-plumed knight crusading against immorality." There was no hint of the specific charges of prosecutorial misconduct that the *Los Angeles Times* itself had reported on previous occasions, such as in the trials of McDougal and Steele. The article appeared to represent the latest version of the propaganda of the impeachment drive.

Once the tide had begun to turn, however, the American press for the first time provided its readers a peek at the striking contradictions, for example, between Lott's statement on the level of presidential misconduct required for impeachment in September 1998 and his statement when he and nine other House Republicans opposed all the impeachment charges against Nixon in 1974: "It is our judgment . . . that the framers of the United States Constitution intended that the president should be removable from office by the legislative branch only for serious misconduct dangerous to the system of government established by the Constitution," he declared back then in their minority report. But the majority of House members and senators who had supported Nixon's impeachment believed the president's conduct had met this description. Twenty-five years later, Lott (who had been advising Gingrich how to proceed) told the press: "I think, frankly, bad conduct is enough for impeachment . . . if you have brought disrepute on the office, that is sufficient. It doesn't necessarily have to be a legal violation" (*Los Angeles Times*, September 30, 1998). Never mind the Constitution.

The same paper's December recollections of Hyde's eloquent defense of lying by operatives of the Reagan administration, such as Oliver North, when they were faced with the Iran-Contra investigation in 1987, were another case in point. "It just seems to me too simplistic," Hyde said back then, to condemn all lying, especially lies in the name of anti-communism; "In the murkier grayness of the real world, choices must often be made." Back then, he also cast scorn upon the "disconcerting and distasteful whiff of moralist and institutional self-righteousness" of the Iran-Contra hearings or, as he put it, the "witch hunt" (*Los Angeles Times*, December 4, 1998). Three days before these statements reappeared, Hyde had said regarding the case against Clinton,

"Lying poisons justice. If we are to defend justice and the rule of law, lying must have consequences." No wonder Europeans found it hard to take the impeachment drive against Clinton very seriously.

At the end of the Senate trial, congressional Democrats urged the Department of Justice to investigate the web of lies concocted by Starr's office in preparing the impeachment case against Clinton. Prominent among them was Starr's assertion, for the purpose of winning Reno's approval to extend his authority from Whitewater to the Lewinsky affair, that his office had had "no contacts" with the Paula Jones lawyers and did not engage in collusion with them to entrap the president. The *Washington Post* and *Los Angeles Times* reported that the Department of Justice put the OIC on notice of an investigation and quoted Senator Tom Harkin to the effect that this had been "a classic sting operation." Faced with this hard evidence of the conspiracy by right-wing attorneys, Democratic House Judiciary Committee counsel Abbe Lowell said: "This impeachment stands on Ken Starr's shoulders, and if there is something weak about those shoulders, it's important that history understands that." Since then, Connecticut public defender Frank Mandanici has moved that Starr be reprimanded or disbarred for unethical conduct during his five years as independent counsel, citing among other things Starr's conflict of interest as independent counsel while representing tobacco company clients. He also produced revealing statements by Steele and by another victim of Starr's investigative methods, Stephen A. Smith, who related: "I was provided a written script [by the OIC], containing false testimony . . . and this script was to be read by me as my testimony under oath to a federal grand jury." Steele and McDougal had earlier made the same assertions about Starr's Mafia methods to extort testimony against Clinton. Mandanici's motion caused all seven federal judges in Little Rock, Arkansas, to recuse themselves from the new effort to disbar Clinton (*Los Angeles Times,* January 4, 2000).

STARR'S PARTING SHOTS

This account of the currency of lies among the advocates of impeachment would not be complete without mention of the parting shots of the spinmeister of this impeachment, Starr himself. Starr had already lied upon his appointment when he reportedly said he "liked Robert Fiske," his predecessor as special prosecutor. When Starr was at his peak in the impeachment drive, repeating the substance of his charges before the House Judiciary Committee in November 1998, he did so under oath. In fact, millions of Americans saw him being sworn in at the beginning, and there is no reason to assume that he was no longer under oath when he answered questions from the Democrats and their counsel on the committee. On this occasion he denied, for example, that the OIC had wanted Lewinsky to wear a device to record conversations with Jordan, Currie, and Clinton himself; it took the irrepressible William Ginsburg, Lewinsky's attorney, to denounce this scheme as "un-American." Starr was also asked whether the OIC had leaked confidential information from the Jones grand jury to the media. His adamant denial induced United States District Judge Norma Holloway Johnson to appoint a master to investigate dozens of such leaks. The judge ruled there was prima facie evidence that a number of news articles had indeed been published from such leaks, and she directed the Justice Department to bring contempt charges against all persons involved. This was a serious charge that could have resulted in substantial fines and the disbarment of several OIC counsels. The most notorious leaks seem to have come from Jackie Bennett to Susan Schmidt and Peter Baker of the Washington Post, but there were others. In the case of Charles G. Bakaly III (who has since been fired), there was the accusation that he had told the New York Times in the middle of Clinton's Senate trial that Starr planned to indict the president even before Clinton left office.

The investigation of some 24 earlier leaks is still continuing and may result in Starr's prosecution for perjury. In the meantime, Starr also tried to blame the grand jury leaks on the White House which, according to newly released court papers "has employed a concentrated strategy of leaking harmful material to the media at an early stage to reduce long-term damage." To block further prosecution—or, some say, to obstruct justice—the special prosecutor in July 1999 turned to the Reagan- and Bush-appointed judges of the federal appeals courts, the usual last line of defense of conservative causes, to intervene and overturn Judge Johnson's findings on various grounds. His appeal, which has meanwhile been sealed, was joined by the Justice Department which is reportedly worried that a precedent might be set that would hamstring its own prosecutors from informing the media.

Predictably, the panel of three federal appeals court judges (two Republicans and one Democrat) squelched Judge Johnson's action, citing among other points that the secrecy of grand jury materials, according to Rule 6-E, applied only to individuals and not to collective entities like the OIC, which could not be held responsible for the actions of its staff. It was a convenient technicality for the federal appeals court which is usually busy overturning the stray decisions of lower courts. The most prominent source of court decisions that fail the litmus test of conservative ideology is the large Ninth District Court (West), which includes a number of Carter appointees and has been publicly accused by the chair of the Senate Judiciary Committee, Orrin Hatch, of being a hotbed of "radical judges" who "pay no attention to what the law is."

In the last weeks of his tenure, Starr undertook to burnish his image before a few carefully selected audiences. In late September 1999 he addressed students at Yale University, emphasizing that he needed to "get his side of the story" before the public so that history could give this "unfortunate chapter" its proper place. He also urged the students not to grow cynical about pursuing careers in public service, an amazing piece of advice considering that it came from Starr. Here as in other venues, as before 500 business and civic leaders at Town Hall Los Angeles, he reiterated his amazement that some people perceived him as having pursued a vendetta against the Clintons and that it was perhaps a mistake for him to have taken on, in addition to Whitewater, the issues of Travelgate, Fostergate, Filegate, and finally Monicagate, each of which should really have had its own independent counsel. He did not mention that he had been the one to request all these extensions of his hunting license. Before friendly audiences, he flashed his charm and worked the crowds, claiming he really admired President Clinton's talent and energy "but was less impressed . . . when [Clinton] took a poll on whether to tell the truth" (*Los Angeles Times,* September 16, 1999).

In an interview on the *NewsHour* with Jim Lehrer (October 18, 1999), Starr was asked what he thought he had accomplished. He answered that "he had served faithfully the principles of our legal system . . . [and found] and assessed the relevant facts in a professional manner." Belatedly acknowledging his ethical adviser Sam Dash's criticism, he added, ". . . once the case was referred [by means of the Starr Report to the House], it became a matter for the American people [and their representatives] to decide, a political matter." Notwithstanding the wording of the Report and his oral presentation in late November 1998 before the House Judiciary Committee, Starr later claimed that in his report he "only meant to say that these were *possible* reasons for impeachment." And the public perception (!) "that the president's offenses rose to the level of impeachment," he said in October 1999, "was wrong." He did not mention that the entire Republican majority of the House and Senate had gotten this same wrong idea from his Report, but added, "It is untrue that I was out to get the president as Clinton said . . . [and] the public thinks. The president could have fired me. A prosecutor acting in excess should be removed, but that was never done."

Spinmeister Starr, of course, did not mention that the president could never have attempted to fire him (as Nixon had done with his Watergate prosecutor, Archibald Cox, with predictable results) and expected to survive in office. His suggestion was on about the same level as that of people who have suggested the president could just have defaulted or taken the Fifth Amendment instead of testifying before the Jones grand jury. Presidents under the gun of impeachment investigations cannot claim the same individual rights as other American citizens. Starr also defended himself against the "totally unfair" charge of "prosecutorial overzealousness," claiming that "the public perception that I was doing one gate after another (Travelgate, Filegate, Monicagate) was completely wrong." An Italian friend watching this astonishing performance on public television, quipped: "Pinocchio, you've got competition."

The same friend also recalled from Al Franken's book about Rush Limbaugh the long list of Limbaugh's lies about all kinds of policy matters. On the whole, however, Limbaugh's lies seem to be based on his abysmal ignorance more than deliberate deception, whereas Starr's lies have been conscious and very deliberate.[19] In public opinion polls by that time, 73 percent of the American respondents considered Starr "a loser," but there were still 20 percent—amounting to millions of Republican grass-roots voters—who thought he was "a winner." A picket at the Town Hall Los Angeles gathering at the Hotel Intercontinental carried a sign, "Hey Starr: Impeach this!" When questioned by a reporter, the picket said: "I feel that Ken Starr is a right-wing sociopath with an abnormal interest in other people's sex lives and no regard at all for the Constitution" (*Los Angeles Times,* September 16, 1999).

It is rather amusing that it seemed to take so many Republican lies and deceptive maneuvers to show that President Clinton may have lied repeatedly and used transparent legal circumlocutions in this sex scandal. This irony did not escape foreign journalists who, of course, had not necessarily expected the principals of a sex scandal to tell the truth. And, of course, all politicians worth their salt do lie a lot, and for good reason. It is simply not possible to hold a national party together, without at least a few statements of misrepresentation. Neither is it prudent for an elected leader to admit that electoral promises frequently exceed what an honest politician can expect to deliver. In the crucible of electoral competition, and possibly to head off rivals who may be more irresponsible, political leadership demands cleverness in word and deed. No one becomes known as a "great communicator" or a mythical leadership figure like General Charles de Gaulle—whose biggest lie was to pretend that he would never set Algeria free—without taking liberties with the unvarnished truth. The great preoccupation of Republicans in 1998 with Clinton's alleged lying was at best a relapse into simplistic requirements of childhood education and naive images of American leaders and politics on the level of Parson Weems's stories of President Washington and the cherry tree. At worst, it was just another bit of hypocrisy—in other words, a Republican lie.

The many lies mentioned still do not exhaust the context of larger, more powerful structures of dishonesty in today's Washington politics, structures on which the intensity of partisan conflict rests. The London *Observer* article focusing on Starr's conflict of interest—being an "independent counsel" investigating Clinton *and* working for the tobacco industry—was at least partially right. For decades now, this industry has had Congress in a double-nelson grip of campaign finance frustrating all efforts to curb the mayhem of tobacco on the nation's health. The irresponsible and extremely partisan choice of Starr by the Sentelle panel of federal judges at the precise time that the tobacco industry was battling against Clinton administration efforts to regulate it, to force it to pay for the damage it causes, and to cease advertising to young people is highlighted further by the reactions of Congress. It was a macabre joke by any measure when the industry argued in 1999 that Congress's decades-long refusal to regulate it—like the congressional refusal to recognize the harmfulness and addictiveness of nicotine for so many years—was proof that the health impact of tobacco was really benign. Even worse, a year earlier the industry had been condemned by a legal settlement to pay hundreds of billions of dollars in compensation, but its congressional lackeys inserted a clause into the federal budget promising the industry a tax write-off of $50 billion for the resultant losses. Our venal Congress, it seems, simply cannot do without tobacco money and, to make sure it remains dependent on it, a majority of Congress resists campaign finance reform.

Similarly, the gun lobby (especially the National Rifle Association) has at least a half-nelson on Congress and, particularly, the Republican party which has enjoyed heavy NRA contributions for many years. Add to this the religious right—suppliers of both money and foot soldiers for election campaigns; the vanguard of the religious right, Randall Terry of Operation Rescue reportedly sported signs calling for the impeachment of Clinton as early as 1993. Add also certain industries and insurance companies that have tended to resist business and environmental regulation, and there emerges a coalition adamant against any campaign reform that would lessen the dependence of elected federal officials on their campaign money and support. It is no accident that these groups have focused on Clinton as a political adversary to be eliminated, a man whose fund-raising prowess and political savvy have made him and his reforms independent of their financial leverage. Public opinion polls have shown again and again that large majorities of Americans favor tobacco regulation, gun control, environmental and workplace regulation, and access to abortion. But the key to the success of this holding action against such reforms remains holding back all efforts at campaign finance reform. As long as "soft money" freely flows to the friends of these special interests in Congress, a system of financial corruption prevails that makes all players scramble constantly for campaign funds. The patent dishonesty of this situation cannot be veiled behind statements that "campaign finance reform is not an issue important to the voters" or behind investigations of past campaign finance violations. It is the future control of financing that matters.

A second structure of political dishonesty involves partisanship and the judiciary. Is it really a mere accident that Chief Justice William Rehnquist, an ardent Republican all his life, prominently argued (with support from Justice Antonin Scalia, another strong Republican) the lifting of presidential immunity in Jones's civil case? And that it was Rehnquist again who appointed the panel headed by Sentelle, another militant Republican, and that this panel (upon the advice of the Republican ultras Helms and Faircloth from tobacco-growing North Carolina) then selected the ultra-Republican Starr as an independent counsel to investigate the Democratic president? How do these judges interpret the word "independent"? The federal judiciary and, above all the Supreme Court, ought to be like Caesar's wife and avoid any shadow of partisan impropriety.

The penetration of our courts, law firms, and law schools by the ultra-right, 25,000-member Federalist Society is as alarming today as were the charges of extreme left-wing subversion of another day. As Jerry M. Landay wrote in the *Washington Monthly* (March 2000): "Starr and the OIC benefited enormously from the [conspiratorial] efforts of a network of well-placed lawyers who, like Starr and other Republican luminaries, are members of, or linked to, the Federalist Society. Most of the self-styled 'elves' who helped Linda Tripp's tapes find their way into Starr's hands had links to the society. And without the 'elves' handiwork . . . Starr's investigation might never have gotten out of the blocks." Far from having anything to do with the Federalists of John Adams's era or the *Federalist Papers,* the agenda of the society seems to be one of Clinton-bashing and conservative revolution in American law and politics. Supreme Court Justices Thomas and Scalia, Robert Bork, and Orrin Hatch are prominent icons, according to Landay. But the society has been most successful at recruiting young lawyers and bringing together a large range of right-wing groups under its aegis.

The sea of lies on which the clipper ship of impeachment pursued its uncertain course naturally attracted sarcastic comment in the European press, which saw in it "a piece of political theatre of which the voters had written the epilog on November 3 [1998]: The 42nd president of the United States will not be removed from office" (*Le Figaro,* November 20, 1998). They saw the humor in "an unpopular and decapitated Congress [without Speaker-elect Livingston], the Republicans demoralized by the public opinion polls, but the president smiling in this 'tragicomedy of impeachment'" (December 21, 1998). But they were also aware how, at the beginning of the Senate trial, "the infernal machine now undertook to push the [dignified] senators into a [similar] excess of accusations and partisan bitterness [as in the House]" (January 8, 1999). *Le Figaro* correspondent Mével even imagined how "sex will reenter the debate after having been banned since the Starr Report of September" as soon as "the voluptuous Monica Lewinsky" was made to testify live about "her stories of alluring underwear, the spiced cigar, and the uncleaned dress," and about "how and where he touched me" (January 8, 1999). Fortunately, he turned out to be wrong.

A MURDERLESS LYNCHING?

European journalists tried hard to cast this sex scandal and its pursuit by the media and the Republicans in Congress into a recognizable simile. The London *Guardian* (quoted in *World Press Review*, March 1999) compared it to the seventeenth century-Salem witch hunt: "the Republicans are pushing on with this Salem-style purge to root out the evildoer in the White House." At about the same time, the *South China Morning Post* of Hong Kong, with a widely current phrase, wrote of "the sexual McCarthyism sweeping through government . . . [that] will spread its poison far beyond the White House." *Le Monde* (September 13-14, 1998) also complained of the "new McCarthyism . . . replacing the panicky fear of communism—an American curiosity that is simply exotic to our Latin culture." In *Scotsman* of Edinburgh, Gavin Eisler wrote, "Washington is a city of cannibals . . . Bill Clinton is the main dish" (December 1998, quoted in *World Press Review*, February 1999). *Le Figaro* of January 1999 (quoted by *World Press Review*, March 1999) spoke of "the United States inventing a new genre, the dirty trial, broadcast live despite the opposition of the majority of the American public." And then, as previously mentioned, there was frequent reference to American sexual Puritanism or neo-Victorian Puritanism (*L'Express*, June 12-18, 1997), in spite of the overwhelming evidence in the polls of large majorities of skeptical Americans who, while expressing a measure of personal criticism of Clinton's conduct, were clearly against the pursuit of the president. We are left to wonder which of these images captures the essence of this dramatic persecution? Which model seemed to persuade European journalists the most?

The dirty trial model presents an image that permits a variety of roles, ranging from the manipulations of ultra-right federal judges and prosecutors over the evasiveness of the accused president and his team of lawyers to the skeptical public, which nevertheless was fascinated enough to watch the prurient spectacle. As Hugo Bütler wrote in the conservative *Neue Zuercher Zeitung* in September 1998 (quoted in *World Press Review,* November 1998): "The bigoted sanctimoniousness with which Clinton's moralistic judges [in the House Judiciary Committee] are pursuing him is as undignified as the president's sexual affair . . . [by turning the Starr documents over to the media and the Internet] they have made show-trial judges of the general public." When we recall other show trials, however, such as the Stalinist purge trials of old Bolsheviks in the thirties, some obvious differences come to mind. First of all, neither the House nor the Senate proceedings had the visual focus of the accused person in the dock. To be sure, there was the Starr Report in newspapers and on the worldwide Internet which put Clinton into a kind of media pillory of the late twentieth century. There was also the purloined grand jury videotape—a fizzle according to most comments in the American press—that allowed Starr and Hyde to put the accused Clinton into a television dock before 20 million Americans. An editorial in *Rolling Stone* (November 12, 1998) even suggested that "the broadcast of this videotape was [Clinton's] just and fitting punishment." But there were no live witnesses (the managers asked for them belatedly and in vain at the Senate trial), no dramatic confrontations between witnesses and questioning attorneys, and no final conviction. Somehow, the model of the Stalinist show trial never materialized. The dubious nature of the legal charges—though this had not stopped the communist purge trials of the 1930s which raised even more unbelievable charges—on the back of a sex scandal in the nineties simply failed to move the public as other show trials had.

The model of Puritanism also fails to fit the profile even though Arthur Miller, the author of the drama *The Crucible* portraying the Salem witch trials of 1696, seems to think it does, perhaps because of the screaming hysteria in the House at the time of the impeachment debate. The pervasive hypocrisy of many key pursuers of the president, exposed effectively by the Internet news journal *Salon*, by Larry Flynt, and, of course, by their own dubious image of saintliness put the lie to comparisons with the Puritans, who in their day were quite sincerely living in a God-centered mental universe. The Clinton-haters of the nineties were no Puritan saints and few people really believed them to be sincere. Puritanism received the vote of several papers, including the *Guardian* of London which, at one time, had portrayed Starr rather charitably as a "Puritan Lone Ranger, representative of an upstanding, God-fearing middle America horrified by the libertine ways of the Clintons" (November 20, 1998). Actually, the non-inhaling, sexually half-hearted Clinton is hardly typical of his protest generation of 1968, as Europeans would call it. Even his resistance to the Vietnam War was tempered by a fear that he might thereby jeopardize his future political career. As far as I can determine, Clinton's dreams and ambitions have always conformed much more closely to those of an all-American boy scout who wanted nothing more than to grow up to be president—a boy scout with some flaws perhaps—than those of the 1968ers. This is not to deny, as Massimo Fini put it in the conservative *Il Tempo* of Rome, "the American obsession with sex in their Puritan heritage and, therefore, in their consummate hypocrisy..." (September, 1998, quoted in *World Press Review,* October 1998). The liberal *Le Monde* of September 23, 1998 followed more closely the Salem witch hunt model when it commented: "Starr makes of his ambitions a terrifying moral order in which sex means sin, and sexual relations, even between consenting adults, are always shameful." But who were the witches in the Clinton-Lewinsky witch hunt? Tripp and Lucianne Goldberg? Gingrich? Starr? Were they the witch hunters, the hunted—as Tripp and Starr claimed to be—or what?

McCarthyism in its day had the good excuse that there had been an immense sea change in American foreign policy from wartime comradeship with the Soviet Union against Nazi Germany to the Cold War. This profound change not only upset the American public and the media. It created a pervasive fear, which at times became hysterical, that Soviet spies and agents had penetrated our cultural life and government, especially in the arts, the State Department, and the military. This did not necessarily make every card-carrying communist or sympathizer a Soviet agent, least of all in Hollywood or in the arts, but Senator Joseph McCarthy and other politicians of the right quickly recognized and seized the possibilities of manipulating the paranoid popular fears for stage effects and a sense of raw power.

The charge of sexual McCarthyism was put into dramatic form by *Le Figaro,* which could hardly be accused of favoring Clinton or wanting to see him spared embarrassment. In an editorial, the conservative newspaper said: "I have a panicky fear of this American innovation . . . a grand inquisitor who is authorized to root around in our most private lives . . . The obscenity of the questions about Clinton's sex life reflects on the entire world" (August 19, 1998). Four weeks later, the same paper spoke of "persecution by a Puritan prosecutor of the extreme right, a legatee of the Prohibitionists and McCarthyites" (September 14, 1998). *Le Monde* (September 13-14, 1998) wrote that the Starr Report on the Internet was "making us all peeping Toms by the choice of the American

Congress. It is on a level with the proceedings of the Inquisition which medievalists read . . . But now *we* have to read it too, the shame of Clinton, just to prove his ignominy . . . the sexual details, [it's] a new McCarthyism." The *Scotsman* of Edinburgh anticipated the salacious proceedings with a live Lewinsky as a witness before the Senate: "We will squirm with embarrassment, yet we will watch . . . fascinated and yet repelled" (quoted in *World Press Review,* February 1999). The aspect of deliberate pornographic titillation by the Republican stage managers behind the presentation and the milking of the Starr Report for prurient effects strip the last veil of pretense from a partisan political campaign. But the image of sexual McCarthyism really lacks all other similarities to the anticommunist McCarthyism of another day, such as the pervasive fears of betrayal in high places.

There was, however, another and very American simile that Europeans would be less familiar with: Representative Rick Boucher's phrase, a "lynch mob atmosphere" in Washington, and Toobin's words, "a decorous lynching," were not just figures of speech. Harry Thomason's image of "a slow-motion assassination" from 1993 to 1999 and *Rolling Stone*'s comparison to "a public stoning" are even more vivid, although the impeachment panic did not bring about Clinton's death as stonings and lynchings usually did. Matthew Parris, whose reaction to the grand jury videotape appeared in the London *Times,* also had it right: "This was medieval. It was cruel. This was like bear-baiting" (September 21, 1998).

A lynching short of death, indeed, otherwise to be put side by side with some 3,600 fatal lynchings—three-fourths of whose victims were African American—in the half century from 1880 to 1930 in America. Although the Clinton-lynching metaphor is perhaps aggressive and offensive to some, the parallels merit closer examination. It was typical of those horrific killings that there was a pervasive belief in the community that such mob justice (without trial or proof) was an acceptable way to punish a person accused of a crime, often rape. Typical as well was a pervasive community belief that the accused, and often the minority to which he or she belonged, was of irredeemably low character. There was usually a lynching chorus of the media, sometimes even of the clergy, echoing the low character theme just as the anti-Clinton propaganda had. Typically also the impatient crowd was convinced of the victim's guilt, but it was not willing to submit the charge or charges to a court trial or due process of law. Victims were often kidnapped from jail prior to a trial and killed. In Clinton's impeachment, there was, of course, a trial process of sorts in Congress, however flawed, and this may have saved him from the unrestrained lethal force of the Washington lynch riot of 1998. But the proceedings were at the wrong level (high crimes and misdemeanors), which is like trying a bicycle thief on murder charges, and were riddled with gross violations of the rights of the accused in any court of law. Typical lynchings often took place in a festival atmosphere and frequently included horrible tortures, sexual mutilations for souvenirs, and the showing off of the (often burnt) body of the victim. Is it really such a stretch to compare the ordeal imposed on the president by the media circus of 1998, the salacious Starr Report, the DNA sample, the grand jury videotape, and worldwide humiliations to the lynchings of the past? This time, of course, the outside world saw a shaming of the United States while the lynchers tried to shame only the highest elected official of the country.

There are further clues that this was indeed a new kind of public lynching without the physical death of the victim: the attitude of the lynchers was all too reminiscent of what one can sense from the pictures in James Allen's book *Without Sanctuary* (1999) or the descriptions in Stewart E. Tolnay's and E. M. Beck's *A Festival of Violence: An Analysis of Southern Lynchings* (1995). There was plenty of celebration and triumph—often under a façade of tongue-clucking and hypocritical expressions of regret at the "decline of morals and family values"—among the activists and sympathizers of the quasi lynching of Clinton. There was the same sociopathic disregard of collateral damage to innocent bystanders and the

Constitution as among the hard-faced lynch mobs pictured in *Without Sanctuary*. And there was the curious anger among the Republican lynchers in Congress and at home at any effort by Clinton's lawyers and defenders to mount defensive countermeasures: "How dare Hillary, the xxx [rhymes with witch, according to Barbara Bush] blame a 'vast right-wing conspiracy'!" I was told by an irate Republican in Santa Barbara. "How dare they use their media skills of spinning and rebuttal!" was the refrain from the media involved in the lynching drive. What nerve for Clinton's lawyers to remonstrate against the denial of his procedural rights as an accused person, for example, for access to the Starr Report and other accusatory materials before they were released to the media! How incredibly cheeky of the Democratic House Judiciary Committee counsel Abbe Lowell to question the special prosecutor himself, or for Blumenthal and others to mount a counteroffensive in the media! Even after Clinton's impeachment by the House and acquittal by Senate majorities, any gloating by him and his team was deemed absolutely unacceptable to the tender feelings of his congressional pursuers. After all, in the bad old days of lynchings, any uppityness or demands for due process of law by a victim triggered immediate physical attack or killing by the sociopaths in the lynch mob.

A final telltale sign of the lynching character of "the hunting of the president," to use the title of the book by Joe Conason and Gene Lyons, was the reaction of the wider community and the media after the event. Just as with the orgies of lynchings of 1880-1930 (and later) or with the race riots of the same period—when such riots often destroyed and drove out entire black communities in our midst—the media and wider public would really prefer to forget the whole thing. It was not that they regretted their roles in the lynchings or riots, even less a sense of having done a shameful wrong, but deep embarrassment and an inclination to blame the victim, especially his alleged character and all the scandals *they* visited upon him. Today, this attitude often expresses itself in the so-called Clinton fatigue, which the media have tried to ascribe to the public and which, during the 2000 presidential campaign, wishful thinking tried to implant in the minds of potential followers of candidate Al Gore. And, just as the lynch mobs of another day, for instance, in the 1921 race riot of Tulsa, Oklahoma, felt no responsibility afterward for restoring the black business district they had burned down or the social order they had destroyed, the anti-Clinton mob of 1998 pretends that no damage was done to American democracy and the Constitution.

It is only natural that our minds should grasp at historical allusions or examples. But the realities of the American attempt to overthrow the president by manipulating a sex scandal do not easily fit any of these models, least of all the presence of a large popular majority that took a dim view of the proceedings of Starr and the congressional majority against its duly elected president. Some of the parts, of course, do fit. But there were no witches and no hunt to find any, unless we want to attach this label to Starr's hunt for Jane Does or his harassment of Hillary Clinton and prosecutions of McDougal and Steele. With the possible exception of charges of a kind of cultural treason by the late-'60s generation, there was no search for treason or treasonable views, as with McCarthyism. Nor were there any sincere Puritan saints among the Clinton-haters today. A lynching without fatal outcome still lacks the chief ingredient. Lynchers, witch hunters, and hanging judges of show trials do share one characteristic: they all appear to suffer a lot more from character flaws than their victims do. The extraordinary amount of hypocrisy among the critics of Clinton's sexual peccadilloes, like the astonishing frequency of lies (strategic, operational, and substantive) behind the prosecutorial and congressional maneuvers also marks this case off from the works of Puritanism and McCarthyism. The charge of frequent lying against the president was particularly prominent, so much so that the preceding compiled list of incidents of lying by his pursuers is indeed lengthy. Quite probably, all these elements contributed in a major way to the public resistance to the attempt to remove President Clinton from office.

SELLING THE LIE

The natural conclusion from these glimpses and reflections is that European attitudes on sex, lies, and audiotaping are not all that different from those of the vast majority of Americans, regardless of what the American media have told us. The zealots of 1998 appear to represent only a small anti-Clinton minority of activists and conspirators that, in turn, has been supported by a large minority of partisans. The sex scandal was a mere smoke screen for the assault of the ultras on due process of law, the presidency, and the Constitution.

On the whole, perhaps, Europeans are still a good deal more conservative on such subjects as gender relations, true family values observed in practice (as contrasted with mere political hype), and the protection of privacy against the prying eyes of neighbors, media, commercial interests, and government agents such as police and loose-cannon prosecutors. We Americans, from childhood on, appear to be more "sexualized" and to be periodically overwhelmed by waves of pornographic adult cultures. In recent years, for example, the production and worldwide distribution of American porno films has risen to all-time commercial record levels. Television and Hollywood movies full of explicit sexuality have been flooding our living rooms and dens, not to mention the movie and television screens of the rest of the world which views these exported manifestations of American morality rather critically. But we must not forget either that, after more than eight decades of American motion pictures shown around the world, American men have a worldwide reputation for modern romance and for treating women with respect and relative equality, features that are still widely admired abroad. Even in today's Europe, where they may snicker about the misogynous new conservatives of America, such consideration between the sexes cannot always be taken for granted. And there are notable patches of glaringly unequal treatment all over the continent, in spite of what European constitutions and law codes may say.

There is also a surprising amount of misunderstanding and anecdotal, mutual recriminations on the surface that can interfere with getting a clear overview. The provincial press in Britain, for example, has long featured columns about shocking or ridiculous phenomena among the "colonials" in America, usually gleaned from the American press. They may include Georgia's laws on oral sex, calves born with five legs or two heads, legislative or school board decisions about the teaching of evolution in public schools, American gun laws and the gun lobby, and shocking hate crimes. Such parades of freaks and horrors, of course, amuse the British and the continentals, even though they are not always accurately or fully reported. It is always uplifting to share a good chuckle or a sincere sense of outrage at the expense of another country. But it would be just as easy to compile such lists of horrors about some of the more backward places in Europe.

Comparing hate crimes between Europe and America, for example, there are attacks on people of color, immigrants, gays, Jews, gypsies, and even the handicapped that can be counted in the hundreds in Britain, France, Germany, and the rest of Europe. There is a depressing sameness to the violent outrages of racists, neo-Nazis, and skinheads that have occurred from Manchester to Marseilles, from Antwerp to Hoyerswerda (East Germany), and in Eastern Europe as well. American hate crimes such as the police torture of a Haitian immigrant in New York, the assassination of a Jewish television host in Arizona, the torture of a black man dragged to his death behind a pickup truck in Texas, or the killing of a gay man in Montana do not stand alone, though some Americans will deny that they are the equal of hate crimes elsewhere. All such incidents and anecdotes, however, are obviously epiphenomena, tales and deeds of individuals, and not of the same magnitude and significance as a political assault on the Constitution, the law, and political institutions of a major democratic country by Congress and the judiciary under the pretext of a sex scandal.

Comparative reflections on political sex scandals in Europe and America show that such scandals are ubiquitous if not necessarily viewed similarly in different places today. But there are also amazing fluctuations over time in how they are regarded: at the present time, for example, Europeans are very tolerant of heterosexual lapses, such as adultery or sexual harassment, though this was not always so. Financial or legal-administrative corruption, such as the recent cases revealed in Italy and Germany, on the other hand, are taken very seriously. France, Britain, and Latin countries differ considerably in their attitudes toward homosexuality in high places.

The Clinton-Lewinsky affair, regardless of what our media were trying to tell us, was not perceived as just a sex scandal in Europe, nor did most European journalists believe that it was really a serious case of perjury and obstruction of justice. Neither the Europeans nor the vast majority of Americans could be expected to buy the great indignation at the sex scandal from the rogues' gallery behind the impeachment drive, least of all from the other philandering husbands. They were, however, deeply shocked by the gross indecency of the Starr Report and by the outrageous invasions of the privacy of the principals—Lewinsky, Clinton—and of others embarrassed intentionally by disclosures in the Report and in the mountains of further unedited and unproven materials, including the secret evidence of Congressman Tom DeLay.

Europeans and most Americans understandably could not accept the condemnation of perjury from DeLay or the categorical denunciation of lying from Hyde in view of his earlier excuses for lying. Finally, they were well aware that Starr lied, once again, when he insisted on the occasion of the impeachment vote in the House: "We must get to the truth. There is no excuse for perjury, none, never, ever." In American law and in social life, there are lies and then there are lies, as we have seen, some obviously much more consequential than others. Lying under oath to protect a criminal or denounce an innocent person is not the same as lying for self-protection, and American judges—probably even Starr—have always treated them differently.

In a civil suit such as the Jones suit, moreover, it is extremely rare for a judge to pursue a case of false testimony, unless the intent of the witness to change the outcome in a material way can be demonstrated. In such an obvious case of prosecutorial manipulation and entrapment as staged by Starr on January 17, 1998, before the Jones grand jury, a judge worth her salt should have intervened. As it turned out, a majority of the final judges in the Senate trial were aware of the miscarriage of justice attempted here and elsewhere, and threw out the case. European and American observers had been aware all along of the sea of lies, especially operational lies and the lies of Starr, that carried the case along throughout the year 1998. The biggest such operational lie, of course, was that impeachment and removal of the president from office were actions intended to defend the rule of law and the Constitution, rather than simply a pursuit of intense personal and partisan hatred on the part of the Republican ultras. Not even the unceasing efforts of dominant parts of the American media were able to sell this lie to the American public and the foreign press.

CHAPTER FOUR

Democracy and the Media Conspiracy

> President Clinton failed to charm the two most flatterable institutions in Washington, Congress and the press.
> —Mark Shields, on the *NewsHour* (March 19, 1999)

> Anonymous sources were used to convict the President and Mrs. Clinton by insinuation . . . and most of those unnamed accusers were in the office of Kenneth Starr.
> —Anthony Lewis, "Nearly a Coup,"
> *New York Review of Books* (April 13, 2000)

> The founding fathers did not guarantee freedom of the press as a means of ensuring the sales and profitability of newspapers or advancing the careers and prejudices of editors and reporters.
> —Robert Scheer, *Los Angeles Times*
> (November 24, 1998)

One of the first major European voices to place a free press near the center of his vision of democracy in general and of American democracy in the 1830s specifically, was Alexis de Tocqueville. Still, Tocqueville was not at all comfortable with the American press. He found it just as "destructive in its principles" and violent in its language as the press of monarchic France but "without the same reasons for indignation" against oppressive, royal authority. The press "constitutes a singular power, so strangely composed of mingled good and evil that liberty could not live without it, and public order can hardly be maintained against it."

The reasons for Tocqueville's uneasiness are apparent: "The journalists of the United States are generally in a very humble position, with a scanty education and a vulgar turn of mind . . . The characteristics of the American journalist consist in an open and coarse appeal to the passions of his readers; he abandons principles to assail the characters of individuals, to track them into private life and disclose all their weaknesses and vices." And, "when many organs of the press adopt the same line of conduct, their influence in the long run becomes irresistible, and public opinion, perpetually assailed from the same side, eventually yields to the attack . . . The power of the periodical press is second only to that of the people."[1]

Tocqueville thought freedom of the press indispensable for democracy, and yet he was under no illusion that it represented majority opinion accurately, and that its journalists were either elected or could be recalled or be threatened successfully with lawsuits for their lies, libel, or defamation of character. Today, the law no longer allows persons in the public limelight to defend themselves unless they can prove deliberate malice. Unlike most other institutions of the American political system, the media are not subject to checks and balances other than from their marketplace. As we have seen again in the Clinton years, these market forces are easily distorted with political pressure from advertisers, media conglomerates, individual owners like Rupert Murdoch, or wealthy individuals like Richard Mellon Scaife, who on a fee-per-service basis commission exposés as in Whitewater and Troopergate.

The press and other media, of course, have changed greatly since the 1830s, further increasing their external controllability. There are far fewer newspapers; there are even a few great papers to rival the centralized press of France or Britain. A significant number of journalists have become well-educated and sophisticated professionals compared to the "humble" and "vulgar" lot of Tocqueville's day—though some reporters around the country are not far from the old description. There are places where reporters and owners of newspapers and radio stations are people of few qualifications other than ego and prejudices of mainly a right-wing sort. Many areas, it seems, have their Rush Limbaugh; their messages are a mixture of misinformation and *ad hominem* attacks on public officials and policies, often with strong reactionary overtones. The new professionals are found mostly on the national programs and newspapers where they may be free-lance pundits, columnists, working reporters and rewriters, or have television programs of their own. Their professionalism rarely penetrates to the executive level of the owners, accountants, and marketing managers who keep the working journalists on a short leash. The entire media apparatus, while impervious to external political or democratic control, is under internal self-restraint only to the extent that owners and editors may be motivated by a sense of responsibility and personal integrity. The professional reporters, with few exceptions, have little opportunity to follow similar compunctions unless they are prepared to risk their jobs.

American newspaper journalism in the nineties has also suffered from excesses of partisanship and a visceral hostility to the president (even more to Mrs. Clinton), both with an intensity not observed since the Republican press went tirelessly after President and Mrs. Franklin D. Roosevelt. With the Clintons, the editors and publishers of major newspapers such as the *Wall Street Journal, New York Times, Washington Post,* and *Los Angeles Times* have engaged in periodic poison-pen attacks or the kind of tricks the tabloid press uses to spike sales. For several years, every two months another great revelation about Governor Clinton's old real estate speculations or his sex life in Arkansas was sprung on a weary public, usually in one-shot fashion—for example, statements by a certain

Little Rock attorney, confessions of Arkansas state troopers, or accusations by a female acquaintance from those days (without any follow-up for lack of proof). As Joe Conason and Gene Lyons (*The Hunting of the President*), and also Jeffrey Toobin, have explained, this usually involved petty, personal, partisan politics on an unprecedented scale, propelled by self-aggrandizing, irresponsible media. Conason and Lyons have pinpointed the beginnings of "the ten-year campaign to destroy Bill and Hillary Clinton" (the subtitle of their book) in 1989 when the late Lee Atwater presciently recognized that the then-governor of Arkansas, Clinton, might become a challenger to President Bush. Atwater had engineered Bush's 1988 election with his dirty tricks to defeat Michael Dukakis.[2]

But as the Romans used to say, *aliquid semper haeret:* something will always stick to the accused, even when there is nothing but the accusation. It is not inconceivable that this concerted assault on public opinion over time may have had the effect described by Tocqueville, the effect of smearing the president, reducing trust, and keeping him from devoting his energy to running the country or promoting his reform program. The sheer accumulation of accusations over the years soon created a new epithet embraced by the media, the scandal-ridden presidency, with one gate chasing another and leaving the widespread impression that somehow the many accusations must represent offenses of the Clintons. To make matters worse, the media along with Kenneth Starr deliberately withheld exonerations of the charges until they did not seem to matter any more—after the November 1998 elections—because they had been replaced with the secondary legal charges of civil perjury and obstruction of justice. The watchdog function of the media was mostly forgotten in the "hunt for the president." Toobin, in his book, concludes that "at some point in the distant future, Americans will likely regard this entire fin de siècle spasm of decadence with incredulity—at the tawdriness of the president's behavior, at the fanaticism of his pursuers, and at the shabbiness of the political, legal, and journalistic systems in which this story festered. Mostly, though, these baffled future citizens will struggle with the same question about Bill Clinton. He was impeached for *what?*"[3] The internal restraints of a sense of integrity and responsibility on editors and publishers of major media had clearly given way to crude partisanship.

Europeans were very much aware of the manipulation of television images, for example, the repetition ad nauseam of the picture of Clinton giving a hug to Monica Lewinsky amid a crowd of well-wishers, or of the president wagging his finger while saying: "I did not have sexual relations with that woman." Foreign journalists, of course, noticed the purpose of this part of the media circus of 1998. Did this have anything to do with Tocqueville's feared "tyranny of the majority," his most quoted thesis about public opinion in a democracy, when these hostile editors, publishers, pundits, and television managers were clearly only a tiny, if strategically positioned, minority of the American public? In this case, many in the media were an integral part of the "vast right-wing conspiracy." In 1998, moreover, they were also conspicuously deaf to the voice of the real American majority that, again and again, spoke through the public opinion polls. Perhaps they hoped to persuade the majority with their slant on the president. They created and maintained a climate of public hysteria for a whole year with the obvious goal not of rational analysis but of generating a lynch mob mentality, as columnist William Raspberry observed, an eagerness to hang the culprit before the real plotters might be revealed.

It was a disgraceful performance by the captains of the American media and it even evoked a curious pity for them from at least one sympathetic, if simple-minded, European voice, the *Economist* (February 7, 1998): "It is hard to believe," the British journal wrote, "that America's media, once popular and even lionized as a check on politicians, now deserve to be resented for assuming too much power. . . . Journalists cannot even be blamed for promoting a general cynicism: in the current scandal, after all, it is they who have taken the moral questions seriously, while the broader public has shrugged." The reference to "taking the moral questions seriously," of course, describes the illusion created by the Washington and media elites that their hypocritical stance ought to be followed by the ignorant, slovenly, and possibly even immoral provincials. On the other hand, given the minimally informed and easily swayed majority of Americans, at least on political subjects, the media chorus did stand a better than average chance to sow doubts and make something stick. To paraphrase Tocqueville, when many media organs controlled by the minority of conspirators—not necessarily the working journalists—adopt the same line, "their influence in the long run becomes irresistible . . ."

The first rehearsal for the media circus of 1998 took place four years earlier, as Anthony Lewis of the *New York Times* has reminded us. Following Vincent Foster's suicide, ". . . a press frenzy developed," and Clinton-haters of the religious right made another videotape (the first was called "Circle of Power"). The libelous "Clinton Chronicles" alleges various crimes including murder and drug dealing; reportedly 150,000 copies were sold at $40 a piece. It was distributed by Jerry Falwell's Liberty Alliance and was shown in evangelical churches (*New York Review of Books*, April 13, 2000). It is difficult to estimate its influence among the media, collectively possessed of a soft underbelly in its opinion formation, through which all kinds of rumors, beliefs, and prejudices are routinely absorbed and may affect crucial decisions.

THE MEDIA CIRCUS OF 1998

"Clinton Accused of Urging Aide to Lie" screamed the headline of the *Washington Post* (January 21, 1998); "Starr Examines Clinton Link to Female Intern" read the *Los Angeles Times* of the same date. Reporters swarmed the office of the Whitewater prosecutor and the press office of the White House. The TV networks carried live updates throughout the day. Top anchor persons returned from the pope's visit to Cuba to cover the sex scandal in Washington. What angry reporters and pundits liked to call the "White House spin machine" promptly swung into action to counter the onslaught of questions and charges. The entire cabinet and staff rallied behind Clinton's line of denial even though, individually, they may have guessed from the beginning that the carefully phrased denial was at least a partial whitewash or altogether false. Clinton foes later made the whole thing into a kind of personal betrayal by the president toward those who believed him and were cruelly disappointed to learn the truth, six months later. The Clinton team was united by the knowledge that they were under furious attack by the president's political and media enemies—the "vast right-wing conspiracy" which at last seemed to have found fodder for its ravenous appetite.

Looking back a year later, Howard Kurtz, media critic of the not-very-self-critical *Washington Post* and author of *Spin Cycle,* a book about the White House spin machine, gave an unintendedly eye-opening account of the battle of wits between that spin machine and the "inside-the-Beltway elitists who had long viewed [Clinton] as a slippery rube from a backwater state." They felt frustrated at finding themselves "unable to hold him accountable [or] to make the public share their outrage at his lack of candor," and derided the popular success of his "small change issues" such as a patient's bill of rights or thousands of additional teachers and police officers for the schools and neighborhoods of America. Leading the media attack were "the high-decibel Sam Donaldson" (ABC), NBC's David Bloom, and CNN's Wolf Blitzer, while press secretary Mike McCurry and his deputy, Joe Lockhart, expertly dodged their sallies, frequently finding themselves "parked in a no-comment zone" (*Vanity Fair,* January 1999). It was a scene fit for a situation comedy, with the same familiar faces always screaming the same familiar questions. Amid copious leaks of grand jury and other privileged information about the Jones case, the journalists tried to play prosecutor and grand jury, badgering McCurry and company with questions about exactly what and how Clinton was supposed to testify.

At a later stage, after Clinton had admitted on television to "an inappropriate relationship" with Lewinsky, Kurtz observes, "the reporters . . . felt that [in January] Clinton had lied to [each of] them personally . . . he had wagged his finger at them." Now, in August, the journalists and pundits took on the role of father confessors: they all trashed the president's admission of guilt within minutes of the broadcast, endlessly discussing how he should make ever more abject apologies, grovel, and confess to serious criminal offenses. The father confessors also wanted to usurp the role of the real confessors: they immediately ridiculed Clinton's apology sessions with clergymen, too. At the same time, six in ten Americans according to the polls were quite satisfied with Clinton's apology. They probably had had their doubts about his earlier dramatic denial. Once again, the Washington media elites had failed to persuade the wider public of their views.

To make things more interesting, the journalists also tried to come up with all kinds of divisions on this issue in the White House. First they shed crocodile tears over the deceived staff, cabinet members, and First Lady. There was dark talk of impeachment and rumors about other intern affairs, hundreds of them. Then they conjured up bitter disagreements between Clinton's political advisers, who were said to be in favor of more abject apologies, and his defense lawyers, who were said to have "seized control of the case" and were said to be concerned about their client's future legal vulnerability in the hands of the malevolent Starr and other ultraconservative enemies. All along in their obsession with the sex scandal, the media ignored pressing presidential responsibilities, such as dealing with Boris Yeltsin and Russia's economic collapse, the expansion of NATO to Poland, Hungary, and the Czech Republic, and the meetings with Mexico's President Ernesto Zedillo and Chile's President Eduardo Frei. Even if World War III had just broken out, the journalists would probably have continued to hammer McCurry on Lewinsky, always in the peremptory style of toupee-clutching Donaldson or the dozens of self-important, conservative Washington pundits. As Todd Gitlin put it in the *Washington Monthly*, Donaldson's "leather lungs . . . his bellow . . . and his selective bullying" were not to be ignored; nor could one overlook the other "barking heads" (December 1998).

Gitlin comments sadly: "In TV news, attitude became the norm . . . easily mistaken for ideological opposition . . . Politics is reduced to criminality," while journalists copy from each other and interview each other rather than talking to the principals of their story. Toobin has dispassionately raised the question whether Clinton's stonewalling for seven long months—along with Starr's inept rejection of Lewinsky's immunity agreement of February—did not in fact save his presidency while the fires of the media had a chance to burn out. Toobin evidently thinks so and I concur, quite contrary to the tirelessly repeated right-wing bromide that if only the president had admitted all (in the midst of the media hurricane), instead of his finger-wagging denial, all would have been forgiven and he would never have been impeached. If Clinton had given in to the pressure back in January 1998, in the middle of a political storm also affecting the congressional Democrats deeply, he would have been forced to resign. "[But by August] the political and legal terrain had been transformed since those frenzied first days of the scandal . . . the months had allowed the country to come to terms with the fact that the president probably did have the affair with the intern—but that he had managed to do a pretty good job anyway."[4]

Once again, the media conspiracy tried to sow the wind: some 140 newspapers called for the president's resignation. Anti-Clinton pundits were screaming the same at the top of their voices. Michael Kelly of the *National Journal* called Clinton "a pig and a cad and a selfish brute" (quoted in *Santa Barbara News-Press*, September 13, 1998). With the impending release of the Starr Report, a flood of illegal leaks had once more reached the news media and was used by NBC's Lisa Myers and ABC's Jackie Judd to rekindle the media frenzy of the beginning of the year. Myers and Judd for years had been aggressively covering Whitewater and appeared to have a pipeline to Starr's office, as did Susan Schmidt of the *Washington Post*. This time, however, it proved much harder to set the media circus in motion. The public had become jaded and tended to turn away from the scandal even though the impeachment process was about to be launched in earnest.

Quite often also, as with the rumors about other affairs with interns, the media picked up and enlarged upon canards or misinterpreted supposed leaks: prior to the public release of Clinton's videotaped grand jury testimony, for example, journalists had reported that the tape would show an enraged Clinton using profanities and storming out of the room in a doomsday atmosphere (the New York *Daily News* and Bob Schieffer of CBS both predicted this). Instead, the president appeared calm, even presidential, according to polls, though obviously uncomfortable. His approval rating, instead of dropping, shot up from 59 percent to 68 percent in a CBS survey. "The president and his defenders had survived a thermonuclear attack by the press and they were still standing. To hell with the Beltway blowhards," Kurtz wrote (*Vanity Fair*, January 1999). But the media continued to insist on exclusively focusing on Lewinsky and burying important presidential activities and issues, such as the first budget surplus in 20 years, on the back pages. Thus, the *Washington Post* dealt with peace in Northern Ireland and with the world economy, and the *New York Times* with rule changes of health maintenance organizations (HMOs) that would affect 120 million Americans. "Why are the media . . . in cahoots with Kenneth Starr to destroy the president?" editor Charles Peters wrote in the *Washington Monthly* (October 1998): "My guess is it's because they've devoted five years to asserting that there's some kind of major Clinton scandal—and they can't let themselves turn out to have been wrong."

If the politics of the impeachment drive had been rational—many political scientists believe in the inherent rationality of politics—the unexpected Republican electoral disaster of November 3, 1998 should have been the turning point. None of the brilliant Washington pundits had predicted this and Starr, in particular, should have felt rather deflated. But the doomsday machine had been set upon its tracks by Gingrich, Hyde, and Starr and was unlikely to stop amidst the hordes of anti-Clinton editors and publishers. Peters quotes a level-headed columnist friend who was trying to start a column with the Los Angeles Times syndicate: "It's a little scary . . . An awful lot of editors are passionately pro-impeachment. They are not likely to take on a columnist who disagrees with them on an issue they feel so strongly about." Arthur Miller, author of *The Crucible,* had already commented on the striking unanimity with which newspapers including the *New York Times* and the *Washington Post,* the tabloids, and television all struck the same supermoral tone on Clinton, "just as if a scattered field of iron filings was uniformly turned in one direction by the presence of an electromagnetic force" (*Sueddeutsche Zeitung,* October 17-18, 1998). Peters added: "The Washington media community is full of people who have [committed adultery and then lied about it] . . . but now seem unable to forgive Bill Clinton" (*Washington Monthly,* October 1998)—shades of the Clinton-hunters in Congress.

The *Washington Monthly* was no less perceptive about other emerging aspects of the media treatment of the Lewinsky affair, beginning with the reported 20 percent circulation loss of the major tabloids (*National Enquirer, Star,* and *Globe*) in 1998 compared to 1997: "This should surprise no one. Their act had been taken over lock, stock, and barrel by the major media, including our most respected newspapers," Peters wrote. He also pointed out that the Watergate committee of 1974, unlike the Starr investigation, specifically omitted charges of Nixon's income tax fraud, "because it did not involve official conduct." He criticized the *Washington Post*'s whitewash of the Starr Report's barefaced lie regarding whether or not Lewinsky had specifically denied that "anyone ever asked me to lie." The *Post* wrote, "Mr. Starr's Report paraphrased her statement and it does not allege any such direct request," a mealy-mouthed, journalistic misrepresentation of the facts. Peters was equally critical of other lapses of the *Post,* such as the "burying" on page 11 of a report about a Justice Department investigation of possible bribery of Republican senators by the tobacco industry (*Washington Monthly,* November 1998).

The most devastating exposé of the media in that year of scandal was Steven Brill's "Pressgate" in his journal *Brill's Content* (July-August, 1998): "The real scandal may be [not the Lewinsky allegations but] the way the news media has covered the story— or, in too many cases, created it . . . What makes the media's performance a true scandal, a true example of an institution corrupted to its core, is that the competition for scoops so bewitched almost everyone that they let the man in power [Starr] write the story—once Tripp and Goldberg put it together for him." Brill raises the question "whether the press has abandoned its Watergate glory of being a *check* on official abuse of power. For in this story the press seems to have become an *enabler* of Starr's abuse of power."

Brill's "Pressgate" review of the first three weeks of media coverage, from January 21 when it "careened from one badly sourced scoop to another in an ever more desperate need to feed its multimedia, 24-hour appetite," is prefaced with Foster's suicide and the earlier scheming of the dynamic duo, Tripp and Goldberg. The Supreme Court deliberations and final decision to let Jones's civil case proceed against a sitting president set the stage for 1998, and for the "secretary now known more for taping than for typing" to take her audiotapes to Starr. Then the media avalanche began, with the Drudge Report, ABC's morning show with Donaldson, *Newsweek,* and the great race for scoops among ABC's Judd, *Washington Post*'s Schmidt, *Time,* and the *Los Angeles Times.* OIC leaks evidently supplied the sources, including secondhand statements about Lewinsky having been told to lie, a crucial element in Starr's later charges of obstruction of justice. Brill supplies a log of the weeks to follow which witnessed, according to Bob Woodward of Watergate fame, "a frenzy unlike anything you ever saw in Watergate . . . we need to remember that for the first eight or nine months of Watergate there were only six reporters working on it full time" (*Brill's Content,* August 1998).

Once unchained, the three networks all claimed anonymous sources, but the information could only stem from the OIC. Starr even admitted to Brill that it was his deputy, Jackie Bennett, who talked to reporters, although the independent counsel denied that the information was potential grand jury witness material and hence protected. In his defense, Starr claimed that such dubious leaking was justified in reaction to "misinformation . . . being spread about our investigation in order to discredit our office and our dedicated career prosecutors" (*Brill's Content,* August 1998). Evidently, Bennett was never named in any of the many media accounts; he seems to have requested anonymity from all reporters. Brill also describes the circus on *Larry King Live* (CNN), CNBC's *Rivera Live,* and MSNBC, all of them feasting purely on the leaks and speculations; Geraldo Rivera's show is described as "a kind of dinner party conversation from hell, in which any and all variety of truth, speculation, fiction, and ax-grinding are thrown together for the viewing public to sort out for themselves."

The journalistic spinning of wheels continued with a great scarcity of confirmed facts, counterpointed by peremptory demands that the president "explain," within the next 24 to 48 hours, "exactly what happened, what kind of relationship he had" (Tim Russert of CNBC). And, "every two or three days throughout the reporting of this alleged scandal," Brill relates, "the press seems to stop, take a breath, and flagellate itself, as if to say to its audience, 'stop us before we kill again.'" In a special bulletin on the fourth day, Brill notes, CNN's Blitzer announced while standing on the White House lawn within earshot of Clinton's astonished senior advisers that "they're talking among themselves about the possibility of a resignation [of Clinton]." He was not the first reporter who, failing to find any news, tried to create some. Russert and Drudge were no pikers in this field of endeavor either, while others, such as the *New York Post* and the *Wall Street Journal,* just used their imaginations. Fortunately for their shareholders at least, *USA Today, Time,* and CNN could boast substantially raised circulation and ratings.

"I think I am beginning to understand the psychology of lynchings now," commented a European student of mine. "But how does it relate to the alleged character problem of President Clinton?" I pressed her for further explanation and she said: "In a real lynching we cannot be sure of the guilt and bad character of the victim, I guess. But we certainly know that the lynch mob is lawless, violent, and of low character. This goes for the journalists who cut to the chase without checking their facts, just as for the other members of the impeachment mob. And for the Clinton-haters outside Washington."

But why was the vast majority of Americans, according to the polls, so impervious to the ranting of the Washington media elites? In his review of Howard Kurtz's book *The Spin Cycle: Inside the Clinton Propaganda Machine,* Robert Scheer gives an answer of sorts. It was not because the Clinton spin masters were so effective in their ready rebuttals to nearly every charge. Scheer points instead to the sense of entitlement, high income levels, and sky-high egos of the top Washington journalists and pundits. They are completely out of touch with the concerns of the average American and how these may relate to Clinton's modest background, his "small bore" policies, and his budget battles (for example, against a tax cut mostly for the wealthy). These celebrity reporters are more likely to identify with "the monied interests of the conglomerates and privileged families who pay their salaries" or with wealthy lawyers and big-time prosecutors with fat tobacco and insurance accounts on the side (*Los Angeles Times,* March 29, 1998). The American journalists of Tocqueville's day at least were poor and understood the public from which they sprang.

ARE THE MEDIA MONSTROUS?

"Whether one hates them or appreciates them," wrote Josef Joffe in an article "The Media—a Monster?" in Munich's *Sueddeutsche Zeitung* (July 13, 1998), "the media are the guarantee of democracy. Without public knowledge," he continued in Jeffersonian fashion, "there can be no political knowledge . . . and hence, no control over those who dominate us." But he also listed a number of glaringly erroneous reports and recent canards in the United States media, including the CNN story about the use of poison gas on American deserters in Vietnam. He commented that quality newspapers really had not changed much in thirty years except for growing threefold in daily volume. A month later, *Sueddeutsche Zeitung* addressed the subject again, reviewing a week's worth of comments on the Starr Report, false scoops, *Newsweek* reminiscences about presidential lies since Warren Harding, and the CNN box score on how long Clinton's televised interrogation was taking before the grand jury. The German daily finally settled on how the story of Clinton's blue and gold Ermengildo Zegna necktie, presumably a gift from Lewinsky, had filled the pages of newspapers and magazines for a lazy week in August of 1998 (August 22, 1998). In the meantime, this tie has been discovered to be more likely a gift from the president's brother and his Italian lady friend. But this did not keep the OIC lawyers from jumping to the conclusion that, by wearing "Monica's tie" on a public occasion in the Rose Garden, Clinton was sending Lewinsky a message not to give in to Starr's importuning. More obstruction of justice! And in the school colors of the University of California at Berkeley yet, a provocation to American conservatives. This line of ruminations, in my opinion, fell considerably short of the role of the media as a triumph of democracy.

In reaction to the media excesses of 1998, the *Washington Monthly* assembled a distinguished cast of journalists to express their views about the decline of objectivity in journalistic reporting. This was done by ostensibly reviewing David T. Z. Mindich's

Just the Facts: How Objectivity Came to Define American Journalism,[5] but also to commemorate the 30th anniversary of the monthly which was originally founded to clothe the "bare-bones objective reporting" of the preceding era with "novelistic flesh," analysis, and a search for solutions. By the 1990s, however, responsible journalists began to recoil from the new opinionated, tendentious, and super-cynical new journalism that had developed in the wake of the end of the Cold War and a series of technological innovations in the news business. The *Washington Monthly*'s symposium (January-February 1999) is well worth rereading, including its spoof (by Art Levine) of how F. D. Roosevelt and his Republican opponents reacted to Pearl Harbor in "wag-the-dog" fashion to distract the nation from a Lewinsky-like affair. The consensus of the journalists was that the profession ought to knock off its excessive cynicism and attitudinizing and return to the standards of objective reporting.

Perhaps the American media of 1998 were too silly to be a monster, but in their "open and coarse appeal to the passions of . . . readers" and in "assail[ing] the characters of individuals" (Tocqueville), they were guilty of considerable measures of sensationalism, puerility, and skullduggery. As the Munich paper reported, *Time* magazine had an elaborate feature on whether it was possible for Lewinsky to have had sex with Clinton, but he not with her. Murdoch's *New York Post* had the headline "He Lied." The *Los Angeles Times* and *Boston Globe*, at least, no longer suggested hypocritically that "if only he came clear, we'd forget it all." But they all continued to engage in a lively trade of OIC and grand jury information "from reliable sources," including, finally, the results of Clinton's DNA test.

During a dinner in 1983, a decade and a half before the 1998 crisis, actor Warren Beatty had asked the members of the American Society of Newspaper Editors, to their great consternation, if their leading newspapers shared the standards and values of supermarket tabloids such as the *Star, Daily News, Globe,* or

National Enquirer. When they indignantly denied this, he went on: "Do you think that the public knows that you feel like this? Irresponsible journalism should be pointed out by responsible journalists." Some of the most critical assessments of the American media during 1998 and earlier came, indeed, from within, as we will show below. But the great American newspapers and networks had already flunked the Beatty test at the time of the 1992 presidential campaign, not to mention at the time of the 1988 presidential campaign of Senator Gary Hart when some of them—for example, the *Miami Herald*—were quick to join the tabloid that had paid for the story of his paramour Donna Rice.

In 1992, a fortnight of disclosures about Gennifer Flowers by the tabloid *Star,* which reportedly paid her a sum between $150,000 and $175,000, may have earned it $800,000 more than usual in newsstand revenues. It quickly attracted the major papers and television channels even though a Yankelovich-Clancy-Schulman poll had shown that 70 percent of Americans thought that private behavior, including extramarital affairs, should be ignored "out of respect for the candidate's privacy" and "regardless of hard proof" (*Time,* February 10, 1992). The same poll also revealed the critical attitude of the public toward the media: 82 percent thought the press paid too much attention to the private lives of politicians and nearly half felt that such media discussions "tend to crowd out discussion of the issues" of the campaign. 50 percent specifically insisted that editors should not print rumors and nearly as many (42 percent) believed they ought to cross-check their facts.

Nevertheless, NBC, ABC's *Nightline* (reluctantly at first), the *Washington Post* (after some hesitation), and the *Los Angeles Times* made a low-key jump into the fray. They were not deterred when they learned that Arkansas papers, such as the *Democrat/Gazette,* had known about Flowers for more than a year and that the Arkansas reporters had already poked a number of holes into her story about a long-time liaison with Clinton. Even the *New York Times* got into the act but buried the story in its back pages. The

Star coverage, in any case, blanketed all discussion of political issues for a full week, according to *Time* magazine, thus putting all 1992 primary candidates at a disadvantage. But this also made the New Hampshire primary a test of the public's opinion of the media. Clinton's eventual triumph as a candidate constituted a defeat for the media. European observers who have their own sassy tabloid press, the "boulevard papers," were hardly surprised by *Star* and the Flowers affair, but they did raise their eyebrows about the descent of many of the respectable American media into the tabloid cesspool.

Respectable European papers like *Le Monde, Le Figaro,* the *Guardian,* the London *Times,* the *Frankfurter Allgemeine Zeitung, Sueddeutsche Zeitung,* Berlin *Tagesspiegel,* or the *Corriere della Sera* and *La Repubblica* are especially careful to maintain the boundary between themselves and the boulevard press. Observing the American aberration in 1992, some European journalists spoke condescendingly of a "media-cracy " in America, rather than a democracy, and the deprecating overtones were quite as apparent as the reference to Tocqueville's thoughts about American democracy. (Even former President Bush, at the beginning of the Senate impeachment trial, spoke not only of "the lack of civility" and "deficit of decency" but also of the "descent of the [American] mainstream press into tabloid journalism.")

Of course, there was worse to come once Clinton was elected in 1992 and the "vast right-wing conspiracy," including certain media elites (publishers, editors, and television managers), began to get organized. Perhaps the five-minute film "They all laughed" by Clinton friend Linda Bloodworth-Thomasson, which was shown at the inauguration gala, made Clinton's reception by the Washington media worse. It featured a rapid progression of media sound bites from journalism celebrities like David S. Broder, Robert Novak, Fred Barnes, and others who had called candidate Clinton "a loser," "unelectable," and "dead meat" during the campaign. In any case, the *Wall Street Journal, New York Post,* and conservative

Washington journals such as *American Spectator* and the weekly *Standard*—with financial infusions from Pittsburgh newspaper publisher Scaife—were Clinton-haters from the start. Some editors of mainstream papers such as the *New York Times, Washington Post,* and *Los Angeles Times,* and smaller papers dependent on the same media conglomerates soon joined them.

Foreign journalists were quite aware of the bias. "The *Washington Post,*" wrote Nicole Bacharan in 1998, "blinded by its own glorious past—*toujours* Watergate—launched its new crusade to clean out, once more, the Augean stables of Washington." After profound editorial disagreements, the *Washington Post* evidently decided that Clinton's faults were equivalent to the conduct of Richard Nixon and that, eventually, "Congress had no other choice but to initiate a process of impeachment . . . the *Post* set the tone." The French commentator counted close to 120 American dailies, including the *Chicago Tribune, Philadelphia Inquirer, USA Today,* and *Atlanta Constitution,* that demanded Clinton's resignation. "From that point on, the scandal and its [ramifications] occupy page one. Nothing else counts, neither budgetary accords . . . education or social security . . . all pass unnoticed." And, of course, "to justify the pornographic [media] display of the Lewinsky affair, a number of media bosses . . . brandished the 'right to know.' But to know what? . . . Does one have a right to peek through the keyhole of one's neighbor? . . . Many journalists without scruples [about the rights of individuals] made quick and cutting judgments, with a contemptuous and cynical attitude . . . as the presumption of guilt of a politician . . . seemed the shortest path to glory. . ."[6]

Some of the prominent weeklies, such as *Time* and *Newsweek,* exhibited a little more detachment at first; other magazines, such as the *New Yorker* and *Vanity Fair* gallantly maintained their independence from the media mania with occasional exposés of Gingrich, Starr, and other principals, and searching essays on the legal and constitutional issues. Still, the rush to judgment of the overwhelming weight of the American media calls to mind

Tocqueville's dire warning: "when many organs of the press adopt the same line of conduct, their influence in the long run becomes irresistible, and public opinion . . . eventually yields to the attack."

The German news magazine *Der Spiegel* (December 7, 1998) was critical of Clinton and similar contemporary figures (Prime Minister Blair and Chancellor Schröder) who make their private lives—family, dog, and cat—public property and of the cynical course of a sex scandal in a "media-cracy." It could also have mentioned Teddy Roosevelt and John F. Kennedy, whose families' stories were public property, although the promiscuity of the latter did not thereby automatically become fair game for the media: "Mean people, of course, pick up the [sex] story and, while expressing their shock about its indecency, insist on telling all about it. Their moral critics in turn attack their judgmental attitude, and themselves go over all the salacious aspects once again. Then the clever set show us how phony all this is, and they too retell the story in full detail . . ." Recalling how conservative opinion in the 1960s had insisted on separating private and public matters in a principled defense against the "sexplosion " of the counterculture of 1968 that insisted that "the personal is the political," *Der Spiegel* said: "The media must learn that this does not sell papers or drive up ratings. It will eventually die down, and then Clinton will be just another cheating husband." During our 1998 crisis, nevertheless, CNN, the soap-opera-formatted MSNBC, and Chris Matthews's nightly *Hardball* not only profited prodigiously but helped to drive the more established media down to the tabloid level.

Beset by the intense competition from the mainstream press, American tabloids had to raise the ante and make higher offers for dirt from the Lewinsky scandal. The *National Enquirer,* for example, reportedly offered as much as $750,000 for a few of the illegal audiotapes of Linda Tripp. The price had gone up dramatically since Gennifer Flowers recorded confidential conversations with Clinton. Lewinsky was offered a million dollars by the *Star* for her exclusive story, before she decided to publish her own account.

There were also rumors of centerfold offers from *Playboy*. It is difficult to estimate what the once-respectable American press gained by its tabloidization although its financial problems in a very competitive world are well publicized. Some papers, especially those from decidedly liberal Democratic cities such as San Francisco or Minneapolis, refused to jump on the impeachment bandwagon. But some liberal papers also felt that they had to bend over backward in a conservative direction on this issue. However, there is massive evidence that the established tabloids lost a good deal of their market share with the tabloidization of much of the mainstream media. The *National Enquirer, Star,* and *Globe* were down to about half of their 1986 combined circulation of nearly ten million. They lost a lot of this in 1998 while tabloid-type TV shows, the Drudge Report, and, of course, the tabloidized big papers gained market share. From January to August 1998, the original tabloids actually cut back on anti-Clinton dirt for fear of offending their readers' sympathy for the president. In a remarkable contrast to the once respectable media, *National Enquirer* editor David Perel was quoted as saying that "the president should not be unduly attacked" (*Los Angeles Times,* September 10, 1998). But it should also be noted that the mainstream papers are not very good at imitating the tabloids; they lack finesse and experience, and their crudeness and presumed deep pockets may invite well-deserved lawsuits. Unlike the original tabloid publications, furthermore, the big interlopers were clearly more interested in exploiting the salacious details of the sex scandal for political gains than in using them for their own sake.

Talking about market shares also draws attention to the fact that since the 1980s America's "independent" media have become a lot less independent, irrespective of the conservative drumfire of propaganda labeling them "liberal," "liberal democratic," or worse. Back then the Reagan administration, the New Right, Young Americans for Freedom, the Heritage Foundation, Accuracy in Media, and the John Birch Society unceasingly complained about the alleged liberal bias, especially of the three television networks and the mainstream press. The very meaning of the word "liberal"—Reagan's "L-word" was evidently meant for those less at ease with polysyllabics—was defined by these self-styled conservatives. This was particularly evident at the time of the takeover of the ABC network in 1983-1984 by Capital Cities with the help of financier Warren Buffett, the son of a Republican congressman. Buffett was a major investor also in the *Washington Post, Boston Globe,* and *Buffalo Evening News,* insurance, advertising companies, financial services, precious metals, and General Foods. Capital Cities/ABC soon came to lead a growing media cartel at the same time that broadcast and cable communications were being deregulated. The concentration among media giants, moreover, continues as the *Chicago Tribune,* for example, has acquired the Times-Mirror Company which published not only the *Los Angeles Times* but Long Island's *Newsday,* the *Hartford Courant,* the *Baltimore Sun,* several smaller dailies, 18 magazines, and, in partnership with Target Media Partners, 25 classified magazines. The *Tribune* already owned 3 other newspapers, 22 TV and 4 radio stations, Tribune Entertainment, 25 percent of the WB Television Network and several Internet companies. Interlocking directorates and linkages among media directors and advertisers have increased the growing stranglehold of the United States broadcasting industry conglomerates over information and culture in America, making the supposed Tocquevillean independence of and fierce competition among companies largely a smoke screen today.

The rightward drift of ABC in 1993, moreover, involved not only greater interconglomerate cooperation but a kind of advertiser-friendliness that broke down the famous wall between the advertising corporations and the editorial offices. Some newspapers, for example, the *Los Angeles Times,* brought in top managers who were completely new to the media and wanted to run a newspaper like any other business, with due respect to the advertisers.[7] Once-great newspapers and independent television networks now routinely began to squelch news and exposés that were embarrassing to or critical of major advertisers. A particularly glaring example was the suppression of ABC and CBS disclosures of exposés on the tobacco industry when Disney and Westinghouse took over ABC and CBS in 1994 and 1996, respectively. This may well have been the path of political influence too—or, at least, this would explain the brazen participation of certain media in the anti-Clinton conspiracy. Even though Clinton's centrism and some of his economic policies were welcomed by many corporate leaders, and he time and again demonstrated his prowess at political fund raising among them, others obviously shared the determination of congressional Republicans and the cabal of right-wing lawyers and judges to get rid of Clinton by nonelectoral means, namely a coup attempt.

IRRESISTIBLE INFLUENCE?

Is it true, as the Mark Shields epigraph for this chapter suggests, that Clinton's bad press in his two terms grew from his failure to charm this "most flatterable institution" in Washington? The answer is yes, but there is a good deal more involved, beginning with the personalities and expectations of American journalists toward politicians. Clinton did himself no favor with the media when he presented himself in his first years as an intellectual, Rhodes scholar, and sage with an extraordinary command of whatever subject he was lecturing on or answering questions about, exhibiting his obvious knowledge and intelligence on many occasions. Reporters again and again found themselves outclassed and grasping at easy formulas for what to them was an astounding high-wire act: they coined verbal defenses against what they could not master: "Slick Willie," high-risk taker, policy wonk, or arrogant outsider from nowhere. Clinton's verbal glibness, empathetic rhetoric, and, finally, his legalistic evasions clearly upstaged the reporters who usually pride themselves on their verbal skills.

Clinton, in this respect, got off to a bad start and shared the experiences of poor press relations with several of his predecessors, certainly Presidents Johnson, Nixon, and Carter. Even Reagan, hardly an intellectual, was not half as popular with the media as everyone would have us believe today. The Clintons were also unwashed outsiders to pretentious Washington society; here they, indeed, needed flattery so as not to bruise fragile, parvenu egos, including the media elites, and they made little effort to make themselves welcome. The media, for their part, exhibited an astonishing degree of dogged persistence, even with the most trivial negative vignettes: to give an example, the *New York Times* managed to extend its distorted discussion of the 1993 Clinton haircut by Christophe on the Los Angeles airport tarmac over no fewer than six issues (May 21, 22, 23, 27, 28, and June 1). The *Washington Monthly* (July-August 1993) was among the few media organs to critically review the press tilt and the heavy television bias—especially Dan Rather (CBS) and Andrea Mitchell (NBC)—against Clinton from the start.[8]

If the American media from day one were almost universally reserved or hostile toward President Clinton, the same media voices, with suspicious eagerness, took to Starr and shielded him from critical scrutiny as Steven Brill, among others, confirmed on the *NewsHour* with Jim Lehrer (November 18, 1998). It was part of the persona created for Starr, by himself and others including the leading media, that he was supposed to be a rather shy, serious, and principled bespectacled scholar and lawyer, a pillar of moral rectitude, who was at a loss among the politically clever crowd and awkward with the media- and spinwise ways of the Clinton White House of the early days. This image also prevailed among early European media reports that called him a Puritan acting mainly on religious grounds, until better judgment and emotional revulsion replaced first impressions. The American media was singularly remiss in pointing out how unsuitable Starr was as an independent counsel. He had no experience as a prosecutor, had considered running for the Senate from Virginia as a Republican, and had shown his strong partisan bias in the other ways mentioned above.

"He was not a wise choice . . . given that background," to quote Louis Fisher of the Congressional Research Service, "it would be hard to defend either his competence or his objectivity." Worse yet, once appointed, Starr "was having trouble finishing his initial assignments . . . [and] completing his investigations . . . Three years after receiving those assignments (Travelgate and Filegate), Starr had yet to report to the public and to Congress." He had fallen behind also because of his numerous activities outside his OIC duties: he continued working at Kirkland & Ellis, handled a big case, taught at New York University's School of Law, and "traveled around the country giving speeches, often to conservative, anti-Clinton groups—again raising questions about his judgment, detachment, and objectivity" (*PS Political Science and Politics*, September 1999).

From the day of his appointment as independent counsel, Starr had eagerly courted the media, particularly the *Washington Post* which bore him a debt of gratitude for his striking down, while an appellate court justice, the 1987 libel suit of W. P. Tavoulareas. In the middle of the scandal, of course, Starr's office became the chief "anonymous sources," perhaps sharing some of that dubious honor with the unholy trio of Tripp, Goldberg, and Drudge. Now he was even less an object of media curiosity. "Why bite the hand that leaks?" writes Todd Gitlin, a New York University professor of culture, journalism, and sociology, who cites typical examples of media blindness. The media had dutifully carried Starr's leaks about the imminent indictment of Mrs. Clinton over Whitewater—a vintage example of Starr's attempts to terrorize people—but then "lifted no eyebrows when Starr's Little Rock jury folded [in May of 1998] without indicting [her]" (*Washington Monthly*, December 1998). Another example was the *New York Times* editorial after Starr had deliberately delayed the official exoneration of the Clintons in Whitewater, Travelgate, and Filegate until after the November elections. The *Times* called this announcement a "desk-clearing exercise," as if it had not been the chief rationale of the hounding of the president for six years. The editorial then turned to the Lewinsky scandal: "Mr. Clinton deserves to be punished in a way that writes his disgrace into the history books" (November 20, 1998). What about the *New York Times*'s disgrace?

On the other hand, for example in Michael Isikoff's *Uncovering Clinton,* Starr was supposed to be a "conservative legal Titan,"[9] deeply steeped in legal studies and profundities. But when we look at his record as special prosecutor, rather the opposite picture seems to emerge: Starr was extremely resourceful in securing political and media support, quite adept at manipulating the media and the public with judicious leaks of information and with his act of shyness, modesty, and understatement. He was not above putting salacious, even pornographic details to work for his political aim of ousting the twice-elected president of the United States. As for being a legal titan, one is, of course, hard put to compare Starr to the great American jurists who have dominated legal history and written some of the great Supreme Court opinions over the decades. Starr appears to lack the appreciation for the majesty of the law and for finding freedom in the interstices of lawful procedure. His interest in legal process, on the contrary, seems to bend toward such low tricks as extorting testimony with threats, entrapping a person in perjury, and trampling the rights of the accused. In spite of his rhetoric, his championship of the rule of law, not to mention the Constitution, does not appear to have risen above the level of Henry Hyde and the impeachment advocates on the House Judiciary Committee and in the rest of Congress. Legal titans all, they outfitted a veritable RMS *Titanic,* armored with arrogance and fueled with sheer hubris, to attack the Constitutional office of the president. Fortunately, this ship collided with a mighty iceberg, the Constitution, and sank before it could complete its task, owing to the common sense of most Americans.

Evidence of attempts to mold anti-Clinton opinion in the years from 1994 to 1997 abounds in the mainstream media. When a media conspiracy is trying to shape opinion in its direction, being direct and confrontational obviously may be far less effective, perhaps even counterproductive, than a subtle approach of undermining trust and preparing the coup itself. The reader may recall the peculiar rationalizations of *Time* magazine in March 1994 to equate Whitewater with Watergate and, then again, to differentiate the two cases. The article "Why It Isn't Watergate" conceded that the Whitewater investigation had not revealed any "evidence of criminality" on the part of the Clintons and yet it was supposed to demonstrate their uncertain "veracity" regarding the health care reform and other policy issues (March 21, 1994). Dick Armey, an influential House Republican leader, was also quoted in the article to the effect that he would see to it that Clinton was somehow "impeached" on the Whitewater charges dating from an ill-fated sixteen-year-old financial speculation.

From that time also, the great media conspiracy evidently triggered a five-year chorus of equating Whitewater with Watergate: "the suffix 'gate' obviously intended to evoke Watergate, that notorious affair which brought about President Nixon's fall in 1974," as Bacharan writes, turns "a suspicion into a scandal."[10] How can we ignore the addition of the suffix 'gate' to every supposed presidential lapse and the continual intimations that impeachment of the president, for whatever reason and regardless of the Constitution, was just around the corner. Like the other small touches, the verbal formulas and presumable echoes of Watergate evidently were meant to soften up the emotional resistance to such an extreme step and, perhaps, to prepare the coup against Clinton by picturing him already fallen. There also were hints that the Republican conspirators were seeking revenge for Watergate, and other slights, but it is not clear why such revenge should target Clinton.

This mind-bending word manipulation was accompanied by more obvious attempts to undermine trust and perceptions of success. This apparently was to be achieved not only by the relentless criticism of the president's policies—which is, of course, perfectly legitimate in a democracy—but also by the constant, mantralike repetition of the formulas "lack of trust" and "character problem" without further explanations, as if a lack of trust and a character problem were foregone conclusions in the case of Clinton. Such formulaic incantations eventually took on ludicrous dimensions; for example, spokespersons for the post-impeachment Senate and House Republican majorities, after *what they had done to him* and to the Constitution, used the excuses of "not trusting him" and balking at his "character" for not cooperating with him. Not trusting him in negotiations, of course, might also have meant that they feared he would once again make fools of them.

Another media tactic to diminish trust and any perceptions of presidential success was to report every achievement at home or abroad as if he did it "only to win the next elections," or "only because he was trying—too hard—to establish his mark in history." Why did he try to bring women and minority appointments into his administration? Not because he believed in it and it was the right thing to do, but to win the next elections. Why did he try to get the vast numbers of uninsured into his health care reform? Why did he try to get thousands more policemen on the beat of the nation's streets or teachers into our schools? To secure his place in history. When repeated often enough to a gullible public, and they were, these phrases would inevitably produce a sour taste in the mouth, suggest a vain personality, a leader incapable of doing anything for its own sake or because he believes it is right for the country. This tactic dissolves a leader's hopes and projects, and reduces them to egomaniacal competitiveness. Just winning the next elections or scoring better in the polls or in parliamentary voting as the sole motive, of course, also distracts the public from the complex substance of the issues and policies.

Time magazine, for example, just could not help sneering at Clinton's State of the Union address in the midst of impeachment proceedings when he cordoned off the burgeoning budget surpluses of the next 15 years for Social Security: "Clinton needed a bold idea in his . . . address to help divert attention from that little matter in the Senate ... By the end of his ... speech [he] had suggested a total of—yikes!—99 policy goals. As a last-ditch, feel-good bid for a legacy, Clinton's 99 for '99 had something for every American, especially the older ones" (February 1, 1999). *Time* editor Nancy Gibbs was obviously nonplused by the fashion in which Clinton had survived a whole year of slow lynching by the media and now elicited "sweet, screaming, Election Day crowds" as he and Vice President Gore went to Buffalo and Pennsylvania. Still believing in the "Republican fortitude" of proceeding with impeachment in spite of electoral rejection and consistently negative polls, Gibbs was furious that the Democrats had organized 200 State of the Union watch-parties to raise support and funds, and that People for the American Way had sponsored anti-impeachment rallies in 23 cities. In a perfectly ordered lynching universe there is no tolerance for such resisters; they should be lynched too.

Calling the newly elected president and his team policy wonks was meant similarly to devalue the ethical substance of the policies themselves and to transform their proponents' desire to work for a better America into personal or intellectual idiosyncrasies: "He is just trying to impress us." For the journalists and politicians committed to an ideology, but woefully ignorant about concrete problems of governmental policy or simply preoccupied with their own egos, it was certainly easier to dodge policy discussions or to insist that the federal government simply be stripped of the power to be active in such complex areas as education, health insurance, poverty, social security, and environmental regulation. Or they could simply stick to discussions of sex, a subject for which a journalist requires no great expertise or investigative research. The media bias of the Clinton years was so heavy that popular jokes soon began to make the rounds. For example—the pope is visiting an American city by a lake and the president escorts him on a walk. A gust of wind carries the visitor's hat off onto the lake. Clinton runs after it, over the waters, and brings back the pope's hat. The next day, the newspapers all carry the headline: "Clinton can't swim."

THE NEW NEWS

One of the many disgruntled news executives, CNN International editor Joseph Manguno in recent public lectures has expressed his dissatisfaction with the decline of newscasting and with CNN in particular. In foreign policy, Manguno said, "TV now sets the agenda with provocative images," but we must do everything to halt the resulting loss of policy control by the official policy makers. There has been an appalling "homogenization of opinion." News reporting, as practiced by nearly all the media, has become mostly entertainment. Journalism quality in the 1980s and 1990s also has declined, according to a wide-ranging survey by Serge Halimi in the French liberal monthly *Le Monde Diplomatique* (August-September, 1998), because the volume of newspaper readership has been shrinking in two-thirds of Western countries. Readership in the United States, for example, dropped from 78 percent of the adult population in 1970 to only 59 percent in 1997. Among young adults (21 to 35 years old), newspaper readership has decreased from 67 percent in 1965 to 31 percent in 1998. The audience for TV news—regardless of the novel concentration on captious sound bites of just 30 or 45 seconds—also has been declining steeply, from 60 percent of adults in 1993 to 38 percent in 1998, while the number of consumers of Internet news more than tripled (to 36 million) since 1995.

On the *NewsHour* with Jim Lehrer (August 26, 1999), Terence Smith confirmed that an ever-growing, estimated 20 percent of Americans were already getting at least part of their news off the Internet. As many, especially of the twenty-somethings, turn away from television and print news, they switch to on-line news including the on-line services offered by many papers, weeklies, and television programs for greater depth. Smith predicted that by the year 2002, at the latest, on-line news will have outgrown print news. Internet news reports such as the quasi tabloid Drudge Report, Microsoft's Slate, and Salon indeed played significant roles in the Clinton-Lewinsky matter. The "unscrupulous Drudge Report" was blamed by *Der Spiegel* (December 7, 1998) for forcing the still-uncorroborated sex scandal out into the open. The immediate release of the Starr Report to the Internet was also criticized by the European press (for example, by the *Neue Zuercher Zeitung*, quoted in *World Press Review*, November 1998) as a way for the House to avoid making an appropriate decision.

Deplorable also is the growing "journalistic myopia" of American print and television media, which has led to the rule of thumb that "[only] if it bleeds, it leads." Three-fourths of all local news programs now start with a crime, fire, spectacular accident, or police action story because, as confirmed by the *New York Times*, crimes and accidents are "the easiest, cheapest, laziest news to cover . . . all [the reporters] do is listen to the police radio, react to it, and send out a mobile camera unit . . . this cut-rate journalism, intercut with eight minutes of advertising every half hour," suits the interests of the multimedia conglomerates (quoted in *Le Monde Diplomatique*, August-September 1998). These have dominated American television since the Reagan administration deregulated the airwaves and, more recently, since Clinton and the Republican Congress gave away enough broadband channels to the networks to retire the entire United States national debt at once. Television is twice as profitable as the printed press which, notwithstanding its complaints, is still doing rather well at this time.

Serge Halimi, naturally, found international news particularly lacking in the United States. Not only are Americans more interested in local news and crimes, but even CNN International (as Manguno confirms) and public television's international news (PBS's ITN) still prominently cover crimes, scandals, and sports along with the hard news. To give a further example, few small-town papers carry news about the United Nations, except in cases of spectacular UN failures. The result is that most Americans know almost nothing about this vital world organization that the United States helped found in 1945, with the exception of the paranoid propaganda they may hear from the radical right about "the black helicopters" and imminent "one-world government" or from Caligula's horse in the Senate, Jesse Helms. For five decades now, the far right in this country has wanted to "get the U.S. out of the UN" and "the UN out of the U.S." Helms and his friends almost succeeded in doing just that through the device of not paying our UN dues for years; they wanted to pressure the UN to suspend all assistance to family planning organizations including those in Africa and countries like China or India.

A tally of *Time* magazine's international cover stories showed a decline from eleven in 1987 to only one in 1997. "It is however not wholly impossible to find serious news about world events in the U.S.," wrote *Le Monde Diplomatique,* tongue-in-cheek; "The *New York Times* [which admits to having assigned up to one-third of its news coverage to sports, sociology, celebrity confessions, and scandals] and the *Los Angeles Times* are quite capable of detailed international coverage on issues of economic restructuring or inequalities of wealth" (August-September, 1998). There is also a curious parallel here in the genuine regret that both Americans and Europeans have expressed about the failures of the American media and of Clinton in the course of the impeachment drama: what a pity it is that Clinton's extraordinary talents to serve America, the West, and the world were buried by the scurrilous and unconstitutional impeachment drive of 1998. And what a pity that rank greed and commercialism, not to mention the secret anti-Clinton agenda, of certain media moguls and editors have rarely permitted their own scores of gifted and able journalists to do the best they could for the good of the country.

Whether in the mainstream press or in television, the once staid and serious business of transmitting political news has witnessed drastic changes: even aside from crimes and accidents, the emphasis on the sensational, personal, idiosyncratic is stealing the political show. As the *Sueddeutsche Zeitung* put it in the midst of the January 1998 revelations about Lewinsky: "An entirely new picture of the media as a bringer and source of the news has arisen . . . a rumor mill . . . an avalanche of news reports outrunning what is known [at the moment]" (January 24, 1998). Or, as it was called by many Americans outside the Washington Beltway, "the runaway media circus" that insisted that the broader American public follow its lead. Of course, the public did just the opposite. Sober comparisons with the Watergate era also bring out the difference. As veteran journalist Haynes Johnson said on the *NewsHour:* "[At the time of Watergate] there were strong, honorable people like Sam Ervin, or Judge John Sirica, and the press was not as ravenous, wild, mad, and hated as we are today" (September 14, 1998). It is difficult indeed to find such "strong, honorable people" among the lynch mob in Congress or in the editorial offices of the nation's media.

This is the "New News," as Jim Lehrer called it, after the election results of November 1998 had splashed a little dose of reality onto the hot faces of the impeachers; "it takes a show business approach to the news" (November 5, 1998). And, as with show business, the name of the game is not bringing the news to the public, but bottom-line profit for the media conglomerates. Political commentator Daniel Schorr called it "the unholy alliance between a new kind of journalism and an old kind of manipulation" and quoted Jay Leno (one of the sad comedians who have lived for years on a diet of aging sex jokes about Clinton), who said he looked at the impeachment process as entertainment (!): "It's like the Jerry Springer Show, except everyone has a law degree." Schorr asks: "What has happened to us, the media? . . . Where did we lose our membership in an identifiable group of professionals, called the Fourth Estate because we stood outside an establishment that we viewed with skeptical detachment?" (*Los Angeles Times,* January 31, 1999). James Fallows, another distinguished journalist, criticized the media's "rush to judgment" after only a few months of the Clinton administration and attributed the contentiousness of 1990s journalism to the new culture of Crossfire and the argumentative John McLaughlin television talk show: "It is the clinching evidence that John McLaughlin has supplanted Woodward and Bernstein as the symbol of Washington journalism" (*Washington Monthly*, January-February 1994). If they are not shouting at each other, it's not a political news show.

Marvin Kalb and several other prominent elder statesmen of journalism blamed the New News for "drowning out any deeper search [for causes and meaning] by their sheer concentration on the Lewinsky story," to the exclusion of State of the Union speeches and the war with Iraq (*NewsHour*, October 30, 1998). Richard Reeves in his book *What the People Know: Freedom and the Press*[11] characterized the New News as the "sensationalizing of stories." Kalb further described the New News of 1998 on the *NewsHour* with Jim Lehrer with five damning characteristics: (1) 70 percent of this news lacked the benefit of the usual sourcing and cross-checking; (2) newscasting was based on sweeping assumptions that the information was "somewhere out there," and hence speculation and guesswork about the facts were enough; (3) editorial bias and slant played a large role; (4) there was an inclination to rush to judgment, a conviction that Clinton was guilty as charged; and, (5) there was the conviction that the news should have the character of entertainment anyway (November 13, 1998). Kalb added that standards of personal privacy had once largely barred journalists from invading that hallowed sphere but that the journalistic standards of thirty years ago had slipped into "an inseparable mix of good, not so good, and bad." He cited polls that found, for example, that 70 percent of American adults felt that the Clinton testimony before the grand jury should never have been released to the public. A former national editor of the *Los Angeles Times*, Norman C. Miller, in an essay entitled "Whatever happened to checking out the facts?," similarly chastised contemporary reporters for skipping the all-important reality test: "Clinton's . . . disgraceful behavior in office is now apparently seen by some reporters and editors as justification that anything goes . . . this demeans politics and shames the press. Politicians, like everyone else, are entitled to the presumption of innocence" (*Los Angeles*

Times, August 26, 1999). As Dick Walsh wrote in the *Irish Times* (September 12, 1998): "[Clinton's impeachment] will be a first for tabloid journalism which has manufactured, managed and marketed an issue on which few of its own practitioners could afford to be tested."

THE *LOS ANGELES TIMES* IN TABLOID LAND

"Are the mainstream news organizations using tabloid methods?" asked veteran journalist Terence Smith on the NewsHour (February 3, 1999); he answered his question in the affirmative and added that even the real tabloids are complaining about it. The venture of the Los Angeles Times into tabloid land with Troopergate is a good example, although other once-respectable papers and the television networks could supply many more illustrations. There is much to admire about the Los Angeles Times, owing to the many fine journalists working for it. Its editorial guidance, however, periodically steers the paper onto the cliffs of political battle, and this is evidently how it became a major vehicle for the drive to go after the newly elected president in December 1993 by means of a sex scandal plus allegations of a cover-up, a formula that by now everybody recognizes.

The *Los Angeles Times*'s Troopergate story began with a very large spread on page one (December 21, 1993), and went on for four more pages, 3,615 words in all. It had pictures of the two principal Arkansas state troopers, Roger L. Perry and Larry G. Patterson, separately and together with their attorneys, Cliff Jackson and Lynn Davis, and a photograph of the Clintons embracing on *60 Minutes* after Bill's denial of the Flowers disclosures in the 1992 presidential primary campaign. One can write a lot in 3,600 words, especially if the format is not constrained by the paper's usual insistence on economy of space, relevance, and confirmed facts. In this case, the paper indulged a number of lurid subplots to the main story about then-governor Clinton using his bodyguards and a state limousine to pursue various amorous liaisons and then offering federal jobs to the troopers to secure their silence. One subplot was the old Flowers story, in case anyone had forgotten it. Another was a sweaty tale of a Clinton paramour picking him up on his regular jogging trail and later bringing him back to the trail, in need of obvious dishevelment and perspiration that would show that he had indeed been jogging five miles. Another subplot involved the elaborate analysis of telephone records revealing numerous calls from and to that same woman. Yet another subplot pictured Hillary sleeping upstairs in the governor's mansion while Bill entertained that same woman in the basement or was on nocturnal outings with his troopers, who would warn him by cellular telephone if Hillary woke up. A real tabloid, of course, would have supplied a photograph of one of the troopers holding the cellular phone in question or, like the Starr Report, described the floor plan and furnishings of the gubernatorial basement.

The first Troopergate report of the *Los Angeles Times* was unable to present testimony from any of the women allegedly involved to confirm the sexual misconduct. It did quote one as saying, "It is infuriating to me that someone is obviously being paid a lot of money to tell you a lie." The paper itself denied ever paying money for such testimonials but indicated that the ever-resourceful Cliff Jackson "had tried [unsuccessfully] to line up a . . . politically conservative financier to guarantee [funds for] jobs and legal defense for the troopers" in case they were fired for telling their stories. Jackson did succeed in getting David Brock to write his hit-piece in the *American Spectator* (January 1994), reportedly with money from Scaife. Both *American Spectator* and Brock's book *The Real Anita Hill: The Untold Story* were funded in part by the ultra-conservative Bradley Foundation for which Starr was an attorney.

The *Los Angeles Times* explained that its foray into tabloid land was motivated by a change in journalistic standards from the days when such scandals would be disclosed only posthumously, to new standards "propelling . . . the media onto uncertain ground." The paper also claimed to be motivated by "a widening belief that personal character may be as important to a leader's performance as political party ideology," a statement the paper did not explain further or put in relation to President Clinton's having been duly elected. The Southern California daily said nothing about the importance of character in publishers and editors, not to mention marital fidelity or truthfulness. Roger L. Perry was quoted by the paper as saying: "If we wanted to go out and sell our stories we could have gone to some big tabloids." Instead, the troopers found the *Los Angeles Times,* although by this time (December 21, 1993), the paper had already been scooped by eager disclosures on CNN and NBC.

The whole affair was quickly dubbed Troopergate. "Cliff Jackson hoped to get $2.5 million to write a book about the [Troopergate] scandal and offered handsome sums to troopers who would help him," wrote Bacharan in *Le piège*.[12] The troopers, too, hoped to write a book that might help them out of financial troubles, present and anticipated. Perry's money problems came to light as the whole scandal quickly began to fall apart in the midst of a credibility crisis: the two principal trooper witnesses had been in a major automobile accident in 1990 after a number of cocktails and then lied about it to insurance investigators. Patterson had driven a state police car first to a nightclub and then into a tree, injuring both Perry and the latter's date, also a state police employee. Apparently, Perry could not meet all his medical bills for treatment of a broken neck even though he had a lawsuit pending against Patterson's insurance for the full personal liability amount.

In the meantime, Clinton's guardian angel Betsey Wright, his long time aide and rescuer in the 1992 Flowers flap, arrived in Little Rock and put out the rest of the fire again. She persuaded a third state trooper, Danny Ferguson, to sign an affidavit revoking his earlier statement that Clinton had promised jobs in exchange for silence about the accusations of sexual misconduct. An exasperated Cliff Jackson fumed that "the issue is not whether in their whole lives [the troopers] never told a lie [but] whether they are telling the truth now about Bill Clinton." He then accused the resourceful Betsey Wright of "orchestrating a White House campaign of deceit and obfuscation." The troopers stood by their earlier statements minus the part about job offers in exchange for silence, but the Troopergate show was over. The *Los Angeles Times* had followed its first spread (December 21, 1993) with a page-one report on Clinton's denial of any misconduct or promises of jobs in exchange for silence (December 23)—"but he avoids specifics," the teasing title said—and then buried the story about the troopers' credibility crisis on page 17 (December 24, 1993).

Hillary Clinton angrily called the charges "outrageous" and refused to be grilled about them on ABC, NBC, and CBS morning shows about Christmas at the White House, which had been scheduled before this "Christmas surprise." The three networks thereupon canceled her appearances; their actions, of course, only served to illustrate their disrespect for the first couple if not their conspiratorial collusion.

Five issues and nearly 7,000 words after its Troopergate coverage began, the *Los Angeles Times*'s first tabloid-style coverage of the presidency had fizzled. There were a few columnists' comments still about Troopergate, by Suzanne Garment, Robert Scheer, and James P. Pinkerton (December 26, 27, and 31), and that was the end. A disappointed Jackson finally wrote a public "letter of apology" to the president, with copies for the media, in which he said: "I feel for your pain and that of your family" and "I have no vendetta against Clinton" (*Los Angeles Times*, December 30, 1993). The second sentence, in retrospect, is eerily evocative of Starr's later words, in a speech to editors and friends in Los Angeles, when he said his greatest regret was creating the erroneous impression that he had been engaged in a "vendetta against Clinton" (*Los Angeles Times*, September 16, 1999). A European friend of mine, on reading about it, guffawed: "No vendetta, Ken? What did you think you were doing, for five years and $50 million of taxpayers' money? Preparing Bill for canonization?"

Anthony Lewis, writing in the *New York Times* (which also carried the Troopergate discussion for a week but without the tabloid flourishes), commented: "The American press faced, and most of it flunked, a test of its resistance to cheap and scurrilous rumors" by repeating the charges of Troopergate. He derisively noted the frequent rationalizations that the editors were concerned not with sex but with the alleged cover-up, for "only someone driven by hate would make the President's most intimate life the test of his Administration" (December 27, 1993). The *New York Times* turned instead to the lurid story of Paula Jones (February 12, 1994) and wallowed in it for most of the month of May and into June. In an editorial (May 25), the paper argued that it was "unwise for the courts to adopt the 'highly dubious' claim of presidential privilege . . . against a civil suit from [Clinton's] Arkansas period" until after the end of Clinton's term. The *Los Angeles Times* filled nearly every issue from January to May of 1994 with Whitewater stories, more than 50 in four months. In fact, the paper kept up the drumbeat until the autumn of 1998, when for some reason it began to advocate restraint. At one point, it even became an advocate of censure rather than impeachment. Nevertheless, through the next year, the *Los Angeles Times* every now and then would favor columnists and cartoonists who were already crowing over Clinton's presumably imminent ouster when, in fact, he persevered as an effective and very active president. The *New York Times* at this point also managed the schizophrenic policy of poison-pen editorials combined with occasional columns advocating a more balanced approach and exposés like Don van Natta and Jill Abramson's story about the right-wing lawyers' conspiracy (October 4, 1998).

One example of the *Los AngelesTimes*'s anti-Clinton favorites were the poison-pen cartoons of Michael P. Ramirez. European cartoonists and caricaturists do not shy away from political controversy and can be biting in their satirical descriptions of the men and women in power. France and Britain, in particular, have a rich and venerable tradition of caricatures. Even the formerly communist countries of Eastern Europe boast excellent reputations for hilarious pictures of the high and mighty, much of it dating from the days when East European humor often flourished, in a fashion, right under the noses and at the expense of malevolent dictators and narrow-minded party censors. But there is also a broad consensus on the limits of good taste and cartooning manners that seems to separate these European cartoons from some of the products of American polemical caricatures. At the outset of the referral of the Starr Report, for example, *Le Monde Hebdomadaire* (August 22, 1998) published a cartoon showing both Clinton and Boris Yeltsin facing each other in their underwear. The American president asks his Russian counterpart: "An intern?" Yeltsin replies: "No, a ruble devaluation," while we can see behind him a back room full of gambling cronies who evidently won his clothes from him (they are draped over a chair). Showing the high and mighty in their underwear to express their embarrassment is considered piquant humor and clean fun in Europe. Let us compare this, however, to a Ramirez cartoon in the *Los Angeles Times* showing two cockroaches scurrying toward each other on a landscape of total devastation, presumably after a massive nuclear explosion. One cockroach cries out, "Bill?," the other "Monica?" (March 5, 1999, and reprinted as "one of the best cartoons of 1999" on December 31, 1999).

To compare the president of the United States and his paramour to cockroaches is crude and certainly not funny to European minds. My European friends in Southern California recoiled in disgust from this egregious display of the evidently pathological Clinton-hatred on the part of the cartoonist and the editor who authorized the cartoon in the public space of the newspaper. "This is how the Nazis used to talk about Jews," said one of them. "It is no surprise that this should come from a man reported to have been connected to the racist Council of Conservative Citizens [which Ramirez has denied], considering Southern resentment of Clinton's rapport with African Americans. People like them probably talk about blacks the same way." The other commented on the evident affinity of the cartoonist and editor for cockroaches, and added: "Speaking of cockroaches, do you remember that movie [*Men in Black*] where the good guys are fighting a secret invasion of giant alien cockroaches that grow to humongous size when they are cornered? And every time the good guys shoot at them, the cockroaches explode into a rain of green slime that slimes the good guys? I think your right-wing conspiracy consists of nothing but such giant alien subversives who try to slime you as soon as you confront them." And the slime, I fear, may adhere forever. *Aliquid semper haeret* (something always sticks).

TALK RADIO HOSTS

Few features of the contemporary American media have drawn as much attention in Europe as talk radio, which has few parallels on the other side of the Atlantic. It was ABC Radio, an offshoot of the Capital Cities/ABC media empire, that sponsored Rush Limbaugh, Barry Farber, and Paul Harvey to bring the Reagan doctrine to the masses. To quote John Arne Markusen of the Oslo *Dagbladet:* "In the United States, reactionary men with media power have been active for years." He pointed to the role of organized radio campaigns, including that of the network of Christian Broadcasting, in Pat Robertson's presidential campaign of 1988: "Today [this] . . . includes conservative radio man Rush Limbaugh who is currently causing more trouble for President Clinton than the Republicans in Congress." Markusen emphasized the high visibility and popularity of talk radio in those days of the health care debate: "By definition [the radio hosts always] are the outsiders. Their favorite target is the stupid government which always does the wrong thing. And so it goes, a constant stream of banal answers to complicated questions, and attacks on gays, blacks, and traffic jams . . . Call-in radio has become a primitive forum for those with cellular phones who sit restlessly in traffic" (quoted in *World Press Review,* July 1994).

During the 1996 election campaign, *Der Spiegel* (April 3, 1995) outlined the mid-1990s dimensions of the phenomenon: Limbaugh was on 660 radio stations with an estimated 20 million regular listeners and also had a television program. The callers were "usually very ignorant, misinformed . . . and belonged to the far right." The magazine attributed the growth of talk radio to 1987 when the Reagan administration rescinded the fairness clause for radio broadcasters. Talk radio programs, relieved of the need for political balance, grew fivefold: "Talk radio is populism in its purest form because it uses direct feedback . . . telephone calls from listeners, to shape political sentiments . . . The result," *Der Spiegel* continued in Tocquevillean terms, "is an ignorant dictatorship of sentiment furthered by Limbaugh & Co. whom the politicians have learned to tiptoe around." The German weekly also told of a racist New York radio host and others dating back to 1949. It described it all as a kind of show business that uses "hate as a hot commodity; this broadcasters' business has nothing to do with the content," only with the financial bottom line. Hate sells.

The *Economist* (August 14, 1993) pointed out that Limbaugh's call-in feature usually drew an army of archconservative callers, his "dittoheads," who then enabled him to skew political debates toward the right-wing position. The British weekly also cited the Times-Mirror survey regarding the nature of the talk radio audience: white, male, well-to-do, elderly, and Republican, in favor of gun ownership and strongly opposed to Clinton, abortion, homosexuals, and women. As many as 42 percent of Americans, according to the survey, "sometimes listen" to talk radio *for news,* and 11 percent tried at least one time to call in themselves. This reflects talk radio's "exaggerated influence," although the hosts usually rely on the established media to pick up their causes or on listeners to call or write Congress or the White House with their complaints. The *Economist* also reminded its readers of the thirties and of the populist radio priest Father Coughlin and his cryptofascist, anti-Semitic harangues. There is indeed a long-established American tradition of right-wing agitation à la Christian Anti-Communist Crusade, which used to be at home mostly in the small-town press and with one-man newsletter (and fund-raising) operations in the fifties and sixties. Given the low level of political information of the average American, such grass-roots right-wing agitation can be very effective. Limbaugh's national prominence got him invited overnight to President Bush's White House—the president reportedly carried the bags of the portly talk show host—and Limbaugh subsequently sang the praises of Bush's policies on his program. When the freshmen of Gingrich's conservative revolution were elected, they reverently listened to a pep talk by Limbaugh and made him an honorary member of their group.

After his reelection in 1996, President Clinton, in a rare response during a press conference, said that "[these radio talk show programs] try to bring people down, to make you look small." He could have drawn chapter and verse from an earlier devastating *Time* magazine feature (November 1, 1993) that compared Limbaugh with the sexually obsessed and socially conservative Howard Stern. *Time* called them both "bombastic, iconoclastic, outlandishly populist rabble-rousers" and associated Limbaugh with youngish, white, grass-roots Reaganites ("he is the ultimate Reaganite"), but also with small-business ownership, taxi drivers, Perot voters, and people devoted to action movies. The news magazine mentioned Limbaugh's two best-selling books and newsletter (370,000 subscribers in 1993), and gave samples of his rhetoric: on Hillary's health care reform proposal, "Bend over, America"; on liberals, "these long-haired, maggot-infested, dope-smoking peace pansies"; and on pro-abortion feminists, the "femiNazis." Limbaugh's diatribes articulate the deep distrust of the average American for elected politicians and "the system," and also his resentment of the hostile, exclusionary national media elite behind them.

In surveys, *Time* reported in 1993, one third of Americans (34 percent) and half the Democratic voters (48 percent) thought the government should censure Limbaugh's sliming attacks on the

Clintons. A year later (April 11, 1994), *Time* again surveyed the right-wing talk radio and newsletter scene, including religious right-wing propaganda such as a 1992 poster that proclaimed "To vote for Clinton is to sin against God." The magazine pointed to the right-wing hate mills of Little Rock, the source of Whitewater and Troopergate allegations without end, and right-wing direct mail pioneer Richard Viguerie, who was quoted as saying about Clinton: "What president since Lyndon Johnson has been so open about his sexual promiscuity."

No one, of course, skewered the Limbaugh phenomenon more effectively than humorist Al Franken in his book *Rush Limbaugh Is a Big Fat Idiot*,[13] in which he ridiculed the considerable comic talents of the radio host for political humor. Exposing, in particular, the reliance of Limbaugh on lies, half-truths, and an abject ignorance about the complexities of social problems and policies, Franken showed the Achilles heel of much of the right-wing assault on the Clinton administration. In some ways, Limbaugh reminds one of the late Governor George Wallace of Alabama, who used to criticize liberals for "coming up with complicated solutions to simple problems." On the other hand, sober voices from our Canadian neighbor have a different take on talk radio in the United States. In the article, "A Bitter, Self-doubting Nation" in *Canadian Business* (quoted in *World Press Review,* October 1996), an unnamed columnist maintained that "talk radio only expresses [public sentiments that are] already there... the voice of the average American." The Canadian paper referred to 800 talk radio stations in 1996 in the United States and an audience that was indeed "self-doubting and deeply divided " about self-contradictory values and preferences. It stated that talk radio tended to be more cynical about Washington than the American mainstream press but, according to the Times-Mirror survey, actually less so than the American public, which gave Washington an even lower ethical rating. The reasons for this attitude were to be found in stagnating incomes and the huge and growing gap between the incomes of the wealthy and the average people in America. A sense of powerlessness and the associated fears of affirmative action, crime, and social problems, *Canadian Business* believed, round out the picture.

TELEVISION: THE EMPTY DESERT

The recent changes in American television newscasting and political advertising—usually by far the costliest part of campaign expenses—have long drawn critical attention in the European press. Europeans have always complained about television's bias, but in their own public, long-time, state-owned television rather than on private channels. Their increasingly independent choices of private television have not even begun to raise problems comparable to American television. To European eyes, to start with, politically relevant television in the United States seems incredibly bland and unpolitical most of the time and a venal racket at campaign time and in between. European state television usually provides candidates for high public office with free time to present their views. It also features frequent political editorials and debates. Daniel Schorr's pertinent comments on National Public Radio about the impact of television on national politics are often cited in the European press, with respect to both candidate selection and the fatal attraction of politicians to television cameras: "You can't run for office if you lisp, have an accent, or can't speak in 45-second sound bites. Whatever happened to issues; where are our Churchills, FDRs, or de Gaulles?" Schorr also explained the political blandness of American television: the fear of offending even 20 percent of the audience creates "this political mush." He called Reagan "our first media president and a model for all to come . . . The secret of his success was sincerity. If you can fake that, you are home free . . . Reagan was a very good liar who never tired of false anecdotes such as the one about the welfare queen in a Cadillac . . . He dreamt big dreams and came to believe in them himself . . . [and then] sold them to us."

For a major constitutional crisis and the moral shocker of all time, the scandal commanded little attention on television. At the height of the impeachment debates in the House in mid-December, impeachment and the constitutional questions involved attained only the sixteenth rank as a national news story: in the polls, only a third (32 percent) of the public was found to be paying "close attention" to them and a few more (38 percent) gave them "some attention." As Hyde and company droned on, some of the major networks had already ceased coverage, wishing the president would just resign and the whole matter would go away and not have to be pursued further. But from the very beginning of 1998 and on certain occasions during the previous four years, television had been deeply involved in the unfolding constitutional crisis in part because of television's inherent flaws, and in part deliberately, as part of the anti-Clinton conspiracy of the media.

The low cost and high profitability of the news and the 24-hour news cycle have long created a paradox. On the one hand, there was now a constant need to fill the empty hours with just-breaking news, often mindlessly copied from the speculations of other media figures, hastily made up from guesswork, and rarely checked against corroborating facts. And there was the upshot of the ever-fiercer competition for leaks and sound bites from the OIC or the White House. The German *Stern* magazine's image of hotly arguing members of Congress in the December 1998 impeachment debates looking like the 19 trained dolphins of Sea World actually better fits the televised 1998 White House press conferences, with their over-eager correspondents, each popping up in turn, trying to ask the same tired questions about the Lewinsky scandal.

It is still an open question whether it is the media who have long been lowering the public's interest in politics or whether the ever-shorter political attention span of that public is the cause of its "tuning out" politics. The director of the Brookings Institution, Thomas Mann, blames the media's emphasis on "covering politics [only] as a game, a forum for celebrity life, and a place for scandal" and notes that they publish few stories about government working well. In television news programs such as ABC World News Tonight and CBS Evening News, according to the Committee of Concerned Journalists, the percentage of government news, good or bad, has dropped by half in the last 20 years. Personal-interest stories and political opinion and analysis have been taking their place. With the rise of CNN, moreover—according to a 1999 *American Journalism Review* study by reporters John Herbers and James McCartney—typical news stories have become very condensed and this has tended to be the new norm of the industry (*Washington Monthly,* July-August 1999). Knowledgeable insiders like former White House press secretary Mike McCurry and *Washington Monthly* editor Charlie Peters, however, concede that government agencies do not always present a full picture of themselves, possibly at once reflecting and encouraging our cynical, negative image of government activities per se (*Washington Monthly,* January-February 1999).

While political news coverage has declined, on the other hand, the more thoughtful segments of the television news audience have been complaining more than ever that the broadcasts are so shallow and superficial (which, however, makes it all too easy to sneak in heavy biases of every kind), so lacking in analytical depth and background that they hardly ever succeed in "explaining the political world we live in." But, if there is so much additional news time to be filled with the 24-hour news cycle, why don't the newscasters fill it with independent news analysis and background in depth? Is in-depth analysis really so much more expensive? Or is the problem the ignorance of the local television personnel? According to an end-of-impeachment count by the *Los Angeles Times* (February 13, 1999), CNN had broadcast no fewer than 144 impeachment-related special reports, although the stories in the three major newspapers were far more numerous: 3,376 in the *New York Times,* 2,456 in the *Washington Post,* and 1,663 in the *Los Angeles Times.* Perhaps Dalton Camp was right when he wrote in the *Toronto Star* (November 18, 1997), apropos of the American media obsession with presidential sex to the exclusion of debating issues and policies: "There is some redemptive value in this lurid business. It is that American television has at last been given a story well within its intellectual resources and editorial competence."

The Murdoch-owned Fox News, CNN, MSNBC, and CNBC obviously prospered with the Clinton-Lewinsky scandal despite the pervasive scarcity of new revelations. Some spectacular canards were also exploited, such as the story of the black teenager who was supposed to be the illegitimate son of Clinton and a prostitute. The European press had a field day with the prejudices of the American media, though they often picked up on the canards right along with the true stories. The weekly *Die Zeit* (January 27, 1998) had called the Gary Hart affair of 1988 an "orgy of [media] hypocrisy" and, regarding Clinton, they again scored "the purity neurosis of the American media." The paper also had a brief assessment of the American press by Marvin Kalb, who proclaimed that "all standards of the U.S. press have broken down in the crazy competition to judge [Clinton] . . . all believe that he is guilty and are copying unproven allegations from each other" (*Die Zeit*, February 12, 1998). At the time of Clinton's impeachment in the House, *Die Zeit* claimed that the press corps had insisted: "Please, Mr. President, don't give us so much political stuff. Give us more drama and emotions, sex and lies, sin and remorse" (December 22, 1998). The next year, in the midst of the Senate trial, *Die Zeit* (January 28, 1999) snickered about the decision to bar all cameras from the chamber: "This is the worst you can do in a media democracy." The *Sueddeutsche Zeitung* (January 23, 1998), in a piece "Sex statt Papst" (Sex instead of the Pope), sneered at the American media forsaking the unique story of the pope's visit in Cuba and rushing to Washington for a little sex scandal. British, French, and Italian television and press expressed similar misgivings about their American colleagues. So did the American public which, according to the polls, was very critical of the tiresome media efforts to get Clinton.

The French television commentator on American affairs, Bacharan, pilloried the hypocrisy of the American media, who in the end blame everything on the insatiable prurience of the public: "It is the public who decides! We only respond to its wishes. It is a voyeur, insatiable, salacious, all of that, this public... It is greedy and devours its idols."[14] She also drew special attention to the "journalistic myopia, even rude dishonesty... of CNN which, under the pretense of giving information... conducted a systematic campaign to beat the president down." She mentioned how CNN's financial expert Lou Dobbs, on the eve of the publication of the Starr Report, suddenly digressed from his financial news commentary to fulminate about the Clinton story: "a story so terrible, so sordid, with an intern half his age! Not a word about the prosecutor's methods... none to explain why the [sexually explicit] testimony given behind closed doors had been made public [where children might see it]." Bacharan also described the dog-and-pony show of Bernard Shaw and Judy Woodruff, the four hours of Clinton's interrogation before the grand jury, "the most grotesque thing to appear in a long time." And the little inserts underneath the televised picture, when the president's testimony was broadcast, ridiculing and contradicting every answer given by Clinton. "And as if this was not enough... several times a day the anonymous appeals of 'Voices' demanding that the president resign... One could not remain impartial any more."[15] This indeed was a CNN performance worthy of Joseph Goebbels, the Nazi propaganda chief. It made even Murdoch's Fox News, another television nemesis of the president, seem professional in comparison.

Perhaps the major networks realized the limitations of their own stars when they began to bring in writers and lawyers of notorious trials, like O.J. Simpson's Barry Scheck, to comment on the unfolding impeachment inquiry in September and October of 1998. However, by design or default, CNN and other channels put on some highly biased legal pundits, personal friends of Starr—

for example, Barbara Olson, Bradford Berenson, and Ann Coulter (who had listened to the audiotapes of Tripp even before they reached Starr)—members of the ultraconservative Federalist Society, and former federal prosecutors appointed by Presidents Reagan and Bush, rarely identifying them by background, party, or financial sponsorship. The networks generally ignored the nation's bona fide constitutional scholars—even those invited to testify before Hyde's Judiciary Committee—who would very likely have disagreed with these others. The 24-hour legal pundit show, predictably, supplied much misinformation and confusion. As Petra Pinzler wrote in a piece called "Sleazy Times" ("*Schmierige Zeiten*") in *Die Zeit* (August 30, 1998): "It is a soap opera without end." Clinton's plea in his televised August statement to the nation to "leave snooping into the private lives of politicians behind us" was followed instantly by "the endless blatherings of all the experts of every political shading, the friends, the enemies, the opponents, the laypersons, all more talkative than ever."

Pinzler thought the reputation of the American media suffered as much of a black eye in the whole crisis as did Congress and the president (*Die Zeit,* February 11, 1999). The news management of the networks was obviously content to let everyone blather on without the slightest effort to resolve any particular point for fear of appearing to give a spin to the discussion. There is some peril in the conservative "pundit culture," as Josh Getlin has dubbed it in the *Los Angeles Times* (December 16, 1998). Not only have the pundits been often wrong and notably unreliable in their predictions, but "the explosion of prime-time punditry raises serious journalistic issues: Is it proper for reporters who cover news stories to moonlight as opinion-mongers?" How representative are the pundits of American society, particularly outside Washington? After the experience of 1998-1999, the only thing that might recommend this "repetitious, often shrill pontificating" on all-news channel television is its cost: it is much cheaper than researching the news and obviously worth far less.

Other broadcasters, of course, were not shy about injecting their bias. In the end, as Paul Campos described it in his book *Jurismania*,[16] these legal "stealth spokespersons" for Starr and Hyde politicized the crucial constitutional questions surrounding impeachment to the point of obliterating them in our adversarial legal culture. If you really hated Clinton enough to want him impeached, the real meaning of the Constitution did not matter. The opening of the Senate trial was covered by the major networks, just as the major newspapers gave it page-one coverage. But they faded and dropped the subject after the first hour or two, although CNN, CBS, NBC, and other news channels continued to supply current information to a shrinking audience: only 15 percent watched all or most of it, and half of the public none of it. All along, some European journalists had unfavorably compared the percentages of television viewers of the landmarks of the Clinton-Lewinsky scandal with the popularity, for example, of the last television broadcasts of *M.A.S.H.* and of *Seinfeld*. The American provincial press often buried the Senate trial on the back pages. Many of the Senators, on the other hand, appeared on television newscasts or interview programs like *Meet the Press* to explain their positions throughout the trial, as did some of the House managers and legal pundits.

JOURNALISTS CRITIQUE THEMSELVES

American journalism during the years of 1998 and earlier often found in its own ranks some of the toughest critics of its sins. A Committee of Concerned Journalists, in fact, went to a great deal of trouble to probe the coverage of the Clinton-Lewinsky affair in the *Los Angeles Times, New York Times, Washington Post, USA Today, Time,* and *Newsweek,* as well as on PBS, CNN, and the three network news broadcasts. The results were both good and bad. Among the good news: the committee found the criticisms of New News coverage, leaks, and fabrications rather exaggerated. The media "*usually* relied on legitimate sources and *often* was careful about the facts" [italics added], although sometimes they got ahead of the facts or printed stories from second hand sources that turned out to be wrong. The bad news was that they often unfairly downplayed denials of those accused and were too quick to rely on Starr's assumptions—as their editors probably had told them to do. Of the published or broadcast statements on Clinton-Lewinsky in the first seven days of the story (January 21-27), 41 percent were not fact but "analysis, opinion, speculation, or judgment," which is not the most discriminating category. Another 33 percent were based on "anonymous sources" or "what other news media had said" (*Los Angeles Times,* February 13, 1999).

"The most damning accusation," wrote Josh Getlin of the *Los Angeles Times* (October 22, 1998), ". . . was that the press may have lost its ethical moorings in a rush to report the story." The journalists' committee chair said that Starr's perceptions "should give us all pause . . . virtually no reporting was done on the activities of the special prosecutor and his deputies, and their treatment of the grand jury process—long considered the role of watchdog journalism." And Benjamin Bradlee, the *Washington Post's* editor in the paper's glory days of Watergate who had been accused by the *Washington Monthly* of having shielded Starr from curious journalists, blamed the 24-hour cable newscasts, the Internet, and careless TV pundits for the lapses of the press. The embattled Anthony Lewis at the *New York Times* commented: "The press, or much of it, can only look back on its performance with embarrassment." And he quoted Russell Baker who had said, "Hanging judges lurk behind every byline, every editorial, every TV reporter, every talking head," as he trenchantly described the media lynching of the president.

Alexis de Tocqueville applauded the crucial role of an independent press in a democracy but had his misgivings about the undereducated, vulgar, and sensationalist American journalism of his day. The function of an independent press in a democracy is undeniable and strongly acknowledged by today's European journalists, many of whom have learned their trade from us back in the 1940s or since. But what can one do when—to borrow Bacharan's subtitle for *Le piège*—"a democracy loses its head," when the media have gone haywire under the pressure of structural changes and the marketplace? When they, instead of critically watching the conduct of our governors and keeping us informed, pursue a vendetta of their own, abusing the law and the Constitution, filling airwaves and print news pages with their not-so-subtle bias? When the media, like the *New York Times*'s Captain Ahab, editor Howell Raines, get carried away chasing the Clinton White Whale to the ends of the earth, forgetting their crucial function in a democracy? "If the president deserves to be punished," wrote Robert Scheer, "what about the leading news organizations . . . ?" In his opinion, "Concealing a private sexual liaison pales in comparison with the media's betrayal of the public trust in a free press" (*Los Angeles Times,* November 24, 1998).

"The news organizations went wrong when they lost sight of their being a public service," said CNN International's Joseph Manguno in one of his public lectures, "and decided they were merely a commercial operation." A past president of the American Society of Newspaper Editors, Sandra Rowe, and Geneva Overholzer, formerly of the *Washington Post,* were exceedingly critical of the cable news coverage of the scandal but warned that even more slipshod coverage as well as more public disparagement of the media was ahead in the future. "People have a pretty sophisticated view of what the press is supposed to do [in a modern democratic society]," said journalism professor Jacquelin Starkey of the University of Arizona, according to the *Los Angeles Times*. "I fear we are in for a period of growing public criticism of the press because people sense that we haven't done enough hard thinking about real news values. They know we have a responsibility to uphold, but do we?" (February 13, 1999). The media captains indeed need to stand back and look at their conduct since 1992. They have little to be proud of. They need to reestablish the boundary between the respectable media and the tabloids, after following them like a herd of sheep, often trying to outdo each other in the search for doubtful or meaningless scoops. Steven Brill in his famous "Pressgate" exposé (*Brill's Content*, July-August, 1998) described the explosive mixture when, in January of 1998, "an author in quest of material [Linda Tripp under the guidance of literary agent Lucianne Goldberg] teamed up with a prosecutor in quest of a crime, and most of the press became a cheering section for the combination that followed." The media captains should also rebuild the barriers between advertisers and the editorial staff.

We have seen the creeping media oligopoly and its stranglehold over press and television in the midst of a strange mixture of deregulation and growing, runaway commercial monopolies with only profit on their minds. The journalistic myopia of the New News, the retreat from traditional approaches to newscasting, and the near-disappearance of international news are enough to give pause to even the staunchest defender of the status quo in the media. The emptiness of television and the mindless propaganda of talk radio surely fail to compensate for the deterioration of the print media. In this chaotic wasteland, it is all the more frightening "when many organs of the press [and other media] adopt the same line of conduct" (Alexis de Tocqueville). Such a media conspiracy against the express will of the people can destroy democracy instead of serving it.

CHAPTER FIVE

Damage to the Constitution?

Why do they all pretend now there was no damage to your constitutional order, the media, the attorneys, the politicians in Washington and their supporters back home? It's like your inebriated neighbor who backed into your parked car last night. Today he is sober and does not want to remember anything about what happened last night. Besides, he says, maybe your car had a dent in the door to start with.

—Anonymous, Munich (June 1999)

In ten, twenty or thirty years, one will think back on this episode as a moment of national folly.

—Carl Bernstein, quoted in *La Repubblica* (August 8, 1998)

Military historians, following the von Clausewitz formulation, speak of the fog of war or of the fog of battle to suggest that in the midst of a massive hostile confrontation, individual combatants, groups of soldiers, and even generals often cannot see very well what is going on until it is too late to take the right action: to attack, go to the aid of comrades fighting superior odds, or to retreat. The fog of the great impeachment battle of 1998-1999 has parted at last, and we can now assess more clearly, against the background of a new, post-Clinton election campaign, what was going on and what damage may have been done by the extremist assault on our constitutional and political system. Thanks to the determined and partisan prosecutorial, congressional, and media efforts to slime the president in order to eject him from office, the quest for a balanced assessment of the impeachment crisis now faces another major obstacle: the American media, the politicians involved on both sides, and even the right-wing and left-wing pundits, are so deeply divided and "talked out" that there seems to be no common ground to attain a balanced view. The media and much of the public, moreover, seem to have responded to this predicament with total amnesia; they do not want to talk about it, and pretend that everyone is so sick of the subject that they have no desire to get to the bottom of it. Americans would rather think ahead toward new electoral choices, some say, than dwell further on the besmirched escutcheon of a lame-duck president. This book never meant to defend the president who made it all too easy for his pursuers. Putting our heads into the sand, however, is no solution to the future dilemmas of partisan showdowns and fictitious moral crusades damaging the fabric of American democracy and of the Constitution.

We owe it to future generations here and abroad and to our venerable Constitution to analyze the crisis, to assign contributory guilt or innocence, and to think of protections against a recurrence of these abuses of our system. "The proceedings to remove the president from office," wrote Dieter Buehl in *Die Zeit* (January 14, 1999), "have awakened doubts about the predictability of Washington. Europeans are uneasy about America's historical drama. What was brewed in a year full of embarrassments and disclosures will now explode [in the Senate trial] . . . The 'irreplaceable' world power will be busy with itself for a long time." The German weekly cited particularly the "disproportionality" of the action, the "hatred and will to destroy [the popularly elected] Clinton," and the disdain for the will of the popular majority as matters for attention. How indeed can our allies feel any "trust" in American leadership of the democratic world when Washington carries on in such a fashion?

To understand the depth of the American debacle before the world, perhaps what is needed are disinterested outside observers, such as the European journalists we have quoted, to restore our sense of political reality beyond partisan hatred and strife. We certainly cannot expect a neutral point of view from the hostile parties involved, including the dominant part of the media, or flawed attempts at a balanced view by Reagan- or Bush-appointed judges and legal authorities. If we had looked into that European mirror while the crisis was in full bluster, and if our own media for reasons of their own had not withheld that point of view from us, we might have seen through the fog of this battle earlier. Many Americans, of course, arrived at a balanced view on their own and registered their conclusions in the public opinion polls of 1998-1999. They were the saving grace in this national disaster.

A VAST RIGHT-WING CONSPIRACY?

"So, what about the vast right-wing conspiracy? Did you spot such a thing while watching the Washington scene before, during, and after the impeachment of the president?" I asked two European visitors.

"Well, yes," replied one of them, a journalist who had observed the media scene closely: "It started with a clique of malevolent scandalmongers in Little Rock and with Arkansas politicians Clinton had defeated in earlier elections. But it was not particularly right-wing ideological although the vast majority of the Clinton-haters are Republicans and many are self-described religious conservatives. Some were Democrats, no doubt. But then, Clinton's policies often followed conservative lines, too."

The other European, a lawyer, nodded vigorously: "Yes, a deep personal hatred of the Clintons comes closer to describing the core of his enemies to this day. And, with all the many partisans and passionate Christian conservatives at the grass roots who were ready to believe anything bad about the Clintons, it was a vast conspiracy rooting for their fall."

The journalist smiled and said: "The runaway excitement of the media, I thought, was a most effective way to organize all these Clinton-haters, stoke their passion, and make them believe they had the president cornered. This was an example of manipulated mass psychology, of the mood of a lynch mob, as you say."

The legal expert became uncomfortable and she protested: "You make it sound as if none of this was happening in a legal context, moving slowly and deliberately like in a kind of trial, even if law and Constitution were flawed and violated. The four-year Starr investigation and the process of impeachment were no lynching passions, no assassination, no quick coup; they were in slow motion."

"But if it was so slow and deliberate, why did they never take the time to stop and think about what they were doing to the law and the Constitution in their violent Clinton hatred?" came the reply.

I reminded my two visitors how Paula Jones's dubious sexual harassment suit had been used by the secretive 'elves' and Starr, "like a kind of after-the-fact election, to use briefs, subpoenas, and interrogations to undo [slowly and] in secret what the voters had done," to quote Anthony Lewis. With furrowed brow, the European lawyer countered: "Sure, but the Starr operation took more than three years of burrowing in Whitewater, Travelgate, Fostergate, and Filegate before happening upon a live case, Clinton's dalliance with Ms. Lewinsky and his alleged cover-up." Regarding the OIC's Whitewater investigation, the deputy counsel in charge of the Little Rock office, W. Hickman Ewing, Jr., was obsessed with the Clintons' past love life. As Anthony Lewis confirmed, the OIC "investigators questioned Arkansas women mentioned in local rumors about Clinton . . . and questioned state troopers. It was a scandalous abuse of power by a prosecutor" ("Nearly a Coup," *New York Review of Books,* April 13, 2000). Lewis, who was a Harvard professor and wrote several important books on American law, also supplied a long list of OIC legal transgressions and harassments. Looking for sex scandals should have been a warning flag for everyone that the Starr investigation had a very different agenda than just looking into Whitewater.

Many Arkansas locals learned to despise the OIC deputies for their high-handed and lawless actions, just as they disliked the antics of the national media which insinuated that Arkansans were corrupt and a bunch of hillbillies. The Resolution Trust Corporation (RTC) had been entrusted with overseeing the resolution of the savings and loan bank failures—for example, Madison Guaranty's failure—of the Reagan and Bush era. Much of the fuel for the original Whitewater stories, according to Lewis, had come from RTC information distorted by one arch-Republican RTC administrator. Finally, the RTC ordered an independent study of Whitewater by a San Francisco law firm, Pillsbury, Madison, and Sutro, which confirmed the Clintons' testimony: the late James McDougal had looted the Whitewater partnership at the expense of the Clintons. Even the anti-Clinton *Wall Street Journal* had the integrity to report this exoneration, but Lewis's own *New York Times* buried it for six months before reporting it. This was also the time when the media erroneously predicted that Hillary Clinton would be indicted in connection with Whitewater (which did not happen) and the empty-handed Starr avenged himself by subjecting her to the media gauntlet, and by charging the uncooperative Susan McDougal with contempt and 18 months in jail.

My European visitors were appalled by the long list of Starr's crucial lies to entrap the president, especially his denial before Attorney General Janet Reno that OIC lawyers had been in prior contact with the Jones lawyers. "If Reno [and her deputy] had known of these connections," writes Lewis, "they surely would have referred the Lewinsky matter to a different independent counsel, if any... Falsities were two-a-penny in the Starr operation." To Lewis, "most astonishing in all this was the fact that a former judge [Starr], a constitutional conservative, showed no respect for the most basic consideration of the separation of powers [between Congress and the president]" that leaves impeachment exclusively to the House and Senate, and allows no advocacy by an independent counsel—the reason for Sam Dash's dramatic resignation—and gave him no authority to order Lewinsky to return to testify before House or Senate: "What business of [Starr's] was that?"

Starr's prosecutors (who of course wrote the pornographic text of the Starr Report) also wanted Lewinsky's testimony under immunity videotaped, particularly an account of exactly when and how she engaged in oral sex with Clinton. No doubt the intention was to distribute this pornographic videotape to the media and around the world. For once the young woman said no, but the resulting deposition, in Jeffrey Toobin's words, was still "a disgrace—to the prosecutors, to Starr, to Lewinsky, and, indeed, to the criminal process."[1] And to America, I would add, as were all the other legal lapses and invasions of the privacy of innocent bystanders by Starr, the man responsible for the entire operation. As independent counsel, Starr's signature on all documents naturally appears as "the United States," as if he represented the American people.

Once the Jones lawyers, Starr, and their cronies from the Federalist Society—the list is endless, possibly extending back to the late Lee Atwater in 1989[2]—had hatched their longstanding conspiracy to nail the president for a sexual indiscretion, Henry Hyde and his zealots in the House became their eager vehicle in pushing for the climax of the slow-motion lynching, the impeachment. Hiding behind heroic postures, they simply ignored the constitutional specifications and the clear signs of public disapproval, both in the elections and in the public opinion polls. On both counts, the abuse of the Constitution and of democratic principles, the two Europeans agreed, every House and Senate member voting for impeachment should be held accountable. "They violated their oaths of office," the European lawyer said.

"And the same goes for the judges and prosecutors who failed to stand up and resist this abuse of your Constitution."

Anthony Lewis drew the final balance line when he wrote: "Even more troubling is the role in this history of the Clinton-haters [everywhere] . . . there is something profoundly disturbing about the way the haters were able to use the power of money and modern communications, in secret, to undo—nearly—our electoral process." Indeed, are we so vulnerable to a rather small number of malevolent conspirators that they can sweep away the rules of our constitutional democracy and topple our highest elective official, just like that? This case was a disaster for our constitutional order and, like all lynchings, for the rule of law. "This is as close as America has come to a *putsch* [since the era of Andrew Johnson]," wrote Lars-Erik Nelson in the *New York Review of Books* (November 5, 1998).

DAMAGE TO THE CONSTITUTION

The December impeachment of Clinton and, oddly enough, his Senate acquittal left his pursuers crowing in triumph in many newspapers. As Doyle McManus wrote in the *Los Angeles Times* (December 20, 1998): "On Saturday, the Republican majority in the House of Representatives ensured that Clinton will be compared [not to his icons Teddy Roosevelt or John F. Kennedy but] . . . to a less inspiring predecessor, Andrew Johnson, the only other president to be impeached." And he cited the historian Stephen Ambrose, another vocal Clinton-hater: "A hundred years from now, this will undoubtedly be the first sentence in the paragraph that is given over to [every president in schoolbooks]." As if anyone could predict that, a hundred years from now (!), anyone would share the media frenzy and lynch mob mentality of 1998-1999, or that historians would not be wise to the transparent manipulations of this crisis. Is it not more likely that enlightened future historians would use the anti-Clinton conspiracy as a textbook example of how unrestrained hatred and partisanship nearly ruined the Constitution?

Clinton managed to soldier on both during and after this ordeal. But, despite what some of our pundits, politicians, and media have tried to persuade us since the Senate trial, it is obviously not true that our constitutional system suffered *no* damage from the five-year effort to overthrow a twice-elected president or from its 1998-1999 climax. After Andrew Johnson was impeached in 1868 for a very weighty cause but not removed from office, it took thirty years for the presidency to recover its strength and self-confidence vis-à-vis Congress. In 1888, Woodrow Wilson, a political scientist and college president long before he became president of the United States, described the entire federal government of his day as "congressional government" in a book by this title. He suggested that it was run by a dominant Congress and its committees, which is, of course, not the interpretation of the *Federalist Papers,* especially not the system envisioned by James Madison, the father of the Constitution. Madison believed in a strong central government composed of well-balanced, largely autonomous branches checking each other's power. He saw no need for impeachment at first and had to be persuaded to add the relevant clause. Wilson described the dominant House and Senate as a petty, spendthrift Congress, dominated by sectional interests and devoid of any larger vision or purpose. But the framers of the Constitution did not intend to make the executive branch a mere errand boy of Congress (as some conservatives suggested during Clinton's but certainly not during Reagan's tenure). As Alexander Hamilton put it: "A feeble executive implies a feeble execution of the government . . . a bad execution; and a government ill executed, whatever it may be in theory, must be, in practice, a bad government" (*Federalist Papers,* no. 70).

The damage to the Madisonian Constitution drew pertinent comment also from constitutional experts abroad. Georg Schild, a political scientist at the University of Bonn, for example, wrote that the "imperial presidency of the Nixon era has yielded to the hegemonial claims of Congress within a single generation. This not only affects the predictability of American policy but reminds us of Thomas Jefferson's 1789 warning that 'the tyranny of the legislature is the thing to be feared the most'" (*Die politische Meinung*, December 1998). As the founders arranged it, our whole system can be made to work only if there is some cooperation between the legislative and executive branches; otherwise stalemate prevails and government stalls. Johnson's impeachment and near-removal had clearly disturbed the balance between the branches by intimidating the presidents to follow and emboldening the special interests represented in the Congress. Probably it also discouraged the most energetic political leaders of the time from running for president.

The resignation of Nixon under threat of removal—the House had already passed three impeachment charges of great weight but dropped the matter when the president resigned—again weakened the presidency, particularly in the area of the president's war powers and general executive privileges. It also created public resistance to a repetition of the impeachment moves among congressional politicians, the media, and the public from which Reagan and Bush received absolution at the time of the Iran-Contra scandals. As a result, they were not impeached even though the accusations were of sufficiently serious character. The present escalation of partisan gridlock to the last extreme under conditions of divided government heralds the worst for the future: a complete breakdown of the system that served us so well for so long.

The anti-impeachment statement by some 400 prominent American historians ("Historians in Defense of the Constitution") in October and November 1998, spelled out the nature of likely constitutional damage. The historians warned of "the most serious implications for our constitutional order . . . mangling the system of checks and balances . . . [and] the presidency permanently disfigured and diminished." In particular, it pilloried the blatant disregard for the Constitutional definition of "treason, bribery, or high crimes and misdemeanors." It added that "the vote of the

House of Representatives to conduct an open-ended inquiry creates a novel, all-purpose search for any offense by which to remove a president from office," a first step down the slippery slope of parliamentary government, and "ties up our government with a protracted national agony of search and accusation." This ominous new "theory of impeachment," they warned, will leave "the presidency, historically the center of leadership during our great national ordeals . . . crippled in meeting the inevitable challenges of the future."

New York Senator Charles E. Schumer—then still a congressman present at the impeachment—warned the House that it was on the verge of becoming a House of Atreus which, in Aeschylus's tragedies, is consumed by "an escalating chain of revenge [between warring factions] such that Atreus serves his brothers a pie that contains his brothers' own murdered children. It was the end of what was once a noble family." A *Los Angeles Times* editorial quoted Schumer and, after the obligatory gesture blaming the president for his "foolish and wrong activities . . . and 'character issue,'" specified particular losses from the impeachment action: "The respect that the presidency ought to command has been terribly diminished." The impeachment process has been abused for offenses that do not "threaten the well-being of the republic," and, quoting Schumer again, "we have lowered the bar on impeachment so much—we have broken the seal on this extreme penalty so cavalierly—that it will be used as a routine tool to fight political battles." The editorial expressed the hope that a senatorial censure would end the process and a full year of "the selfish, intemperate, and dishonest behavior of public officials . . . in Congress no less than in the presidency." A short list of bad precedents of 1998 followed: (1) "obsessively pursuing alleged presidential criminality arising from . . . private sexual misbehavior"; (2) "diminish[ing] the tradition of confidentiality between a president and his lawyers . . . and his Secret Service protectors"; (3) A congressional "majority respond[ing] to the most solemn constitutional responsibilities by abandoning good sense in a rush to humiliate and destroy a president of the opposing party." The editorial concluded with Schumer's words: "History will not view this day [of impeachment] kindly . . . Let's not become a House of Atreus . . . for the sake of our republic" (*Los Angeles Times*, December 20, 1998).

Other American voices have added further details to the list of bad precedents to be avoided. Many saw the ultra-right impeachment venture as a "dangerous threat to the separation of powers that is the Constitution's structural heart," as law professor Ronald Dworkin put it in an essay tellingly entitled "The Wounded Constitution." Impeachment should be reserved only for true emergencies, "wrongful conduct so threatening to [our system] that we must endure a grave shock to the balance of powers," such as months of hearings, debates, and trial, weakening the presidency, preoccupying Congress, and monopolizing public attention.[3] Senator Pat Moynihan introduced legislation to overturn the Supreme Court decision allowing civil litigation against a sitting president to proceed. Many others, like Harry Gelman of the Rand Corporation and Stanford historian Jack N. Rakove have added their names to the list of those who question the propriety and good sense of that decision. The historian also raised the questions: (1) "Has [the impeachment and acquittal] lowered the bar against other impeachments, or will it leave future Congresses reluctant to deploy so unwieldy a weapon . . . ?" and (2) what seems to be the "damage . . . inflicted on the Constitution . . . and the system of governance it still sustains?" Rakove disagreed with the statement "that [with the end of the Senate trial] the Constitution has worked," and deplored that "one of the least useful (and least used) provisions of the Constitution . . . [was] placed . . . at the center of a prolonged, embittered struggle [with predictable outcome]" (*Los Angeles Times*, February 14, 1999).

There is no doubt that the constitutional system would have suffered major damage, and been transformed in the direction of parliamentary government, had the impeachment forces succeeded in removing Clinton or bullying or shaming him into resignation. Despite the spin propaganda of the ultras after the fact, they did intend to drive him from office in a series of efforts spanning five years. This was also the perception of all foreign press observers. European journalists, of course, had been impressed by the rise of Republican majorities in the House and Senate and, at least until 1996, rather expected a kind of quasi parliamentary takeover by Speaker Gingrich, who was already "steering the canoe from the front," but by electoral means, not the low legal tricks of a Starr. However, Gingrich's revolution fizzled and Clinton won reelection in 1996.

Alexander Hamilton gave an almost prophetic description of the unfolding process of Clinton's impeachment scene in 1998: "The prosecution of [political impeachment charges] . . . will seldom fail to agitate the passions of the whole community, and to divide it into parties more or less friendly or inimical to the accused . . . It will connect itself with the preexistent factions, and will enlist all their animosities, partialities, influence, and interest on one side or the other; and in such cases there will always be the greatest danger that the decision will be regulated more by the comparative strength of parties [in the House] than by the real demonstrations of innocence or guilt." And because the strength of the parties in the House "rest[s] entirely on . . . periodical elections . . . the most conspicuous characters in it will . . . be too often the leaders or the tools of the most cunning or the most numerous faction, and . . . can hardly be expected to possess the requisite neutrality toward those whose conduct may be the subject of scrutiny" (*Federalist Papers*, no. 65). Hamilton expected more dispassionate judgments from the Senate—which was not elected in his day—but considered also the likelihood that "firm and faithful execution of their duty might have exposed [the Senators or other judges sitting as a court in impeachment proceeding] to the persecution of an intemperate or designing majority in the House of Representatives . . . [moved by] the demon of faction" (ibid.).

Because Clinton was impeached but not removed, and the ultras' spin propaganda later sought to claim this curious half-cocked version of impeachment was their intent at the outset, we have another set of questions to answer. Aside from the spurious nature of the charges, the Clinton impeachment resembles that of Andrew Johnson more than that of Nixon and, therefore, we might expect the damage to be more in the nature of the thirty years of presidential enfeeblement following Johnson's impeachment. Angry congressional majorities from now on, perhaps, will not expect to oust duly elected presidents with trivial charges, but they can harass and disrupt their conduct of office at will with never-ending legal shenanigans. There was also the thoughtful comment of Barney Frank during an earlier House debate that starting a process of impeachment without likelihood of removal of the president "demeaned the constitutional process as well as the House" (reported by R.W. Apple of the *New York Times* in *Santa Barbara News-Press,* December 13, 1998).

Foreign journalists always thought that the attempts to humiliate Clinton inevitably involved the presidency itself. As the *Manila Standard* wrote, "What's happening to Mr. Clinton is really an assault on the dignity of the office of the president of the United States" (quoted in the *Irish Times,* September 14, 1998). In the same fashion, *Le Monde* argued when the Starr Report was submitted: "Whatever the outcome of the Clinton-Starr battle, there is already one loser: the American presidency. Without a doubt the institution has been weakened forever . . . the system being put in place risks eliminating from high office those who are the most talented simply because they may not be the most virtuous. The legacy of this psychodrama will weigh heavily on American institutions" (quoted in *World Press Review,* October 1998).

Not only has the Constitution's emergency measure of presidential impeachment been trivialized and a step rendered much easier than ever intended, but the delicate executive-legislative balance is, once more, in disarray. What is to keep a vengeful future Democratic congressional majority from attacking, say, a possible President George W. Bush with low legal tricks and sensational charges about his colorful past? They might unearth a failed Texas oil exploration loan from 15 years back to harass him, add a booze-gate, coke-gate, and assorted bimbo- or party-gates. The allegedly liberal media might forever repeat, mantralike, that he had a "character problem," lacked "gravitas," and failed to inspire trust. All his policy initiatives might be reported as motivated solely by the next vote in congress, or his reelection, or his fatuous desire to make his mark on history. Surely, the Democratic camp followers could find the dirty money and sleazy lawyers to entrap him in some illegal action. Why shouldn't they do to a Republican president what the Republicans did to Clinton in 1998, in fact, ever since December 1993? This could go on forever and at the expense of our Constitution, if we don't get to the bottom of it.

Experts on constitutional law disagree about the damage done to the constitutional system. Akhil R. Amar, for example, concluded in *The New Republic* (March 8, 1999) that the "scandals have done considerable damage to the presidency, leaving us with an office weaker in key respects [an 'unimperial presidency'] than the one the founders envisioned." Robert J. Spitzer, on the other hand, argued that unlike Watergate, the Clinton crisis involved "no reformulating debate over the power . . . or internal functioning of the executive branch." But he too admits, in addition to invasions by an "imperial judiciary," that "the proceedings against Clinton did indeed lower the bar for subsequent congressional impeachment [efforts becoming] . . . more routine and more partisan . . . with Congress increasingly tempted to pursue impeachment in order to remove a president with whom they had mere policy differences" (*PS Political Science and Policy*, September 1999). Thanks to the great conspiracy, in other words, we are well on our way toward a parliamentary system in which a congressional majority can simply push a president out of office.

The damage to our Constitutional system was worsened by the callous intervention of parts of the federal judiciary which, seeing the executive under siege, quickly conducted its own raids upon the separation of powers. There is now a crucial need for future Congresses to pull the "imperial" Supreme Court back from its expansionist mode and into its own rightful domain. For decades conservative critics pilloried an allegedly liberal and excessively activist Court under Earl Warren, a liberal Republican. Since the appointment of Chief Justice William Rehnquist and other very conservative judges, the Supreme Court and the federal appeals courts have become a hyperactive conservative judiciary that frequently intervenes in defense of states rights to invalidate decisions of Congress, striking down federal laws on clean air, smoking by youths, gun control, and the right of rape victims to sue their attackers, as well as the rights of employees and consumers to sue corporations. In the Fourth District, a lily-white appeals panel has set the guiding mark for extreme conservatism in the nation. Its presiding judge contends that such "ideological" considerations as the one-sided composition of the court are totally irrelevant measures by which to judge the quality of justice rendered there. North Carolina's senior Senator, Jesse Helms, for his part, has blocked appointment hearings for any additional judges from his own state for fear of putting any more female or African American liberal judges on the panel.

For some time now, the Supreme Court has neglected much of its traditional bailiwick, for example, in the arena of controversial individual rights, and concentrated instead on the hobby-horse of states rights which, ever since the Dred Scott decision of 1857 and through much of the post–Civil War era, were the ramparts of slavery and segregation. Rehnquist himself, before his Supreme Court days, used to defend segregation and headed an organization, Operation Eagle Eye, that reportedly sought to discourage newly enfranchised minority voters from voting. Recently, in a 1995 case eerily presaging the school shootings of 1999, the court struck down a federal law barring anyone from bringing a gun within 1,000 feet of a school. As the *Economist* (May 6, 1995) reported, "Rehnquist, a fierce conservative, and four others say this is not interstate commerce," as if gun traffic and trade in the United States did not cross state lines. Court critics like Peter Irons, the author of *A People's History of the Supreme Court,* point to the recent resegregation decision in the case of Linda Brown (of Brown v. Board of Education) in which the court simply declared that federal jurisdiction in this matter had ended and now the subject of desegregation was solely in the hands of the states. The Council of Conservative Citizens must be very happy: just like old times. Irons suggests that the present court has reversed most civil rights cases not because of an ideological belief in states rights, but because it has tried to shield recent conservative state laws from the effect of more liberal federal statutes. If future Democratic state administrations begin to take advantage of this situation by passing liberal legislation, will the courts then reverse themselves to champion federal powers?

Many lower court federal judges were appointed when the Reagan and Bush administrations launched all-out efforts to change the allegedly liberal federal judiciary by appointing only the most arch-conservative nominees. They clearly overdid what may have made some sense to begin with. Now, some of these judges do not seem to understand that an excess of partisanship in either direction—and the standards of liberal and conservative were mostly made up by ideological Reaganite conservatives—is a form of judicial corruption. In some cases indeed, impeachment and removal from judicial office may be the only remedy against the new "demon of faction" in the courts.

The transparent policy of the current Republican-dominated Senate Judiciary Committee and of Helms to block all but the most conservative nominees to the federal judiciary, and especially to deter women and minorities from receiving hearings, leaves little hope that the one-sided slant of federal justice will be remedied anytime soon. In the year 2000, there were 64 federal judicial vacancies and 34 pending nominations in limbo, obviously waiting for a future Republican president to further pack the federal judiciary. A recent study also established that the Senate Judiciary Committee under Orrin Hatch takes about 50 percent longer to process women and minority judicial candidates than whites which, perhaps, is Senator Hatch's idea of a kind of "white male affirmative action." His committee allows individual senators, apparently, to blackball a candidate under cover of anonymity. Knowledgeable observers expect that the next president will have an opportunity to appoint at least three new justices to the Supreme Court, but who will they be? On the occasion of the death of Supreme Court Justice William Brennan, who was no narrow partisan but a man of universal vision, the *Economist* (August 2, 1997) commented: "No doubt the court will have liberals again. What it may never have again is Justice Brennan's belief in the essential goodness of men and women, and in the purity of their intentions."

Neither the House of Representatives nor the federal judiciary covered themselves with glory in the 1998-1999 constitutional crisis, but for the elected representatives, and the senators too, there is always the electoral remedy. On the other hand, it should be pointed out that many of the impeachment-minded House members, especially the House managers, and some Senators, had previously served as federal prosecutors, judges, and attorneys. Being so closely associated with the law should have made it especially incumbent upon them to understand and respect the formulations of the Constitution and the time-hallowed procedures of due process of law. How could they support so many egregious violations in their pursuit of the "demon of faction"? How could they give a standing ovation to the special prosecutor, knowing of his lies and his legally dubious prosecutorial actions and pornographic presentations? "Whatever happened to the American Bar Association's ethics committee?" European friends asked me. "Aren't they supposed to maintain the standards of the profession in the presence of such glaring violations?"

The highly ideological beliefs of contemporary American conservatives are most unusual in an America long known for a spirit of political compromise and moderation. As one continental lawyer told me, these zealots reminded him of his native communists of another day: "If the communists said ten times in a row that the sun rises in the west, it became the gospel truth among the faithful. And if their opponents said the opposite five times, that only showed how prejudiced *they* were." European observers, as we have seen, also were particularly scandalized by the manner in which the House majority chose to ignore the advice (on the definition of "high crimes and misdemeanors") of the nation's finest constitutional scholars solemnly testifying before it. In all European countries, except under Nazi and communist dictatorships, such academic expertise has always enjoyed the highest respect.

DAMAGE TO AMERICAN DEMOCRACY

The impeachment of the president in December 1998 was a watershed in American democracy. Large segments of the American public shared their shock at the excesses of partisanship in Washington that left deep tears in the fabric of American politics. To quote a letter by veteran journalist and writer Frank K. Kelly in the *Santa Barbara News-Press*, "The bitterness generated by the partisan procedure will endure for a long time" (December 17, 1998). The premier scholar of the American presidency, Richard Neustadt, said in a PBS series on the American president that "partisan divisiveness [has] never [been] as great" as in 1998-1999. Stanford historian Rakove wondered out loud "whether the deep partisanship that has scarred these [impeachment] proceedings foretells continuing ideologic trench warfare that will further sour the electorate on Washington" (*Los Angeles Times*, February 14, 1999). Such extreme partisan divisiveness, of course, is a major form of damage to the normal functioning of American democracy.

To be fair to both parties, however, we should also take into account their internal divisions and struggles in the midst of five years of nonelectoral battles to remove a very controversial but duly elected president. On the Republican side, it was the great transition toward becoming an overwhelmingly southern party with a southern conservative following that had once, before Franklin Roosevelt, dominated a solid Democratic South. After decades of overt disrespect for their "eastern establishment" and of efforts to woo the South (plus a string of Democratic-to-Republican conversions of southern representatives and senators), the Republicans have almost succeeded too well. They have nearly completed the transformation of the grand old party (GOP) of Abraham Lincoln into the party of Jefferson Davis, president of the Confederacy, or into something like the Old Southern Democrats of the years of Jim Crow and segregation. It seems ironic to hear young Republicans chant the mantra "What would Abe [Lincoln] do? (WWAD)" in the face of moral challenges. Early in January 2000, staging a major Republican presidential primary debate in Charleston on the same weekend as a rally of 6,000 passionate defenders of the Confederacy commemorated four decades of flying the Confederate flag over the state capitol of South Carolina certainly set a mark and a symbol. Along with this role reversal have come new frictions with the last liberal Republicans, such as the northeastern Republican senators who voted to acquit Clinton in the impeachment trial. And, as conservative zealots threaten to retaliate against defecting Republican nonsoutherners, they literally risk confining the future loyal Republican electoral base to the South. To make matters worse, even in the South, recent elections have given the Democrats a comeback of sorts, for example, in Georgia and in the South Carolina gubernatorial elections. This may contribute in the future to a possible permanent Republican minority status not unlike that of the post–Civil War Democrats prior to 1933.

If we see today's southern Republicans as a covert revival of the segregationist rear guard of another day, say in the era of young

George Wallace or Orval Faubus, filled with deep hatred of black and white civil rights leaders, perhaps we can understand better the profound personal hatred against Clinton. Clinton himself said in the PBS series on the American president that "civil rights was the first defining interest of my early years." What other president had close African American friends and made such a point of selecting women and minority secretaries for his cabinet? As the *Economist* (July 22, 1995) remarked apropos of Clinton's strong endorsement of affirmative action in the face of the passage of a California initiative that prohibited it: "Mr. Clinton is at heart a liberal on race . . . whose statements of conviction rarely seem as persuasive as they do when he speaks on matters of black and white." Affirmative action is vital to African Americans, especially businessmen, and the black electorate amounts to a sizable share of the Democratic vote. In 1996 affirmative action suffered a major defeat before the Fifth Federal Court of Appeals (Texas, Louisiana, Mississippi) which held that "[mandating] diversity [in hiring and public contracts] fosters, rather than minimizes, the use of race . . . [it] may promote racial stereotypes, thus fortifying racial hostility." In other words, affirmative action may make prejudiced people even more prejudiced. Forty years ago, opponents of desegregation and of African American voting rights used to warn that an end to discrimination might intensify [white] prejudice.

It was the same dubious reasoning as that of the California initiative (#209) that claimed to uphold the civil rights of the majority (!) over those of women and minorities, and it was used also in the resegregation of many southern schools. Against this background, Clinton is a southern renegade who shares neither the South's mainstream attitudes toward military traditions nor their attitudes toward a traditional role for women. At the time of his impeachment by the House, Karen Grigsby Bates raised the question in the *Los Angeles Times:* How much of the hatred of Bill Clinton is rooted in his civil rights record? She answered her question: ". . . whenever I hear Trent Lott speak, I immediately think of nooses decorating trees. Big trees, with black bodies swinging from the business end of the nooses." She referred to Lott's and Barr's contacts with the "Council of Conservative Citizens (CCC), an intellectual version of the KKK" (*Los Angeles Times*, January 26, 1999). William Raspberry, another black journalist, also discovered "a lynch mob mentality" among the impeachers of Clinton who believed that "Clinton simply does not deserve to be president and therefore ought to be impeached, convicted and thrown out of office" (*Santa Barbara News-Press*, December 4, 1998). The lynch mob attitude, we might add, was also confirmed by the curious anger of many Republicans that the president dared defend himself with the assistance of lawyers against the charges. A lynch victim, in the opinion of his lynchers, is supposed to keep still and suffer his well-deserved fate.

Tomorrow's post-Clinton Democrats, conversely, may have a better chance to form national majorities again than at any time since Roosevelt, provided they overcome their own internal divisions and timidity. Their wrenching internal transition is from the Old Democratic establishment and its positions to the New Democratic centrism of the Democratic Leadership Council and Clinton, and it has been almost as bruising as the internal disagreements in the Republican party. The ire of the Old Democrats in Congress at Clinton's centrist policy focused particularly on his foreign trade policy—NAFTA (North American Free Trade Agreement) and GATT/WTO (General Agreement on Tariffs and Trade/World Trade Organization)—and on his welfare reform. "His tax reforms," as Thomas Walkom wrote in the liberal *Toronto Star*, "by favoring the well-to-do, have increased the gap between rich and poor ... the income gap in the United States is now wider than it ever was during Ronald Reagan's so-called era of greed" (quoted in *World Press Review*, October 1998). The two leading Democratic presidential candidates of 2000, Bill Bradley and Al Gore, charted courses between the Old and the New Democrats, just as the two Republican front runners, George W. Bush and John

McCain, chose a noticeably more moderate conservative path than the Republican zealots of 1994-1998.

An important consequence of both parties' internal divisions: neither party was likely to set its exclusive trust in majority counts but would play every angle and maneuver in Congress. The new Republican majority of 1994, in particular, capitalized on its control of committee chairs and on the availability of the Senate filibuster, hitherto used only by numerical minorities to defeat threatening majority action especially on civil rights issues. Eventually, the ultras-dominated majority got around to pressing the impeachment procedure into service for their anti-Clinton campaign.

Aside from the personalities and their confrontational character, the most striking change in the 1990s to the once-admired American democracy as seen by Europeans was the extraordinary degree of partisan and ideological polarization in a country long known for the opposite, namely for political consensus and a nonideological spirit of compromise. Europeans observed with amazement when, at long last, the determined onslaught of the Republican ultras had united the divided and apathetic congressional Democrats to rally around their embattled president—after many of them, as recently as September 1998, appeared ready to abandon him to the wolves. The second feature most noted by foreign journalists, as we have seen, was the demonstrated Republican disdain for electoral verdicts—in 1992, 1996, and 1998—coupled with their expressed disgust for the consistently critical public opinion polls. Europeans were nonplused: "What kind of democracy is this?" was the consistent refrain among my European friends. "Don't elections matter any more?" In America, "is it the determined minority now that calls the shots in politics?" That this determined minority tried to get its way with a never-ending succession of charges over a span of six years did not lend its quest more dignity or validity in European eyes. The tolerance, even collaboration, of courts and judges with the impeachment campaign further alarmed Europeans.

Finally, the perception that this nonelectoral harassment of the president was intended to interfere with his pursuit of certain policies, such as health care reform and holding the tobacco industry liable for the lethal consequences of its products, played a big role regardless of policy preferences. For obvious reasons, we have tried as much as possible in this book to stay out of the discussion of values and the policy debate. But many European and Commonwealth journalists, as we have seen, again and again thought the defeat of certain policies was the real goal behind the various charges and the drive to oust Clinton. "For months," wrote the weekly *Die Zeit* (December 16, 1998), "discussions of domestic policy have been postponed and pressing problems ignored" while the House pursued its impeachment drive. "There must be relief in the United States," wrote the conservative *Hindu* of Madras after the Senate acquittal of Clinton, "now that the sordid drama that has held Washington hostage . . . has ended and the Clinton administration is free to spend the rest of its term concentrating on critical domestic issues" (quoted in *World Press Review,* April 1999). Of course, there was also the nexus of the aborted congressional campaign finance reform and certain policies: as long as Republican resistance to reform keeps the campaigners' thirst for money unquenchable, even unpopular but well-heeled interests like the tobacco industry, the gun lobby, health insurance, and others can forestall any effective regulation of their industries and products. The prevention of campaign finance reform keeps the Congress venal and corrupt, and it may also be used to maintain Republican party cohesion.

BLAMING THE OIC STATUTE

The 1978 Ethics in Government (OIC) Statute grew out of Nixon's Saturday Night Massacre, the firing of Watergate special prosecutor Archibald Cox that triggered the resignation of Attorney General Elliott Richardson, who had appointed Cox. The statute was designed to restore public trust in government by creating an independent agency to investigate ethics charges in the administration. It was received rather critically by, among others, Supreme Court Justice Antonin Scalia and journalists like Edwin M. Yoder, Jr.; both predicted that it would concentrate action against targeted persons rather than on violations of laws.

An independent counsel—whether statutory or not—is needed because the Justice Department cannot investigate some matters inside its own cabinet without creating a conflict of interest. But critics of the OIC statute have seen independent counsels with unlimited (taxpayers') funds abuse their power in witch hunts. In the aftermath of the Senate trial of Clinton, a major debate ensued concerning the statute establishing the OIC, which had sponsored 20 special prosecutors to investigate prominent figures of the Clinton administration. "The hair-raising Independent Counsel Law of 1978," wrote Klaus Lutterbeck in the German weekly *Stern* (February 11, 1999), "gives the special prosecutor powers that are really intolerable in a democracy." If the statute had not compelled Attorney General Reno to appoint so many independent prosecutors, if it had not permitted the various independent counsels such excessively broad authority, many argued, they would not have provoked such universal public criticism for their actions. Former Iran-Contra prosecutor Lawrence E. Walsh and Watergate counsel Sam Dash, for example, called for major revisions in the law to reduce both the number of persons being investigated and the scope of the inquiries. Walsh, in particular, proposed that only the president and the attorney general should be on the list of targets of investigation, leaving all other federal executive officers to the prosecutors of the Department of Justice. He agreed with much of the criticism directed at independent counsel Starr by the White House and Democratic critics. Conduct that occurred before a president was elected should be off limits to the inquiry. The expense and intensity of an independent counsel's investigation should be reserved for major abuses of public office requiring specific and credible evidence that the president or attorney general committed a crime in connection with their discharge of official duties.

Dash defended Starr's tactics, which were under investigation by the Justice Department, but preferred that the law specify only counsels with "extensive experience in criminal law," a qualification that Starr did not possess (*Los Angeles Times,* March 25, 1999). It would also help if the counsel knew the Constitution better and promised to stay within its precise limits. Attorney General Reno simply wanted to let the statute expire on June 30, 1999, restoring investigative authority to the Justice Department. But at the last minute, the chair of the Senate Government Affairs Committee, Fred Thompson, intervened. He had long feuded with Reno over her refusal to appoint a special prosecutor to investigate the 1996 campaign finance charges against Clinton and the Democrats. He also wanted Congress to have the power, within 60 days, to approve or reject the attorney general's decisions to launch investigations. Alternatively, Thompson insisted, the Justice Department should have the sole authority to launch investigations and be completely responsible for them, rather than being able to blame its decisions on the panel of three federal judges. In spite of some efforts to save the statute with amendments, it expired in mid-1999.

The *Economist* had commented two years earlier that such investigations often were a necessary but thankless and unpopular job. "Kenneth Starr notwithstanding, special prosecutors do it best ... [but] the public aids and abets [the official's evasions], finding most investigations of public figures unwarranted, and (unless sex rears it head) plain boring" (July 12, 1997). It is true that "20 congressional task forces and subcommittees investigating the White House," as Gingrich had threatened in October 1994, would have even more likely been partisan fishing expeditions of the worst kind. When he finally stepped down, Starr himself claimed that "one of my regrets is not to have done enough to make people understand the responsibilities of the OIC." He rejected charges of a Republican bias and blamed the "personalization and politicization" of his investigation on the nature of the OIC statute and on the inherent character of the undertaking. This last point, of course, is well taken: how could investigations of the president and half the cabinet be other than political? But his rejection of the charge of partisan bias is ridiculous. As for blaming the OIC statute, Starr was in the company of many a pundit, including some of his critics—for instance, former Attorney General Griffin Bell, former Senate leader Howard Baker, Common Cause, and the American Bar Association—but the charge was somewhat dubious: any law or institution, of course, is imperfect and subject to misinterpretation and abuse. But it was not true, as many critics had claimed, that the OIC statute created prosecutors without checks and balances: every new investigative mandate as well as particular prosecutors had to be specifically authorized by the panel of high federal judges and by the attorney general, who also had to authorize any change or expansion in the mandate.

The horrendous failures of these checks in the case of Starr and his associates were clearly attributable to the liberties taken with the very words "independent counsel." Arch-Republican Rehnquist appointed David Sentelle to head the panel of judges and they picked Clinton-hater Starr, who now blames Reno for his taking on the Lewinsky investigation. It goes without saying that the chief responsibility lies with Starr, who actively sought to expand his list of targets regardless of what he may say today, and whose spinning and fabrications attempted to conceal his neglect of his duties and cavalier disregard of lawful procedure. But it is also true that Reno and the federal judges should have known better than to give in to Starr's ceaseless pursuit of ever-new sets of charges.

After Clinton's acquittal, a quick survey by the General Accounting Office undertook to sum up the results and costs of the operation of the OIC statute. There had been 20 separate investigations, 13 of which produced no indictments. The investigations resulted in 41 guilty pleas and 21 convictions (five of them overturned), eight acquittals, and six pardons so far. Only one "impeachment referral" was sent to Congress. There had been an earlier Starr Report in 1997 when he was ready to quit his quest for the smoking gun. The cost of all this, since 1978, was $168 million. Of this, the numerous investigations of the Clinton years were at least $95 million, Starr's alone $52 million, and his eager successor Robert Ray talks about $3.5 million more to prosecute Clinton after his term ends. Perhaps, the access to unlimited funds under the statute is a hard-to-resist invitation to open up more and more investigations. Prior to Clinton, the biggest probes involved Reagan's Housing secretary Samuel Pierce, Jr., during whose tenure, according to news reports, over $4 billion disappeared, and the previously mentioned Iran-Contra investigation under Lawrence Walsh.

We also must not forget that in addition to the taxpayers' expense of the OIC investigations, there is also the private expense of high-priced attorneys not only for the accused but for the numerous witnesses. Nicole Bacharan mentions, for example, the legal debts of George Stephanopolous ($100,000), former chief of staff Harold Ickes (at least $200,000), former White House spokesperson Deedee Myers ($50,000), and Hillary Clinton's assistant, Margaret Williams ($100,000), not to mention the millions in lawyers' fees owed by the Clintons, and all "for a nonexistent crime."[4] The amounts mentioned are probably far less than the final cost to each person, no matter how innocent. It would appear that Starr's OIC intended to punish and drive away Clinton's team, one by one, because they could not afford this expense. It certainly adds an obscene note to Starr's parting exhortation to the students at Yale University to go into public service. He should have told the Yale students to earn a few million dollars first so that they could survive the ordeal of public service in our time.

Starr's conduct and abuse of his vast power drew widespread criticism and probably doomed the OIC statute. But the other OIC investigations were hardly above criticism either and, taken together, were a transparent scheme to tie up the entire Clinton administration in busywork and extraordinary personal legal expenses so that it could not concentrate on its executive tasks. European observers, looking at the larger picture, immediately noticed also that almost all the investigations targeted minorities or women: Commerce secretary Ron Brown, Agriculture secretary Mike Espy, Housing and Urban Development secretary Henry Cisneros, Interior secretary Bruce Babbitt (the only Caucasian), and Labor secretary Alexis Herman. Many were driven from office while answering spurious charges and undergoing great private expense.

In the case of Espy, $21 million was spent, as the *Washington Monthly* (November 1999) disclosed, subpoenaing, among other things, Espy's high school transcripts and interviewing his old girlfriends. What crime did independent counsel Donald C. Smaltz expect to unearth with these methods? Smaltz reportedly gave watches engraved with Espy's name to the OIC staff the way participants in lynchings used to take away grisly mementos. Upon Espy's final acquittal—on charges no more incriminating than his having accepted football tickets as gifts—journalists asked Smaltz whether this boondoggle had been worth $21 million of taxpayers' money. His answer was: "Yes, it sent a message: the mere indictment of a public official has as much deterrent value as the conviction of a public official." The *Washington Monthly* commented: "What it really deters is the entrance of decent people into public life. Why should they subject themselves to the possibility of being prosecuted by a jerk like Smaltz?" We are left to wonder whether Smaltz's statement is another version of the novel impeachment-sans-removal doctrine—investigations at taxpayers' expense without the expectation of finding anything, just to send a message. As with the other independent counsels, Smaltz's role in court proceedings and documents appears as "the United States."

Independent counsel David M. Barrette's $10 million case against Cisneros fared no better when his chief witness, Linda Jones—already serving a 42-month prison sentence for an unrelated case of bank fraud and money laundering—was revealed to have doctored the secret tape-recordings of allegedly incriminating telephone conversations with Cisneros. Jones had been Cisneros's mistress while he was the mayor of San Antonio; she was evidently trying to extort more money from him. He had deceived FBI investigators about the size of the payments made to her when they terminated the relationship. By admitting that he had lied to the FBI and pleading guilty to a misdemeanor, Cisneros avoided trial and paid a $10,000 fine. His investigation cost $12 million. Ron Brown died in an airplane accident in Bosnia, whereupon independent counsel Daniel Pearson dropped all charges. Babbitt was acquitted of perjury charges brought by independent counsel Carol E. Bruce in connection with an Indian casino license, after examination of 450 witnesses and 630,000 records evidently failed to provide evidence for further prosecution. Alexis Herman was also cleared in April 2000 of the charges against her, after two years and $3 million in public expense. All of this confirms the impression that it was not necessarily the statute or the institution of the OIC but the incompetence or the partisan ill will of the supervising agencies and the overzealousness of highly partisan lawyers that were at fault here.

In September and October 1999, in parting from the public scene to return to his once-lucrative law practice (he is no longer a senior partner with Kirkland & Ellis), Starr once more expressed his criticism of the OIC statute. He blamed the "nature of the OIC statute" for the degree of politicization of his investigation: "The statute simply does not work. The Congress was trying in effect to create a separate branch of government" (*Los Angeles Times*, September 16, 1999). He never quite said, as the House managers did at the end of 1998, that impeachment without removal served a worthwhile purpose, but he showed a curious ambivalence about the process in relation to the president. When asked if he was disappointed with the outcome of the Senate trial, he emphatically said "no" in his awkward legalese: "The facts did not burden the president's discharge of his duties so as to warrant his removal . . . a reasonable judgment [regarding removal] could be made either way" (*NewsHour,* October 14, 1999).

Regardless of the phrase making of the conspirators, the impact of the impeachment crisis on American life was apparent to many observers. In a thoughtful essay, "The Legacy of a Scandal," Richard T. Cooper and Alissa J. Rubin laid out the most important signs of the damage to American public life. They thought the crisis ostensibly waged over the rule of law would "leave a deep bruise on the legal system." Public perceptions of Starr's abuses and his politicization of the investigation, they said, would probably prevent the renewal of the OIC statute and the stain might spread to all prosecutors, federal, state, and even local, who would face "public suspicion of . . . excessive zeal or . . . politic[al motives]." The presidency will be "at least temporarily diminished" for Clinton and his successors in the twenty-first century. "Cynicism about government [and] . . . politicians," will grow. "The American media have been indelibly changed" and "the attitudes and values of Americans in their personal and communal lives" will reflect the impact of this crisis as Watergate never did (*Los Angeles Times,* February 13, 1999). Indeed, anyone could see that 1998-1999 with its venom had brought about a "corruption of the media" and "pollution of the national discourse" (Lars-Erik Nelson in *New York Review of Books,* November 5, 1998).

THE PERILS OF BEING IN THE MIDDLE

Some commentators have blamed Clinton's impeachment on his attempt to chart a centrist course between the Old Democrats and the Republicans from whom he allegedly stole such policies as welfare reform and law and order. Was this why Republicans hated him so and the Democrats at first would not come to his assistance? Clinton was not the first president to practice triangulation. Dwight Eisenhower, Richard Nixon, Gerald Ford, Ronald Reagan, and

George Bush frequently charted compromise courses between the two parties to generate bipartisan support for their legislative projects. They chose this route particularly when their party did not firmly control both houses of Congress, which was most of the time. In Clinton's case, however, there is a new perspective, if not exactly unprecedented in the annals of the American presidency. When Clinton became president, the Democrats in both houses were deeply divided and dominated by Old Democrats and their following, whom their detractors had characterized variously as tax-and-spend liberals, New Deal Democrats, and defenders of the embattled welfare state.

The public, moreover, was weary of partisan hostility and gridlock between these Old Democrats and the Republicans, both Old and New, and wanted new leadership to break the stalemate and concentrate on pressing problems of the nation. We would not go far wrong if we attributed the landslide of 1994 in large part to the voters' disgust with partisan gridlock in Congress and with the stand-pat attitudes of the Democratic establishment, rather than to the discreet charms of Gingrich and his Contract for America. This was an obvious opportunity for Clinton, a prominent member of the centrist Democratic Leadership Council, but it was also a moment fraught with great dangers. For, as we know, the Democratic establishment met him with disdain and little cooperation, leaving him friendless and exposed, whereas Republicans were outraged that he seemed so "opportunistic" and "brazenly stole their issues."

Since then, however, the rationale of Clinton's centrist course has become much clearer than his early opportunistic compromises and vacillations seemed to suggest. The clarification has come, in particular, in the wake of a series of apparent imitations in other major Western democracies such as Britain, Germany, France, and in smaller countries like the Netherlands and Denmark. All these cases, of course, differ from each other according to national preferences and relative success or failure. But they all originated in response to similar problems and dilemmas that resembled the American situation of the early 1990s. For that reason, a comparative sketch might shed some light on what columnist Lexington in the *Economist* so tellingly called the "lonesome" and uncomfortable perch "on top of the triangle" of triangulation (November 18, 1995).

In all the countries mentioned, a dominant left-of-center party had run out of options and the patience of the voters. The ballyhooed "social democratic consensus" of the 1970s between left and right—the Johnson, Nixon, and Ford years in this country—no longer seemed capable of solving social problems and satisfying the increasingly sophisticated public in the advanced democracies. Under the impact of two major energy crises and rising environmental concerns, the European governments of this social democratic consensus—those of Helmut Schmidt, James Callahan, and François Mitterand—also began to run out of the money that they used to throw at problems. There was a sudden awareness that industrial development and economic growth, the engines of well-being of Western societies, could not go on forever. Gradually, the public mood grew frustrated and sour. The parties and groups of each system became more antagonistic in the 1980s than they had been in the 1970s. One Western government after another discovered that its increasing public indebtedness—even without involvement in wars such as Vietnam—often forced it to say no to groups of social beneficiaries of the traditional welfare state, or at least to cut back their benefits. Group antagonisms intensified and gridlock followed. The perception, right or wrong, that some people (the well-to-do, the professional classes, or certain new industries) were flourishing while others had to do with even less than they had received in the past reawakened social resentments long believed dead.

Nowhere was this as true as in the United States. The deep recession of the early 1980s coincided with the negative, antiwelfare rhetoric of the Reagan administration, an era of greed, and a wave of megamergers against a background of bankruptcies and rising unemployment, as manufacturing companies moved operations and jobs to Third World countries, especially Mexico. The well-paying industrial jobs, for example, in the steel and auto industry, that had sustained American prosperity for nearly 30 years, became a rarity while new fortunes were made and flaunted. Consequently, the degree of economic inequality in America grew astronomically after the '70s. If we divide American families into five groups, for example, the average annual income of the richest one-fifth grew by close to one-third from the late '70s to the mid-'90s. The one-fifth poorest in income, on the other hand, lost nearly a fourth of its buying power in the same period. In New York in the mid-'90s, the average annual family income in the top one-fifth group was over $132,000, or almost twenty times the average of the bottom fifth (*Economist*, December 20, 1997).

The famous 1981 tax cut, much as Republicans try to deny it, was of disproportionate benefit to those in the upper brackets. It opened the gates, as it were, to the Trojan horse of economic royalism. The spectacular rise of the index of the stock market of the Clinton years, for that matter, had an even more dramatic effect on the incomes of those with substantial investments in the form of stocks, at the same time that unmarried teenage mothers were pilloried and welfare clients compelled to work. The result of all this, by 1999, was a society in which the extremes of wealth and poverty were pulled apart, a society in which the top one percent owned the lion's share of what there is to own while the situation of those earning less than $20,000 a year had barely improved over the previous six years. Unemployment has declined, and employment has risen spectacularly, but wage levels have not risen as much as might have been expected.

The impact on politics of these dynamic changes is not easy to assess. Political analysis of trends in voting and in voter loyalty to parties over the last quarter century has shown the increasing dealignment of voter loyalties: only about 60 percent of the voters now identify with one of the two major parties. A more sophisticated generation of voters has broken with much of the traditional Democratic or Republican loyalties of the postwar era; they vote however the spirit seems to move them over time or over local issues. The socioeconomic changes of the last 25 years, and especially of the years since the recession of the Bush years, have also confused the voting trends with contradictory moments of partisan appeals and profound voter alienation. In a massive recent national polling operation, the Pew Research Center for the People and the Press learned that the antigovernment sentiments of the American electorate had peaked back in 1994—when nearly 70 percent of respondents agreed that anything "run by the government [was] usually inefficient and wasteful" and 54 percent thought that "people like me don't have any say about what the government does." This coincided with the Republican congressional landslide. In more recent years, the hostility toward the government has decreased. A sense of economic contentedness has grown; the reader will remember how the tax cut promised by Republican candidate Dole in 1996 fell flat. It should be mentioned, however, that the social and economic frustrations of the early-'90s only explain the widespread hostility to the federal government, not the visceral, personal hatred for Clinton in particular. Could that have been a revenge for Watergate and the impeachment of Nixon, the source of many a mantra invoked by the president's political and media enemies? Clinton had little to do with Watergate (although Hillary Clinton had a minor staff position with the House Judiciary Committee at the time). Or was it the much-ballyhooed cultural wars of the 1980s and 1990s that somehow became crystallized in anti-Clinton hatred?

An avid reader of history, Clinton likes to compare his role at the helm of state with the time of Teddy Roosevelt who "also helped American society to make the difficult transition into a new technological age" (*NewsHour,* April 13, 1999). The turbulent scenes of 1994 and 1998, however, seem curiously reminiscent of another time of latent culture wars when the dramatically rising stock market raised the fortunes of a minority to unprecedented levels while the vast small-town and rural majority of Americans did not do especially well. This occurred at the time of the presidential election campaign of 1928 when Herbert Hoover opposed Alfred E. Smith, governor of New York and former New York City mayor. A fever pitch of hatred, on the stump and in the media, burned everywhere but in the big cities against Smith, an Irish Catholic of very modest origins among the immigrants in the Fourth Ward of the city. As governor, Smith was the architect of a New Deal-like interventionist regime that, for the first time in New York history, had regulated business and protected the interests of the workforce.

During that campaign, the powerful Ku Klux Klan fulminated against Smith, picketed his rallies, and planted burning crosses all along the Oklahoma railroad tracks he was scheduled to follow. Protestant ministers denounced him from the pulpit as a subordinate of a foreign power (the Vatican), and as a representative of New York Mammon (big capital), race mixing (the multicultural melting pot), and immoral entertainment (the Harlem Renaissance). The Republicans made the most of this wave of anti-Smith attacks and Hoover buried him in a landslide, especially in upstate New York. Smith's only support came from other metropolitan areas where his track record in the New York legislature and governor's office was appreciated. Clinton, of course, is no Catholic—the barrier against Catholics in the White House fell with John F. Kennedy and the civil rights revolution soon made tremendous inroads against segregation and racism in America—and the agenda of urban concerns now commands a majority of Americans. But the sudden concentration of hatred toward government and the president in 1993-1994 (especially during the health care debate), the Republican landslide of 1994, and the emotional wave of 1998 (focused on impeachment) present some similarities. Although their base has shrunk in spite of the multiplier effects of talk radio and other media, the same kind of people were hellbent on attacking and impeaching the president no matter what the Constitution said. They were the kinds of people who are preoccupied with the unfettered use and possession of guns, prayer in schools, putting the ten commandments on schoolroom walls, outlawing abortion, and keeping women and minorities from the benefits of affirmative action.

The other Clinton-like centrist regimes in Western democracies do not share the American cultural antagonisms of 1928 and 1998. The similarities also appear to lie less in the economic trends or in the distinctive antigovernment sentiments typical of the United States. Economic stagnation and frustrations have long prevailed on the continent, if less in Britain, but are unlikely to target the government per se. On the other hand, bearing in mind the different systems, European centrist leaders have faced problems quite similar to Clinton's. In a striking parallel to Clinton's difficulties with securing the support of the Old Democrats in Congress, for example, Tony Blair from the outset had to confront and overpower the more leftist, ideological wing of his British Labour party. But, whereas the Old Democrats still dominated Congress in 1993-1994, Blair's Labour party had been whipped again and again in parliamentary elections: it was willing to accept his new centrist course, therefore, and has supported him ever since.

In contrast, German chancellor Gerhard Schröder, despite a similar series of Social Democratic electoral losses to Kohl since 1983, barely managed to establish control over his own leftist party and, since taking office in 1998, has been confronted with the contentious resignation of his leftist finance minister, Oskar Lafontaine, a string of state election losses (that cost his party the majority in the upper house, *Bundesrat*, and restive left-wing elements both in his own party, the SPD, and in his coalition party, the Greens. By sheer luck, a major corruption scandal involving Kohl and the Christian Democratic opposition saved Schröder's government from its own imminent crisis at the beginning of the year 2000. Uneasy lies the head that wears the centrist crown.

It is not easy for these European centrist leaders to break their respective parties' umbilical cords to century-old traditions of European socialism. Under Premier Lionel Jospin in France, the centrist policies adopted by his socialist (P.S.) government have been carefully re-labeled so as not to wake the sleeping dogs of party orthodoxy within or of its traditional opposition outside, the Gaullist party. So far, only Blair and, perhaps, some government figures in the Netherlands and Denmark, have had the fortitude to express their bold new departures in party-defying terms. The British prime minister, for example, credited former Prime Minister Margaret Thatcher with the origins of many of his economic policies, including his independence from the trade unions. British Conservatives could have complained that he stole these policies and public credit from them, as the Republicans have said about Clinton; but, perhaps they have less of a proprietary sense about their policies, which were often controversial within their own party as well. Schröder only went so far as to say, during his successful election campaign of 1998, that if his party won against Kohl's Christian Democrats, "things [in general] would not be very different [from what they were under Kohl] but some things should be much better."

Both Schröder and Blair, who have expressed admiration for America and free enterprise, however, have refused to follow Thatcher all the way to a completely untrammeled market economy. They preferred instead a kind of market economy with a social conscience or, as Schröder's former chief of staff (and guru of centrism) Bodo Hombach put it, a "return to the social market economy" of Ludwig Erhard of the early decades of the Federal Republic. Erhard's old formula stated that market competition would benefit the economy but only after the government first intervened against cartels and monopolies to create an optimal environment for competition. Hombach added to that his vision of the "activizing state"—this clearly was not the Republican idea of minimal government—that in many ways, especially by training and education, would stoke the entrepreneurial spirit and encourage individual initiative and responsibility.

Among other measures, the Blair-Schröder-Hombach formula sought to facilitate, by retraining redundant employees, the circulation of jobs and personnel in a rapidly changing economy. Hombach also proposed the recruitment of, and assistance to, new entrepreneurs invited to take over thousands of German family enterprises whose owners retire without successors. Tax cuts and the privatization of certain aspects of social security and medical insurance also play a role in this centrist program, but not quite along the ideological lines of America's New Republicans. European centrists are pragmatic to the point of opportunism; they will emphasize only the policies for which they can generate enough political support—no doubt requiring extensive reliance on public opinion polls—and will gauge their policies to the greatest good of the greatest number rather than to small self-interested elites and special interests. On the basis of these democratic criteria, too, European centrists find self-styled American conservatives wanting rather than worthy of imitation. In fact, there are more parallels among the centrists of leading Western countries than among the conservatives reacting to their challenges. As of this writing, British and German conservatives are in great disarray and not likely to rally again for years to come.

Since the political turmoil of the early half of the '90s, the demand for sweeping political reforms in the United States has receded. Thus, the Republican impeachment campaign of 1998-1999 not only was rejected in public opinion polls and by the voters of November 1998, it also seems to have threatened the electoral fortunes of congressional Republicans for the year 2000. The GOP's popular approval rating has dropped to record lows (one-third) while lame-duck Clinton's approval still hovers around 60 percent. On the other hand, there is a sense of fatigue with the problems and scandals of the Clinton administration that undeservedly appears to tar Clinton's vice president and post-Clinton presidential candidate Al Gore as well. Republican presidential candidates, by the same token, may benefit from Clinton's impeachment but only if they can detach themselves from its Republican promoters. The upshot of these contradictory trends may well be more divided government and conflict between Congress and the president in the future, possibly including Democratic impeachment efforts, fair or foul, of a Republican president. Now that the barriers have been so drastically lowered, any charge seems within the pale.

DAMAGE TO AMERICAN WORLD LEADERSHIP

"Yes, there is bewilderment in England [about the House vote on an impeachment inquiry]," S. Malachy of the *Economist* said on the *NewsHour* (September 17, 1998), "but it is really that America's legal and political machinery makes such a meal out of it," compared to compelling a disgraced cabinet minister to resign. "And if Americans are making so much of it, please can they get on with it. We want a leader who can lead." The world would not stand still while America had a tantrum.

Similar expressions came from Irish newspapers, from Egypt, and from a Mexican journalist on the same show who said: "A weakened American president [vis-à-vis Congress] is bad news for Mexico." European journalists may have been uncertain of the impact of the impeachment drive on American domestic politics then and in the future. But there was no mistaking their fears of what it might do to American leadership in the world. "We know that Saddam and Milosevic are addicted to CNN, we know [North Korean leader] Kim Jong Il watches CNN, and they can't help but think command authority is distracted," a congressional staffer in Washington said. Most of the fears concerned a lapse in American leadership per se, not Clinton's conduct, because the United States suddenly seemed to be in wrenching turmoil over what was widely perceived as a bagatelle. As the deputy director of the French Institute of International Relations in Paris, Dominique Moissi, put it: "All those who would wish for a paralyzed America are totally satisfied, and those who were expecting America to play a leading role are totally disappointed" (*Los Angeles Times,* February 25, 1998).

But a few conservative newspapers agreed with the *Frankfurter Allgemeine Zeitung* in September 1998: "The . . . question now of interest for the United States, its allies and its opponents is: How capable of acting is the morally discredited president of the U.S.?" (quoted in *World Press Review,* November 1998). The conservative German paper was particularly concerned at the time about the escalating Serb violence in Kosovo: "The timid initiatives of Western diplomacy seem totally incapable of stopping [Milosevic's] bombs and machine gun fire." Jochen Siemens, writing for the liberal *Frankfurter Rundschau,* covered both constitutional and foreign policy damage when he wrote: "The Republicans, with their sights set on the November [1998] elections, are trying to milk the crisis for everything they can get out of it. Aside from the damage that they're doing to their country's political system, they are paralyzing America in foreign affairs, and on the world stage . . . Clinton's resignation [also] would damage the office, and impeachment could be a long drawn-out and presumably very dirty process" (ibid.).

Clinton's foreign policy experience and expertise had been questioned by his Republican opponents from the very beginning in 1992, and for good reason. His GOP opponent, incumbent George Bush, boasted a long apprenticeship as Reagan's vice president, UN ambassador, and CIA chief. As president, Bush had masterfully directed the Western alliance through the challenges of the fall of communism in 1989-1990, eased the Soviet-Russian transition, and orchestrated the Gulf War, no mean achievement under the circumstances of post–Cold War anarchy. But it was not fair to deduce from candidate Clinton's campaign slogan "It's the economy, stupid" that a President Clinton would be exclusively focused on the domestic scene. Once elected, in fact, he proved himself highly effective in the area of foreign economic policy, exercising United States leadership particularly in the promotion of worldwide free markets and agreements such as GATT/WTO and NAFTA. In reaction to the submission of the Starr Report, for example, the *Irish Times* called for "strong effective international leadership from the U.S. on the world economy, the Middle Eastern and Russian [situations]—and not the least in helping to consolidate the progress that has been achieved [in Northern Ireland]." Toward the end of his first year under the new Republican-dominated Congress in 1995, the *Economist* (October 14, 1995) even credited the president with having become a "foreign policy president" who provided United States leadership in the world and against the forces of isolationism in America.

The balance of Clinton's conduct of foreign relations, however, was a record of uneven accomplishments, often lacking in timeliness of action and follow-up on particular regional problems. In the midst of his reelection campaign, the *Economist* (September 7, 1996) wrote: "On balance there has been enough [of foreign policy successes] for Mr. Clinton to brag about, but not enough for him to inspire confidence." The British weekly spoke of "halfway triumphs" and of winning only "halfway support" for his ventures. He was also criticized by pundits for lacking a grand, overall vision for America's role in the world and for a future world order. However, these criticisms ring hollow against the background of overwhelming complexity of the post–Cold War world with its neonationalist upsurges, rogue states, and humanitarian crises. There has also been a noticeable reaction to American hegemony and a resulting decline of good will toward Americans around the world (*Los Angeles Times,* March 26, 2000).

On the occasion of one of the Clinton administration's major congressional defeats, the denial of fast track authority in negotiating free trade agreements, Lexington of the *Economist* actually thought Clinton had such a larger vision, namely globalization. Globalization was not only inevitable but good for America; it held tremendous opportunities and Clinton had shown great willingness to help the losers in this process (December 20, 1997): "The Clintonites sensibly recognize that many big things in life, such as economic globalization and technological advance, cannot be resisted by laws or other means, so they might as well be welcomed. At the same time, the Clintonites are not totally laissez faire: they want to 'empower' citizens, to 'help people help themselves,' so that everyone is equipped to deal with the inevitable transitions" (December 6, 1997). Needless to say, this position did not endear Clinton to organized labor or the Old Democrats, who were concerned about the effects of globalization on labor standards and the environment. The Cold War days indeed had been vastly simpler and, as long as the two superpowers did not clash militarily, much easier to manage.

Regarding Republican criticism of Clinton's handling of foreign policy, we also need to consider the steep decline in Republican foreign policy statesmanship from Nixon and Henry Kissinger to the Reagan years, when the president appointed, in place of the towering figure of national security adviser Kissinger, William P. Clark, an obscure rancher from rural California who was unfamiliar with the names of the leaders of our principal allies. President Bush's obvious expertise was scarcely appreciated by the Republican chiefs who at first opposed his candidacy. This decline was also true of Republican foreign policy in Congress where the rare, knowledgeable foreign policy leaders—for example, Senators Richard Lugar, John McCain, or Jack Warner—have received little respect for their expertise. Astonishingly, the inexperience in foreign policy of the Republican presidential candidate of 2000, George W. Bush—the genes of his father evidently do not carry the foreign policy knowledge—was treated like a joke in the media, because "most average Americans could not identify the names of many foreign leaders either," as newscasters put it on television.

But then, we hope that "most average Americans" will be spared making decisions for all of us on national security questions. To European journalists who consider diplomacy among the highest of political arts, such amateurishness in Washington is a frightening prospect. And when the yahoos threaten to impeach the American president, the outcome is truly alarming.

As early as January 1998, European media fretted that the distractions of the Lewinsky scandal interfered with American leadership. Suzanne Moore, writing in the London *Independent*, commented that "... an affair with Monica Lewinsky may diminish him. Whether it calls into question his ability to lead is highly debatable." Leo Wieland, in the conservative *Frankfurter Allgemeine Zeitung*, complained, "how can the world be governed by a man who is the brunt of nightly jokes on television" (both quoted in *World Press Review*, March 1998). The German weekly *Die Zeit* (January 29, 1998) wrote, "The world worries how we shall meet the crises, especially in the Far East and the Near East, if this American president is preoccupied with saving his own skin." Its foreign policy expert, Christoph Bertram, questioned how the world power, America, could get along with "only half a president ... What happens if Clinton should order a strike against Saddam Hussein? The whole world will think it is his attempt to divert attention from his troubles" (ibid.). This was, indeed, what many American pundits and newspapers said when the Iraqi dictator, after weeks of defying the UN weapons inspectors the following fall, evidently thought he could take advantage of the prolonged American crisis. He underestimated Clinton's readiness to take action.

"Wag-the-dog," some media voices cried when Clinton finally struck Iraq on the eve of the impeachment vote, but over 70 percent of Americans, again, were smarter than the pundits and supported the military action. Many European and some American media had been eyeing the Iraqi dictator for months, wondering when he might make another attempt to break out of his confinement. The House grudgingly put off the impeachment debate for one day and resumed it the next, while American and British bombs and rockets continued to fall and American pilots were clearly in harm's way. When Lott, the isolationist, opposed Clinton's decision vociferously, it was a defining moment for the collision between the pressing and constantly erupting problems of the world and the convulsions of American domestic politics. The world would not wait while American leadership was tied down like Gulliver, unable to rise to its challenges.

Further collisions of this kind concerned the long-overdue payment of the United States' dues to the United Nations and the ratification of the nuclear test ban treaty. After years of wrangling with the obstreperous chair of the Senate Foreign Relations Committee, Jesse Helms, President Clinton finally managed to obtain $926 million in the budget for the year 2000, about half of what was originally owed. The turning point came when the UN threatened to take away the United States seat and vote in the General Assembly (though not in the UN Security Council). Republicans in Congress exacted both a reduction of the American share of UN expenses in the future (from 25 percent to 22 percent) and a pledge that the funds would not be used to support foreign family planning agencies that might facilitate abortions. The antiabortion rider was written by Republican House members and had, of course, nothing to do with the national security interests it threatened to jeopardize; its effect is also doubtful. Other payments to the UN, for example, large assessments totaling $2 billion in 1998, have been paid by the United States. Another of Helms's demands, that the UN trim its budget and reorganize its administration, had long been met, though not necessarily to his satisfaction. Spiteful Republican senators had also held up the appointment of Richard Holbrooke as UN ambassador for fourteen months to make their political points.

"The U.S. has already lost influence in the UN," the British UN ambassador said, "Its voice has been muffled and its reputation stained. I believe that people can't quite take it that the world's richest country is the UN's biggest debtor" (*Los Angeles Times,* November 7, 1999). Spokespersons for our European allies, indeed, were not very polite about the deadbeat Americans and their antiabortion blackmail in foreign policy. On the other hand, to quote Marc Thiessen, Helms's press spokesman, "few Republicans lose sleep if we lose our seat in the General Assembly" (*New York Times,* October 24, 1999). And, thanks to the media's ignoring the UN, neither would many Americans outside Congress.

As for the nuclear test ban treaty, the domestic political impact of its Senate defeat has already been discussed in "Impeachment, Act Three." Its effect on the American leadership role abroad was infinitely greater because, owing to the international negotiating environment, it was exceedingly important for the United States to be able to persuade countries still sitting on the fence, such as India, Pakistan, and others. A positive Senate vote would have sustained the international momentum to sign up the undecided and would have put more effective pressure on the rogue states. The Republican counterarguments about the "unverifiability," "unenforceability," and "inapplicability to rogue states" such as North Korea totally miss the point. They also misrepresent the nature of international treaties—which are not like domestic law enforced by a sheriff but rather resemble promises or voluntary commitments—and international law, revealing the ignorance and prejudices of some members of Congress, presidential candidates, and sections of the public at large. The controversy over the test ban treaty vote, in fact, was almost immediately drawn into the presidential primary campaigns for the year 2000 while it was still reverberating abroad.

As *Washington Post* correspondent T. R. Reid reported from London on *Washington Week in Review* (October 15, 1999), Britons snickered about American leadership. They lumped this ridiculous display of personal hostility toward Clinton with other laughable aspects of American life, such as the ban by a South Carolina school district of the very popular Harry Potter children's books, presumably because the books' protagonist attends a school for wizards (read, witchcraft). An analyst for Britain's International Institute for Strategic Studies, Andrew Brooks, reportedly said: "This is the chance for the biggest superpower to freeze the nuclear [arms race] mechanisms, and [the United States] is behaving like a small child" (*Los Angeles Times*, October 15, 1999).

The Blair, Schröder, and Chirac administrations declared the Republican Senate's scornful fecklessness a true disaster for the fragile structure of post–Cold War arms control negotiations, opening the door to a possible new nuclear arms race. Germany's defense minister Rudolf Scharping called the vote "absolutely wrong" and "highly regrettable." NATO Secretary General Javier Solano called it "very sad for [nuclear] proliferation." China and India—India was already in a nuclear arms race and in an explosive Kashmiri border showdown with unstable Pakistan—expressed alarm at the destabilizing implications of the Senate vote. The Russian foreign ministry said: "This decision delivers a serious blow to the entire system of agreements in the field of nuclear disarmament and proliferation." Other Russian voices warned that this egregious lapse of American leadership would encourage nationalists and rogue states with nuclear ambitions, possibly leading to the establishment of many more than the current five nuclear powers. Russian action on several pending arms control agreements, such as START II and III and the Anti-Ballistic Missile Treaty of 1972, may also be stymied by the Senate's display of childishness, a sample of what a future Republican administration might present as foreign policy. Jesse Helms as a possible Secretary of State?

A frustrated Clinton responded by denouncing the "new isolationism" among the Republicans and called upon the current nuclear powers to refrain from nuclear testing, just as the United States would do under his leadership. He also mentioned the refusal of the Republican-dominated Congress to fully pay the UN dues, to fund programs for the Middle East, and to pay enough for the destruction and safeguarding of Russian nuclear materials. He could have added also the failure to fully support the participation of American troops in Kosovo and East Timor. Lott rejected the label of isolationism and countered that Republicans didn't "want to be international cowboys." Cowboys or Caligula's horse, there was no mistaking the implacable hostility of the "handful of spiteful old men in the Senate" (Mark Shields, *NewsHour,* October 15, 1999) who still wanted to get in their licks regardless of the worldwide consequences. The public was left to wonder if these messages of personal animus could not have been delivered in a way that did not damage American interests and reputation abroad. The European press shudders to think that the one remaining superpower may not be up to its role of leadership.

Some of the foreign responses to the American crisis of 1998-1999 were off the mark. The *Irish Times* (September 14, 1998), for example, speculated that "if Clinton had asked for pardon right after his first [finger-wagging] lie, he might have been able to have [Prime Minister] Benjamin Netanyahu keep Israel's promises to the Palestinians." The Israeli leader had just expressed his support, somewhat belatedly and surprisingly, for the beleaguered president. Asian newspapers voiced the fear that Zippergate might further destabilize the world economy. Even the staid *Le Figaro* (September 14, 1998) claimed that "ten years after crushing communism, the power of the United States collapsed before the Internet [which carried the Starr Report worldwide] . . . If Clinton had preferred discreet ladies of the night to overly talkative interns, [perhaps] he could have convinced Boris Yeltsin to hunt down the robber barons [of the Russian Mafia] who, after stripping Russia, now risk throwing it back into the communist noose." The Arab media found the culprit for the Lewinsky imbroglio in a conspiracy of the Israeli Mossad (secret service) to stem the advance of the peace process, according to Sheikh Ahmed Yasin and Syrian and Palestinian papers. The Iraqi *Al Iraq,* on the other hand, thought that Clinton had ordered the bombing of Iraq in early 1998 in order to divert attention from his unfolding scandal (*Ma'ariv* of Tel Aviv, January 25, 1998).

THE LIBERTY TREE

There is something very engaging about the concern expressed by knowledgeable European observers regarding the state of our Constitution. It has truly become a sacred document of the world. Nicole Bacharan in her book, *Le piège: Quand la démocratie perd la tête* (*The Trap: When Democracy Loses Its Head*), even added to the book's dedication to her assistant the words: "Jefferson, Lincoln, wake up. They have gone mad!" In a review of Jeffrey Toobin's book by the *Economist* (March 11, 2000), the reviewer looked back on Clinton's acquittal, one year earlier: "Viewed calmly and with hindsight, it seems extraordinary that a lie about sex . . . should almost have capsized a president." Admitting that his own journal looked in vain for proof of "anything that was actually criminal" about Clinton's conduct, and surveying the range of his enemies and their actions, the reviewer finally conceded that "even as president [Clinton] was entitled to some privacy in his sexual affairs." Except for his pursuers, "motivated Republicans, overweening lawyers, and a yawning cultural divide," this affair did not have to turn into "America's gravest constitutional crisis for 25 years."

But what about our own citizens? How much do they care about this constitutional crisis? How much do they know about our marvelous and venerable system? Recent tests conducted by the Department of Education among the nation's three million high school seniors have shown that only about a fourth has a solid understanding of how our Constitution and system of government are supposed to work. Only about 30 percent of the seniors know, for example, that the Supreme Court's power to review the constitutionality of laws is intended to protect the rights of individuals. More than a third lacks the most basic civics information about our form of government at the moment in their lives when they are about to become active citizens and voters.

"For a democracy like ours to flourish, it is crucial that citizens are prepared to participate in making decisions through rational discussion and debate," Diane Ravitch, a member of the National Assessment Governing Board and a New York University professor, commented (*Los Angeles Times,* November 19, 1999). This sorry state of civic knowledge among the citizenry of tomorrow is probably not far below the level of general political ignorance today, at least among high school graduates of the last twenty years. It represents an ideal climate for the right-wing fly-by-nights of the media, the talk radio hosts, the lawyers, and members of Congress to peddle their misinterpretations of the Constitution. A constitution is a living thing that must be kept alive by the awareness and active engagement of all the citizenry or it will die. Ours has lived for more than 200 years to come to this sorry passage.

For more than a century, the commencement exercises of St. John's College in Annapolis, Maryland, were held under a mighty tulip poplar tree that by the 1990s was said to be 400 years old. During the War of Independence, in fact, the local chapter of the Sons of Liberty convened under it, plotting action in the war, as other chapters met throughout the colonies under similar stately trees. Old age, storms, and disease unfortunately caught up with these trees, one by one, and, in the fall of 1999, the Liberty Tree at St. John's was the last to succumb to the chainsaw. The college commemorated its passing with a solemn ceremony, the singing of the national anthem, and the tolling of a bell before they cut it down.

Our living Constitution, with most of its working parts still intact—and a few new branches like the party system and the triumph of democracy—lives on despite the assault of meanspirited men and women, and the failures of the judicial checks on the House of Representatives and the expiring Office of Independent Counsel. The death of the last living Liberty Tree is a sad moment in the life of the republic. The death of the living Constitution, however, would be a catastrophe of unimaginable proportions, not only for this country but for all our friends and allies throughout the world of democracy.

Notes

INTRODUCTION

1. Jeffrey Toobin, *A Vast Conspiracy* (New York: Random House, 1999), p.5

CHAPTER 1

1. Nicole Bacharan, *Le piège: Quand la démocratie perd la tête* . . . (Paris: Éditions du Seuil, 1999), p.38
2. See also T. Hamburger, T. Marmor, and J. Meacham, "What the Death of Health Reform Teaches Us About the Media," *Washington Monthly,* November 1994, pp.35-41
3. Lars-Erick Nelson, "The Republicans' War," *New York Review of Books,* February 4, 1999, p.6

The following books were consulted for this chapter:

——— Joe Conason and Gene Lyons, *The Hunting of the President: The Ten-Year Campaign to Destroy Bill and Hillary Clinton* (New York: St. Martin's Press, 2000)

——— Michael Isikoff, *Uncovering Clinton: A Reporter's Story* (New York: Crown, 1999)

——— David Maraniss, *First in his Class: A Biography of Bill Clinton* (New York: Simon & Schuster, 1995)

——— Dick Morris, *Behind the Oval Office: Getting Reelected Against All Odds* (New York: Random House, 1997)

——— George Stephanopolous, *All Too Human: A Political Education* (Boston: Little, Brown & Company, 1999)

——— Bob Woodward, *The Choice* (New York: Simon & Schuster, 1996)

I also benefited from reading Gail Sheehy, "The Inner Quest of Newt Gingrich," *Vanity Fair,* September 1995, and other American periodicals.

CHAPTER 2

1. Nicole Bacharan, *Le piège. Quand la démocratie perd la tête* . . . (Paris: Editions du Seuil, 1999), p.69
2. *Ibid.,* pp.91, 94-95
3. Jeffrey Toobin, *A Vast Conspiracy* (New York: Random House, 1999), p.190
4. *Ibid.,* pp.195, 204

5. Bacharan, *op. cit.,* pp.70-71
6. Toobin, *op. cit.,* pp.116-117
7. Bacharan, *op.cit.,* p.75
8. See also William H. Rehnquist, "The Impeachment Clause: A Wild Card in the Constitution," 85 *North Western University Law Review* (1991), pp. 903-918. Chief Justice Rehnquist points out, among other things, how impeachment could cause severe damage to the separation of powers between executive and legislature.
9. Michael Isikoff, *Uncovering Clinton: A Reporter's Story,* (New York: Crown, 1999), p. 287
10. *Ibid.,* p.287
11. *Ibid.,* 352
12. Bacharan, *op.cit.,* pp.73, 85
13. *Ibid.,* p.86
14. *Ibid.,* pp.96-98
15. Toobin, *op.cit.,* pp.207-209
16. Isikoff, *op.cit.,* p.245
17. Bacharan, *op.cit.,* p.117
18. Isikoff, *op.cit.,* pp.218, 231
19. *Ibid.,* p.303
20. *Ibid.,* p.301
21. Quoted by Bob Woodward, *The Choice* (New York: Simon & Schuster, 1996), p. 210

The following books were consulted for this chapter:

——— Raoul Berger, *Impeachment: The Constitutional Problems* (Cambridge, MA: Harvard University Press, 1973)
——— Charles L. Black, Jr., *Impeachment: A Handbook* (New Haven, Conn.: Yale University Press, 1974)
——— Eleanor Bushnell, *Crimes, Follies, and Misfortunes: The Federal Impeachment Trials* (Champaign-Urbana: University of Illinois Press, 1992)
——— *The Federalist Papers: Alexander Hamilton, James Madison, John Jay* (New York: New American Library, 1961)
——— Michael J. Gerhardt, *The Federal Impeachment Process: A Constitutional and Historical Analysis* (Princeton, NJ: Princeton University Press, 1996)
——— Peter C. Hoffer and N.E.H. Hull, *Impeachment in America, 1635-1805* (New Haven, CT: Yale University Press, 1984)
——— Richard A. Posner, *An Affair of State: The Investigation, Impeachment and Trial of President Clinton* (Cambridge, MA: Harvard University Press, 1999)
——— William H. Rehnquist and Clyde Adams Phillips, *Grand Inquests: The Historic Impeachments of Justice Samuel Chase and President Andrew Johnson* (New York: Quill, 1999)

I also benefited from a number of articles, such as:

——— Renata Adler, "Decoding the Starr Report," *Vanity Fair,* December 1998
——— Ronald Dworkin, "The Wounded Constitution," New York Review of Books, March 18, 1999

——— Anthony Lewis, "The Prosecutorial State: Criminalizing American Politics," *The American Prospect,* January-February 1999
——— Lars Erik Nelson, "The Not Very Grand Inquisitor," *New York Review of Books,* November 5, 1998
——— Jeffrey Rosen, "Kenneth Starr, Trapped," *New York Times Magazine,* June 1, 1997

And from many issues of *The New Yorker* and the *Washington Monthly.*

CHAPTER 3

1. Jeffrey Toobin, *A Vast Conspiracy* (New York: Random House, 1999), pp.5-6
2. *Ibid.,* pp.173-176
3. Nicole Bacharan, *Le piège: Quand la démocratie perd la tête* . . . (Paris: Éditions du Seuil, 1999), p.95
4. *Ibid.,* p.141
5. *Ibid.,* p.177
6. Michael Isikoff tellingly describes the mixture of reportorial curiosity and editorial hypocrisy in *Uncovering Clinton: A Reporter's Story* (New York: Crown Publishers, 1999), pp.57-61
7. Joe Conason and Gene Lyons, *The Hunting of the President: The Ten-Year Campaign to Destroy Bill and Hillary Clinton* (New York: St. Martin's Press, 2000), p.308
8. Bacharan, *op. cit.,* p.137
9. *Ibid.,* pp.97-98
10. *Ibid.,* pp.128-129
11. Jeffrey Rosen, "Jurisprurience," *The New Yorker* (September 28, 1998), p.34
12. Bacharan, *op. cit.,* pp.118-119
13. *Ibid.,* pp.28-29, 113, 146-147
14. *Ibid.,* p.57
15. *Ibid.,* p.119
16. Toobin, *op. cit.,* pp.266-279, 286-288, 304, 321-322
17. *Ibid.,* p.287
18. Bacharan, *op. cit.,* p.187
19. Al Franken, *Rush Limbaugh Is a Big Fat Idiot and Other Observations* (New York: Island Books of Dell Publishing, a division of Bantam Doubleday Dell, 1996), pp.61-65

The following books were consulted for this chapter:

——— James Allen, *Without Sanctuary* (Santa Fe, NM: Twin Palms, 1998)
——— Alan M. Dershowitz, *Sexual McCarthyism: Clinton, Starr, and the Emerging Constitutional Crisis* (New York: Basic Books, 1998)
——— Al Franken, *Rush Limbaugh is a Big Fat Idiot and Other Observations* (New York: Island Press, 1996)
——— Michael Isikoff, *Uncovering Clinton: A Reporter's Story* (New York: Crown, 1999)
——— Monica Lewinsky, *Monica's Story, as written with Andrew Morton* (New York: St. Martin's Press, 1999)

―――― Catherine A. MacKinnon, *Sexual Harassment of Working Women: A Case of Sex Discrimination* (New Haven, Conn.: Yale University Press, 1979)
―――― Stewart E.Tolnay and E. M. Beck, *A Festival of Violence: An Analysis of Southern Lynchings, 1882-1930* (Champaign-Urbana: University of Illinois Press, 1995)

I have also benefited from pertinent articles and commentary in *The New Yorker*, the *Washington Monthly*, *Vanity Fair*, and other magazines.

CHAPTER 4

1. Alexis de Tocqueville, *Democracy in America* (New York: Harper & Row, 1966), vol. 1, pp.191-195
2. Joe Conason and Gene Lyons, *The Hunting of the President: The Ten-Year Campaign to Destroy Bill and Hillary Clinton* (New York: St. Martin's Press, 2000), pp.1-10
3. Jeffrey Toobin, *A Vast Conspiracy* (New York: Random House, 1999), pp.399-400. See also pp.284-285 for his account of the *Washington Post*'s deceptive news-mongering of February 5, 1998.
4. *Ibid.*, p.304
5. See also David T. Z. Mindich, *Just the Facts: How 'Objectivity' Came to Define American Journalism* (New York: New York University Press, 1998)
6. Nicole Bacharan, *Le piège: Quand la démocratie perd la tête* . . . (Paris: Éditions du Seuil, 1999), pp.191-196, *passim*
7. See also Blake Fleetwood, "The Broken Wall," in *Washington Monthly*, September 1999, pp.40-44
8. See also Christopher Georges, "Bad News Bearers," in *Washington Monthly*, July-August 1993, pp.28-34. There is also the analysis by Tom Rosenstiel, *Strange Bedfellows: How Television and the Presidential Candidates Changed American Politics* (Westport, CT: Hyperion, 1994). Rosenstiel describes the campaign year of 1992 as the year of the New Media which grew from journalists' perceptions of the tabloid methods of the Bush campaign of 1988.
9. Michael Isikoff, *Uncovering Clinton: A Reporter's Story* (New York: Crown Publishers, 1999), p.104
10. Bacharan, *op. cit.*, p.31
11. Richard Reeves, *What the People Know: Freedom and the Press* (Cambridge, MA: Harvard University Press, 1998
12. Bacharan, *op. cit.*, p.31
13. Al Franken, *Rush Limbaugh Is a Big Fat Idiot and Other Observations* (New York: Island Books of Dell Publishing, a division of Bantam Doubleday Dell, 1996)
14. Bacharan, *op. cit.*, p.191
15. Bacharan, *op. cit.*, p.194-195
16. Paul Campos, *Jurismania: The Madness of American Law* (New York: Oxford University Press, 1998), preface

The following books were consulted for this chapter:

―――― Ben H. Bagdikian, *The Media Monopoly* (Boston: Beacon Press, 2000)

——— Michael Isikoff, *Clinton Uncovered: A Reporter's Story* (New York: Crown, 1999)
——— Howard Kurtz, *Spin Cycle: How the Media and the White House Manipulate the News* (New York: Touchstone, 1999)
——— Gene Lyons, *Fools for Scandal: How the Media Invented Whitewater* (New York: Franklin Square Press, 1996)
——— Dennis W. Mazzocco, *Networks of Power* (Boston: Southend Press, 1994)
——— David T. Z. Mindich, *Just the Facts: How 'Objectivity' Came to Define American Journalism* (New York: New York University Press, 1998)
——— Richard Reeves, *What the People Know: Freedom and the Press* (Cambridge, MA: Harvard University Press, 1998)
——— Tom Rosenstiel, *The Beat Goes On: President Clinton's First Year With the Media* (Washington: Brookings Institution, 1994)
——— Alexis de Tocqueville, *Democracy in America* (First edition, New York: Harper & Row, 1966)

I have also benefited from the continuous coverage of the media in the *Washington Monthly* and *Brill's Content*, not to mention direct observation.

CHAPTER 5

1. Jeffrey Toobin, *A Vast Conspiracy* (New York: Random House, 1999), p.322
2. Joe Conason and Gene Lyons, *The Hunting of the President: The Ten-Year Campaign to Destroy Bill and Hillary Clinton* (New York: St. Martin's Press, 2000), pp.1-10. The antecedents certainly go back to Cliff Jackson of Little Rock and the right-wing conspirators of 1993 and 1994.
3. *New York Review of Books* (March 18, 1999), p.8. See also his essay in the January 14, 1999 issue of the same journal.
4. Nicole Bacharan, *Le piège: Quand la démocratie perd la tête . . .* (Paris: Éditions du Seuil, 1999), p.189

I also consulted the following sources:

——— Joe Conason and Gene Lyons, *The Hunting of the President: The Ten-Year Campaign to Destroy Bill and Hillary Clinton* (New York: St. Martin's Press, 2000)
——— Ronald Dworkin, "The Wounded Constitution," *New York Review of Books*, March 18, 1999
——— Symposium: "The Independent Counsel Act: From Watergate to Whitewater and Beyond," *Georgetown Law Journal*, 86 (July 1998), 2011 ff.
——— Peter H. Irons, *A People's History of the Supreme Court* (New York: Viking Press, 1999)
——— Jerry M. Landay, "The Conservative Cabal That is Transforming American Law," *Washington Monthly*, March 2000
——— Anthony Lewis, "Nearly a Coup," *New York Review of Books*, April 13, 2000
——— Stephen Pomper, "The Gipper's Constitution," *Washington Monthly*, December 1999
——— Cass R. Sunstein, "Unchecked and Unbalanced: Why the Independent Counsel Act Must Go," *The American Prospect*, May-June, 1998

Index

ABC radio, 289
ABC television, 255, 257, 260, 271
    and Capital Cities, 270
    on Flowers, 265
    on impeachment, 299-300
    and tobacco industry, 271
    on Troopergate, 286
abortion issue, 58, 234, 338
Ackerman, Bruce, 103, 107
affirmative action, 322, 338
Amar, Akhil R., 316
American Journalism Review, 295
American Society of Newspaper Editors, 264-265, 301
American Spectator, 28, 284
American world leadership, 171
anti-impeachment rallies, 277
Arkansas Democrat-Gazette, 72, 265
Armey, Dick, 28, 74, 78-79, 118
Atlanta Constitution, 169
Atwater, Lee, 252, 308
Bacharan, Nicole, 37, 95, 97, 301, 350
    on American media, 297
    on Starr, 123-125
balanced budget amendment, 46
Baltimore Sun, 270
Barr, Bob, 7, 117-118, 120, 202
    on coup attempt, 150
    motion to impeach, 78-79
Beer, Samuel H., 106
Bennett, Jackie, 97, 160, 220, 229, 261
Bennett, Robert, 42
Bennett, William, 13, 121, 150
Benoist, Alain de, 116
Berliner Morgenpost, 11
Berlusconi, Silvio, 40
Bernstein, Carl, 99-100, 303

Bildzeitung (Hamburg), 185-186
Blair, Tony, 5, 268, 338-340, 348
    election of, 59
Blumenthal, Sidney, 220, 242
Boren, David, 22
Boston Globe, 146, 264, 270
Bradley, Bill, 323
Brill's *Content,* 260
Brown, Floyd, 42
Brown, Ron, 66, 331
Buchanan, Pat, 53, 58, 115
Buffalo Evening News, 270
Buffett, Warren, 270
Burton, Dan, 7, 76, 120
Bush, George Herbert Walker, 30, 76, 266, 333
    and foreign policy leadership, 342, 344
    and international politics, 24-25
    and Iran-Contra, 42, 100, 108-109
    on Arthur Laffer, 59
    on Limbaugh, 290
    lying by, 18-19
    in 1992 election, 21-22
Bush, George W., 118, 316, 323, 344-345
    military service of, 30
campaign finance issues, 69-71, 77-78, 233-234
    Clinton accused of, 34
    Congressional, 325
    Thompson on, 327
Canadian Business, 292-293
Capital Cities/ABC, 270, 289
Carter, Jimmy, 100, 221
cartoons about Clinton, 287-289

CBS television, 258, 271-272, 286, 299-300
censure, 119, 146, 150, 166-167
centrism, of Clinton, 55, 75, 323, 332
   European parallels, 59, 63, 333-334, 338-340
   and Old Democrats, 24-25, 48-49
   see also New Democrats *and* Democratic Leadership Council
Chase, Samuel P., 102, 105
Chicago Tribune, 270
Chirac, Jacques, 5, 199, 348
Cisneros, Henry, 66, 76, 330-331
civility, decline of, 71-72
Clinton Chronicles, 25, 205, 254
Clinton fatigue, 8-10
Clinton, Hillary Rodham,
   and commodities futures, 68
   European perceptions of, 216-218
   Foster's suicide, 80
   in Gallup poll, 6
   and health reform, 40-41
   media hostility to, 20, 251, 257-258
   role in 1998 elections, 140, 216-217
   and Starr, 243
   and talk radio, 19
   and Travelgate, 65, 80
   and vast right-wing conspiracy, 7, 242
   and Watergate, 336
   and Whitewater, 26-27, 34-35, 71-72, 80, 307
Clinton, William Jefferson, 5-7, 13
   apologies of, 207-208, 256
   appointments of, 24
   background of, 20-21
   budget policies of, 24, 36, 258, 262
   in cartoons, 287-289
   censure of, 119, 146, 150, 287
   character issue of, 20, 62, 109, 120, 241, 262
   and civil rights, 19, 322
   and deficit-cutting, 80
   entrapment of, 124-125, 131, 247
   executive privilege of, 134, 157
   failing, 43-44
   and foreign economic policy, 343
   and Gingrich landslide, 38-40
   and globalization, 344
   and government shutdown, 48-52
   and grand jury videotape of, 258
   haters of, 305-306
   historical legacy of, 276, 309-310
   impeachment of, 137, 138-140, 241, 253
   investigations of, 76-78, 80-81, 110, 165
   and job creation, 24, 42-43, 57, 335
   on Limbaugh, 291
   lying by, 18-19, 222, 232-233
   lynching of, 240-243
   media hostility to, 10, 80, 251, 255-259, 271-277, 305
   and middle class issues, 55
   and military issue, 29-31
   national service, 24
   1992 election of, 21-22
   and 1998 congressional election, 138-141
   and Old Democrats, 324
   political weakness of, 23-24
   and press on Whitewater, 26-28
   public opinion polls on, 13, 60, 110, 154, 168
   reelection of, 53, 55-65, 79-80, 90
   resignation of, 167-169, 257
   resurgent, 45-46, 48
   scandal-proneness of, 26
   Senate trial of, 107, 145-149
   and Al Smith, 336-338
   Starr Report and American press, 127
   State of the Union speech, 168, 276-277
   and stock market, 57
   and Teddy Roosevelt, 336
   trust issue, 61-62, 276; *see also* character issue
   Watergate analogies for impeachment of, 274
   welfare reform and, 25, 36; *see also* welfare reform

Whitewater investigation, 27; *see also under* Whitewater
and world leadership, 341-349
worldwide esteem for, 199
CNBC television, 261, 296
CNN television, 261-262, 268, 278, 285, 301
on foreign policy, 277, 279, 341
on impeachment, 295-300
Committee of Concerned Journalists, 295, 299
Congressional elections of 1998, 138-142
Republican expectations, 139-140
Congressional investigations, 66
conservative revolution, 115-118, 140, 235
Constitution, American, 110, 242-243
abuse of, 7, 9, 308-309
damage to, 303, 309-317, 332
European admiration for, 9, 16, 83-84
on impeachment, 99, 102, 106-107, 111
on investigations, 66
popular knowledge of, 350-351
vulnerability of, 9
Contract for America, 38-39, 55, 63, 71-75, 88, 333
fulfillment of, 45-46
Conyers, John, 11, 83
Corriere della Serra (Milan), 39-40, 110, 266
Cosmopolitan, 213
Council of Conservative Citizens, 117, 170, 288, 323
coup d'état, 9, 11, 150-154, 162-166, 275
against 1996 elections, 109, 271
in America, 309
by House Judiciary Committee, 34, 83
Dagbladet (Oslo), 217, 289
Dagens Nyheter (Stockholm), 183
Daily News, 258, 264
D'Amato, Alphonse, 28, 36, 68, 140
Daschle, Tom, 171
Dash, Sam, 130-131, 224, 326-327

Dean, John, 101
DeLay, Tom, 7, 30, 74, 117-120, 148
Democratic Leadership Council, 22, 323, 333
Democrats, Old, 63, 115, 323, 332-333, 338
contrasted with New Democrats, 55, 91
on NAFTA, 344
Dole, Robert, 44-47, 56-65, 73, 79, 119
defeat in 1996, 53
and government shutdown, 51-52
on health reform, 40
on Whitewater, 28, 35-36
World War II record, 30
Drudge Report, 260, 269, 278
Dworkin, Ronald, 313
Economist, The (London), 22, 25, 29-30, 39-40
on abolishing cabinet departments, 45
on American media, 253-254
on American sexual mores, 175
on campaign finance, 69
on Clinton's resignation. 163, 188
on Clinton's resurgence, 45
on Congress, 85
on employment, 42-43
on foreign policy leadership, 343-344
on Gingrich's revolution, 63, 74-76, 89-90
on government shutdown, 49-52
on Helms, 44
on incivility, 72
on investigations, 68-69, 76-77, 327
on Jones' suit, 66-68
on Justice Brennan, 319
on Limbaugh, 290
on 1994 elections, 38
on 1996 elections ,47, 53-55, 56, 58-59, 61, 73
on privacy, 193-194, 350
on religious right, 210
review of Toobin, 350
on Supreme Court, 318

environmental protection, 55, 75-76, 90, 234
Erhard, Ludwig, 339
Espy, Mike, 66, 76, 145, 330
Ewing, W. Hickman, Jr., 96-97, 160, 306
Express, L' (Paris), 65, 119, 148, 204, 237
Faircloth, Lauch, 42, 132, 140
fairness clause
Falwell, Jerry, 7, 25, 205-206, 254
federal judicial appointments, 67, 169-170, 230, 317-318
federal judicial bias, 318
Federalist Papers, 99, 103, 310, 314
Federalist Society, 7, 118, 159, 235, 298, 308
    Jones attorneys in, 67
feminism, 209-210, 291
Figaro, Le (Paris), 97, 118, 128, 131-132
    on American democracy, 84
    on anti-Clinton campaign, 13
    chronology in, 120-125, 133-135
    on Clinton's apologies, 207-208
    foreign policy speculations, 349
    on impeachment, 143-144, 164, 199, 203, 235
    on judicial tyranny, 155
    on 1998 elections, 140
    on Puritanism, 239-240
    on Senate trial, 147, 150, 175, 236-237
    on sexual attitudes, 182, 210-213
    on Starr Report, 199-202
    on tabloids, 266
Filegate, 36, 80, 96, 231
Financial Times (London), 44, 188, 217
Fiske, Robert, 28, 35-36, 41, 81, 132
Flowers, Gennifer, 18, 21, 80, 265, 268, 284
Flynt, Larry, 148, 194, 202
Foley, Tom, 43
Forbes, Steve, 53
Ford, Gerald, 100, 119, 129, 332
Foster, Vincent J., 118, 120, 231, 254
    re: charges against Clinton, 80
    in Clinton Chronicles, 25-26, 37
    and Fiske, 41
    and OIC, 96
France-Soir, 199
Franken, Al, 292
Frankfurter Allgemeine Zeitung, 164, 207, 342, 345
    on impeachment, 10, 154
    on 1994 elections, 39, 44
    on polls on Clinton, 14
    on Starr Report, 5, 128
    on tabloids, 266
Frankfurter Rundschau, 140, 342
Gephardt, Dick, 44, 108
Gergen, David, 24, 25
Gingrich, Newt, 69, 169, 205, 209
    anti-Clinton drive of, 7-8
    decline of, 46, 58, 63-64, 74, 174
    on drugs in the White House, 44
    European admiration for, 15
    Gingrichites, 39, 54-55, 117, 169, 291, 324
    government shutdown, 49-53
    investigations threatened by, 60, 327
    military record of, 30
    1994 election victory of, 22, 28, 30, 33, 38, 45
    and Perot, 56
    revolution of, 73, 79, 88, 89-90, 115, 140
    support for NAFTA, 23
Globe, 259, 264, 269
Globe and Mail (Toronto), 143, 156
Goldberg, Lucianne, 8, 121, 178, 302
Goldwater, Barry, 74
Gore, Al, 45, 74, 277, 323, 341
government shutdown, 49-53
Guardian, The (London), 94-95, 108, 126, 128, 136
    on Clinton's apologies, 207, 217
    on Clinton's problems, 43
    on impeachment, 163-166, 175, 188, 236
    on Monica Lewinsky, 193, 212
    on 1994 elections, 39
    on 1998 elections, 140
    on tabloids, 266

on Puritanism, 238
Guardian Weekly, 188, 217
gun lobby, 58, 70, 234, 245, 325
Hamilton, Alexander, 68, 310, 314
Handelsblatt (Duesseldorf), 14, 92
Hardball, 268
Harkin, Tom, 203, 228
Hart, Gary, 296
Hartford Courant, 270
Hatch, Orrin, 169, 192, 230, 235, 319
hate crimes, 245-246
health care reform, 22-23, 35-37, 46, 291, 325
   failure of, 40-41
Helms, Jesse, 131, 169, 280, 317, 319
   in firing of Fiske, 42
   and isolationism, 54
   on nuclear test ban, 170-171, 348
   threats to Clinton, 44
   on US debt to UN, 346
Hindu (Madras), 10, 325
Holden, Matthew Jr., 104
Huang, John, 66, 69, 77
Hussein, Saddam, 13, 25, 60, 170, 345
Hustler, The, 194, 202
Hyde, Henry J., 101-102, 106-107, 113-114
   abuse of rule of law, 274, 313
   admission of defeat, 149
   and checks and balances, 310-311, 313, 315-317
   and Democrats, 136
   extremism of, 7, 117-119, 308
   of federal judges, 100, 102, 104
   impeachment, 78-79, 86, 92-99, 142, 143, 308
   impeachment without removal, 108, 142-145, 315
   initial reluctance of, 79
   level of impeachable actions, 101-105, 156, 231, 311
   lying by, 223, 227-228
   Madison on, 310
   marital infidelity of, 120, 195-196, 202
   and 1998 elections, 139-141, 165
   partisanship of, 138
   purpose of, 100-101, 119, 144
   and Republicans, 319
   and Starr Report, 126
   weakening presidency, 310-315
   and world leadership, 342-349
imperial judiciary, 317
incivility, 71-73
Independent (London), 113, 187-188, 209, 345
Independent on Sunday (London), 16, 204
Indian Express (New Delhi), 143
Internet news, 278-279
Iran-Contra investigation, 100, 109, 112-114, 311
   Bush innocent of, 19
   Reagan's polls after, 13
   and Walsh, 42
Irish Times (Dublin), 149-150, 188-189, 212, 343
   on Middle east, 349
   on Starr Report, 128-129
   on tabloid journalism, 283
Isikoff, Michael, 26, 67, 121-122, 160-161
isolationism, 54, 348-349
ITN television (PBS), 279
Jackson, Andrew, 20, 87
Jefferson, Thomas, 67-68, 310
Johannesburg Mail and Guardian, 190
Johannesburg Star, 48
Johnson, Andrew, 12, 99, 105, 107, 109
   censure of, 167
   aftermath of impeachment, 310-311
Johnson, Haynes, 281
Jones, Paula Corbin, 28, 95, 98, 105, 161, 287
   attorneys of, 121-125, 135, 157, 159, 178, 308
   motives of, 66
   motives of Jones' lawyers, 7, 66
   and Starr, 42
Jordan, Vernon, 95
Jospin, Lionel, 339
judicial supremacy, 155-157
Judiciary Committee, of House of Representatives, 113, 124, 126, 229

denial of Clinton's due process, 99
   and impeachment, 34
   and Starr, 131, 136, 142
   and witnesses, 102-103
Kalb, Marvin, 282, 296
Kelly, Frank K., 320
Kemp, Jack, 58
Kendall, David, 27
Kennedy, John F., 20, 268
Kinsley, Michael, 69, 77
Kohl, Helmut, 4-5, 338-339
Kosovo, 31, 342, 349
Leach, James, 68
Lewinsky, Monica, 101, 120
   abuse of sex scandal of, 95
   Clinton's denial of involvement, 13, 101, 134
   detention of, 124, 131, 142, 158, 160, 214
   friend Tripp, 120-122
   immunity agreement of, 125, 131-132, 213, 219, 257
   lack of discretion of, 196, 213
   media storm over, 133
   OIC threats to mother of, 122, 214-215
   pillorying of, 212-215
   pretend concern about, 121
   privacy of, 204, 212-214
   sexual relations with, 96, 137, 201
   and Starr, 120
   and Starr Report, 7-8, 101-102, 202
   sting of, 95, 122
   tabloid offers to, 269
Lewis, Anthony, 131, 249, 254, 287, 300
   on Clinton-haters, 309
   on impeachment, 306
   on OIC misconduct, 306-307
Lewis, Marcia, 214-215
Libération (Paris), 94, 191
Limbaugh, Rush, 19, 41, 74, 232, 251, 289-293
Lincoln, Abraham, 12, 154, 224, 321
Livingston, Bob, 119-120
Los Angeles Times, The, 109, 196-197, 226-228, 231-232, 254, 264

   on American world leadership, 344, 347-348
   cartoons of, 31, 288-289
   on censure, 312
   on civic knowledge, 350-351
   on executive privilege, 312
   on Flowers, 265
   Gamble in, 52
   on girl-child Lewinsky, 121
   hostility to Clinton, 251, 267, 283, 301-302, 309, 323
   on impeachment, 223, 295, 312-313
   international news in, 280, 342
   on journalists, 281-282, 299-300
   market share of, 269
   McGovern in, 203
   on media bias, 301
   on OIC Statute, 327, 331-332
   on partisanship, 320
   on pundit culture, 298-299
   race for scoops of, 260
   Schumer in, 312
   on star journalists, 262
   in tabloid land, 283-287
   Troopergate in, 28, 72, 283-287
Lott, Trent, 117, 170-171, 322-323, 346
   and campaign finance, 78
   and Dick Morris, 49
   and isolationism, 54
   and Senate trial, 145
   see also isolationism, nuclear test ban
Lowell, Abbe, 142, 228, 242
lying in politics, 220-228, 232-233, 243, 246-247
   by Bush, 18-19, 108
   by Clinton, 18-19, 222, 232-233, 243
   by Reagan, 108, 293
lynching, 262, 277, 309, 323
   in history, 240-243
   media role in, 163, 241-242, 300
   quasi, of Clinton, 119, 173, 240-243
Ma'ariv (Tel Aviv), 349

Madison Guaranty, 18, 25-26, 35-36, 69, 307
Madison, James, 87, 103, 106, 310
Manila Standard (Manila), 315
McCain, John, 71, 78, 323, 344
McCarthyism, 7, 236, 239, 243
McConnell, Mitch, 70
McDougal, James, 26, 35, 69, 307
McDougal, Susan, 29, 35, 69, 218-219, 243
McLean's, 65
media advertiser-friendliness, 270
media bias, 251-254, 269-272, 277, 294, 299-305
  see also media conspiracy
media circus, 253-254, 281
media concentration, 270-271, 302
media conspiracy, 251-258, 266-267, 274-277, 302
Miami Herald, 265
Mills, Cheryl D., 148
Mittelbayerische Zeitung (Regensburg), 201
Mitterand, Francois, 183-184, 334
Monde, Le, 84, 108, 118-119, 127-128
  on Clinton's apologies, 208
  on French sexual attitudes, 176, 184-185, 192, 212
  on impeachment, 315, 105
  on 1998 elections, 139, 140
  on Puritanism, 239
  on Republicans, 210
  on sexual MacCarthyism, 236, 239
  on Starr, 182
  on Starr Report, 198-199, 101-102
Monde Diplomatique, Le (Paris), 278-280
Monde Hebdomadaire, Le (Paris), 199, 288
Morgenpost (Hamburg), 128
Morris, Dick, 23, 36, 49, 61
Moynihan, Pat, 22, 35, 48, 170, 313
MSNBC television, 261, 268, 296
Murdoch, Rupert, 250, 264, 296
National Enquirer, 259, 265, 268-269
National Journal, 257
National Review, 216

NBC television, 255, 257, 265, 272, 285-286, 299
Neue Zuercher Zeitung (Zuerich), 107, 110, 205, 237, 279
Neustadt, Richard, 320
New Leader, 59
New Republic, The, 8, 316
news as entertainment, 278, 281-282, 294
Newsday, 270
Newshour with Jim Lehrer, 231, 272, 281-283, 332, 336
  on American foreign policy leadership, 341
  Clinton on, 26
  Oliphant on, 146
  Shields on, 349
News of the World (London), 187
newspaper readership, 278
Newsweek, 161, 260, 263, 267, 299-300
New Yorker, 94, 267
New York Review of Books, The, 195, 254, 306, 309, 332
  Lewis in, 33
  Nelson in, 143
New York Post, 118, 262, 264, 266-267
New York Times, The, 36-37, 71-72, 207, 216, 254, 257
  on buying commodities futures, 41
  on crime, 279
  Flowers, 265
  hostility to Clintons, 26, 251, 259, 267, 272-274, 301
  on impeachment, 295, 299-300
  on international news, 280
  nuclear test ban ad in, 170
  Rich in, 175
  and Starr Report, 127
  on Troopergate, 287
  on US debts to UN, 347
  on Whitewater, 18, 26-27, 307
Nixon, Richard Milhouse, 93, 99, 101, 105, 231
  background of, 20
  campaign finance of, 62
  impeachment charges of, 12

polls upon threat of impeachment, 13
and Watergate, 109, 267, 311, 325
North American Free Trade Agreement (NAFTA), 23, 36, 323
Nuclear Test Ban Treaty, 170-171, 347
Nunn, Sam, 22
Nussbaum, Bernard, 27-28, 65
Observer (London), 11, 132, 165, 233
   obstruction of justice, 129, 142-143, 246, 260
   as a bogus charge, 203
   as impeachment charge, 126
   Isikoff on, 122
Office of Independent Counsel (OIC), 42, 96-98, 101, 120, 125
   appointment of, 105
   Arkansas office of, 29
   bias against minorities, women, 330
   checks on, 328, 351
   contacts with Jones's lawyers, 224, 307
   criticisms of, 166, 193, 306-308, 325-329
   leaks of, 125, 224, 229, 257, 260-261
   investigations under, 328-329
   private legal expense of, 329
OIC Statute, 111, 325-326, 331
Pais, El (Madrid), 127, 199
Paris Match, 183
parliamentary government, 85-93, 103-108, 312, 316
partisanship, 320., 324, 333
peace process,
   in Middle East, 57, 343, 345, 348-349
   in Northern Ireland, 57, 258, 343
People for the American Way, 277
perjury, 84, 94, 101, 104, 106, 122, 246
   alleged of Lewinsky, 131
   civil, 17
   in impeachment charges, 142, 203
   redefinition of, 123, 130, 143
   as secondary offense, 162, 252
   in Starr Report, 126, 137, 198

Perot, Ross, 18-19, 21-22, 36, 40, 56-57, 65
Playboy, 269
Powell, Colin, 53
Prescott, John, 59
presidential immunity from civil suits, 67
privacy, 191-197, 204, 244, 246, 265, 268, 282
Prodi, Romano, 6, 199
public opinion polls, 19
   on anti-government sentiments, 336, 340
   on Clinton in 1995, 44
   during the crisis, 13-14
   on Gingrich, 46, 54
   on government shutdown, 51
   on impeachment, 144
   on 1992 elections, 21
   on 1996 elections, 60
   on 1998 elections, 140
   after Oklahoma City, 48
   on privacy, 265, 282
   on Republicans, 340
   on Whitewater and health reform, 41
Puritanism, 173-174, 204, 237-238, 243, 272
Quayle, Dan, 30
Ramirez, Michael P., 31, 288
Reagan, Ronald, 67, 221, 291, 293
   Central American wars of, 100, 112
   era of, 111-115, 270, 334-335
   and foreign policy leadership, 344
   and Iran Contra, 12-13, 42, 100, 108-109, 112
   military service of, 30
   Teflon president, 43
   and triangulation, 332
Reeves, Richard, 282
Rehnquist, William, 234, 317, 328
   and appointment of OIC, 42, 156
   on impeachment, 105
Reich, Robert, 55
religion in America, 204-205
religious right, 146, 203, 205-207, 234
   and Contract with the American Family, 210

in 1996 election, 47
and Republican party, 118-119
Rutherford Institute of, 67
on talk radio, 292
Reno, Janet, 66, 307, 327
and Whitewater, 35, 95
Repubblica, La (Milan), 184, 190, 303
on Gingrich wave, 44
on November 1998 elections, 141
on Starr Report, 128, 135, 199-201
on tabloids, 266
Repubblica Oggi, La (Milan), 168, 174
Republican campaign finance, 69, 233-234
Republican electoral defeat of 1998, 91
Republicans, 33, 36-37
Congressional leaders of, 7
on Dole and religious right, 47
Gingrich wave, 39, 43, 45, 50
on health reform, 40
and impeachment, 10-12
after 1992 election, 22-23
in 1996 election, 53
tax cuts, 48-50, 55
Republican tax cuts, 76, 335-336
and Gingrich, 64, 73-74
n 1996 election campaign, 55, 58-59
Republican transformation, 321-323
Republican voters, 62
resignation, of Clinton, 98, 167-169
advocacy of, 168-169
and Starr Report, 126-129
Rolling Stone, 237, 240
Roosevelt, Eleanor, 119, 251
Roosevelt, Franklin Delano, 33, 56, 65, 251
Roosevelt, Theodore, 268
Rosen, Jeffrey, 94, 104
Rossitskaya Gazeta, 196
Rostenkowski, Dan, 22, 43
Rubin, Robert, 50
Ruff, Charles, 148
rule of law, 108, 154
abuse of, 7, 9, 101-102
criticisms of American law, 161, 203, 309
European admiration for, 83

and legal expense, 157
pretend issue of, 7, 223, 274
Rutherford Institute, 67, 118, 159
and Starr, 274, 308, 331
and videotape of Clinton's testimony, 129-130
Salon, 194, 278
Santa Barbara News-Press, 163, 315, 320, 323
hostility to Clinton, 37, 257
Raspberry in, 156
Scaife, Richard Mellon, 7, 118, 158
and *American Spectator*, 28, 250, 284
bankrolling anti-Clinton exposés, 202
Scalia, Antonin, 105, 234, 326
Scheer, Robert, 263, 286, 301
Schippers, David, 120, 148, 195
Schlesinger, Arthur Jr., 106
Schmidt, Helmut, 334
Schorr, Daniel, 281, 293
Schroeder, Gerhard, 268, 338-340, 348
Scotsman, The (Edinburgh), 143, 236-237, 240
Senate trial of Clinton, 145-150, 247, 299
Sentelle, David, 233, 235
appointment of Starr, 42, 328
partisanship of, 81, 105, 132, 156
separation of powers, 81-82, 85-88, 97-98, 313
sex scandals, 166, 176, 183-190, 246, 268
sexual attitudes, 178-190
sexual harassment, 130, 191-193, 210
sexual McCarthyism, 236, 239-240
sexual relations, 96, 134, 143, 168
60 Minutes, 200
Slate, 278
South China Morning Post (Hong Kong), 236
Spiegel, Der, 213, 220-221
on Bill Bennett, 121
on Clinton's empathy with blacks, 119
on Limbaugh, 290
on Cheryl D. Mills, 148

on privacy, 268
on Reagan, 111
on Starr Report, 279
on Starr's coup attempt, 164
Spitzer, Robert J., 316
Star, 259, 264-266, 268-269
Starr, W. Kenneth, 254
   abuse of power by, 134, 260, 273, 308, 329-330
   appointment of, 42, 81, 235, 328
   contacts with Jones' attorneys, 131, 158, 235
   criticisms of, 160, 161, 174, 195, 215, 217-221
   disbarment of, 228
   disregard for Constitution, 308
   European curiosity about, 7, 28-29, 37-38
   European perceptions of, 8, 130, 155-156, 178, 272-273, 306
   evasiveness of, 94
   extension of jurisdiction of, 81
   and Filegate, 66
   ineffectual head of OIC, 97
   on leaking, 261
   legal weakness of, 101, 104, 155-156
   lying, by, 221, 223-226, 228-233, 246, 252, 307
   manipulations of, 122-125, 129-134, 138, 156-157, 228, 247
   media image of, 272-273
   on OIC Statute, 328, 331
   partisanship of, 130-132
   on pornography, 200-201
   and presidential resignation, 167-169
   style of, 108-109, 118, 158, 162, 166, 203
   and tobacco industry, 42, 132, 228, 233
   and Travelgate, 66
   tricks of, 119, 130, 134
   and Whitewater, 66-69, 76
Starr Report, 108-111
   and children, 125-129, 137, 200
   and impeachment, 101, 108-111
   indecency of, 5-6, 16-17, 246, 101-102, 137
   publication of, 84, 127, 135-136
   salacious nature of, 126-130, 137, 177, 197-198, 241
   uncorroborated evidence in, 121, 224
State of the Union addresses, 22, 44, 57, 276-277, 282
states rights, 317-318
Steele, Julie Hiatt, 218-219, 243
Stephanopolous, George, 24, 27-28, 34-35
Stern, Der (Hamburg), 111, 120, 147, 196, 294, 326
Sueddeutsche Zeitung, (Munich), 14
   on American media, 263-264, 280, 296
   on American sexual attitudes, 185
   criticisms of American law, 162, 215
   on impeachment fervor, 133-134, 137, 142, 144, 259
   on 1994 elections, 38-39, 43-44
   on 1996 elections, 53, 58, 60-64, 89
   on 1998 elections, 91
   on Reagan policies, 112
   on Starr Report, 137-138, 197-198, 263
Sun (London), 98, 187-188
Sunday Telegraph (London), 118
Sunday Times (London), 15
Sunstein, Cass, 104-105
Supreme Court, 105, 156, 158
   decision to abrogate presidential immunity, 81-82, 97-98
   expansive judiciary, 317
   and resegregation, 318
   restoring presidential civil immunity, 313
Sydney Morning Herald, 89
Tagesspiegel (Berlin), 266
talk radio, 289-293
Tempo, Il (Rome), 238
Temps, Le (Geneva), 102
Thatcher, Margaret, 112, 114-115, 339
Thompson, Fred, 76-78, 327

Time, 264-265, 276-277
  on Clinton, failing, 24
  on health reform, 37, 41
  international news in, 280
  on journalists, 299-300
  on Lewinsky, 213
  on Limbaugh, 291-292
  on lying, 18-19, 221
  in media circus, 260, 262
  on 1992 elections, 18-19, 21
  on 1996 elections, 62, 65-66
  on Whitewater, 37
Times (London), 188, 196, 240
  on Clinton's acquittal, 148-149
  on impeachment, 11, 165, 169
  on 1996 elections, 46
  on Starr Report, 6
Tocqueville, Alexis de, 68, 249-252, 264, 266-268, 300, 302
Toobin, Jeffrey, 125, 257
  on Jones' suit, 67
  a legal-political revolution, 18
  on OIC personnel, 96-97
  on ultraright lawyers, 158
Toronto Star, The, 15, 190, 209, 296, 323
Travelgate, 65-66, 80, 96
  Clinton on, 26
  media exaggerations on, 34
  travel employees' dismissal, 24
Tripp, Linda, 8, 178, 260, 302
  contacts with OIC, 121
  deposition of, 125
  immunity for illegal taping, 95, 159-160, 193
  plot to write book, 121-122
  sting of Lewinsky, 95, 120
  tapes recorded by, 268, 95
Troopergate, 28-29, 36, 80, 223
TV filth and violence, 4
24-hour news cycle, 294, 300
United Nations (UN), 6, 16, 279-280, 346-347
USA Today, 262, 299-300
U.S. News and World Report, 162-163, 192
Vanity Fair, 126-127, 205, 255, 258, 267

Vietnam war, 29-31, 114
voting trends, 335-336
Wallace, George, 292
Wall Street Journal, The, 72, 251, 261, 266-267
Walsh, Lawrence E., 42, 96, 326
Warner, John, 170, 344
Washington Monthly, The, 26, 28, 257-260, 330
  on Federalist Society, 235
  on Larry Flynt, 202
  on journalistic objectivity, 263-264, 272, 282
  Peters in, 295
  on Starr's manipulations, 273
Washington Post, The, 72, 212, 228, 251, 254-255
  American foreign policy leadership, 347
  and Warren Buffett, 270
  on Flowers, 265
  hostility to Clinton, 267, 300
  on impeachment, 295, 299-300
  international news in, 258
  on journalists, 299-300
  pro-Starr bias of, 260, 273, 300
Washington Times, 26
Washington Week in Review (PBS), 121, 347
Watergate, 93, 260-261, 281
  and campaign finance, 69
  legacy of, 65, 76, 80
  nature of, 99-100, 111, 130, 259, 261
  and OIC Statute, 325-326
  privacy limits to, 41
  revenge for, 30, 36-37, 160, 275, 336
Weekendavisen (Copenhagen), 194
Weekly Standard, 28, 267
welfare reform, 98, 209, 332-333
  Clinton-style, 55-56, 59-60, 65
Welt, Die 14, 216
Whitewater investigation, 18, 66, 76-77, 80, 118
  and Robert Fiske, 41
  in *Los Angeles Times*, 287
  media circus over, 34-37

political storm over, 25-28, 68-69
and Starr, 7, 95
in *Wall Street Journal,* 307
Watergate analogies, 38, 99, 274
Wilentz, Sean, 8, 106
Willey, Kathleen, 218-219
Wilson, Woodrow, 310
Wirtschaftswoche (Duesseldorf), 56
Wright, Susan Webber, 98, 123, 135, 159
Yeltsin, Boris, 11-12, 256, 288
Zeit, Die (Hamburg), 134, 215-216
on abuse of rule of law, 129-130
on American leadership, 305, 345
on American media, 298
on American Puritanism, 207, 208, 296
on Clinton's background, 20
on Gingrich's failure, 140
on impeachment, 14, 142, 145, 164
on privacy, 175-177, 189
on Starr Report, 201
Zhu Ronji, 77